Fielding Derrida

John D. Caputo, *series editor*

PERSPECTIVES IN
CONTINENTAL
PHILOSOPHY

JOSHUA KATES

Fielding Derrida

Philosophy, Literary Criticism,
History, and the Work
of Deconstruction

FORDHAM UNIVERSITY PRESS
New York ■ 2008

Chapters 1, 5, 6, and 7 appeared in a variety of different forms in the *Journal of the British Society for Phenomenology*, *Philosophy Today*, and *The New Yearbook for Phenomenology* (6, 7), respectively. A version of Chapter 2 appeared in *Husserl Studies* 19.2 (Summer): 101–30 as "Derrida, Husserl, and the Commentators: Introducing a Developmental Approach" and appears here with the kind permission of Springer Verlag. Chapter 3, first published as "A Transcendental Sense of Death? Derrida and the Philosophy of Language," *Modern Language Notes*, 120.5 (December 2005): 1009–43, appears with the kind permission of Johns Hopkins University Press.

Library of Congress Cataloging-in-Publication Data

Kates, Joshua.
  Fielding Derrida : philosophy, literary criticism, history, and the work of deconstruction / Joshua Kates.—1st ed.
      p.   cm.— (Perspectives in continental philosophy)
   Includes bibliographical references and index.
      ISBN 978-0-8232-2946-8 (cloth : alk. paper)—ISBN 978-0-8232-2947-5 (pbk. : alk. paper)
      1. Derrida, Jacques.   I. Title.
   B2430.D484K385   2008
   194—dc22

                                                              2008026058

Printed in the United States of America
10   09   08   5   4   3   2   1
First edition

To Jennifer and Zeke

Contents

Abbreviations

AFT	Jacques Derrida, "Afterword: Toward an Ethic of Discussion," in *Limited, Inc.*, trans. Samuel Weber (Evanston, Ill.: Northwestern University Press, 1988).
DG	Jacques Derrida, *De la grammatologie* (Paris: Editions de Minuit, 1967).
ED	Jacques Derrida, *L'écriture et la différence* (Paris: Editions du Seuil, 1967).
FTL	Edmund Husserl, *Formal and Transcendental Logic*, trans. Dorion Cairns (The Hague, Netherlands: Martinus Nijhoff, 1969).
GMT	Jacob Klein, *Greek Mathematical Thought and the Origins of Algebra*, trans. Eva Brann (New York: Dover, 1992).
IOG	Jacques Derrida, *Edmund Husserl's Origin of Geometry: An Introduction*, trans. John Leavey, Jr. (Stony Brook, N.Y.: Nicholas Hays, 1978).
LI	Edmund Husserl, *Logical Investigations*, 2 vols., trans. J. N. Findlay (London: Routledge and Kegan Paul, 1970).
LOG	Edmund Husserl, *L'Origine de la Géométrie*, traduction er l'introduction par Jacques Derrida (Paris: Presses Universitaire de France, 1962).
LT	Jacques Derrida, *Le Toucher—Jean-Luc Nancy* (Paris: Galilée, 2000); *On Touching—Jean-Luc Nancy*, trans. Christine Irizzary

(Stanford, Calif.: Stanford University Press, 2005). All references are to the original French.

LU   Edmund Husserl, *Logische Untersuchungen* Husserliana XVIII and XIX (I and II), ed. Ursula Panzer (The Hague: Martinus Nijhoff, 1984).

OG   Jacques Derrida, *Of Grammatology,* trans. Gayatri Spivak (Baltimore: Johns Hopkins University Press, 1974).

PG   Jacques Derrida, *Le problème de la genèse dans la philosophie de Husserl* (Paris: Presses Universitaire de France, 1990); *The Problem of Genesis in the Philosophy of Husserl,* translated by Marian Hobson (Chicago: University of Chicago Press, 2003). All references in the text are to the original French edition unless otherwise noted.

POS   Jacques Derrida, *Positions,* trans. Alan Bass (Chicago: University of Chicago Press, 1981).

SEC   Jacques Derrida, "Signature Event Context," in *Limited Inc.,* ed. Gerald Graff (Evanston, Ill.: Northwestern University Press, 1988).

SM   Jacques Derrida, *Specters of Marx: The State of the Debt, the Work of Mourning, and the New International,* trans. Peggy Kamuf (New York: Routledge, 1994).

SP   Jacques Derrida, *Speech and Phenomena and Other Essays on Husserl's Theory of Signs,* trans. David B. Allison (Evanston, Ill.: Northwestern University Press, 1973).

"TT"   "Time of a Thesis: Punctuations," in *Philosophy in France Today,* ed. Alan Montefiore (Cambridge: Cambridge University Press, 1983).

VP   Jacques Derrida, *La voix et le phénomène: Introduction au problème du signe dans la phénomenologie de Husserl* (Paris: Presses Universitaire de France, 1967).

WD   Jacques Derrida, *Writing and Difference,* trans. Alan Bass (Chicago: University of Chicago Press, 1978).

Fielding Derrida

Introduction

Fielding Derrida

Jacques Derrida's death, now several years past, brought to the surface a question that had already been stirring concerning the fate of his own work and of Derrida studies generally: will Derrida's thought continue to be central to intellectual life across the globe in the absence of Derrida himself? Will his works continue to be read and studied—and how will they be read and studied—when the unique personhood, the forceful individuality, of Jacques Derrida, so dear to so many, is no longer with us, and his incredible, ongoing productivity has come to an end?

The fact that Derrida's enterprise is best designated by his own name—as attested to by the numerous works consisting of some form of it simply as their title—already shows how much research and debate in this area is owed to Derrida's singular life and personality. Such reliance on Derrida's extraordinary individuality, in the long run, however, potentially sits uneasily with the impersonal nature more usually associated with ongoing scholarly endeavor.

Derrida himself, with typical acuity, already raised such concerns in a late interview in *Le Monde* in 2004. He averred, "smiling and immodestly," that "people have not even begun to read me." Yet he added that the day for his own work might also soon be past: he believed his corpus' disappearance was imminent in light of his own impending mortality. "I feel that two weeks after my death, nothing at all of my work will be left," Derrida said, "except what remains in the copyright registration library."[1] Derrida here envisions at once both his work's first authentic reception (the beginning of its genuine interpretation) and its complete disappearance, following immediately upon his demise. And the lesson for us, his interpreters, is that Derrida himself thus suspected that a new phase in the reading of his work was required if his writing were to continue to maintain that pivotal position in the humanities it had occupied for so long. Derrida's remarks suggest that a new tack must be taken today toward his corpus, lest it be relegated someday to "the copyright registration library."

One possible response to Derrida's demand for a new approach to his work is offered by the present collection of essays. Inserting Derrida's work into such fields as analytic philosophy or Marxist / post-Marxist theory, connecting it explicitly to the thematic subtexts it often merely implies—to skepticism, or certain positions in the philosophy of language, to phenomenology, debates in literary criticism, or the category of the modern—establishes the positions Derrida took or presupposed within larger, previously established contexts and controversies. Is deconstruction a form of skepticism? What assumptions in philosophy of language did Derrida actually hold? Does Derrida believe that modernity represents a radical discontinuity in knowledge, as well as in political and social life—as do thinkers as disparate as Michel Foucault, Leo Strauss, and the pioneering historian of mathematics and interpreter of Plato, Jacob Klein—with whose interests Derrida's own often overlap in surprising ways?

The present work aims to draw bright lines around Derrida's positions, brighter lines than often have previously been drawn. Nevertheless, it would be wrong to see this occurring at the cost of simplifying Derrida's positions, by dint of reducing his writings to the concerns of already existing debates or disciplines. On the contrary, by initially questioning some of the terms of Derrida's self-presentation, and placing his writings in already constituted contexts, the actual complexity of Derrida's own stances can be captured with a new specificity and precision.

Indeed, the following essays all assume that the most viable solution to the issue, so often raised throughout his career, of how satisfactorily to read and comment on the writings of Jacques Derrida, is to insert his thought and work into already existing fields. By starting from a different frame than that which Derrida himself provides, by thus "fielding Derrida" (since a break with the field in all its forms doubtless results from Derrida's own way of working), an unraveling of Derrida's writings becomes possible, which simultaneously takes us deeper into these works' real concerns and their dynamic center. Unearthing buried positions and presuppositions, framing field-specific assertions and truth-claims, and then correcting and nuancing these assertions in turn, such exegesis necessarily overflows the boundaries of Derrida's own texts, even as it reaches into the depths of the mechanics and texture of his writings.

Such fielding or contextualization, by forcing his work to make contact with other research already in progress, also answers to Derrida's own expressed concern about whether and how his thought will continue to play a significant role in the humanities in the future. Now, explicitly connecting Derrida's work to the argumentative contexts provided by an array of ongoing research—Husserlian phenomenology, analytic philosophy of language, literary criticism, and the intellectual history of modernity—what Derrida's project indeed holds for the future, what his project can contribute to keeping alive a certain heritage of thinking, as well as to confronting problems, and indeed a world, still unknown and yet to appear, can emerge and be tested in a dialogue at once newly concrete and unprecedentedly wide-ranging.

Part I: Jacques Derrida's Early Writings Alongside Skepticism, Phenomenology, Analytic Philosophy, and Literary Criticism

The interpretation of early deconstruction (found in texts such as *Of Grammatology* and *Speech and Phenomena*) as a new, more radical skepticism remains a common one. Chapter 1, "Deconstruction as Skepticism," examines canonical treatments of these early texts, such as those of Jonathan Culler and Christopher Norris, as well as specialized ones focusing on the philosophical problem of skepticism (Anthony Cascardi, David Wilmore, Robert Bernasconi, Simon Critchley, and Ewa Ziarek), in order to argue that Derrida always wished to keep a distance from all forms of skepticism, and that he repeatedly turned to Husserl's phenomenology in order to do so.

At the same time, the longstanding view of Derrida as some kind of skeptic turns out not simply to be wrong. A radically skeptical standpoint is built into the order of presentation of Derrida's first deconstructive writings, despite Derrida's intention to the contrary. To this, I believe, is owed the instability of our understanding of Derrida's first work even today, early deconstruction often being taken as a radically skeptical enterprise, focused on *language*, while also somehow simultaneously conceived as providing quasi-transcendental conditions for the whole of philosophy. This impasse thus invites us to further examine the emergence of Derrida's thinking from his early intensive engagement with Husserl's thought.

Chapter 2, "Derrida, Husserl, and the Commentators: A Developmental Approach," responds to the task set out in the conclusion of Chapter 1, by turning to what is known as the Husserl / Derrida debate. While mounting a defense of Derrida as an interpreter of Husserl, it introduces a new mapping of Derrida's corpus and a new approach to the interpretation of his 1967 works. "Derrida, Husserl, and the Commentators" shows, in particular, that still-unrecognized significant change does take place in Derrida's thought between his 1962 "Introduction to Husserl's *Origin of Geometry*" and the advent of deconstruction proper in 1967. Derrida's positions, especially his understanding of writing and language, thus start out closer to Husserl's than others have previously believed. So, too, the occasion that led Derrida to invent or institute deconstruction can be identified: namely, the impossibility of maintaining the transcendental significance that Husserl assigns to writing alongside a broader, more common and more empirical construal of this notion.

Chapter 3, "A Transcendental Sense of Death? Derrida and the Philosophy of Language," sets forth Derrida's actual presuppositions in the philosophy of language (tackling head-on Richard Rorty's questions about where Derrida stands in respect to nominalism, the status of the concept, and Frege's revolution in logic). It focuses on two places where Derrida speaks of a transcendental sense of death associated with writing and language: one in his "Introduction to Husserl's *Origin of Geometry*" and one in *Speech and Phenomena*. In the second instance Derrida's handling of indexicals (terms like "here" and "now," "I" and "this") is compared with that of so-called direct reference theories in analytic philosophy. In addition to clarifying Derrida's philosophy of language, this lets me articulate the precise fashion in which Derrida broke with the transcendental historico-linguistic teleology of Husserl's last writings in *Speech*.

Chapter 4, "Literary Theory's Languages: The Deconstruction of Sense vs. the Deconstruction of Reference," follows up the work of Chapter 3 by exploring the impact of these two alternative models of language (analytic and Husserlian) on developments in that field in which Derrida's thought has been most influential in the last twenty years: namely, literary theory and literary criticism. Here I plump for a return to an older style of literary theory that inquires into questions of language (and its relation to literature), by identifying a previously unsuspected split between semantic and referential approaches in literary theory itself, as well as in actual criticism—specifically, in the neopragmatism of Stanley Fish, Walter Michaels, and Steven Knapp, the queer theory of Eve Sedgwick, and the new historicism and its heirs. Derrida's "Signature, Event, Context" provides the keystone of this demonstration, read in the context of the working out of a broad overview of Gottlob Frege's thought and its influence on all subsequent treatments of language in the analytic tradition.

Part II: Jacques Derrida and the Problem of Philosophical and Political Modernity

Chapter 5, "Jacob Klein and Jacques Derrida: The Problem of Modernity," introduces the notion of modernity to the discussion of Derrida's thought—modernity understood as entailing novel epistemic, institutional, and political formations, as well as presumably referring to a species of historical occurrence. Modernity provides the overarching context for all of the essays of Part II, and this setting comes forward thanks to taking up, along with Derrida's own, the work of Jacob Klein, an intellectual historian and philosopher, currently receiving more attention, whose interests dovetailed in a surprising number of respects with Derrida's.

The most notable feature of Derrida's relation to modernity, of course, may be the distance his own thinking kept from it as an operative category. Yet even as Derrida gives almost no privilege to this notion (perhaps less than Husserl, and far less than Klein), the examination of Klein's work, in particular Klein's treatment of the modern innovation to which he believes number was subject, allows Derrida's early deconstructive endeavor, including his signature notion of *écriture*, here to be understood as a response to what Klein so saliently identifies as the "modern rupture."

Chapter 6, "Jacob Klein and Jacques Derrida: Historicism and Historicity in Two Interpretations of Husserl's Late Writings," treats the intellectual context that explicitly united Klein and Derrida: namely, an engagement with Husserl's last writing on history. They are, in fact, the only two authors of whom I am aware (arguably, apart from Dorion Cairns), who published detailed, extended interpretations of Husserl's late fragment "The Origin of Geometry" during their own lifetimes.

This chapter thus investigates their very different treatments of this fragment, a comparison that permits a new specificity concerning how Derrida interpreted Husserl in 1962. This comparison also allows a deepening of the problematic of modernity, thanks to the oddly complementary role Husserl's recasting of history ultimately played in the thought of both authors. Husserl's treatment of history allowed Klein's own history of mathematics to leave behind empirical history and come to grips with the true conceptual (yet also genetic) roots of the problem of number and of modernity itself. For Derrida Husserl's work, due to some of the same features that Klein valorized, ultimately showed the fealty of all history to the metaphysics of presence, thus establishing the demand that history as such be overcome in its entirety. In both cases, however, in these enormously different ways, the engagement with this phase of Husserl's project permitted these authors to bypass empirical history as such, thus raising the question of whether Klein's and Derrida's recourse to Husserl does not itself attest to modernity as a more profound and recalcitrant category than either author was ultimately prepared to recognize.

Chapter 7, "Derrida's Contribution to Phenomenology: A Problem of No Species?," explores two major facets of Derrida's thought, both early and late. One is Derrida's longstanding distance from the category of the human, his insistence on blurring the line between humans and other animals, as well as between the animal and machine, the living and the dead—what some call his post- or meta-humanism. The other is Derrida's consistently unique departure from Husserlian phenomenology, especially when viewed in the context of the more general response Husserl's thought has received in the phenomenological tradition. An estimation of this response is here gleaned through a comparison of Derrida's interpretation of the constitution of intersubjectivity in *Ideas* II with that of Merleau-Ponty's. Derrida emphasizes the transcendentalist, rationalist, and even essentialist side of Husserl's project, over and against most of the phenomenological tradition, which turned to facticity and the category of the human as the basis for its own renovated phenomenological investigations (as in Merleau-Ponty, Sartre, Scheler, Schutz, and even, though to a lesser degree, Heidegger and Levinas). These gestures are related; for, only by dint of a (deconstructed) transcendentalism does Derrida find the leverage to exceed the sphere of empirical humanity. The recognition of this unique interlacing of Derrida's project with Husserl's thus prompts an investigation of whether Husserl himself within the confines of *Ideas* II actually managed to successfully coordinate the various phases of his own project devoted to the naturalistic, personalistic, and absolute standpoints. Furthermore, it suggests that Derrida's contribution to phenomenology may consist most of all in having taken up a version of Husserl's own flexible, open, "enlightened" stance toward the regional disciplines and the sciences (e.g., in comparison to Heidegger's)—yet one which, thanks to its greater fluidity, its anti- or hyper-foundationalist mode of proceeding, may be to many in our own time more credible than Husserl's.

Chapter 8, "Foretellese: Futures of Derrida and Marx," investigates Derrida's late political thinking in the critical instance of its engagement with Marxism, here understood not only as including Marx and Engel's writings, but also contemporary Marxist / post-Marxism. The Marxist tradition remains today our richest line of revolutionary political thinking, and it here represents more than a mere example for evaluating Derrida's own political project.

The first job of this chapter, accordingly, is to ward off the uncharacteristically reactive or high-handed dismissals of Derrida's project some contemporary self-avowed Marxists have made, by focusing on Derrida's longstanding diagnosis of our (historical) present, of what is coming to pass around us. This diagnosis, including the hauntology that Derrida juxtaposes to Marx's ontology, does not in itself represent a decisive deviation from at least some strands of contemporary Marxist / post-Marxist thinking. Derrida's *response* to this diagnosis, however, his reworking of history itself, along with his demand, most clearly set out in *Politics of Friendship*, to reconceive the political as such (his interest first and foremost neither in understanding the world nor in changing it, but in changing our understanding) does separate him from even the most experimental quasi-Marxian initiatives. These differences come forward in my examination of the role of the ana-chronistic present and the quasi-messianic to-come in Derrida's late writings. And this chapter ends by joining up with the common theme of this section, modernity, thanks to identifying what Derrida and Marx above all *have in common*, which I (following Wallace Stevens) call foretellese: namely, an appeal to a permanent matrix of permanence and change, for the sake of further change, made in the course of diagnosing the present and summoning the future. Such foretellese, however, this way of doing politics and of thinking politically, disturbingly, itself seems to originate with modernity, to be a quintessentially modern political invention.

PART I

Jacques Derrida's Early Writings

*Alongside Skepticism, Phenomenology,
Analytic Philosophy, and Literary Criticism*

Deconstruction as Skepticism

The Development of Derrida's thought spans his earliest writings, from *The Problem of Genesis* and his "Introduction" to Husserl's *Origin of Geometry* through his trio of books published in 1967: *L'écriture et la différence*, *De la grammatologie*, and *La voix et le phénomène*. In the course of composing these works, Derrida evolves from a daring commentator on Husserl to become one of the foremost thinkers of his age. This development has begun to receive more attention in the literature[1]; its importance, however, remains obscure, especially to those in fields like literary criticism or history who mainly know Derrida as an avatar of linguistic relativism.

Why is a developmental approach focused on Derrida's early work necessary, especially at this late date? To begin, I will approach Derrida through his interpreters, particularly those whom I call the "first wave" of Derrida critics. English-language practitioners of this criticism focused primarily on *Of Grammatology* and paid little attention to Derrida's prior works. The "first wave," nevertheless, has rippled the farthest, and the form in which it portrays deconstruction still holds sway in popular representations of Derrida's thought.

The first wave of criticism is vast; it includes all literary deconstruction. In debates in the literature the first-wave position has gotten fixed, somewhat retrospectively, on critics like Jonathan Culler and Christopher Norris. Taking deconstruction as the center of Derrida's thought, the first wave, in a nutshell, claims that deconstruction (1) introduces a new way of reading; (2) focuses on writing and language; and (3) draws negative, or skeptical, conclusions about philosophy, reason, and truth.

To first-wave critics, the skepticism part is crucial. No genuine knowledge is possible, deconstruction asserts, as the first-wave construes deconstruction. No knowledge *can* exist, the first wave says deconstruction says.

The first wave grasps Derrida's thought partially at best, but the point is not to blame, or even correct, the first wave, as other commentators have done.[2] Admittedly, the first wave took deconstruction as skepticism, as arriving at or promulgating skeptical insights, as denying thought's ability to get at truth; but this movement—Culler and Norris, particularly—understood deconstruction in other ways as well: Derrida was a skeptic *and not*, as these critics read him.

These critics, however—Culler, Norris, and much of the first wave—could find no way to square this view of Derrida as a skeptic[3] with the other stances that Derrida took; they couldn't make their multiple views of Derrida's project cohere. These critics couldn't say how Derrida's discourse functioned as a whole; and that, in my view, is the first wave's predicament with bite, for its difficulties pose questions about Derrida's thought that remain unanswered even now, pointing to a problem all interpreters continue to have. The first-wave reading indicates an unclarified area in Derrida's writings themselves, and that, most of all, is why it is important here to understand the first wave's approach.

Derrida himself, after all, claims that he is *not* a skeptic; he states this repeatedly and unequivocally. Yet how Derrida's project really avoids skepticism is very hard to see. Skepticism—whether as a premise or a result—threatens to fragment Derrida's work and make it difficult to sort out how Derrida's project is to be conceived as any sort of coherent whole.

The problem of skepticism proves intractable in Christopher Norris's and Jonathan Culler's now canonical presentations of Derrida's project. How skepticism does that, in what way it proves problematic for Culler's and Norris's discourses, shows how in Derrida's own work this theme arises as an issue. Christopher Norris's commentary in his *Derrida* begins to reveal where this problem emerges in Derrida's thought and how it functions.

Early on in *Derrida* Norris writes: "To think logocentrically is to dream of a 'transcendental signified,' of a meaning outside and beyond the differential play of language that would finally put a stop to this unnerving predicament. Deconstruction defines its own project by contrast as a perpetual reminder that meaning is always the sign of a sign, that thought cannot escape this logic of endless supplementarity. . . ."[4]

Norris here offers a representative first-wave account of Derrida's thinking. So sketched, Derrida's thought consists in identifying limits, something "thought cannot escape," its entrapment in an "unnerving predicament." Moreover, language is this unnerving predicament's locus. Language, the play of the sign ("the sign of a sign"), according to the first wave, threatens thought with "endless supplementarity."

Deconstruction, then, produces a negative, skeptical insight based on language's consideration.[5] And this lesson must be drawn again and again in a way that makes the practices of reading and writing crucial. Because deconstruction itself eschews any so-called "transcendental signified," more specifically, its teaching, its lesson only surfaces and dissolves again in the course of readings, themselves necessarily repeated. For this reason, too, deconstruction takes writing as its theme, since writing, understood as the "sign of a sign," is especially resistant to "logocentrism's dream" of bringing an end to discourse in the telos of truth.[6]

Norris's view is so familiar by now as to be almost not worth characterizing further; yet it remains the view of Derrida's thought that still circulates outside narrow circles of Derrida scholarship. Deconstruction is a way of reading-focused-on-writing that brings forward a fundamentally skeptical insight: there is no stop to the play of meaning, motored by the enchainment of signs, and thus no authoritative truth. Paradoxes of language debunk reason's claims. That's deconstruction.

Norris's account, to be sure, is partial at best; what's critical is that Norris himself knows this—he recognizes that his account is partial. For him all this is but the beginning: "This is still to understand 'writing' in the narrow familiar sense," writes Norris.[7]

For Norris, an emancipatory, quasi-Kantian side of deconstruction exists in addition to deconstruction's negative, skeptical one, a theme that Norris will expand on in the future; Derrida's emancipatory side is the core part of Derridean deconstruction that is *not* skepticism.

This emancipatory side suffers an odd fate in Norris's hands, however, a fate that begins to show how the skepticism problem arises in Derrida's 1967 writings and what place it has in Derrida's own first deconstructive work.

Norris, as we have seen, begins his exposition from a discussion of writing and its concomitant language-oriented skeptical insight; only later in his text does Norris address the question of truth as such. More specifically, in order to bring forward deconstruction's non-skeptical side, Norris finds it necessary to distinguish Derrida's views on truth from those implied by Richard Rorty's pragmatism and Rorty's reading of Derrida.

Norris, opposing Rorty's Derrida interpretation, thus declares: "It is simply not the case—as Rorty would suggest—that Derrida . . . rejects all forms of epistemological critique and treats philosophy as just one kind of writing among others. . . ."[8]

And not only is Norris right, but it is important that Norris is right. Derrida *doesn't* take "philosophy as one kind of writing among others." Rorty's Derrida is *not* Derrida's Derrida. Derrida does *not* subscribe to "psychological nominalism," is *not* an "historicist," "naturalist," "antifoundationalist," "nominalist," as is Rorty.[9] In particular, Derrida is not a skeptic in respect to all philosophical knowledge.[10]

Derrida himself, after all, explicitly rejected Rorty's interpretation of him some time after Norris's book was written. Derrida disavowed Rorty-style antiphilosophical skepticism to Rorty face-to-face. Addressing Rorty, Derrida declared, "I maintain that I am a philosopher and that I want to remain a philosopher and this philosophical responsibility is something that commands me."[11]

Norris is right, then: Derrida does not think of himself as a skeptic. He is not an historicist or relativist like Rorty. Nor does he hold a pragmatist truth theory more standard than Rorty's own.

What Norris can't say, however, is how Derrida avoids these outcomes. What pact with the "enlightenment" (Norris's term) has Derrida arrived at, such that his work does not fall prey to any of these things? What model of truth and reason does function in Derrida's work, such that skepticism, relativism, historicism, nihilism are bypassed by Derrida?

Though Norris supplies no convincing account of this, what is crucial is why Norris's failure is necessary, given his understanding of Derrida.[12] This failure is programmed in advance by the skeptical reading of deconstruction set out above. Because, according to Norris, Derrida sets aside truth from the beginning, Norris himself has no convincing way to bring it back now. Norris, that is, is unable to say how Derrida, having debunked, decried, and denounced "logocentrism's dream," will be able later on to take seriously philosophical arguments of any kind, and thus to bring about what Norris takes as deconstruction's emancipatory goals. Indeed, Norris himself, continuing to address Rorty, concedes that "he [Derrida] may regard such [philosophical] questions as beyond hope of definitive answers, at least on the terms laid down by traditional (logocentric) reason. . . ."[13]

Norris, even now, then, starts from the premise that "logocentric reason" ultimately fails to function. All these questions, according to Norris, are already known to be beyond hope of definitive answer. Given this, how, then, to go any further? How to take another step? Have not skepticism, relativism, even irrationalism already cut Derrida's project off from further elaboration? Does not Derrida's logocentrism talk, as Norris takes it, make all further work, including emancipatory work, moot?

That's the clash in Norris's own thought on which we need to focus. (A similar clash exists in Culler's thought.) Norris knows there is another side to Derrida's discourse; he can't, however, really get at this other side in any convincing fashion, given the side of Derrida's discourse Norris does get. Derrida's thought is skeptical from the outset for Norris. And thus, by the time philosophical truth is explicitly affirmed and any non-skeptical goals broached, it's too late.

The role of skepticism in Derrida's thinking that Norris's account highlights—how certain of deconstruction's arguments entail skepticism, apparently in conflict with some of its other avowed goals—is a problem for almost all Derrida criticism, not just that of Norris or Culler. Such an impasse is not confined to these somewhat more general or at times introductory accounts of Derrida's work.

For some of Derrida's most fastidious commentators—for Robert Bernasconi and those who follow his pioneering work in bringing Derrida's and Levinas' thought together, for instance—this problem also remains unresolved. Bernasconi avers in his pathbreaking essay "Skepticism in the Face of Philosophy" that one should "think of Derrida as occupying a place *like* that held by skepticism."[14] Whether this place "like . . . skepticism" entails actual skepticism, discounting all truth and any resting point for discourse, in the sense that we have just seen Norris specify (and if not, how Derrida avoids this), Bernasconi himself never really makes clear. Does this "place . . . like . . . skepticism" mean that Derrida's own thinking implies skeptical conclusions, and thus that the difference Derrida himself once saw as crucial between his work and that of Emmanuel Levinas is really insignificant?[15]

Of course, for his own reasons, perhaps good ones, Bernasconi's aim was in fact to downplay this last difference.[16] Yet even Ewa Ziarek, who explicitly treats this theme in her powerful first book, in part building on Bernasconi's interpretation, does not resolve this issue. Ziarek similarly concludes that deconstruction proceeds "in a manner parallel to skepticism."[17] The " 'truth' of skepticism," not skepticism as such, is deconstruction's ally (88). Yet what the former entails for the latter, whether the "truth of skepticism" entails actual skeptical conclusions, is never really clarified by Ziarek. This is in part because Ziarek, who brings forward this "truth" through a discussion of Cavell's treatment of skepticism, and then of Levinas's, wants to show that a still deeper, more radical skepticism is conceivable than any Cavell would allow.

Of what this difference consists, then, what this distance in the parallelism between Derrida's thought and skepticism entails, is never made plain by Ziarek. And not only does this show that she and Bernasconi share Norris's and Culler's problem, but in her case especially, where skepticism is an explicit topic, this may well be because Ziarek is assuming as known a more standard response to how deconstruction and skepticism differ. An account of how the skeptical side of Derrida's thought is supposed to function has long existed in the literature; after all, an explanation of deconstruction's relation to skepticism was explicitly given by some of the commentators who comprise what I call the first wave. Many of these authors did try to explain why Derrida's talk of logocentrism and phonocentrism is not simply skepticism.

From Christopher Norris let me turn to Jonathan Culler, in order to reprise one version of this explanation. Culler offers a very respectable discussion of why logocentrism talk isn't skepticism talk when he, as Norris, differentiates deconstruction from pragmatism. There he writes the following:

> Deconstructive readings identify this paradoxical situation in which, on the one hand, logocentric positions contain their own undoing and, on the other hand, the denial of logocentrism is carried out in logocentric terms. Insofar as deconstruction maintains these positions it might seem to be a dialectical synthesis . . . but these two movements do not, when combined, yield a coherent position or a higher theory. Deconstruction has no better theory. It is a practice of reading and writing attuned to the aporias that arise in attempts to tell the truth.[18]

Culler here offers a "first-wave reading," it should be noted. "Deconstructive *readings*"—"a practice of reading and writing"—are in question here. And what results are "aporias . . . in attempts to tell the truth."[19]

Most importantly, though, is why Culler thinks these results aren't straightforward skepticism. The difference is this: Culler believes that in deconstruction "the denial of logocentrism is carried out in logocentric terms." Deconstruction speaks against reason only through reason. And it does so since it does not believe that an outside of reason is simply or straightforwardly available. Deconstruction wards off skepticism due to its recognition of reason's unavoidability.

Derrida's claims about language, writing, are claims, after all. As claims, they refer back to truth. Derrida's setting out of the limits to truth, his debunking of logocentrism's dream, thus also depends on this dream. Deconstruction never asserts that one can make a final step outside of truth. Or, to put this in the school's jargon: deconstruction doesn't presume that any *absolute exteriority* to philosophy, to metaphysics, exists, or even that one is possible.

Let us leave aside for now whether Derrida in fact construes deconstruction this way. That question will return. Does this sort of account, which is indeed representative, really get us out of skepticism? Culler's treatment of an actual skeptic is enlightening on this point. Early on, he distinguishes Hume's treatment of causality from a deconstructive one offered by Nietzsche. Deconstruction's difference is this, according to Culler: the deconstruction of causality *uses causality*. More specifically, it involves a "double procedure of systematically employing the concepts or premises one is undermining," which "puts the critic in a position not of skeptical detachment but of unwarrantable involvement. . . ."[20]

That's the standard response. Deconstruction is not skepticism, because deconstruction lacks even skepticism's *security* in reason's denial. Deconstruction lacks skepticism's own confidence that skepticism is even possible—a confidence still exhibited by a traditional skeptic like Hume. Deconstruction doubts there is an "outside," and thus must employ the very "concepts or premises one is undermining."

Such an approach, arguably, does differ from Hume's, and the traditional skeptic's, self-understanding. Deconstruction, in Culler's view, trusts reason less: it doubts that reason may even arrive at definitively skeptical results. Deconstruction uses reason more, however: deconstruction uses reason even as reason's ability to conclude anything at all is brought into doubt.

That may be right. Is Derrida's position as glossed by Culler less skeptical than Hume's on that account? Does deconstruction differ with skepticism's conclusions in any way, however deconstruction arrives at the statement of these conclusions?

Culler's use of the term "unwarrantable" gives the show away here. Deconstruction's "involvement" with reason is "unwarrantable," according to Culler. It is said to be unwarrantable from the first. Accordingly, far from departing from skepticism, deconstruction, according to Culler's account, is skepticism's thoroughgoing generalization. Radical, thoroughgoing skepticism here precedes everything else. Reason has no intrinsic rights whatsoever, according to this reading. From the first reason, truth, and meaning are known not to function. And the fact that appeals to reason, truth, and meaning are subsequently made only deepens the charade: it extends and ramifies the thoroughgoing skepticism already posited.

As here understood, reason's, truth's employment at every moment indeed confirms skepticism, rather than refuting it. Already knowing reason somehow to be false, involvement with it to be unwarranted, in Culler's scenario, one is nevertheless forced to use it anyway, because no outside exists. The very appeal to reason, to truth or argument, is thus construed as the function of an entirely nonrational demand. By presenting reason, discourse, as under the sway of an entirely unknowable necessity, this scenario makes the employment of reason itself a delegate, a stand-in of unreason. A need, a force exceeding reason here founds the appeal to reason, such that reason is both coerced and coercive. On Culler's construal, reason is endlessly ventriloquized and ventriloquizing.[21]

Does Derrida believe this? Is Derrida a skeptic in the fashion asserted here? Is deconstruction radical, thoroughgoing skepticism, as many believe? This question is the central one this chapter poses. Before trying to answer it, however, before deciding if Derrida believes deconstruction is radical skepticism, it first needs to be asked whether the skepticism question is appropriately put to Derrida's discourse at all.

Another account appears to exist as to how all this stands, after all. Derrida explicitly labels his own discourse *undecidable*. Isn't the problem of skepticism, then, really addressed by undecidability? Is not what appears to be skepticism but a facet of such self-avowed, overarching undecidability?

This objection has some force. Derrida's thought is deeply complicated, and skepticism does concern undecidability in some way. Undecidability doesn't resolve the problem of skepticism as a whole, however, and our discussion of the first wave clarifies why this is so.

Most simply put, undecidability characterizes Derrida's discourses' *outcomes*, their results. It concerns the way Derridean notions like trace, archi-writing, supplement, and others function. The role of skepticism in Derrida's thought, however, as we have begun to see, precedes these issues. It concerns Derrida's starting point: the first move in his best-known texts, and the problems it poses. It thus precedes any undecidability that Derrida may finally attribute to his thought. Skepticism, this first phase of Derrida's thought, may indeed lay a groundwork for an undecidability that emerges later; but for just this reason, skepticism reaches beyond undecidability. In a nutshell, skepticism concerns deconstruction's presuppositions. Norris's and Culler's treatments, the first wave's problem, as I am about to show, indeed makes that plain.

Norris and Culler, the first wave, are right about a lot, after all. The first wave is right about the scope and positioning of the problem of radical skepticism in Derrida. Derrida's notion of logocentrism is as broad as the first wave says it is. It truly is all-encompassing.[22] Logocentrism is a claim about the character of all speech, all discourse: that these have illicitly been defined with an eye to telling the truth, held within the hegemony of the veridical. Further, writing's and logocentrism's delimitation, just as Culler's and Norris's treatments present them, indeed precede all concerns pertaining to philosophy, including Derrida's appeal to a transcendental of any kind.

In all of his 1967 works, Derrida begins by discussing the themes of writing, language, and the sign. He begins by discussing writing in its specificity, "regional writing"; before this term, "writing" has become a "paleonym." And because Derrida makes a claim about the *logos as such* on the basis of an interpretation of the sign (specifically, the written sign as embodying every possibility of signification as the sign of a sign), this invites, indeed perhaps even requires, his project's construal as skepticism. This combination—of writing regionally construed, as a linguistics might treat it, with the limitless generality of logocentrism's scope—is the very thing that opens Derrida to the skeptical, relativist, empiricist charges Derrida himself always rejects.

Of Grammatology is an especially important text in this regard. It remains perhaps Derrida's best-known work, and in it Derrida indeed starts from this theme of writing—quite evidently, since that's why *Of Grammatology* is called *Of Grammatology*.[23] The second section of *Of Grammatology*'s first half, which introduces the reading of Saussure, makes writing's role clear, as well as the role of these quasi-skeptical assertions.

This section is the beginning of Derrida's argument proper.[24] Writing has been discussed. Grammatology has been discussed. And, at this moment, before turning to Saussure, Derrida pauses to reflect methodologically and ask about the "ontophenomenological question of essence, that is to say of writing's origin" (*OG* 28).

Now, though this is not always widely recognized, for Derrida Socrates' question, *tí esti*, the question of essence, is a fundamental starting point for thought. It is the root of all philosophy and philosophical responsibility, a point to which Derrida himself returns again and again.[25] Accordingly, were the question of the essence of writing addressed at this moment by Derrida, philosophy's rights, reason's priority, would be preserved, and skepticism of any sort would be definitively avoided.

In this one case in *Of Grammatology*, however, Derrida will *pass* on this question. The examination of writing's essence, the answer to the question "what is writing" (what do we mean when we speak of writing, what concept of writing is in question here) is deferred, delayed, never to return. Instead, Derrida turns to linguistics' treatment of writing, to his reading of Saussure. Further, Derrida's reading begins by assuming that writing as a theme must be essentially suppressed—that such suppression *indeed defines an epoch*, though one with no dateable beginning and end.

Thus, introducing his discussion of Saussure, Derrida announces that Saussure's "declared purpose confirms . . . the subordination of grammatology, the historico-metaphysical reduction of writing to the rank of an instrument enslaved to a full and originarily spoken language. . . ." (*OG* 29). Accordingly, Derrida posits writing's repression from the start, prior to linguistics' reading, a reading that itself takes the place of philosophy's question of essence.[26]

This development, let me again underscore, comes before any philosophical considerations are directly raised. It comes before any talk of transcendentals, quasi-transcendentals, and truth.[27] Thus, while this framework, again, may contribute to a later setting out of undecidability, an undecidability that pertains to Derrida's results, that undecidability can transpire only because the theses concerning phonocentrism and logocentrism have been postulated already. Accordingly, these theses— writing's repression, an illicit logocentrism undermining all claim to tell the truth—*on their own* have standing. They have meaning on their own, and they themselves have been said to be true initially. Numerous critics have taken them this way, as Culler's and Norris's works witness.

The apogee of the skepticism problem, its greatest extension, it should be noted, doubtless comes in Derrida's talk of binary oppositions. In *Positions*, and in his other 1972 publications, Derrida formalized the possibility of the theses of logocentrism and phonocentrism. The history and system of the language of metaphysics is a system of binary oppositions, Derrida declares. More specifically, in *Positions*, in the course of presenting "a general strategy of deconstruction," Derrida offered the canonical version of his notion of binary oppositions. "I am attempting to pursue . . . a kind of general strategy of deconstruction," Derrida writes. "The latter is to avoid simply neutralizing the binary oppositions of metaphysics and simply residing within the closed field of these oppositions. . . . To do justice to this necessity is to recognize that in a classical philosophical opposition we are not dealing with a peaceful coexistence of a vis-à-vis, but rather with a violent hierarchy. One of the two terms governs the other . . . or has the upper hand. To deconstruct the opposition, first of all, is to overturn the hierarchy . . ." (*POS* 41).

Derrida declares that it is necessary to begin by reversing philosophy's violent hierarchies. Let me emphasize—that is a thesis *about* philosophy; it's not a thesis *within* philosophy. The standard reading, the account of Derrida's thought as engaged in "double reading," thus gets this wrong, no matter how salutary it has proved in other ways. The standard reading claims that Derrida begins from philosophy, from philosophy's dominant reading of a text, and then goes elsewhere.

That's not right. In the 1967 writings Derrida begins from theses *about* philosophy. Those theses are not philosophy's own, by any means. Derrida's work with philosophy presupposes a perspective foreign to philosophy from the beginning. Derrida's entrance to philosophical discourse is based on claims that no philosophy authorizes, nor can authorize.

More specifically, as stated by Derrida himself, binary oppositions arise as his discourse's presupposition. They function as logocentrism and phonocentrism do in *Of Grammatology*—as broad, sweeping posits or hypotheses from which the rest of deconstruction begins. Their region (what science studies them), subject (the medium in which they inhere), and evidence (on what grounds these claims are true, on what grounds one should believe that there *are* binary oppositions) are far from clear, however. Some readers seem to have taken these claims as odd sorts of linguistic or historical facts.[28] Are they, however, historical or linguistic theses? Are they really true? Are they even meant to be? What kind of knowledge does or even could know them?

Whatever their status, given their postulation, how to avoid the radical skeptical, relativist conclusions that Norris, Culler, and so many others draw from them? How to rule out historicist and linguistic relativist results like Rorty's from deconstruction? How to declare such skeptical, relativist deconstruction interpretations false? Where, if anywhere, in short, have Norris and Culler really gone wrong?

Whatever else, this much is clear: Derrida insists that these conclusions are false; he insists such results are to be avoided. Derrida denounces "relativism, psychologism, empiricism, skepticism and historicism" always. He often groups them together: "skepticism, empiricism, even nihilism" (*AFT* 137). Derrida is not an historicist, a relativist, a skeptic, he claims. Derrida takes philosophical responsibility seriously; he repeats this, first to last.[29]

How to understand these repeated denials by Derrida? Does he simply have in mind the standard first-wave account? The question returns: is deconstruction radical skepticism *according to Derrida*?

It's difficult to say. There is something right about Derrida as a radical skeptic. There is something right about the first-wave view. Derrida does talk like Norris and Culler talk on some occasions.[30] He does sound very much as Culler presents him at times. There's no denying this. Reason is an ultimate strategic necessity. Its values are to be given only lip service. Reason's very employment is itself the sign of radical coercion.

Sometimes Derrida sounds like Culler and Norris. Other times, however, he makes a different, perhaps more disturbing claim. Derrida says that such a reconstrual of reason is itself part of the carrying out of philosophy's and reason's own responsibility. Derrida is commanded by philosophy *throughout*, says Derrida, even if what he carries out no longer answers fully to reason's and philosophy's name. His undertaking is *philosophy's responsibility's heir*. Derrida said that to Rorty, it seems. Derrida claims he is being responsible to all philosophy somehow, even at these moments in his text where reason is most in question: when logocentrism, phonocentrism, binary oppositions are postulated.

The matter is very vexed. For, Derrida, finally, seems not to distinguish between the two accounts that have come forward. Derrida doesn't distinguish between first-wave–style forced reason talk and the claim to philosophical responsibility throughout. The one just seems to be the other in Derrida's eyes.

Derrida's failure to distinguish these different responsibilities in a 1994 roundtable discussion at Villanova sheds further light on his relation to skepticism. When asked about the way he reads, Derrida rejected as "caricature" the assignment to him of a "lack of respect for reading." "I have constantly tried to read and understand Plato and Aristotle and I have devoted a number of texts to them. . . . So I think we have to read them again and again and again and I feel that, however old I am, I am on the threshold of reading Plato and Aristotle. I love them and I feel I have to start again and again and again. It is a task which is in front of me, before me."[31]

Derrida went on: "Now nevertheless the way I tried to read Plato and Aristotle and others is not a way of commanding, repeating and conserving, this heritage. It is an analysis which tries to find out how their thinking works or does not work, to find the tensions, the contradictions. . . . So to be true to Plato and this is a sign of love and respect for Plato, I have to analyze the functioning and disfunctioning of his work."[32]

Derrida means more at this moment, however, than he says. All philosophical discussions, after all, ask whether the philosophers discussed "work or not." The "tensions," the "contradictions," the "disfunctions" Derrida talks about here go farther than this. They in fact refer to the logocentrism, phonocentrism, binary opposition side of Derrida's thought. The disfunctions, according to Derrida himself, concern reason's and philosophy's project as a whole. As with his talk of writing's suppression above, Derrida believes that structural and genetic limits, from the first, haunt thought's, reason's, philosophy's very possibility and aims.

How these conclusions comport with a "love and respect" for Plato and Aristotle is very hard to see, however. *Why* would one keep reading Plato and Aristotle, why would this be a task "in front of" one, once these theses have been promulgated, once these internal and unavoidable limits of the projects of these authors are known?

It's equally clear, however, that *Derrida* himself finds no discontinuity between the two. "To be true to Plato and this is a sign of love and respect . . . I have to analyze the functioning and disfunctioning," he states. That Derrida doesn't distinguish between first-wave–style forced responsibility to philosophy and responsibility to reason and philosophy in truth is obvious. Derrida's belief in his entire body of work's total responsibility to philosophy's ethos, this "love and respect" for philosophy and tradition, is evident in all his writings, and it is doubtless genuine. The one really is the other, as far as Derrida is concerned.

Again, what to make of this? Is Derrida perhaps right?

No one can say he understands Derrida better than Derrida understands himself. The problem is not with Derrida at all, perhaps, at first remove. A kind of parallax arguably exists between Derrida's project, viewed from Derrida's perspective, and Derrida's project viewed from its receivers' point of view. Derrida's responsibility to philosophy looks different to Derrida's readers than to Derrida himself.

Here's where what I call a developmental perspective can step in. Such a perspective avoids this perhaps inevitable parallax by returning to Derrida's thought's development: by returning to deconstruction's genesis. Derrida decides on deconstruction *and* its undecidability, it is often said.

How did Derrida come to make that decision? More specifically, how did Derrida begin to conceive of his deconstructive transformation of philosophical responsibility, and why was such a transformation in the first place deemed desirable by Derrida? So, too, what led Derrida to believe philosophical responsibility *could* be transformed, and that something other than skepticism could result? These are the questions a developmental approach pursues.

We've already seen that Derrida denies skepticism, first and last. At times, he construes the denial of skepticism in the same way as his first-wave commentators. But the refutation of skepticism also takes another form in Derrida, which is absent from first-wave construals. It's absent for the most part from Derrida's better-known writings, to be fair. It's not highly evident in the 1967 publications, though his early essays on Foucault and Levinas are crucial exceptions.

Skepticism's other refutation has its roots in Husserl's thinking. Whenever Derrida speaks of his anti-relativist, anti-empiricist, anti-historicist

stance, he refers to Husserl. "Something that I learned from the great figures in the history of philosophy, from Husserl in particular, is . . . not to
be held within the fragility of an incompetent empiricist discourse. . . ."[33]
"I have . . . drunk my mother's milk on the breast of transcendental phenomenology, which first of all was a rigorous critique of relativism, empiricism, skepticism, and historicism. . . ."[34] "Husserl has shown better than
anyone else, relativism, like all its derivatives, remains a philosophical position in contradiction with itself" (*AFT* 137).

Can Husserl's role in the development of Derrida's thought show how
deconstruction's strategy answers to philosophy's responsibility as a
whole? Can what appears to be radical skepticism be shown to be something else, thanks to tracing the development of Derrida's thought
through Husserlian phenomenology?

These questions are less far-fetched than they seem. Husserl shaped
Derrida's thinking on history from the first. Genesis was the question Derrida wanted to put to Husserl from the very beginning. Derrida's last predeconstructive writing, Derrida's "Introduction" to Husserl's *Origin*, reconsiders Husserl's interpretation of history from the ground up.

Derrida devoted years of study to Husserl and Husserl's thought, particularly in relation to history. That's what keeps Derrida from historicism, relativism, skepticism, Derrida himself seems to think. Derrida
confirms this in a decisive footnote he appended to an interview in
Positions:

> I had forgotten that Scarpetta's question also named historicism. Of
> course the critique of historicism in all its forms seems to me indis
> pensable. What I first learned about this critique in Husserl . . .
> seems to me valid in its argumentative framework, even if in the last
> analysis it is based on a historical teleology of truth. On this last
> question the issue is to be reopened. The issue would be can one
> criticize historicism in the name of something other than truth and
> science. . . ." (*POS* 58n32)

Derrida insists on his thought's debt to Husserl; he still insists on Husserl's influence even when Derrida is articulating deconstruction's grand
strategy. Derrida's response provides a road map for investigating the development of Derridean deconstruction.

First, the role of the critique of historicism in Derrida's own thinking
must be examined from the ground up. How Derrida's thought differs
especially from Heidegger's should be established here.[35] This difference
can be made clear thanks only to an understanding of the roots of Derrida's thought in Husserl and Husserl's critique of historicism.

Secondly, a developmental approach must flesh out Derrida's break with Husserl. Husserl's critique of historicism depended on a theory of history and truth, "a historical teleology of truth." Ultimately, Derrida questioned that theory, *Positions* informs us. Derrida leaves Husserl's thought's framework, his teleology, behind. Derrida leaves this framework behind, yet retains what depends on that framework: Husserl's historicism critique. That's Derrida's claim.

How does that work? How does that function? What shape did this break from Husserl take? How did Derrida break with Husserl, yet still retain some of Husserl's conclusions?

Exactly what sort of a break with Husserl did Derrida make, then? How does Derrida go from his 1962 phenomenology work to the 1967 works, and particularly to *Of Grammatology*'s opening pages? Does this break supply the premises of Derrida's 1967 works?

The study of Derrida's development, of deconstruction's singular genesis, tries to answer these questions. It tries to quiet the fruitless, yet perhaps inevitable, debate that shrouds Derrida's work even to this day. It confronts Derrida's own question head-on: "can one criticize historicism other than in the name of truth and science?" The study of Derrida's development will aim to determine, once and for all, how deconstruction differs from skepticism . . . if in truth deconstruction does so.

Derrida, Husserl, and the Commentators

A Developmental Approach

This chapter begins where the previous one left off, by attempting to establish what Derrida inherited from Husserl. Apart from the specific motivation brought forward in Chapter 1—the unstable character of the part played by skepticism in early deconstruction—the need to plumb Derrida's engagement with Husserl seems self-evident. Derrida worked on no one else for nearly fifteen years, and Husserl's thought was the milieu in which the project of deconstruction was forged. Indeed, throughout his career, when Derrida was pressed on concrete philosophical points—the status of concepts, of the sentence and its use, the relation of sense to reference—it was to the teachings of Husserl that he returned.[1]

Not only, however, have the most prominent commentators on Derrida devoted relatively little attention to this relationship, but this facet of Derrida's corpus has long been fraught with controversy.[2] Indeed, with a few highly significant exceptions, those interested in Derrida and Husserl even today can be divided into two separate and opposing camps.[3] One of these is largely composed of Husserl scholars, often latecomers to Derrida's thought, who tend to extrapolate detailed individual positions from a particular text, largely in isolation from broader hermeneutic and interpretative concerns. These critics, when it comes to Derrida's work on Husserl, are interested above all in whether Derrida gets Husserl right, usually on quite specific, albeit often important, points. They want to know whether what Derrida is saying about Husserl is correct,[4] and they take for granted, for the most part, that the standard of correctness will be supplied by the sort of analyses current in the field of Husserl studies in the U.S. today, in contrast to the way work was done on Husserl in France or Germany thirty to forty years ago, when Derrida himself engaged in these studies.[5]

More significantly, this camp wants to know if Derrida gets Husserl's claims right *before* they attend to Derrida's own deconstructive aims—to Derrida's own interests and program.[6] Whether Derrida understands Husserl correctly is the first and often the sole topic of discussion for such interpreters.

The Derrideans, by contrast, by and large read rather than argue, and tend to have more care for the broadest aims of the author under discussion, at least if that author happens to be Derrida. This camp cares most about what Derrida thinks; Derrida's intentions are key. In turn, though there are some notable exceptions, these readers tend to give short shrift to Husserl's own thought, to any prolonged investigation of Husserlian phenomenology, whether in Derrida's own style or another's. For the Derrideans, Husserl's hard-won positions and insights too often serve as a mere medium for the expressions of Derrida's own concepts and aims.[7]

This second camp has a quite different view of where any discussion of Derrida and Husserl must begin. In their eyes, Derrida's own intentions, his own project and ambitions, must be understood first, before anything else. Indeed, this second camp claims, I believe persuasively, that even if one wants what the Husserlians want—to see whether Derrida gets Husserl right—Derrida's own broader aims must first be grasped. Derrida's statements about Husserl are everywhere a part of Derrida's articulation of his own program; their context is provided by the exposition of Derrida's own aims. For this reason, it is impossible to understand the sense, the significance of Derrida's claims about Husserl (and thus their correctness) without coming to grips with Derrida's own intentions, which continually inform that sense.[8]

The two camps, then, disagree about nearly everything. They don't read one another often. And when they do, they don't understand or convince each other; the Derrideans' argument does not persuade all, or perhaps any, of the Husserlians.[9] And to return to the broader point, the one that most concerns me, no current approach to Derrida's writings on Husserl promises to treat these works in a truly comprehensive manner, or in a way potentially convincing to all concerned. Those who tend to know Husserl best are highly skeptical of Derrida's own approach, even to the point of being unable to identify with any specificity what this style of treatment may be. Those more sympathetic to Derrida's work in turn find themselves unable to engage with Husserl, upon whom Derrida comments, and to whose works and thoughts Derrida devoted some fifteen years of study.

There is then, a deep divide, a dysfunction besetting Husserl / Derrida studies generally, and this begins to indicate that a deeper deficiency exists: that an obstacle largely unrecognized even now impedes engaging with Derrida's thought on Husserl in a wholly satisfactory way. Of course, specific reasons may well account for this division and some of its intransigence—differences in training among the participants in the debate, disdain for one another's scholarship, and so on. Yet those who have taken part in these debates are some of Derrida's most able interpreters, and almost all have proceeded with the best of intentions. The persistence and depth of this split suggests that something more substantial is at work here, something that affects even the best of Husserl and Derrida commentators.

Theoretically speaking, the solution to this problem of how to read Derrida on Husserl is rather easy, after all. On the surface, the resolution of the impasse that exists between Husserlians and Derrideans concerning where commentary on Derrida and Husserl must begin is in principle achievable. Neither camp's perspective has priority over the other; neither side is completely right on its own. Instead, understanding Derrida and seeing if he gets Husserl's claims straight must proceed together; these tasks can only be approached simultaneously if comprehensive work and any conceivable resolution to these disputes are to emerge.[10]

At the same time, if what is needed here is in theory available, the persistence of the problem indicates that a deeper impediment is also at work. Granting that the appropriate stance for commentary has not been explicit until now, genuinely common ground between Husserl and Derrida has yet to be uncovered in these debates. For the stated theoretical perspective to work, however, an area of interest genuinely shared by both thinkers must be apparent. If Derrida's deconstructive aims and Husserl's phenomenological claims are to be respected together, their *interests* must clearly line up somewhere; thus it must be recognized, in tandem with the absence of theoretical clarity about the overall standpoint commentators should take, that the deepest points of philosophical contact between Derrida and Husserl have yet to be fully disclosed in a working, practical way.

What this failure to uncover a common working ground for Derrida / Husserl studies suggests is that a deeper, underlying impasse indeed has hold of Derrida studies, and that Derrida himself may have something of a hand in such an impasse. These matters are very difficult, however, and may only be approached slowly. Indeed, the one thing fully clear is that no one has an approach at present by which any definitive judgment of any sort about these matters may be reached. Thus, if the criterion set out is to be fulfilled—if Derrida's aims and Husserl's claims are to be approached together—extraordinary steps, an unusual course of presentation will be required. Setting aside for now what is perhaps the deepest aspect of this problem, let me further explore the discussion among the commentators, detailing the strictly occasional causes of this impasse and how these function, since an approach to Derrida's *Speech and Phenomena* by way of Derrida's thought's development begins to look highly promising in that context.

The Case for Weak and Strong Development in Derrida's Early Writings

Some rather obvious motives exist for adopting a developmental perspective on Derrida's thought and work. Yet, a certain paradox, a certain irony lies latent in all this controversy among his commentators. A massive, thoroughgoing split has hold of much of Derrida / Husserl studies; nevertheless, an equally vast, albeit largely tacit, agreement turns out to be shared by both camps: namely, the belief that no substantial change or development takes place in Derrida's thought throughout the four works he wrote on Husserl over the course of fifteen years.[11] Almost all commentators on both sides treat Derrida's Husserl writings as if they propose a single, unitary interpretation of Husserl, and thus the possibility of real change in Derrida's relation to Husserl—both in Derrida's actual interpretation of Husserl and in his stance toward Husserl's goals—is something neither camp has really taken seriously so far.[12]

Of course, I do not wish simply to call into question the priority often granted to *Speech and Phenomena* as such. This priority was reasonable enough, given that *Speech and Phenomena* was one of the three publications of 1967, works for which Derrida remains best known even today. At the same time, this assumed priority often bore a set of corollaries in its wake, and these I *do* intend to question as a means of showing the need to take seriously the possibility of real development in Derrida's work. Not only was *Speech and Phenomena* given priority, but it was often believed to be the goal, the single culminating *telos* toward which all of Derrida's other Husserl writings tended—such that no serious temporal differentiation among any of Derrida's Husserl works was thought to be required.[13] All of Derrida's writings were believed to lead up to *Speech and Phenomena* and thus to agree with Derrida's 1967 Husserl work, as well as with one another in almost all essential respects, this often to such an extent that *Speech and Phenomena*'s theses have been read back into the earlier works, and the claims of the earlier works read forward into *Speech and Phenomena*.

I would argue, however, that recognizing the specificity of Derrida's different engagements with Husserl over time is essential to any attempt to remedy the impasses in the field of Husserl / Derrida studies just sketched—central to the ability to take into account, together, Husserl's claims and Derrida's aims. At a minimum, these early works must be examined and their differences registered in order to find such missing common ground and, in the case of *Speech and Phenomena*, to find a way to pay attention to Derrida's aims and Husserl's claims. Nor may the results of either partisan Husserlians or partisan Derrideans be pronounced convincing until such work has been done.

Two key points may give a better idea of what this attention to Derrida's development would mean as pertains to the background and context of *Speech and Phenomena*. First, the relation of Derrida's 1967 work on Husserl to Derrida's 1954 *Le problème* would be given more attention than is currently the case. *Le problème* certainly foreshadows *Speech and Phenomena* in some respects, as commentators have recognized, and both works undertake a project ultimately aimed at Husserl's thought as a whole. Yet the mere fact that Derrida's corpus contains two complete texts aimed at total interpretations of Husserl's thought indicates that significant differences must also exist between *Le problème* and *Speech and Phenomena*. Two works devoted to the entirety of Husserl's project show that important changes must have taken place in Derrida's own standpoint, as well as his actual interpretation of Husserl, between 1954 and 1967; yet these so far remain almost wholly unspecified in the critical literature. Attending to Derrida's development in this sense would thus entail getting a clearer account of the relation between these two works than we have at present, preliminary to any decision about what Derrida does or does not accomplish in *Speech and Phenomena*.

A second basic developmental feature, also so far neglected, informing Derrida's work in *Speech and Phenomena*, and upon which much potentially rests, is where *Speech and Phenomena* stands in the sequence of Derrida's writings on Husserl. Specifically, when held up against the unfolding of Husserl's own corpus, *Speech and Phenomena* turns out to occupy an almost opposite position in the series of Derrida's works on Husserl than it does in Husserl's own thought. Derrida addresses almost last in his own itinerary those matters on which Husserl worked on nearly first in his, the logical considerations contained in his *Investigations*; similarly, Derrida works first, or at least earlier, on those matters to which Husserl devoted the final phase of his thinking: the historical considerations to be found, above all, in "The Origin of Geometry." The movement of Derrida's own thought through Husserl's corpus thus traces out Husserl's own almost in reverse.[14] This reversal, accordingly, affects the status of *Speech and Phenomena* and its claims in significant ways, though, once again, this has for the most part been ignored by the commentators. It suggests at the least that Derrida's reading of Husserl in *Speech and Phenomena* may be heavily sedimented—a technical Husserlian term for conclusions and premises that continue to operate in a discourse even after their actual grounds, the reasons for holding them, have fallen from view. Thus, Derrida may well take for granted in *Speech and Phenomena* interpretations he has carried out in previous works and which he does not necessarily feel the need to restate at this later moment.[15]

These, then, are but two singular features of Derrida's development—from many that might be offered—that clearly inform Derrida's engagement with Husserl in *Speech and Phenomena*, and to which insufficient attention has been paid in the literature. Their investigation would be a propaideutic, a necessary first step, for arriving at any truly definitive judgment concerning Derrida's treatment of Husserl in that work. Only by taking Derrida's extensive and multisided engagement with Husserl into account prior to *Speech and Phenomena* can an interpretation of this work be offered meeting the criteria set out above. Both of these concerns, however, speak only to a first sense of development. A second, stronger sense of development is also possible, though it should be noted that the preceding arguments would still hold good no matter what readers may make of what follows. According to this stronger sense of development, the moment of deconstruction's advent, the appearance of the publications of 1967 would be assigned far greater importance than has been the case thus far. According to this second developmental hypothesis, all of Derrida's 1967 thought would be presumed to be the site of a highly singular, perhaps unparalleled innovation. These works would represent a moment of radical, even discontinuous change in relation to Derrida's earlier pre-deconstructive writings—the 1962 "Introduction" and those that come before.

With this we come to the most decisive matter. A radical shift, a moment of unprecedented innovation, could mark the work for which Derrida remains best known. And this second, strong sense of development would begin to explain why truly satisfactory comprehension of all of Derrida's 1967 work has not been achieved, as well as why the deepest philosophical ground for Derrida's work has not yet been found, since the latter may only be available in a traditional form in Derrida's earlier works. So too, some of the other anomalies we have just brought forward with respect to *Speech and Phenomena* would also be explained: why Derrida writes on all of Husserl a second time around, and why his path through Husserl's work is so different from Husserl's own.

Remaining still with *Speech and Phenomena*, and with our own perspective on it as commentators, this work, as this second hypothesis presents it, would turn out to be not just another, second interpretation of Husserl's thought in totality, but one framed from the point of view of Derrida's newly construed approach to *all philosophy*, an approach having all the other 1967 writings as its context.[16] Just on the face of it, Derrida's aims in *Speech and Phenomena are* clearly very different from Husserl's. Derrida there is not engaging with Husserl's first phenomenological writings preparatory to an encounter with the rest of his phenomenology; rather, he is taking leave from Husserl's thought as a whole and writing on his work for what turns out to be almost the last time.[17] Derrida from the first in this text aims at those concealed features of *all philosophy and all thought* that permitted Husserl's project to spring forth in the first place: what ways of viewing signs and language led Husserl toward the reductions and perhaps destined them in advance to an illicit set of limitations. Derrida thus is not interested in arriving at authoritative distinctions among species of signs, nor asking whether, on their own terms, with Husserl's aims in mind, these may have cogency—a matter that Derrida takes as already settled.[18]

This isn't to say that *Speech and Phenomena* itself would ultimately be unimportant or even unintelligible. It may mean that considerable preparation is needed, however, before Derrida's work in *Speech and Phenomena* may be successfully engaged in a satisfactory way. It may also indicate that what is demanded most of all at this moment, given the impasse commentary faces, is the opposite of what *Speech and Phenomena* offers when taken on its own. This work provides Derrida's view of Husserl primarily from the perspective of how Derrida now sees all philosophy. In *Speech and Phenomena*, Derrida starts from the perspective of phonocentrism and logocentrism that the first half of *Of Grammatology* provides, thus coming at Husserl from decisions about philosophy as a whole that Derrida had reached *prior to Speech and Phenomena*—most notably decisions that constitute variations of Heidegger's theses on the history of metaphysics and its privileging of presence.

Given the originality, the complexity, and the difficulties of Derrida's core thought, what may be needed most, however, is not Husserl's thought seen in light of Derrida's views on philosophy, but Derrida's views on philosophy seen in the light of his own earlier work on Husserl. Derrida came to his mature positions, after all, by way of a prolonged engagement with Husserl's thought. Husserlian phenomenology provided Derrida with the tools and the most immediate motives for his considerable innovations—for what came to be known as deconstruction, according to Derrida's own repeated testimony. What readers in both camps may most need to grasp, then, is how and why Derrida was led to invent deconstruction in the first place. What in his engagement with Husserl led Derrida to devise this singular way of working, a way that we have still perhaps failed to fully comprehend? What specific points in Husserl made Derrida feel deconstruction was needed, and that it was possible?

These are the questions posed by a developmental approach, in the sense that I intend, and they may well be the key questions for Derrida/Husserl Derrida studies and for the study of Derrida's early writings generally. Such an approach reaches no decisions in advance concerning the legitimacy and validity of deconstruction itself; its intention would be neither to celebrate Derrida's work nor to denounce it. Rather, more modestly, it seeks a comprehensive understanding of Derrida's project, in living contact with Husserl, the author upon whom his thought most depends, prior to arriving at any other results.

Derrida Speaks of His Own Development—or Does He?

Approaching Derrida's thought through its development in both senses just presented should eventually make possible significant progress in understanding Derrida's own early project, as well as in definitively adjudicating the status of Derrida's Husserl interpretation. Later in this chapter, Derrida's "Introduction to Husserl's *Origin of Geometry*" is explored and my theses surrounding deconstruction's invention developed. The grounds that led Derrida to this innovation, what made him think deconstruction was possible as well as necessary, begin to emerge, and with this, some of the actual results this style of investigation attains become clear.

Yet all this, in turn, presupposes that Derrida's thought does indeed develop in significant ways, and in particular that Derrida's "Introduction" is the turning point of this development. Thus, before turning to the "Introduction" itself, I must first come to grips with another dimension of the present problem, a further aspect of what has prevented Derrida's development from receiving careful scrutiny.

So far I have only treated one aspect, the first prong, of what might be called "a two-pronged unity thesis" underlying all extant approaches to Derrida's early work. This first prong centers on *Speech and Phenomena* and the relation of all of Derrida's early works *on Husserl* to it, as well as to one another. The second prong, however, extends this unity thesis further. According to this hypothesis, all Derrida's early works, including all the 1967 works, are of a single piece and to be seen as the product of a single consistent intention: *Of Grammatology* and *Writing and Difference*, as well as *Speech and Phenomena*, agree with *Le problème*, the "Introduction" and "'Genesis and Structure' in Phenomenology."[19] This second claim, that all of Derrida's early writings form a unity, has often buttressed the first claim, such that commentators like Bernet or Dastur, who are most aware of some of the problems in asserting the first, downplay them, thanks to the second.

This second, broader assumption, that all of Derrida's early writings form a single whole, typically focuses on the relation of Derrida's "Introduction" to *Of Grammatology* rather than to *Speech and Phenomena*. It depends on an understanding of Derrida's early work about to be sketched, a sketch that will eventually lead us to re-think Derrida's early thought and confront the development that may take place there.

An account already exists of how Derrida's early reading of Husserl led Derrida to deconstruction, to all of the 1967 writings. In its existing form, however, this account actually *supports* the neglect of development and of changes in Derrida's thought. On this standard account, Derrida discovers the core notion of all his thought, the problem of writing, in his 1962 "Introduction" to Husserl's work. Now, no one, obviously, could quarrel with the claim that Derrida first encounters the theme of writing in the "Introduction." On the view in question, however, how writing is understood, and the stance taken toward it by Derrida in the "Introduction," is essentially the same as in Derrida's 1967 texts. Writing's status is posited as identical in all of Derrida's early work, Derrida's treatments of writing in 1962 and 1967 being essentially fungible; this belief underpins the notion that Derrida's outlook across all of his early works is unitary. This rather monolithic view comprises the second, broader prong of our unity thesis, and with it, a difficult issue emerges; for the fact is that Derrida himself has lent credence to this standpoint. Derrida's own occasional remarks do appear to endorse this continuist scenario in some fashion, and it must be conceded that those who have failed to take Derrida's development seriously have often only been heeding what they believe to be Derrida's own prescriptions on this matter.

The evidence from which Derrida's endorsement has been gleaned, however, proves to be more ambiguous than it first appears, and than many commentators have supposed. Whether Derrida himself does or does not endorse such a view of his own writings ultimately remains fundamentally in doubt.

Nevertheless, particularly in the first case that I am about to examine—a passage to which most commentators have looked for guidance as to how Derrida's early works are to be understood—Derrida does seem at first glance to confirm the standard view of his corpus. "In this essay," Derrida states, referring to the "Introduction," "the problematic of writing was already in place as such, bound to the irreducible structure of 'deferral' in its relationships to consciousness, presence, history and the history of science, the disappearance or delay of origins, etc." (*POS* 5).

This passage occurs in an interview Derrida originally gave in 1967, which was first published in book form in 1972 in *Positions*. And this single sentence has been the authority for most construals of the development (or lack thereof) of Derrida's early thought. In it, Derrida appears to say what the vast majority of critics have believed: that "writing" in the "Introduction" and the 1967 works is fundamentally the same—that writing's conception, and Derrida's own stance toward it, are essentially identical in 1967 and 1962. Nevertheless, a single sentence may seem scant evidence for matters of such importance, especially when "Time of a Thesis: Punctuations" ("TT") is taken into account. This work, which Derrida gave as a prelude to his 1990 doctoral dissertation defense, offers a far more detailed account of his corpus. Overall, "Time of a Thesis" paints a more complex portrait of Derrida's early works and their relations that renders all judgments about Derrida's development immediately more problematic.

Yet at first glance, even "Time of a Thesis," it must be conceded, while clearly expanding on Derrida's account in *Positions*, may still seem to confirm that account. In "Time of a Thesis," reviewing his corpus to date, Derrida broaches the "Introduction" by referring to "something like an unthought axiomatic of Husserlian phenomenology." Derrida then links this unthought axiomatic to what seems to be the very same theme we have just encountered, namely "a problematic of writing," "a consistent problematic of writing and the trace," as Derrida here calls it. "This unthought-out axiomatics," Derrida continues, "seemed to me to limit the scope of a consistent problematic of writing and the trace. . . ." ("TT" 39)

Matters turn out to be more complicated than they appear at first glance, however, as Derrida's talk of "a consistent problematic of writing and the trace" itself begins to indicate, since Derrida never speaks of the trace in the "Introduction" at all. Moreover, such an "unthought axiomatic" pertaining to all of Husserl's phenomenology would by no means be the first matter to which the "Introduction" as a whole is dedicated, though this description surely pertains to Derrida's 1967 *Speech and Phenomena*. So, too, the issues Derrida inventories under this heading of the unthought also make one wonder to what extent Derrida is assigning to the "Introduction" alone such a labor of thinking this unthought. Derrida goes on to speak of "intuitionism, the absolute privilege of the living present, . . . the problem of its own phenomenological enunciation . . . ," and though each of these topics are doubtless touched on in the "Introduction," especially the last, none of them are major themes—none are central concerns of the 1962 work.[20]

Fortunately, however, more than internal evidence exists to support the concern that Derrida may not be addressing solely his 1962 work at this moment in "Time of a Thesis," which is how it may first seem and which most commentators have assumed; for in "Time of a Thesis" Derrida does not in fact assign these themes to the "Introduction" itself; he never claims that in the "Introduction" he himself thought this "unthought axiomatic" or decisively addressed any of its subcategories. Rather, Derrida says his 1962 "Introduction," let him *approach* all this ("m'avait permis d'approcher").[21] The "Introduction" permitted Derrida to draw nearer to some of these matters, to make a start on them—issues whose full conception Derrida, in fact, as with the trace, clearly only arrived at later.

Here a very large issue emerges that we can touch on only in passing. Features of the *Positions* interview also support this notion that Derrida does not intend to give a straightforward account of the role the "Introduction" plays in his development, but rather, that, in both places, he views this text along with his later work and presents what the "Introduction" and *Speech and Phenomena* accomplished *together*.[22] Both discussions of the "Introduction" and *Speech and Phenomena* may take place from a perspective that sees each as part of a single whole—as two sides of a single page, "recto and verso," as Derrida himself in fact puts it in *Positions*, right before the remark cited above (*POS* 5). Derrida in both thus may be presenting the "Introduction" retrospectively, from the standpoint of its contribution to his mature thought—from an essentially teleological vantage.

I do not wish to assert that this gloss is necessarily right and that it is certain that the standard view is wrong. Only this much is evident: we cannot be sure in either passage that Derrida is ruling out significant development, since we cannot tell whether Derrida means to comment on this possibility at all, to give any real testimony one way or the other. Fortunately, "Time of a Thesis" provides a further service when it comes to this issue. Though we cannot be sure Derrida is denying that his thought develops, this same passage of "Time of a Thesis" does give us a straightforward *criterion*, thanks to which we can decide this matter for ourselves. As is becoming plain, in "Time of a Thesis" Derrida links what he calls "a consistent problematic of writing and the trace" to the "unthought axiomatic of phenomenology" ("TT" 39). Derrida thus implies that framing "a consistent problematic of writing and the trace" is only possible once the limits of Husserl's thought have been decisively broached. A truly "consistent problematic of writing and the trace," Derrida affirms, requires thinking this "unthought axiomatic of all Husserlian phenomenology"; the discovery of the one, of such an unthought axiomatic, turns out to be the necessary condition for the other, for a consistent problematic of writing.

This correlation drawn by "Time of a Thesis" thus provides a standard by which we may measure for ourselves whether Derrida's thought does indeed develop. Did Derrida in the "Introduction" really present *the unthought axiomatic* of all of Husserl's thought and really arrive at a truly "consistent problematic of writing" (and the trace)? Did Derrida already, in this radical a manner, break with Husserl in the "Introduction" and thus treat writing in a way genuinely identical with his later work, such that the kind of development I have been suggesting would be ruled out? Or did Derrida in the "Introduction" perhaps begin to see that such a task was possible, perhaps even that it was necessary—that Husserl's treatment of writing was arguably inconsistent, and that something like an unthought was there at work, yet without Derrida himself thinking either this unthought or a more consistent writing as such—with the result that real change, significant alteration must indeed be acknowledged to take place in Derrida's own thought across these early works?

The Interpretation of Writing in Derrida's 1962 "Introduction"

With these questions in mind, let us turn to the "Introduction," clearly the decisive text for all these matters, and to Derrida's treatment of writing in its section VII, in order to decide them for ourselves. The key issue for determining how close Derrida's treatment of writing in his "Introduction" in 1962 is to his 1967 work is how writing is precomprehended in the 1962 text, and what sort of role is assigned to it. Is the writing at issue here the same writing as in *Of Grammatology*, for example—regional, worldly writing, as most people understand it, potentially the subject of an empirical science, such as, for example, Saussure's linguistics? Is this sort of everyday conception of writing Derrida's starting point in the "Introduction" as well? Most commentators have believed this to be so; section VII of the "Introduction," they aver, starts out from writing understood as it is treated in the 1967 works. Yet that such commentators are right, that section VII understands writing in this sense, turns out to be far from evident.

In fact, it can be quickly established that this is simply not so. To be sure, Derrida doesn't specify writing's status at the outset of section VII, and this has caused some confusion. Not only, however, does his opening discussion clearly assume the discussion of language already in progress in VI and all the stipulations that attach to it; but, five paragraphs into section VII, referring to what's come before, Derrida makes clear how writing is to be understood and decisively sets out the status it has had in his text up until this point. "All this can be said," writes Derrida, "only on the basis of an intentional analysis which retains from writing nothing but writing's pure relation to a consciousness which grounds it as such, and not its facticity which, left to itself, is totally insignificant. . . ." He continues, a bit later in this same paragraph, the fifth paragraph of section VII of the "Introduction": "If the pure juridical possibility of being intelligible for a transcendental subject in general, and if the pure relation of dependence on the gaze of a writer and a reader is not announced in the text, . . . it is only a chaotic literalness, the sensible opacity of a defunct designation deprived of its transcendental function" (*LOG* 85 / *IOG* 88, translation altered).

Writing thus has been viewed from a transcendental-phenomenological perspective from the very beginning of VII, according to Derrida. Writing is subject to an "intentional analysis": it must be "intelligible for a transcendental subject in general," and must stand "in *pure* relation to a consciousness"; nor may its "facticity" in any way be considered on its own account. Worldly writing, pertaining to a real empirical factical language (inscriptions in French or English, for example), is not the issue, but writing transcendentally understood, and it has indeed been spoken about in this way from the beginning of this section, the sole one in the "Introduction" in which Derrida explicitly discusses writing.[23]

A deep-rooted, crippling, long-standing misunderstanding has had hold of the Derrida literature when it comes to this key point. To be sure, complicating features relating to these themes, to which I will attend shortly, do arise later in VII. Nevertheless, lest there be any doubts, note that Derrida, in his following paragraph, further specifies the manner in which writing and language are to be thought, bringing the first phase of his discussion in VII to an end. At this moment, Derrida, expanding on the reference to an "intentional analysis" we have just cited, further stipulates that only writing as "living flesh, *Leib*, as spiritual corporeality, *geistige Leiblichkeit,"* can make a transcendental contribution to truth (*LOG* 85–86 / *IOG* 88).

Derrida, then, concludes this portion of his discussion by returning to Husserl's long-standing views, not about writing but about language and discourse. Husserl always subordinated discursive acts of signification (what might be called in other contexts speech-acts, or *parole*) to the speaker's intentions animating them.[24] Derrida recalls Husserl's doctrine at this moment in VII, stipulating that only writing so considered, as enlivened by such intentional acts, is able to perform the sort of transcendental labor that has previously been specified. The merely conventional sign, the mere *Körper*, the simple body of the conventional worldly sign does not enter into these considerations at all; the factical, worldly, empirical side of writing must be reduced and only the intentionally animated body, the spiritual flesh, *the geistige Leiblichkeit*, in principle subordinated to an active intentionality, and with that, to a transcendental subject, may make any sort of transcendental contribution to truth.

This further stipulation caps off Derrida's discussion of writing in these opening paragraphs; it rounds out writing's transcendental contribution and how writing functioning as a transcendental condition of truth must be conceived. In the absence of these conditions, it thus seems clear, Derrida believes that none of the claims he has made about writing in Husserl would have any cogency at all.

Of course, in VII, Derrida's argument traces a difficult and tortuous path. That this view of writing as spiritual flesh, and as remaining intelligible for a transcendental subject, is in question at every point where the transcendental contribution of writing to truth is at issue, seems to me to brook no doubts. Yet while acknowledging these results, Derrida himself may well be made uneasy by them, as Bernet for one has already suggested.

Derrida's discussion in VII, as we are about to see further, doubtless twists and turns; it may even be said to thrash about, as Derrida repeatedly comes face-to-face with the limitations these transcendental-phenomenological stipulations place on writing's functioning and conception. Nowhere in VII of the "Introduction," however, does Derrida break in any decisive way with any of the provisos he lays out at the beginning of this section.

In order to further clarify matters, to nail down that Derrida in the "Introduction" stands at a distance from his mature positions, as well as exactly how far Derrida may be at this moment from his later thought, I want to examine one key point later on in VII, one especially vertiginous juncture where the interpretation of VII has repeatedly seemed to go off the rails. This point, which to my knowledge has never before been fully appreciated, should give us a definitive view of where Derrida in fact stood in 1962 in respect to writing, and this will make it possible for me to very briefly nail down a sketch of deconstruction's invention, or discovery, or advent, and the development of Derrida's engagement with Husserl overall.

Let me make clear: I do not doubt that Derrida at this point may well already be kicking in his traces, as we sometimes say; Derrida, that is, may indeed sense the limits of these Husserlian conceptions in a way that Husserl did not, and Derrida may even have started to glimpse from time to time some of the work that must be done to free himself from them. Nevertheless, this work itself never takes place in the "Introduction": nowhere does Derrida break with Husserl's framework in any decisive fashion—or even question it radically, at least in respect to the themes of writing and language—and arrive at a truly general conception of writing in its radical positivity, a really "consistent problematic of writing and the trace," of the sort that he spoke of above.

Two themes in VII clearly provide confirmation of this, though only one of them will be treated here in any detail. Let me mention the other theme in passing, however, since it arises before the central one in VII and thus can provide a useful bridge to the latter.

This first theme is the book. Derrida in 1962 affirms the book as a preeminent mode of inscription, one uniquely reflecting writing's mode of existence.[25] This highly positive treatment of the book clearly differs from the book's role in Derrida's later thought. It thus makes manifest Derrida's distance from his later work in the "Introduction."[26]

That Derrida in the "Introduction" sees a specifically transcendental writing, and only this, contributing to the transcendental-historical establishment of truth and ideality, is also confirmed by the book, for the book's proper specificity can be thought, according to Derrida, only in a context owed "to a *pure tradition* and to *pure history*" (*LOG*, 88 / *IOG* 90; my emphasis). Thanks to a history and tradition so conceived, Husserl lays the ground for thinking "an original spatiotemporality, escaping the alternative of sensible and intelligible, empirical and metempirical." And this original spatiotemporality opens the way to grasping "the book's proper volume and duration," which themselves "are neither purely sensible nor purely intelligible noumena" (*LOG*, 89 / *IOG* 91).[27]

These claims are the outcome of a debate with Eugen Fink, which I cannot review further here.[28] Suffice it to note that, for Derrida, Husserl's analysis of writing's role in the historicity of truth makes conceivable the identification of an original spatiotemporality specific to truth's written and linguistic signs, and thus founds the "space" of the book, of the "*biblioumenon*," as Derrida will speak of it here, following Gaston Bachelard. Derrida's affirmation of the book thus assumes that writing, as it is at issue throughout section VII of the "Introduction," is writing transcendentally understood, writing pertaining to the "history of truth," to a "pure history and a pure tradition," something obviously not the case in a work like *Of Grammatology*.

Moreover, only this stillborn effort to found the volume of the book in Husserl's late transcendental history really lets the reader grasp the reasons Derrida makes so much of the book in his later writings—a concern whose urgency is not always totally clear when encountered in the later work. Precisely because the book in the "Introduction" proved the exemplary instance of a novel spatiotemporality, one pertaining to a specifically transcendental language, writing, and communication, Derrida, later wishing to contest these same transcendental-historical conceptions, this same subordination of writing to truth, must question the book as well. In 1967, Derrida thus continues to believe that the book, its "proper duration and volume," has a spatiotemporality specific to transcendental history and the teleology of truth; at this later date, however, Derrida, wishing to exceed this same transcendental history in its totality, denounces the book as being this teleology's most proper instance and enforcing writing's fealty to truth.

Derrida affirms the book in the "Introduction," then, and this begins to make plain how far he stands in 1962 from his better-known, later thought in respect to writing and language. In the case of the book, while a new spatiotemporality, suggestively enough, neither intelligible nor sensible becomes possible, thanks to a writing and language transcendentally conceived, later on in VII, by contrast, Derrida puts forward an instance where these transcendental conceptions themselves, writing and language as Husserl here understands them, *do come directly into question*; and it is to this stretch of Derrida's text that most commentators have attended.

Here, not a supposedly new, original spatiotemporality but the possible reliance of transcendental writing and language themselves on an explicitly sensible and worldly spatiotemporality becomes the issue. Even at this moment, however, Derrida does not intend to abandon Husserl's transcendental-phenomenological restrictions entirely. Rather, Derrida envisions a moment in which these restrictions by necessity come to be coordinated with that of a worldly writing and the sensible body of the sign. Derrida suggests that a parallelism would be in effect at this moment between transcendental, intentionally animated writing and language and the worldly empirical body of their signs—yet one that implies at least the possibility of the former, transcendental writing and language, coming to be embodied in the latter (worldly, sensible signification). And this complex coordination of the transcendental and the worldly, according to Derrida, does call into doubt Husserl's philosophical commitments as a whole.

Let me cite this development at the moment it takes shape in Derrida's text. "The authentic act of writing is a transcendental reduction operated by and toward the we," writes Derrida. "But, since, in order to escape from worldliness, sense must from the first *be able* to gather itself into the world and to dispose of its sensible spatiotemporality, it is necessary for it [this authentic act of writing] to put into peril its pure intentional ideality, that is to say its sense of truth. One thus sees appear in a philosophy which, at least by certain motifs, is the contrary of empiricism, a possibility which, up until now, accords only with empiricism and non-philosophy, that of a disappearance of truth" (*LOG* 91 / *IOG* 92–93, translation altered).

Here, then, Derrida considers a moment when Husserl's conceptions of writing and language finally break free, it seems, of their transcendental limitations. Transcendental writing and worldly writing in some fashion do imply one another, Derrida claims, and their mutual implication now brings into question just that ideality of truth that hitherto has set the parameters for transcendental writing's conception.[29]

This crossroads in Derrida's text has indeed proved the decisive one for the majority of commentators; yet it nevertheless seems clear that the claim I have just made, that certain specifically transcendental limitations have been ascribed to writing by Derrida all along, from the beginning of section VII of his "Introduction," is confirmed, not denied, by what here transpires, since the very fact that Derrida now makes an argument to be rid of just these limitations shows that he has seen them as in effect until now.

Moreover, perhaps even more critically, having entertained this scenario whereby a "disappearance of truth" is hypothesized, Derrida on this basis subsequently launches a more specific inquiry into the possibility of truth's disappearance, an inquiry that subdivides into three distinct phases and whose discussion occupies the remainder of this chapter. In none of these three cases, however—under none of the three subhypotheses according to which Derrida considers this possibility—will Derrida ever affirm that such a disappearance is really possible. Truth cannot disappear in any of the three senses under which Derrida actually contemplates this possibility in depth, after it has momentarily come forward here, and the intersection that Derrida proposes at this moment thus fails to take on any ultimate significance at all in his account, to offer any genuine resistance to the force of Husserl's claims and conceptions; it fails to break with the totality of Husserl's thought in any fundamental way. The limited, mutual yet decisive dependence that Derrida seems to envision at this moment between the act of authentic writing—operative of and by the transcendental reduction, as it takes responsibility for truth and meaning at the moment it comes to give them their last horizon of objectivity—and the worldly sensible spatiotemporality this act must assume as its disposal when it performs its inscription—even this mutual limited interdependence will never be cashed out in the "Introduction," since Derrida will never be able to affirm the disappearance of truth that should follow from it in any of the three cases he goes on to consider.[30]

Finally, all of this—the failure to affirm this empiricist possibility of a disappearance of truth and thus to find transcendental writing, the authentic act of writing, as ultimately implicated in sensible spatiotemporality—is owed to that possibility upon which Derrida depends to formulate this hypothesis of truth's disappearance in the first place. This is the most decisive point, one that has been neglected by all commentary up until now; for Derrida has indeed laid the ground for this moment, the moment of truth's putative disappearance, by dint of Husserl's own analysis and distinctions.

More specifically still, Derrida invokes Husserl's own construal of the sign in the first of his *Logical Investigations* to articulate the supposedly necessary conjunction between the transcendental and the worldly, the spiritually animated sign and its sensible spatiotemporality (a conjunction that appears to, but never quite does, bring truth into question). Indeed, the sign as such, the very concept of the sign, is only really attended to, only even mentioned, I believe, once in VII, and this takes place at the moment right before Derrida floats this hypothesis of the disappearance of truth. Two sentences earlier, Derrida had begun a paragraph by declaring: "In effect, from then on, as is prescribed for it, sense is received into a sign, this becomes the exposed and worldly residence of a truth. . . ." (*LOG* 90–91 / *IOG* 93) And Derrida, in order to explain the workings of the sign and what it entails, footnotes Husserl. He footnotes those very distinctions pertaining to signification at the outset of the first *Investigation* that will turn out to be the object of Derrida's *own deconstruction* in *Speech and Phenomena*: "We take this word ['sign'] in the broad sense of significant-sign [signe-signifiant] or 'sign-expression' (graphic or vocal), in the meaning that Husserl gives this term by opposing it to the 'indicative' sign (*LI* II, 1, §§1–5, 269–75)" (*LOG* 90n3 / *IOG* 92n96, translation altered).

It should be no wonder, then, that Derrida's analysis will never attain that radicality at which Derrida himself perhaps already aims in the "Introduction," and no wonder that Derrida turns to the opening section of the first of the *Logical Investigations* at the moment when he wishes to take his leave from Husserl and launch deconstruction some five years later. Derrida had recourse in the "Introduction" not just to the Husserlian notions of a transcendental writing intelligible for a transcendental subject, and of the living flesh of language as subordinated to an animating act of intention, but finally to Husserl's own notion of the sign, and the relation of its signification to its materiality, as Husserl sets this out in *Logical Investigations* 1.

The answer to the broadest question, the leading question of this chapter, thus emerges. In the "Introduction," Derrida self-evidently did not frame a more "consistent problematic of writing and the trace" than Husserl's own. He continues to depend on Husserl's doctrines and demonstrations pertaining to writing, language, and the sign at the most decisive moments of his own arguments. Nor can he be said to have broken with the appurtenance of writing and language to the rest of Husserl's transcendental-phenomenological project in any decisive sense. Derrida indeed may twist and turn; he may wish to question Husserl as radically as possible in respect to writing and language. Yet when he attempts this most explicitly in the "Introduction," Derrida in fact ensnares himself further in the net of Husserl's own distinctions and the teleology possibly commanding them. Nowhere, when it comes to writing and language at least, does the "Introduction" ever break free from Husserl's guiding distinctions: between transcendental and worldly, factical and ideal. Though he may push them to their internal limits, Derrida is not yet able to conceive a space beyond them, one genuinely exceeding the framework of Husserl's philosophy.

So, too, equally clearly, this experience will, of course, inform all Derrida does with writing and language hereafter. Arguably, Derrida himself encounters in the "Introduction" how Husserl's construal of the sign has a commitment to truth built into it and has remained within the purview of a teleology. Derrida found it impossible to question Husserl's suppositions radically on their own basis, simply from within, in the "Introduction," and doubtless for this reason Derrida returned to these matters in 1966–67, starting directly with the sign and Husserl's treatment of them. This is why Derrida must write again on the whole of Husserl's thought, why *Speech and Phenomena* comes last, and why Derrida's path through Husserl's thought is, and must be, the reverse of Husserl's own.

The Invention of Deconstruction

Where, then, have we arrived? First of all, an answer to our leading question has indeed become plain. Derrida's thought does develop, and develops decisively, I have shown. Derrida is unable to think of a writing that goes definitively beyond Husserl's own conceptions in the "Introduction," unable to set forth a truly consistent problematic of writing and the trace at this era. Derrida may well have tested the limits of Husserl's thought at key points, probed its architectonic, especially at the end of the "Introduction," when concerns pertaining to the infinite idea and the teleology of Husserl's transcendental history return. Nowhere in the "Introduction" are these themes ever fully coordinated with those of writing and language, however; nowhere are the problematics of transcendental history and transcendental writing articulated together in a way that decisively frees them from Husserl's own framework.[31] Significant development thus takes place between the "Introduction" and Derrida's more mature thought, according to Derrida's own standard.

Moreover, recognizing all this, a sketch of the trajectory, the path, that Derrida takes to arrive at deconstruction can begin to emerge. Having established the status of writing in the "Introduction," the single decisive occasion that led Derrida to invent deconstruction can be brought forward—and with this, the depth of Derrida's innovation, the extent and the parameters of his invention, can be grasped.

First of all, to see what occasioned the invention of deconstruction, it should be noted that nothing in the argument just made contradicts what Derrida and his commentators have so often asserted: namely, that in the "Introduction" Derrida did confront the "absolute novelty" of Husserl's analysis of writing ("la nouveaté absolue," *VP* 91). That is, for the first time in Husserl's work, in his commentary in the "Introduction," Derrida encountered writing conceived as making a genuinely positive, even necessary, contribution to the inauguration or establishment of truth. Writing "found[s] absolute objectivity" itself, as Derrida says at the outset of VII. At the same time, this discovery of a novel role of writing in respect to truth takes place solely in the context of Husserl's understanding of writing and language and of truth, as well as of history—and within Husserl's unique transcendental historical approach more generally to the foundations of scientific knowledge and tradition.

This gives the reason why deconstruction had to be invented. Derrida contrived deconstruction to break writing out of the boundaries he encountered in the "Introduction," in order to generalize its function and existence beyond Husserl's stipulations. Deconstruction was necessary to think writing in terms of a "general," rather than limited economy, as Derrida sometimes puts it. In the "Introduction" Derrida had already encountered a possibility of writing that he believed pointed beyond Husserl; he doubtless did glimpse the possibility of a radically new relation between writing, language, and truth, as is commonly held. What occasioned deconstruction's invention or "discovery" was Derrida's desire to further this nascent insight—to conceive of a writing broader than either transcendental or mundane writing, and to see this more global writing function as both the condition of possibility of truth as well as its genuine disappearance.

At the same time, the depths of the problem facing Derrida at this moment ought not be underestimated. The difficulties in capturing the force of Husserl's insights beyond Husserl's framework are grave. After all, it is far from clear how the confines in which writing is held in Husserl are to be overcome—and transcendental and worldly writing brought together—without this resulting in relativism or historicism, in a new kind of skepticism or nihilism. This is a surpassingly difficult problem, as the "Introduction" itself shows, perhaps impossible to resolve, according to any standard forms of philosophical argumentation, obviously including those of phenomenology itself.

And this is why, I would suggest, the invention of deconstruction, of such an absolutely singular way of working, was required. Deconstruction, this unprecedented operation, had to be invented so that Derrida could articulate fully what he believed had started to come forward in the "Introduction": a more global functioning of writing, yet one that would not simply cancel Husserl's transcendental insight, would not turn away from truth entirely and slide over into simple skepticism. The trio of publications of 1967 thus turn out to have marked an innovation of an entirely singular sort, something to which Derrida himself at times refers—as in "Time of a Thesis," where Derrida writes that "during the years that followed, from about 1963–1968," he "tried to work out . . . a sort of strategic device, opening onto its own abyss, an unclosed, unenclosable, not wholly formalizable ensemble of rules for reading, writing, and interpretation" and thanks to this *Of Grammatology, Speech and Phenomena*, and *Writing and Difference* came about ("TT" 40).

Derrida, then, would have invented such a singular way of working just because no other mode of preserving Husserl's novel analysis of writing, while exceeding Husserl's own framework, was available to him, for reasons that an exploration of Derrida's predeconstructive works alone may bring to the fore. While giving such emphasis to the invention of deconstruction and what occasioned it, however, I do not mean to suggest that Derrida had no prior preparation or precedent for this invention at all. Indeed, to bring the sketch of the development of deconstruction overall to a close—one in which continuity and discontinuity must both be recognized, as Derrida has long taught—in *Le problème*, Derrida had already devised a schema that permitted him to retain Husserl's standpoint, to preserve the starting point of transcendental phenomenology while also taking Derrida beyond Husserl, to attempt to think what no phenomenology could think. Though this matter is difficult—Derrida until 1967 insisted on the post hoc nature of his questioning and thus the post hoc character of the excess at which he arrives beyond Husserl (and had not yet invented the first, broad, opening gesture of all deconstruction or the schema that he speaks of in "Time of a Thesis"), nor had any of Derrida's later concerns yet stepped forward—not language and writing nor historical teleology—nevertheless, Derrida may well be seen, as he himself has recently suggested, as taking up *Le problème*'s overall program again in 1967 and transforming, as well expanding its operation on the new sites that the "Introduction" bequeathed to him.[32]

A general sketch of the rather difficult and contorted path that finally led Derrida to deconstruction thus comes into view. Derrida started from *Le problème*'s approach, expanded and altered it in light of the issues that the "Introduction" made urgent, and on this basis *Speech and Phenomena* and *Of Grammatology* result. By taking into account *Le problème*, alongside the specific issues and variations the "Introduction" brings with it, a developmental perspective thus can uniquely register the unparalleled innovation that the 1967 writings represent.[33]

Such a treatment of Derrida's major breakthrough, here barely sketched, is, moreover, both valid and necessary. Valid, since, with this notion of development, as I began to suggest, I have done nothing but follow Derrida himself in his own explorations of Husserl in *Le problème* and in "Genesis," as well as in his path-breaking studies of Rousseau and Emmanual Levinas. Mine is by no means a teleological treatment of the sort that Derrida criticizes, for example, in "Force and Signification," but an aporetic or quasi-aporetic investigation that has recourse to a developmental or diachronic axis in order to gain a standpoint complex enough to map the different dimensions of Derrida's early treatments of writing and language.[34] While opting for neither a continuist nor a discontinuist hypothesis (or perhaps both at once) in regard to Derrida's early writings as a whole, I have aimed to disclose a moment of still more radical genesis, an event of coming into being, still not exhausted, that finds its precise analogue in the work that Derrida attempted in regard to Husserl in *Le problème*, in the preface to which these concerns and paradoxes pertaining to development were first set out by him.[35]

Such an approach is not only valid in a Derridean context, but also necessary, because Derrida's thought did indeed develop, change, alter. The broader second prong of the unity thesis, that a single approach to writing everywhere informs Derrida's early work, turns out to be demonstrably false. Better reasons have now emerged for readers to take into account the hermeneutic situation of the 1967 texts, especially *Speech and Phenomena*. If Derrida's aim and Husserl's claims are both to be honored, an examination of the 1967 texts in light of Derrida's development today becomes unavoidable.[36]

After all, a real problem, a radical singularity, does hold Derrida / Husserl studies in its grasp, one that ultimately coincides with the name "Jacques Derrida," as attested to by the number of studies of this work that invoke this name in its title. Even today, then, a perspective that would make this singular standpoint clearer, at once in its structural complexity and in its genesis, ought to be welcomed by Derrideans and Husserlians alike, indeed by all concerned, to see twentieth-century thinking, especially that which Husserl pioneered and Derrida adapted and transformed, continue to resonate in times already so manifestly different from their own.

A Transcendental Sense of Death?

Derrida and the Philosophy of Language

One advantage of standing on the cusp of a new century is that the considerable intellectual achievements of the previous one can be approached in a new way. Today sufficient distance exists from the projects of the last century to render commentators less dependent on which side of various divides they happen to find themselves—analytic or Continental, formalist or historicist, Marxian or democratic, to name but a few. A far greater solidarity of concerns, methods, and questions has become apparent among what once were taken to be opposing movements, of a sort already customary when treating earlier eras. At the same time, we are still close enough to these divisions and programs of an earlier time that the new shuffling of the deck made possible—the new filiations and limitations discovered where previously only open vistas beckoned—cannot help but change our understanding of our own projects, working methodology, and present intellectual commitments.

This chapter undertakes this style of rearrangement, or revisionism, if one must, with regard to the field of what might be called post-philosophy (to what was sometimes meant simply by "theory" at certain periods in the Anglo-American academy), and it does so, in particular, with regard to Jacques Derrida's work.

The trajectory from the "Introduction" to *Speech and Phenomena* established in Chapter 2 as crucial for understanding deconstruction's advent is examined here in further detail, focusing particularly on Derrida's stance in the philosophy of language. Derrida's first deconstructions depend on his taking far deeper and more controversial positions in the philosophy of language, of affirming or holding them as true, I will argue, than is recognized almost anywhere today.

The ultimate aim of such a demonstration is not, of course, to suggest that Derrida's project is therefore invalid, his initiative an uninteresting or even dispensable one. A central goal of this essay, running parallel to the aim just mentioned, in fact, is to make clear, on this basis, precisely how certain signature moments of Derrida's thinking function: to offer new and more precise renderings of articulations long taken to be definitive of his project as a whole. Even if Derrida's stance were to some degree brought into question, however, it would not be in a manner any different than other initiatives that characterize twentieth-century thought. For the concern that forms the ultimate horizon of this chapter, put most simply, is whether post-philosophy—that departure or transformation in respect to reason and truth characteristic of so much work of the preceding century—truly exists in the manner currently imagined, as an ongoing enterprise of its own, with an autonomous living future. Are any of the endeavors by which the twentieth century remains marked from beginning to end, whether they be that of Heidegger or Adorno, Wittgenstein or Deleuze (to take some provocative pairings)[1] able to do without quite definite commitments in the fields of traditional philosophy, and thus without that truth whose ultimate authority and possibility they are commonly thought to question? Are not their projects, even as they seek to exceed or transform truth or reason, only able to go forward if they are right about these matters foundational for their own thought?

If the answer to these queries is yes, this raises the possibility that post-philosophy, or theory, does not exist, at least in the fashion usually assumed—not because there is no need for it, because philosophy somewhere has been established as a successfully achieved science, but for the precise opposite reason: because philosophy, too, has never existed in this sense. No working version of philosophy is at hand, no single set of philosophical commitments has been stabilized, such that one can talk about what comes after these foundations, or in any way build upon them—and this is so, regardless of whether such building entails the finding of further philosophical truth, or instead intends to depart from this program and head in other directions. This remains the case even when that departure takes the strange, yet somehow now seemingly familiar, form known as deconstruction.

Of course, the validity of these concerns can only really be judged after the single instance of them here in question in Derrida's work has been explored. Derrida's project, however, has always had an exemplary, perhaps more than exemplary, value in respect to just these issues. No one more than he has asked how to take leave responsibly from philosophy, from reason and truth—what such an excess, transformation or departure, which is not merely precipitous or phantasmatic, should look like. In turn, this specific concern has always been tied, especially at the outset of his thought, to a focus on language. It may, then, be time to ask: where does Derrida actually stand in respect to language? What philosophy of language, if any, does Derrida in fact hold? What perspective on language do his works imply?

To pose such questions to a body of work whose discussion has been associated with language in some form for nearly forty years may seem rather unexpected. However, not only does a split concerning just this issue, dating back to the first reception of Derrida's work, continue to be with us today—some critics even now seeing Derrida as primarily concerned with language and related themes in his first works, while others long taking him as focused on topics more closely connected to the philosophy of reflection and to an alterity associated with Levinas or Heidegger—but assuming that these two possibilities are not necessarily mutually exclusive, as many of the more sophisticated treatments of Derrida's work have argued, the occurrence of both linguistic and transcendental or near-transcendental themes in Derrida's corpus does not in itself resolve these questions, but instead invites them and makes them pertinent.

Early on Derrida himself doubtless acknowledged both a semiotic (or linguistic) as well as a transcendental dimension to his own thought. He articulates the relation of these themes within his work, at this same early stage, by insisting that language, the sign-function in particular, provides a necessary gateway to "ultra- transcendental" concerns (as Derrida already labeled them in 1967, with specific reference to Husserl),[2] insofar as thinking the sign in its utmost radicality demands removing it from its confinement within a "metaphysics of presence." In turn, however, such removal or withdrawal, requiring the deconstruction of this metaphysics as such—itself only able to be accomplished by traversing a certain inside—leads to a thought of radical alterity, bringing with it the very disappearance of the concept of the "sign" (a generalization of its function beyond its usual bounds, resulting in the loss of its specific identity, and its relegation to an old name), thus signaling this metaphysics' closure.[3]

This complex intent may well be why it has always been so difficult to know what philosophy of language Derrida holds or whether he has one at all. For, assuming this account is right—and as the term "deconstruction" itself already might suggest—Derrida never seems to have aimed to establish any *positive* doctrine of language or signification. Instead, Derrida has always wished to extract and somehow generalize a possibility that lies latent within these fields, and to use linguistic themes to present a previously unknown thematic, at once historical (or epochal), and ontological or phenomenological (or at least close to these last).

With this, however, the actual question concerning language I here seek to pose and eventually to answer can be made clearer. The question all this raises is: how is a sign to be recognized *in the first place* when it is encountered in Derrida's world? Even if Derrida does finally aim to withdraw the sign from its prior enclosure in metaphysics, eventually employing it as an old name for something new, what decisions in linguistics or philosophy of language prompt him to do so? How is the sign understood, and with what status—as an element in a language or a speech act, corresponding to a word, a phoneme, an expression—according to what criteria of identity more generally, such that it stands as the object in what may well later prove merely an opening gambit within Derrida's own concerns?

These questions take on special relevance, moreover, insofar as they have been the very ones repeatedly posed to Derrida's project by the two primary versions of philosophy that today still understand themselves as *research* (rather than proceeding by way of commentary or dialogue): namely, analytic philosophy and Husserlian phenomenology. As documented in Chapter 2, numerous phenomenologists over the years have argued against Derrida's interpretation in *Speech and Phenomena* of Husserl's treatment of the sign. From an analytic perspective, John Searle and Richard Rorty, most notably, have time and again expressed doubt and perplexity in respect to Derrida's actual positions in philosophy of language. Rorty in particular, while of course sympathetic to the negative side of Derrida's results to which allusion has just been made—to those conclusions, however Derrida arrives at them, that seem to lead to a complete break with philosophy of language—has wondered why one should complement or supplement this with a positive doctrine of any sort (thus "beating the philosophers at their own game," as Rorty sometimes puts it), even one that goes under the heading of alterity and professes to be as mobile as does Derrida's.[4]

What I propose to do, most proximally, then, is to answer these longstanding questions concerning Derrida's stance toward language, to discover where Derrida's project stands within the broad spectrum of positions available today within the philosophy of language. This endeavor, which breaks with some of the hermeticism that has long marked discussions of this work (granting that such hermeticism has also often led to some of its most significant achievements), will eventually come to focus on the topic of meaning, on the status of semantics in Derrida's work—this being, among other things, the question that most prominently divides these two philosophical schools, and thus the one most important for situating Derrida with respect to them. Accordingly, the two sections into which this chapter divides will start, respectively, from two *loci classici* in Derrida's work, each of which speaks of meaning or sense, and does so in relation, on the one hand, to the intentional subject, and, on the other, to death. Both have proved crucial to now canonical interpretations of Derrida's early thought, including his views on the sign and language. The first is to be found in Derrida's 1962 "Introduction to Husserl's *Origin*," the other in his 1967 *Speech and Phenomena*.

A Transcendental Sense of Death?

The first passage to be examined is that from which my title comes. Derrida's explicit proclamation of a "transcendental sense of death" is found in the same section, section VII of the "Introduction," in which writing becomes an explicit theme for the first time in Derrida's entire published corpus. And not surprisingly, given its context, Derrida's formulation, despite its brevity, has been assigned enormous significance. In the literature, including of late, it has been seen as deeply portentous, often taken to encapsulate all of Derrida's views on writing.

More specifically, one prominent commentator, Peter Fenves, has recently linked Derrida's talk here to Derrida's discussion in another early work of "lost and mute" signs,[5] and he has understood this theme, of illegible significations, to be critical to Derrida's complex stance toward history, both in his first writings as well as thereafter.[6] Perhaps still more typically, another leading interpreter, Leonard Lawlor, has identified in this early remark a core feature of all Derrida's thought on writing. After declaring, perhaps a bit extravagantly, that Derrida's statement "tells us what death is for . . . death is for the transcendental; the reason why we die is for the transcendental 'We,'" Lawlor outlines a variant of the claim that writing, and such death, plays the role of a "quasi-transcendental," a condition of possibility and impossibility both—here, in respect to Husserl's transcendental subjectivity and intersubjectivity.[7]

Without suggesting that either commentator's contribution can be reduced to the schematic accounts I give here (Fenves', to which I shall return, is especially rich and far-ranging), the question that I seek to pose to these and similar interpretations can be quickly stated. Both authors see in Derrida's remark an absence, loss, or death brought by *writing*, which

Husserl's endeavor requires even as it brings his project into doubt. What understanding of linguistic signification, however, makes this kind of double-sided analysis possible in the first place? Language understood in what way, signs seen how, permit writing, and thus death, to function as a premise, a transcendental condition within Husserl's own undertaking, yet also to represent a certain outside or limit, thus inscribing this undertaking's breakdown in the form of an "endless flight" of meaning,[8] or "the transcendental's failure"?[9]

This question is all the more pressing since, as it happens, precisely these issues concerning how writing is to be conceived are being addressed by Derrida at the beginning of the same paragraph. Derrida begins the paragraph, in which he announces "a transcendental sense of death," by asking under what conditions writing may be assigned the value given to it by Husserl and, in response, it is worth noting, he insists that "all this can be said" only when writing is viewed "solely in *pure* relation to a *consciousness* which founds it as such." Writing, he continues a little later in the same vein, must keep "the pure juridical possibility of being intelligible for a transcendental subject in general" (*LOG* 85 / *IOG* 88).

Thus, after having specified at the start of this section the transcendental significance Husserl gives to writing in his very last works, and after having explored some of its consequences, Derrida here lists those conditions under which it alone may so function. Before further investigating these conditions, however, let us turn to the end of the same paragraph, and witness Derrida explicitly announcing this "transcendental sense of death."

Part of the problem in interpreting this particular statement of Derrida's is due to a mistranslation with which this paragraph closes, and to which I shall return. Embarking on this theme, however, Derrida indeed declares that "a transcendental sense of death is disclosed in the silence of prehistoric arcana and of submerged civilizations, the entombment of lost intentions and of guarded secrets, the illegibility of a lapidary inscription" (*LOG* 85 / *IOG* 88). Death appears with a transcendental sense, Derrida suggests here, in illegible inscriptions, silent and lost signs, when these are no longer able to be read or reawakened due to the disappearance of the language and civilization from which they arose.

In what way, specifically, then, do such lost inscriptions pose a threat to Husserl's own project? For Lawlor and Fenves, this threat consists in the radical loss of (linguistic) intelligibility such inscriptions appear to bring. A death of *meaning* shelters in such signs, and this is what is believed to cast Husserl's program so deeply into doubt.[10] Indeed, staying just with Fenves' discussion for the moment, the role of writing more broadly in Husserl's analysis for Fenves consists in supplying a place for what otherwise has no place of its own: what are called in Husserl's lexicon "ideal objectivities," the validating objects of theoretical knowledge.[11] In turn, this function of writing, as a surrogate place for what has none of its own, opens for Fenves the possibility of an even more radical wandering of truth, of the sort that we have already seen him mention. Writing gives a place to truth, yet thanks to harboring this possibility of losing all meaning or intelligibility that Derrida seems to describe, writing also allows a radical loss of all place, and in this way, again, it is at once a threat to, even as it forms a condition of, Husserl's project.

The main problem faced by Fenves' interpretation (which, again, is one of the best we have, both of this passage and of these themes) is that it simply does not square with the stipulations we have just seen Derrida set out above, nor with those he is about to bring forward—the ones that in fact most interest us here, since they concern precisely Derrida's philosophy of language. At the beginning of this same paragraph, Derrida states that writing, inscription of any sort, can play *no* transcendental role *at all*, apart from standing in relation to a *pure* consciousness and being intelligible to a transcendental subject in general. Only if related to a *pure* consciousness—"pure" meaning independent of all factual and worldly determinations—and referred back to a specifically transcendental intelligibility, can writing assume the role Husserl assigns to it.

Accordingly, beginning his next paragraph, Derrida sets out that broader interpretation of language, of linguistic signification as such, that makes these stipulations possible. "It is by thinking the juridical purity of this intentional animation," Derrida writes, "that Husserl always speaks of a linguistic or graphic body that is a flesh, a body proper (*Leib*), or a spiritual corporeality" (*LOG* 85–86 / *IOG* 88).

Writing must be understood with reference to a pure consciousness and to a transcendental intelligibility, in order to function transcendentally in Husserl's thought, to give some kind of place to truth and to ideal objectivities in just the way Fenves describes. In turn, this requires recourse to a more general "intentional animation" and to its "juridical purity," and such recourse is only possible to the extent that such animation finds a correlate in the body of expression itself (whether oral or written): namely, a construal of the (linguistic) sign ("of a linguistic or graphic body"), which takes the sign of language as *Leib*, as a *living* flesh, or as a specifically *spiritual* corporeality.[12]

Here we return, then, to those issues concerning the more general interpretation of language and the work of meaning alluded to above, and the stance that Derrida holds in the philosophy of language begins to emerge. To explain how writing can play any sort of transcendental role in Husserl's thought, Derrida has set out a highly singular, yet entirely orthodox Husserlian interpretation of the linguistic sign—as a kind of living flesh, enlivened by an "intentional animation" in its "juridical purity"—one which, it turns out, has undergirded his and Husserl's analysis all along. On such a construal, writing can never depart from meaning and intentionality once and for all, since these stand at the basis of all signs, of all linguistic signification, of every "linguistic or graphic body," spoken or written. So, too, whatever talk of a transcendental sense of death signifies, it cannot be equivalent to a complete loss or death of sense itself on the transcendental plane.

To get clearer about what Derrida intends with this notion of death, as well as what kind of threat writing really does pose to Husserl's project in Derrida's eyes in 1962, the interpretation of the linguistic sign to which Derrida here alludes must be grasped in more detail. With this notion of *Leib*, Derrida is referring to a doctrine Husserl made explicit in one of his last published writings, *Formal and Transcendental Logic* (*FTL*). There, Husserl set out an analysis that assigned to linguistic signs generally a very special mode of being. All objects that remain identical without regard to spatiotemporal individuation for Husserl have an existence he calls "ideal." (His favorite example of this is the literary or musical work of art: reading Melville's *Moby-Dick*, you and I read the *same* work, not similar ones, not works somehow only merely alike.) And in *Formal and Transcendental Logic*, after setting out this ideal character, he writes: "Now it is quite the same in the case of all *verbal formulations* . . . they concern such [ideal] formations even with respect to the verbal corporeality itself, which is so to speak, *a spiritual corporeality*. The word itself, the sentence itself, is an ideal unity, which is not multiplied by its thousandfold reproductions" (*FTL* 25 / 21).

The entities comprising language, for Husserl, are thus neither real natural individuals, nor even real psychological ones, but *ideal individuals* only possible at the level of culture (or spirit). They have their authentic existence not in their numerous distinct factual reproductions, but in an *individuality* that is identically the same (not similar) across their spatio-temporally individuated embodiments. The linguistic sign thus has a mode of existence all its own, different from all natural objects and even all real artifacts. This entire doctrine lay at the heart of Derrida's first dissertation proposal,[13] and it plays an enormous, though hitherto underappreciated, role in all of Derrida's early writings, including in his first deconstructions.

According to Husserl, an actual physical mark or object, a real spatio-temporal thing can, and often does, underlie the actual body of the sign; this mark or mere body (*Körper*), however, is finally in no way determinative for its status as a sign, for its character as any sort of genuine signitive entity. An intentional act, an act of meaning originating in an intentional subject, must be adjoined to this body, fused with the *Körper*, in order to make the "sign-thing" (*Körper*) into a genuine sign (*Leib*), a genuine "verbal corporeality." Without such intentional animation, without the employment of the sign as a vehicle for an act of meaning, such marks (*Körper*) lack any status as signs.[14]

In sum, for Husserl, then, and for Derrida, who follows him here in 1962, the linguistic sign as such is an *ideal individual*, ultimately belonging to culture and history, only able to be accessed through repeated intentions and acts of intention. These, in turn, necessarily bring with them higher-order acts of meaning and intending—both toward the objects at which they aim (*Gegenständen, Objekte*) as well as the logically articulated conceptualizations (*Bedeutungen*) through which these objects are presented. The sign thus stands in a total complex comprised of: (1) merely spatiotemporal bodies (*Körper*); (2) living spiritual corporealities or flesh (*Leib*); and (3) acts of meaning (*bedeuten*) and meanings (*Bedeutungen*—specifically logical conceptualizations); and this is indeed how Derrida conceived the (linguistic) sign, both spoken and written, in 1962. Nor should it be a surprise that Derrida stood as close as he did to Husserl on these matters at that moment. Derrida, after all, was himself a young philosopher, relatively unknown, with almost no prior publications.[15] And his work presently in question is an *introduction*: an introduction to a translation of a late work *by Husserl*.

Derrida's own orientation at this point toward language and linguistic signification was thus thoroughly Husserlian, and only by understanding this are we able to clarify his remarks concerning a transcendental sense of death. Dan Zahavi, one of the leading Husserlians of the current generation, recently has argued for something like "a transcendental sense of sleep": a notion of sleep that does not cancel but instead *flows from* Husserl's unique construal of transcendental subjectivity and intersubjectivity in his last works.[16] Derrida should be seen here, then, as conceiving something similar in the case of death. "The silence of prehistoric arcana and of submerged civilizations, the entombment of lost intentions and of guarded secrets, the illegibility of a lapidary inscription" would "disclose [*decelent*] a transcendental sense of death," in a sense that belongs specifically to Husserl's late transcendental thinking, and that it alone makes possible.

Specifically, Husserl himself in his late works thinks of transcendental subjectivity as having a transcendental historicity proper to it, something only possible thanks to the unique construal of language and writing that is also his. And because this is so, in those instances when an *entire language* is lost, and an inseminating sense already put to work becomes no longer recoverable—the circulation of this ideality specific to language and spiritual corporeality, at the lowest level of meaning, coming to a rest or halt—a stasis ensues which would indeed gesture toward a novel, specifically transcendental *sense* or meaning of death. Death would find a transcendental foothold or force, a sense of its own, with reference to this transcendental plane, insofar as the movement of signification is checked in respect to its "flesh" or spiritual corporeality, yet without meaning as such, or Husserl's transcendental perspective correlative to it, coming into any kind of radical doubt. Indeed, death can gain a *sense* as *death* on the *transcendental plane* only thanks to the ongoing relevance of Husserl's own assumptions, thanks to this particular construal of language and the positing of a transcendental history. Death would thus indeed stand "*united* to the absolute of an intentional right even in the very instance of its check," as Derrida's French is here better translated[17]—without, as Derrida himself acknowledges, ever simply canceling the presumption of this absolute right as such.

In sum, Derrida in 1962 by no means conceived of an absolute, radical loss or death of meaning—a transcendental *death of sense*—coming to Husserl's enterprise at writing's hands, and implying the failure of his project as a whole. He indeed conceived the opposite: a transcendental sense of death. And only if this is recognized first can the actual threat writing poses to Husserl's thought, as Derrida truly understands it, at this epoch be grasped.

The threat posed by writing (and this remains to some extent true even in Fenves' account),[18] often has been taken to be clarified by a development later on in the same section of the "Introduction," one that also falls under the heading of a "transcendental sense of death" (or even a transcendental death of sense). There, writing—now understood, thanks to the associated *Körper*, as the specifically *worldly* and *sensible* locus of the inscription of truth—is posited as making possible a wholesale loss or disappearance of truth at the hands of the destruction of truth's *inscriptions*, a default of truth owed to the possibility of a complete disappearance of all its worldly signs, sometimes referred to as "the destruction of the archive." Such a possibility of destruction—which "even here accords only with empiricism and non-philosophy," as Derrida notes (*LOG* 91 /

IOG 93)—clarifies and echoes, it is said, the transcendental sense of death of which he has previously spoken.

Not only, however, does Derrida himself, coming to the end of his discussion of this topic, reject this possibility outright, deeming it "the most grave of confusions" (*LOG* 97 / *IOG* 97),[19] but the grounds on which he does so are the same ones that make possible the true threat posed by writing. For Derrida will indeed consider further how truth might disappear, but he will do so only after he has reaffirmed the interpretation of the linguistic sign as *Leib* sketched out above. The final hypothesis Derrida frames in respect to the possible disappearance of truth (the only such scenario to which Derrida will ever unequivocally assent within the covers of the "Introduction"[20]) starts by returning to just this same construal of the sign and its life, and the distinction between *Körper* and *Leib*—and by giving to these, in fact, an even greater weight. A "new reduction," Derrida writes, "is going to isolate the intentional act which constitutes the *Körper* into *Leib* and maintains it in its *Leiblichkeit*, in its living sense of truth." Thus here commences, he claims, "an analysis" that "has no need of the *Körper* as such" (*LOG* 98 / *IOG* 97).

The true threat posed by writing, then, in section VII of the "Introduction" (and VII is the only section in the entire "Introduction" in which writing is discussed) is the threat that Derrida is about to examine: one that has nothing at all to do with the body of the sign, or any possibility of writing's physical or sensible destruction. Rather, it takes place wholly on the plane of *Leib*, and accordingly, concerns those *meanings* and acts of meaning to which the status of the sign as so understood is owed.

What, then, briefly, is this threat? Using a phrase Derrida employs, it is the threat posed by a "*pure* equivocity" (*LOG* 107 / *IOG* 104)—not a threat that meaning would be extinguished, or permanently lost at the hands of a foreign medium, but rather a threat that comes to meaning *through meaning*: thanks to a transformation, even an extension it undergoes, through that medium to which it here becomes fused and that continues to depend on it as well (namely, writing).[21]

Derrida here, more specifically, speaks of "singular puttings in perspective" (*LOG* 106 / *IOG* 104) within pure transcendental history as such, and, with that, a "sort of pure equivocity that grows with the rhythm of science" (*LOG* 107 / *IOG* 104). The acts of meaning (*bedeuten*) of a subject now know the possibility of *a virtual propagation to infinity*, Derrida argues, thanks to the transcendental contribution of writing—here specifically understood as the *Verleiblichung*, the embodiment, or enfleshment, of sense.[22] As thus conceived, the meaning-endowing acts of an intentional agent, for instance those of the proto-geometer and his or her successors, are now situated in a moment of a principledly infinite transcendental history—an ongoing history that, as infinite, has not brought the truth of its objects, nor their total sense, to a final stabilization (an *Endstiftung*).

From this, in turn, follows both of those consequences just noted. Those acts of meaning and the meanings themselves—in principle stabilized by the objects at which they aim—thanks to being situated in this ongoing infinite historicity of meaning, indeed become open to an unexpected kind of singularity, which Derrida here dubs a "singular putting into perspective" (*LOG* 106 / *IOG* 104). Secondly, the more general possibility of what Husserl calls the "reactivation" of all meaning and acts of meaning (the returning of these to light) comes into doubt. Some meanings may originate in wholly singular acts. In all cases, however, thanks to this open-ended infinite history, the recovery of meaning will have to traverse a chain infinite in principle in order to secure the total univocity of a given scientific discourse—with the result that even if such reactivation could be undertaken, it would freeze all further inquiry on the part of a science's practitioners. Thus, the attempt in which Husserl himself is here engaged, that of the recovery of an originary meaning—the return to the moment of an *Urstiftung* (inauguration, or "originary establishment") of the objects of a science (here of geometry) in order to refound it by clarifying its possibility and sense—encounters a limit, due to this proliferation of meaningfulness, owing to the latter's fusion with writing.

Precisely on account of the *bond*, then, between meaning, inscription, and the linguistic sign, the possibility of purely equivocal and potentially infinitely *sedimented meanings* appears at this moment in Husserl's own analysis. A side of discourse bearing an irreducible, ongoing equivocity, a proliferating infinitude of possibilities of meaning, emerges over and against the assumption of univocity and the stabilization of the objects of the science, as a possibility inherent in the very work of meaning itself within a stratum only able to be delineated thanks to Husserl's own transcendental and linguistic assumptions. "A transcendental sense of practice," it could thus be said—a transcendental or pure weight of scientific or theoretical *praxis* as such—makes itself felt on the inner face of Husserl's transcendental history, within Husserl's last, most exploratory, and most far-reaching construal of *theorein* as a whole.

The true threat posed to Husserl's thought by writing, as Derrida sees it in the "Introduction," thus emerges. And this threat turns out to be all the more urgent, due to Husserl's own response to this possibility. This is the facet of Derrida's own discussion that has received the most attention in the literature. Yet, though important—playing a central role in Derrida's truly systematic and thoroughgoing break with phenomenology in *Speech and Phenomena*, as we shall see—the scope of Derrida's remarks have often been exaggerated and their implications for Derrida's stance in the "Introduction" blurred.

On the one hand, Husserl, faced with such pure equivocity and infinite transcendental discursivity, will indeed state that a further idealization, a passage to infinity, can be performed that allows these practical impediments to be overcome and theory to retain its rights. In the final sections of the "Introduction," Derrida, in turn, questions this supplemental moment of idealization—a moment that also turns out to stand at the origin of geometry's objects and has its possibility in "an Idea in the Kantian sense." As has often been noted, Derrida doubts the congruence of this possibility with the rest of the architecture of Husserl's thought, specifically with Husserl's principle of principles: Husserl's claim that all phenomenological functions and assertions are to be grounded on first-hand present evidence—since how this stipulation is to be fulfilled in the case of even an *idea of infinity* is by no means clear.[23] Derrida thus opens a question at the end of the "Introduction" concerning this moment when *theorein* is here rescued back from *praxis*—when an idea in a Kantian sense, a regulative ideal, comes to articulate scientific theory back onto an unlimited, pure discursivity—a question that indeed stretches back to his first work on Husserl and forward to his subsequent writings.[24]

Nevertheless, Derrida's position here in 1962 cannot and ought not be assimilated to the position at which he will arrive in 1967, as so often has been done. For on the other hand, he will bring those issues he raises at the end of the "Introduction" back into line with Husserl's overall intentions,[25] and he has done the same thing here at the end of section VII itself. The univocity of transcendental historicity and a certain equivocity may turn out to be coordinate possibilities (and the now-famous comparison of Husserl with Joyce arises from this). Yet, as Derrida himself makes plain, they are never symmetrically so. Equivocity refers to univocity for its own sense in a way that univocity does not refer to it. Thus, only thanks to the continued presumption of sense, of meaning's boundless rights (themselves cashed out by this univocal and infinite transcendental historicity), are equivocity and finitude in the first place, even able to take on their force as exposing a certain limit to Husserl's project (*LOG* 107 / *IOG* 104–5). These problems only emerge at all on the *inner* face of Husserl's transcendental history, within the domain of transcendental historicity, thanks to the underlying presupposition of sense and the reduction of all signification to the activities responsible for its *Leiblichkeit*; thus the privilege given to univocity, and with it the priority of meaning, cannot be and never are radically questioned within the framework that the "Introduction" sets out.

Moreover—and this may be the most decisive point—the presupposition of sense and its rights has been at work from the very beginning of Derrida's discussion. Husserl's late intentional history ultimately may have need of recourse to a *telos*, as Derrida argues in the final pages of the "Introduction"; yet the sense this *telos* guards must already have been established in its own right for Derrida's entire analysis to get under way. Husserl's own "Origin," as well as Derrida's "Introduction," presupposes that the meanings, essences, and objects known by geometry have already been given and that these have been further clarified and established by the so-called "static" phase of Husserl's phenomenology. Without the existence of these guiding threads and guardrails, the return to geometry's origin and the investigation of transcendental history and historicity could never take place.[26] These meanings open the entire plane of history and the possibility of thinking writing's transcendental role in the first place, and their validity in their own terms is never questioned here, either by Derrida or Husserl. Within the space of Husserl's sense analysis, "within the limits of a regional investigation," "a bold clearing" may have come about that "transgresses them" toward "a new form of radicality" (*LOG* 14 / *IOG* 34). Yet the acknowledgement of these meanings and their unquestioned authority remains the ground of both Derrida's and Husserl's treatment.

Derrida, Demonstratives, and Death

Where, then, do matters stand? Derrida, at the most decisive junctures in 1962, it turns out, wholly relied on Husserl's views of meaning and the sign, even as he had begun to explore certain fault-lines in Husserl's project. Derrida's construal of the sign, meaning, language, and writing were themselves strictly Husserlian, anchored in this notion of the linguistic sign as *Leib*, as flesh or spiritual corporeality. Were different starting points in the philosophy of language valid—should Husserl's interpretation of the linguistic sign as a living flesh come into doubt—none of Derrida's own findings would remain: neither those concerning a transcendental (and thus potentially quasi-transcendental) writing, nor a purportedly "transcendental sense of death," nor even that of a pure equivocity and the perhaps problematic teleology that remedies this.

In turn, this proximity to Husserl generally, especially around this notion of *Leib*, as the previous chapters lay out in far more detail, may well explain why Derrida, a few years later, came to invent "deconstruction." Precisely insofar as Derrida in 1962 found himself constrained by the limits of Husserl's late thought, even as he had begun to probe them, Derrida in 1967 turns to Husserl's treatment of the sign in *Logical Investigations*, convinced that Husserl's thought is held in a unique form of confinement, one that can only be deconstructed (not rebutted), in a fashion requiring questioning the entire conceptuality of Western metaphysics as such, including especially that pertaining to the sign.[27]

I do not wish here to rehearse the argument that Derrida pursues in the whole of *Speech and Phenomena*, however.[28] Instead, I want to begin by focusing on a moment late in this work, where what could well be called a transcendental sense of death again steps to the fore. This will let us gauge how much Derrida's stance toward Husserl has altered, as well as eventually letting his views on the linguistic sign be grasped and be compared with those of the analytic tradition in particular. Granting that Derrida now does aim at the larger deconstruction of Husserlian phenomenology and the entirety of the "metaphysics of presence" (a deconstruction, some of whose terms will be reviewed here), I also want to show that Derrida, bringing to a climax his questioning of the reference points anchoring Husserl's project, which permit it to understand itself as a species of presuppositionless knowledge aimed at absolute truth, nevertheless still draws on assumptions found within Husserl's own interpretations of language and meaning. Derrida even here must embrace at a very fundamental level a linguistic analysis specific to Husserl, in a way that proves decisive for the relation of his work to analytic philosophy, as well as for his standpoint within the philosophy of language more generally.

The moment I have in mind, then, comes in Chapter 7, the final chapter of *Speech and Phenomena*. In much scholarship on Husserl and Derrida, it has been associated with the passage from the "Introduction" just discussed, one example of this being Lawlor's comments cited above. In *Speech and Phenomena*, Derrida does not explicitly speak of a transcendental sense of death. He does, however, claim to deduce "my being dead" as a condition of possibility of saying " 'I' " and saying " 'I am alive,' " in one of the most famous treatments in all of his corpus. This moment has been taken as a sort of signature argument for giving writing priority over speech, and thus to encapsulate Derrida's entire contestation of phonocentrism and the so-called metaphysics of presence. All speech, all discourse, Derrida is believed to have shown, entails the structural possibility of the speaker's absence (i.e. his or her death), an absence itself most apparent in writing.

Thus, at the climax of this development, Derrida rather provocatively declares: "The utterance 'I am living' is accompanied by my being dead and its possibility requires the possibility that I might be dead; and inversely" (*VP* 108 / *SP* 96–97). Another prominent commentator, Geoffrey Bennington, has summarized with admirable brevity the reasoning underlying Derrida's conclusion. "It can be shown," he writes in "Derridabase," "that, like any other term, 'I' must be able to function in the absence of its object, and, like any other statement (this is the measure of its necessary ideality), 'I am' must be understandable in my absence and after my death. It is moreover only in this way a discourse on a transcendental ego is possible, which again shows the link between transcendentality and finitude. The meaning, even of a statement like 'I am,' is perfectly indifferent to the fact that I be living or dead, human or robot."[29]

"I" "must . . . function in the absence of its object"; it must be able to be read and understood even in the absence of the author. Its intelligibility, its meaning, thus has built into it an objectlessness (*Gegenstandlosigkeit*), which entails my possible absence, or the possible death of whoever is speaking. So too, such death or absence—making of writing the true virtual or effective condition of all discourse—here takes on a transcendental, even quasi-transcendental role, specifically in respect to Husserl's enterprise. As Bennington points out—letting us gauge how far Derrida has come from his 1962 stance—Husserl's phenomenology would be dependent on such death or absence, insofar as these subtend the intelligibility of "I." "I" and "I am" must retain their meaningfulness for Husserl's own thought to be expressed in speech; and death, or "finitude" (as Bennington also puts it), would thus be foundational for Husserl's own discourse, even as these, as radical conditions, remain foreign to the rest of his thinking.

Unlike in the "Introduction," then, death here—as the condition of meaning in general, and of the meaning of Husserl's speech in particular—really is presented as an impossible condition of possibility, a so-called quasi-transcendental (in the technical sense of this term).[30] And thus, with this teaching, which Bennington faithfully captures, Derrida's own intentions have shifted: Derrida here is clearly engaged in a much more radical break with Husserl than anything to be found in the "Introduction."

Nevertheless, without doubting its accuracy, Bennington's argument, especially when seen from the perspective of the analytic tradition, raises some key problems. This is not to say that the alternative perspective analytic philosophy provides is itself necessarily the right one, of course. Invoking it will, however, permit clarity about what both Bennington's and

Derrida's argument implies—what construal of language and meaning it presupposes—and thus let Derrida's more mature approach to philosophy of language eventually become clear.

The major problem, then, is this: on what basis is "I" said to have *meaning* in the first place? Bennington's argument presupposes that the word "I" is indeed a term "like any other," and that as such "I" does carry *meaning* (*Bedeutung*)—meaning, which Bennington further tells us, always takes the form of "necessary ideality." But this is by no means self-evident: neither (1) that "I" *is* a term like other terms such that its function is to express or bear *meaning*; nor (2) that meaning's mode of existence is generally that of *ideality*.

The issue of ideality may be put aside for now, since Derrida himself also questions this presupposition in *Speech and Phenomena*, and it is a point to which I will return. As to the first, the claim that "I" really *is* a term "like any other," and that it does express or carry meaning, is highly controversial. Terms like "I"—but also "today," "now," "here," as well as the demonstratives "this" or "that," which are dubbed "occasional expressions" by Husserl, others calling them "token reflexives" or "indexicals"—are expressions whose function is *not at all* to mean, it has been argued, but solely to refer, to refer directly. They are constituents of what are sometimes called singular propositions—statements that contain a reference to a particular, without any mediation by a concept or a sense.[31]

As a class such terms thus distinguish themselves from other sorts of referring expressions such as those found in "the man on the lawn is yelling," in which case reference indeed depends on understanding a thought or sense, or even a set of concepts, those contained in, or expressed by, the phrase "the man on the lawn." In the case of indexicals, this is doubtful, however, and why this is so is made most readily apparent by the issue of *paraphrase*: by the problems involved in *saying* what sense "I" and the other indexicals *do* have, if indeed they have one.

After all, a proper name, or even a possible gloss on the meaning of "I," such as the phrase "the person now speaking," can by no means stand in for "I." To take an example, an historically informed, yet amnesiac, Bob Dole, sitting at the Republican convention, listening to Trent Lott orate, may say that "the person presently speaking was the Senate Minority leader," without expressing or even knowing the same fact about himself. Dole might, in fact, even be able to agree with the statement that "Bob Dole was the Senate Minority Leader," yet still not know that "I was the Senate Minority Leader" was true of him. Thus neither his own name nor a stable reference to the one speaking can replace "I." *Nothing*, it can be plausibly argued, in fact supplies a successful paraphrase or substitute for any of these expressions, and for this reason it is questionable that these terms can be construed along the lines of sense or meaning at all.

Bennington's and Derrida's argument, then, presupposes quite a lot. Their conclusion, specifically, assumes that the "role" of the indexical, as this is sometimes called (the possibility of its application as predelineated in language: in the case of the "I," roughly, to refer to the speaker or the agent of expression; in the case of "now," to fix a moment of time), is to be identified with an actual meaning. For this argument to go forward, the role and the meaning of "I" must indeed be one and the same.[32]

Only because "I" is taken to be meaningful in this way, after all, can their conclusion asserting the subject's necessary death or absence be reached. Only because the referent in question is seen here against the backdrop of this sort of meaning—of a universal sense, expressive or significant in itself—is the *necessity* of its absence or death (not just the contingent possibility of one or the other) affirmed as a co-condition of such meaningfulness, and the meaningfulness of all other discourse.[33]

Accordingly, should this presupposition fail, should meaning not be relevant in the case of the "I," this phase of both Bennington's and Derrida's argument would fail as well. A set of linguistic, specifically semantic assumptions stands behind this argument—an argument that, again, presents one of Derrida's signature positions. Without the assumption that all parts of discourse, all words or sentences, ultimately can be construed as terms like any other, and that all these have meanings—a claim far from self-evident, as we now see—Bennington's and Derrida's results would be impossible.

Before drawing whatever broader conclusions may be implied here concerning Derrida's general approach to language, however, it is necessary to restore this phase of Derrida's argument concerning the "I" to its larger context. What has so far been discussed is part of a more general treatment of occasional expressions, on Husserl's part as well as Derrida's. And for the sake of doing justice to the complexity of Derrida's own thought, as well as to let the broader orientation toward language informing his analysis become plain, we must see what positions Derrida is taking more generally with respect to Husserl's text: specifically, both how Derrida's discussion relates to his earlier stances on these matters in *Speech and Phenomena*, as well as how it relates to Husserl's own solution to this problem—to the way Husserl himself tries to give "I" a meaning, to which the above argument is indeed a response.

For Derrida, following Husserl as he introduces this entire class of expressions, at this moment indeed recurs to an issue that arose at the beginning of *Speech and Phenomena*: Husserl's treatment of *indication*. Derrida tells us that "indication penetrates . . . everywhere" occasional expressions function (*VP* 105 / *SP* 94). This theme of indication, as others have suggested,[34] is indeed crucial to Derrida's overall treatment of language in *Speech and Phenomena* and, as we shall shortly see, its occurrence here has far-reaching implications for Derrida's future stance on these topics, especially in "Signature Event Context," in the ensuing brouhaha with Searle, and in matters pertaining to Derrida's relation to analytic philosophy more generally.

To recall this theme briefly, indications, or indicative *signs* (*Anzeigen*)—such things as a knot made on my finger or the canals of Mars—according to Husserl are signs characterized by their dependence on a *real existing* circumstance or object to perform their signifying function (the knot *must be there* to indicate to me what I need to remember, which it shows but does not itself express). In turn, in the opening chapters of *Speech and Phenomena*, Derrida had contested Husserl's construals of meaning and linguistic expressions on the basis of this notion. Extending his analysis of indication to all those aspects of the sign that Husserl had distinguished from its capacity to bear ideal meanings and thus function as a genuine expression—so-called intimation between speaker and interlocutor, facial expression, tone of voice, and so on, in short, all the elements bound up in the real, factual, situation of communication and discourse—Derrida had argued that Husserl's exclusion of these factors rooted in indication was owed to an illicit, albeit unconscious, teleology. All the functions of language, including its capacity for expression, Derrida claimed, in fact were infected by "an indicative web," thereby drawing into question Husserl's ability to arrive at ideal meanings and the signs that express them in their purity.[35]

At the present phase of Derrida's analysis, however, what becomes apparent is that Derrida's stance is undergoing a subtle alteration, doubtless in part under the pressure of Husserl's own treatments. Though Derrida in this later moment in *Speech and Phenomena* continues to valorize indication in the most general sense, to privilege indication as an "originary" possibility at the very border between linguistic and nonlinguistic signs, as a function *within discourse itself* he starts to link indication to the work of presence, specifically a supervening presence of, and to, the subject. Discussing these occasional expressions, which, as so defined, contain an indicative moment, he states: "the root of all these expressions, one sees it very quickly, is the zero-point of the subjective origin, the I, the here" (*VP* 105 / *SP* 94).

Derrida now sees this indicative dimension of the linguistic sign in use as redounding to the presence of the subject and thus to the metaphysics of presence—in particular, in the case of the use of "I"—and clearly, on these same grounds, Derrida would also steer clear of the alternative "analytic" treatment of the "I" set out above. Moreover, Derrida's decision to reject indication within language in this way will have far-reaching significance: his understanding of this matter at the end of *Speech and Phenomena* augurs his future stance toward this topic generally. Derrida's distance from the zone of the indicative or pragmatic as it pertains specifically to language first emerges here in its incipient form, and this distance, in the reading of Austin and then Searle, will only continue to grow.[36]

In one way, furthermore, Derrida is surely right. This indicative dimension within language is indeed the crux of the analysis of indexicals brought out above. To it is owed the removal of indexicals from anything that might be genuinely called a meaning. Thanks to functioning in the factical and the real, thanks to being at work within the particular circumstances of discourse and communication in which they occur, indexicals are indeed claimed to be able to refer to particulars without any conceptual mediation. The work of *indexicals*, one might say, is simply the work of the *indicative*, the work of *indication* through language (all the terms being cognate).

Nevertheless, without wishing to foreclose the remarkable further results that Derrida reaches along this path, it should be noted that his suspicions concerning a reliance on presence may be overly broad, especially when it comes to the analysis just brought forward. To be sure, in some developments that give weight to the speech-situation, communication, or pragmatics in the analytic tradition—as in Searle's version of speech act-theory or certain analyses following from H. P. Grice—a dependence on presence and a supervening intentionality will be discernible in the way that Derrida claims.[37] Yet this is not necessarily the case in all.

In particular, in the analysis set out above, the ability of indexicals to refer should not be seen as a function of the presence of the referent to a consciousness, or as depending on the acquaintance of the speaker. Rather, the character of these terms, their *grammar* is such that they always directly refer; and only for this reason, in fact, on occasion do issues related to acquaintance in the most general sense arise—issues that flow from these terms' linguistic roles, rather than these roles from such acquaintance, as David Kaplan, perhaps the primary originator of this standpoint, made clear long ago.[38] "I" indeed on this account *never* functions as a general term, even in the absence of its referent, and it thus continues to indicate, or, as this is sometimes put, "rigidly designate" a singular referent, including on those occasions when this referent is in fact absent or unknown. "I" already refers individually and directly, as in the case of a note found on the ground, or a will with the first and last pages missing. And only thus may further information, such as that this is Ben Franklin's stationery (again not necessarily tied to presence at all), secure the identity of the referent in question.

Derrida, then, has perhaps gone a little too quickly, when it comes to extrapolating from this phase of the indicative or the pragmatic in Husserl to classing all such initiatives under the heading of presence. Doubtless, Derrida in his next texts of this era will plumb all the more provocatively that indexicality and even referentiality in the form of repetition, iterability, and spacing, which first emerges at the outer edge of language at the outset of *Speech and Phenomena*—functions that Derrida believes to be embedded in, or extractable from the possibility of semiosis generally. Nevertheless, Derrida simultaneously also comes to affirm, perhaps erroneously, that the indicative, or pragmatic dimension specific to language (not to mention pragmatism as such) is wholly tributary to the privilege of presence, specifically presence to a subject, in line with his analysis here set out.[39]

To see the broadest stakes of this decision and this interpretation, however, we must finally take into account the suggestion that Husserl himself offered concerning the "I" and Derrida's grounds for rejecting it. This is a matter of the greatest consequence for Derrida's own position; for, with this, among other things, the other issue raised above, the status of ideality—the conviction not only that there is meaning, but that such meaning is necessarily ideal—returns.

Husserl, like the other great logician of this period, Gottlob Frege, supposed that every (complete) sentence must have a meaning or sense complete in itself. And faced with the difficulties in giving sense to the "I" here reviewed, both Husserl and Frege chose the same solution, one which could well be said in this one instance indeed to opt for presence, even a pure or absolute presence. Both logicians, lacking an obvious meaning for "I," claimed that this consisted in a representation authentically given to the speaker alone. The true and fundamental meaning of "I" was a wholly private sense, a singular representation of his or her own self, uniquely known to the one employing it.

This solution, of course, is not really viable, as well as being contrary, as Derrida also notes, to Husserl's own assumptions (as well as to

Frege's).[40] Equally telling for our purposes here, however, is Derrida's response to Husserl's alternative. Derrida contests Husserl's solution, his appeal to pure presence and a private sense of the "I," but he does so only by appealing to *the rights of meaning generally,* in a gesture I have already begun to examine. Indeed, at this juncture (at which the subject's death, her or his necessary finitude emerges in the face of the requirements for "I" to be meaningful), Derrida relies on a more a general semantic analysis of language, explicitly owed to Husserl. As will be true in "Signature Event Context," where parallel considerations are raised, Derrida in fact appeals to an architectonic distinction Husserl himself draws between a pure logical grammar, focused on meaning alone, and a higher-order logic taking in validity, the object, and truth. Husserl, committed to the independence and autonomous rights of meaning, isolates a semantic realm complete in itself, able to stand apart from all concerns with truth and reference.[41] And Derrida, depending on this analysis to support his claim that the "I" is meaningful in the argument reviewed above, in fact, at this moment rejoins that construal of language that he had questioned at the start of *Speech and Phenomena.* Derrida, in order to argue that "I" must have a meaning like any other term, that is, recurs to Husserl's own belief that all discourse can and should be understood in terms of *meanings* themselves *ideal,* that all speech is governed by ideal meanings and functions essentially as expression.

A decisive crossroads, discernible in all of Derrida's future work, thus emerges here. Derrida may well wish to claim that the indicative or pragmatic dimension of language is tributary to the privilege of presence and the subject. Yet, as here, doing so, he will have no choice but to have recourse to Husserl's own semantics in order to avoid and counter this alternative. There really are only two working alternatives in philosophy of language: the way of reference or the way of meaning. At this critical juncture, as in future ones, where Derrida must choose, he indeed chooses meaning. None of his subsequent philosophy, or post-philosophy, none of his subsequent deconstructions of these *topoi,* prove possible without his reliance on Husserl's own semantic presuppositions, as becomes evident here.

Of course, to be clear, my point is not that Derrida makes these appeals for the sake of affirming Husserl's own outcomes. Undoubtedly, his ongoing reliance on Husserl's conception of language and semantics can be deemed tactical, strategic, or "micrological," as this is also sometimes put. Yet, it is not simply so. Not only is this return to meaning (and ideality) indispensable to the declaration of a quasi-transcendental role for death or absence—thus to Derrida's entire argument that all discourse depends on an absence of the subject especially manifest in *writing*, an argument long taken to be a cornerstone of his thought—but the final phase of the deconstruction of Husserl's thought about to be undertaken by Derrida, in which he explicitly announces or inscribes the so-called "closure of metaphysics," also proves impossible apart from this presumption—apart from the invocation of Husserl's models of language and meaning, and the return to ideal meanings and expressions that Derrida himself has already questioned. At the core of Derrida's own results thus remains an unavoidable recourse to Husserl's philosophy of language—and because this is so, and in fact will always be the case, and because viable alternatives to this construal do exist, the role of these presuppositions in Derrida's own thought cannot be said to be merely tactical or local.

Indeed, after his treatment of occasional expressions and his discussion of the "I"—after his proclamation that to say "I am" is to say "I am dead," "I am mortal"—Derrida again confronts those claims concerning the teleology of univocal sense that surfaced earlier in our discussion of the "Introduction" in the previous section of this chapter. More specifically, Husserl, having assigned the "I" a meaning, yet a wholly private one, had wanted to know whether his own analysis therefore implied that meaning itself might change, and thus its status as an ideality come into question. Husserl had asked "whether these important facts of fluctuations of meaning are enough to shake our conception of meanings as ideal, i.e. rigorous, unities, or to restrict its generality significantly?" (*LI* Vol. 1, 321 / *LU* II, 94).

To this question, Husserl answers no, as Derrida points out, seemingly in conflict with his earlier analysis of the "I." Yet most importantly at this moment, Derrida connects this rejection with the discussion of univocity, pure equivocity, and idealization that we examined above. Husserl, it turns out, bases the rejection of shifting meanings, his insistence on the stability of all *Bedeutungen*, itself a claim that functions entirely in principle, by arguing that to posit such stability is finally but to posit "the unbounded range of objective reason" (*VP* 113 / *SP* 100; *LI* Vol. 1, 321 / *LI* II, 95). Noting that "the *Origin* takes up under a literally identical form these propositions upon the univocity of objective expression as ideal" (*VP* 113 / *SP* 101), Derrida thus concludes that the entire network of distinctions Husserl has made up to this point relating to the sign, language, expression, and meaning are purely teleological. "In its ideal value, the whole system of 'essential distinctions' is therefore a purely teleological structure" (*VP* 113 / *SP* 101), he declares.

Husserl, at least as Derrida reads Husserl, by his own admission at this moment admits a radical difference between the practice of discourse in its entirety and the system of distinctions he has applied to it all along, between discourse, with all its vicissitudes, and the ideality of objective meaning. This distinction depends for its resolution, in turn, on the same open-ended possibility and rights of an objective reason in general—the stipulated ability eventually to fix all that exists in objective, univocal expressions—that came forward in the "Introduction" when the univocity of theoretical discourse was in question. The possibility of univocal sense is once again assumed as what gives confidence that the objective and ideal character of all meaning may be maintained, and it is again explicitly posited as a goal, a *telos* coordinate with the project of objective reason in general, of the complete scientific or theoretical determination of all objectivity.

Due to where we now stand in Husserl's own itinerary, however, thanks to the plane on which this *telos* is invoked and on which this whole argument currently takes place, this *telos* and its invocation proves even more problematic than in the *Origin*, and Derrida's commentary on it, correspondingly, more potent. Here this *telos* of an objective reason, an Idea in a Kantian sense, *opens* all of Husserl's distinctions, as Derrida emphasizes. It opens the entire system laid out in Husserl's *Logical Investigations* and therewith the rest of phenomenology. Derrida can indeed thus assign to this opening—still exceeding the purview of strictly phenomenological evidence, as in the "Introduction"—an ultra-fundamental status, an absolutely primary role, since, in contrast to the earlier work, the distinctions secured on its basis (those concerning the sign, meaning, and so forth) themselves *precede* all other phenomenological distinctions and provide the framework on which the others emerge.

Correspondingly, *différance* at once infinite and finite here manifests itself, according to Derrida. A work of an "originary," "primary," "essential" deferral and delay comes forward at the ground of all this work, making possible the first articulation, at the basis of the rest of Husserl's thought, between a theoretical *telos* of objective meaning and the actual practice of discourse. In Derrida's view, all of Husserl's thought, the totality of Husserl's actual enterprise, turns out to be based on a set of concepts that themselves live off this difference between the practical and the theoretical, itself founded by *différance*—Husserl's entire initial logico-linguistic conceptuality in its "pure possibility" thus itself being "deferred to infinity" (*VP* 112 / *SP* 100).

A radical work of *différance*, of originary deferral and delay, thus opens the very project of *theorein* as such, Derrida believes he has shown, and thinking this infinite *différance*, which is at once also finite *différance* (since from the start it implies absence, deferral, delay)—thinking the infinite rights of reason as finite / infinite *différance*—the "history" of an infinite reason is not ended, but closed. Starting from the interpretation of ideality as the infinite recursive economization of an interlinked chain of substitutes (the sign, the linguistic sign, the perceived object, its preconceptual sense, the object's intended meaning, this meaning's ideality), the infinite rights of theoretical reason has had its limits, internal and external, essentially sketched (*VP* 111–13 / *SP* 99–101).

Yet, granting that these are Derrida's goals—and granting that his outcomes, now, in the future, and perhaps even always, will give us much to think about—it should also at this moment be clear that such closure can be declared, *différance* said to play this role, only because Derrida had previously honored Husserl's views of language and meaning. *Différance* here takes center stage insofar as it articulates a total theoretical model of language, meaning, and its rights, on to an undifferentiated plane of discursive practice, onto the practical employment of language and speech in general. However, were this interpretation of language not able to be affirmed in the first place—if this general semantic assumption had already been denied, for example, in the case of indexicals—Derrida's analysis could never take this next step and assign to *différance* this founding role. *Différance* here indeed steps forward as a kind of meta-articulation of the ideal onto the real, of the rights of a universal and infinite reason onto all discourse generally, but had linguistic signs *that do not mean* already emerged within language, this meta-articulation would be impossible to conceive, and a very different relation would result *within language* between the theoretical and the pragmatic, constative and performative, meaning and reference. Thus, only because Derrida goes Husserl one better—in fact, solidifying all in Husserl's discourse that renders such semantic assumptions doubtful, granting ideal meanings to all language, to all items of discourse across the board, including the "I" and indexicals generally—may he think the opening of theory within practice in this admittedly novel and radical way, and declare the conceptuality of all philosophy of language, and indeed all philosophy, closed.

Both in 1962 and in 1967 (as well as beyond), then, we now see, Derrida's philosophy of language is essentially that of Husserl. Derrida's work in 1962 on Husserl's late transcendental history depends on an interpretation of language, writing, and (transcendental) discourse that has as its core Husserl's doctrine of the sign as *Leib*, as a living flesh. Again, in 1967, Derrida ultimately appeals to Husserl's own "pure logical grammar," which permits all language and discourse to be seen in terms of an autonomous realm of ideal meanings and as describable apart from any regard to reference or truth.

Does this, then, bring into question Derrida's own project? Does his enterprise become invalid as a consequence of its ongoing, if largely strategic, reliance on Husserl's work? By no means. What is true, however, is that Husserl has to be right about *some* things for Derrida to be right about *other,* often very different things, and thus that the line between these endeavors, the divide between philosophy and post-philosophy, as it were, should begin to be understood quite differently than it is in some quarters. Indeed, perhaps this line should really not be drawn at all.

For no border genuinely exists, it seems, at which the one endeavor may be said to stop and the other begin. As the case of Derrida lets us see, philosophy and post-philosophy today and always form a single, still indeterminate, seamless field. Such a conclusion, it must be conceded, may well come as less of a surprise to these authors, to these theorists and post-philosophers themselves, than they do to us, their interpreters and heirs. Derrida himself, for one, often insists on just this continuity of his thought with philosophy,[42] even while at other times, he seems to speak in a far different voice, or at least to let his emphases fall elsewhere.[43] However this finally stands, nevertheless, all these initiatives are in truth more dependent on what is today often taken to be an older style of inquiry—on argument, on phenomenological descriptions, on conceptual, linguistic, and logical analysis—than many of us recognize today. And thus, if I am right, and there really is no post-philosophy precisely because there never was any philosophy in the first place, then, in tandem with our ongoing discussions of Derrida, Deleuze, and others, it will indeed be necessary, in order to go forward, to return to the study of Husserl and to the ongoing consideration of those questions of logic and language that he shares with the analytic tradition.

Literary Theory's Languages

The Deconstruction of Sense
vs. the Deconstruction of Reference

Near the conclusion of her influential essay on Henry James, "The Beast in the Closet," Eve Sedgwick, the noted literary critic, speaks of meaning. Addressing the "totalizing insidiously symmetrical view that the '*nothing*' that is Marcher's [James' protagonist's] unspeakable fate is necessarily a mirror image of the 'everything' he could and should have had," Sedgwick suggests that "a more frankly 'full' *meaning* for that unspeakable fate might come from the centuries-long historical chain of substantive uses . . . of negatives to void and at the same time to underline the possibility of same-sex genitality."[1]

Confronted with such an assertion today, very few practicing literary critics ask what theorization of language lies behind it. Yet much of what is powerful in Sedgwick's work comes from an effect inseparable from her view of language: specifically, the experience one has here and elsewhere in her work of unexpectedly finding one set of putative meanings (in this case the puzzling *nothing*, and its ambivalent values, supposed to lie at the core of the life of Henry James's character, John Marcher) being mapped on to another (here the nothing, the concealment, of male same-sex desire, in the face of what Sedgwick calls the male homosocial, whose specific form in the figure of the "closet" Sedgwick's essay sets out).

Though the question of what notion of language is at work is not raised, Sedgwick's criticism, to employ the distinction in my title, clearly privileges and starts from the presumed capacity of language for sense—its ability to mean, and to mean in surprising ways—over against its capacity to refer. This is one reason, doubtless, that Sedgwick's interpretations are so often resisted by more traditional literary critics, since, believing they already know what themes and topics her authors treat, what the works she discusses talk about, they reject such novel meanings for such well-known works—Sedgwick often in fact treating highly canonical authors and texts.

Sedgwick's approach, moreover, is exemplary for the paths literary criticism has trod in more recent years; for if her work implicitly appeals to a theory of language that gives great weight to the possibility of meaning (and meaning in its capacity to undergo continuous transformation and reappropriation)—something this example shows, along with numerous others in her work, perhaps most particularly her concern with what she calls "binarisms"—nevertheless, this does not prevent it from also asserting (and perhaps achieving) a very specific form of reference, from laying claim to a new sort of "reality" that James's work and others map: a formation in the real, a novel historical and cultural moment, preeminently identifiable, thanks to the cluster of semantic traits that it turns out to share with its literary avatars (here of silencing and barring, of a concealment never quite total that allows itself to be penetrated precisely through tropes of penetration, violation, etc.).[2]

By giving a privileged place to the disclosure of novel meanings, Sedgwick retains the importance of something like the literary text (which still today may appear to be made of meanings through and through), even as she reveals new areas within the real for it to disclose. Doing so, Sedgwick's work furnishes a paradigm for a certain type of engagement with history and culture more generally. And indeed, returning to these questions of language, further pursuing this distinction between sense and reference, one thing the present chapter hopes to achieve is to establish a context in which the treatment of language by a variety of recent movements in literary studies, not only Sedgwick's, may be mapped.

Before arriving at this context, however, it is necessary to be a little clearer about my own aims overall. My enterprise might potentially be deemed a "retro" one, since, as the Sedgwick example shows, taking up these topics related to language, I intend to return to themes that by no means occupy the forefront of literary studies or even much of the humanities today, though the time is not long past when this was otherwise. I want to reopen these issues, pursue a reflection on language in an older, perhaps even outmoded, sense (what was once meant by "literary theory"), in order to clarify the paths literary criticism has taken in recent years, but also on account of a crisis that criticism, perhaps all textual interpretation, today seems to me to face. The overwhelming success in the humanities of historicist approaches and methods (among which I include sociology as well as that cultural studies stemming from British Marxism),[3] while in many ways all to the good, nevertheless raises questions about the future of the study of literature as such—whether it will retain any specificity as a pursuit, and, if so, under what conditions.

I discuss this problem further at the end of this piece. At the moment, however, I wish to emphasize in respect to literary *theory*, that, despite the possibly "retro" character of my endeavor, I do not believe it is simply possible or desirable to return to theory in the form in which it was once previously conducted. At issue here, first, is what links the moment sometimes called "high theory" (associated primarily with the deconstruction of Jacques Derrida and Paul de Man), as well as post-structuralism more generally, to all the major movements in criticism that come after it, it being well attested that these latter were decisively influenced by both de Man and Derrida. This is a rather delicate point; for, speaking broadly, as Sedgwick's work witnesses, even beyond any single view of language that post-structuralist or deconstructive approaches may or may not have shared, in much of the humanities the legacy of post-structuralism consists primarily in the belief that the proper stance toward language and all related concepts is to undo or deconstruct them. Both high theory and post-structuralism questioned the ability of preceding structuralist approaches to gain closure as knowledge; they doubted the scientificity of these so-called regional sciences (of which their founders, in cases such as Saussure, Freud, and even Marx, were especially proud). Thus despite their enormous investment in philosophical and other sorts of theoretical discourse, deconstruction and post-structuralism proved themselves to be the first moment "against theory," as their undertaking indeed implied the barrenness of further scientific or philosophical inquiry, into language especially, in favor of a radically volatized textuality and a radical genesis or productivity, entailing an engagement with a variety of genres (literary, philosophical, historical, and political). Such an essentially negative and syncretistic standpoint toward language found endorsement by an unexpectedly wide range of scholars thereafter, such as Stephen Greenblatt and Homi Bhabha, as well as Sedgwick herself.[4]

The belief that language as a study and a theme was to be dissolved into a wider spiral of economic or strategic negotiations (including language, thought, speech, meanings, referents, speakers, and even epochs) is the broadest self-evidence that post-structuralism bequeathed to the initiatives that followed after it, and this conviction, correspondingly, needs to be overcome, and new, concrete problems for a more direct style of questioning rediscovered, if theoretical debate is to be renewed. Such reopening of questions, accordingly, is something toward which this essay moves in its middle section, by bringing forward some hitherto often unrecognized presuppositions related to language, on the one hand in Jacques Derrida's early program—specifically, in his encounter with J. L. Austin—and, on the other, in Michel Foucault's writings, thus pitting a (Derridean) "deconstruction of sense" over and against what will be termed an alternative (Foucauldian) "deconstruction of reference."

In turn, a second, more principled impediment to the renewal of literary theory at present exists, coming from the movement known as neopragmatism. The literary critics assembled under this heading argue that the very practice of literary theory, the pursuit of a fundamental reflection on language, is either otiose, without purpose and hence undesirable (the case first made by Stanley Fish), or, even more radically, not even possible (as Stephen Knapp and Walter Michaels argue in their first "Against Theory"). This claim, which first surfaced within literary theory itself (on the basis of certain interpretations of language), must also be engaged with and surmounted if theory is to have any future. Thus, in the two final sections of this chapter, I turn to the neopragmatist position in order to argue that a split or tension between sense and reference also informs this work: specifically, that Stanley Fish as a theorist relies on a deconstruction of sense over and against Steven Knapp and Walter Michaels' deconstruction of reference.

For literary theory as a subdiscipline of literary studies again to become viable (a possibility whose realization I by no means take for granted), perhaps even if literature itself is to continue to be meaningfully discussed, theory, I believe, must conceive itself differently, both "theoretically" (with reference to post-structuralism's and high theory's undoing of theory's standpoint) and as a "practice" (over and against neopragmatism's claims that theoretical inquiry is useless or impossible). To begin to address both these demands, I will here appeal to the same remedy: namely, the setting out of a broader matrix for the investigation of theory's canonical questions concerning language than has hitherto been readily available, one that brings to light the decisions made about language by all these participants—by Michel Foucault or Jacques Derrida, on the one hand, by the neopragmatists, or Eve Sedgwick, on the other—and thus again allows these to be seen as questions, as genuine problems requiring further thought and investigation.

The field of theory's inquiry must indeed be made wider, more comprehensive, if issues capable of spurring theoretical debate and research are again to arise. To accomplish this expansion, I begin by reviewing a relatively unknown approach to language (at least to a majority of literary critics and perhaps to many humanists): namely, that of analytic philosophy.[5] Analytic philosophy starts from a different set of decisions about how to inquire into language, and yields a fundamentally different way of thematizing language, than that to which many scholars in the humanities are accustomed—one which, above all, privileges language's capacity for reference over sense.

Moreover, it will eventually be shown that not only the new pragmatism of Knapp and Michaels, but also the new historicism and work deriving from it, finds its footing, consciously or not, in this relatively little-known approach. A straight line leads back from many current historicist treatments of literature (and related developments in other disciplines, such as history) to the analytic approach to language. Bringing forward this connection can thus give new life to theory's pursuit, not only because new questions for theory are thereby raised, but because their relevance to contemporary literary studies is assured, as such unresolved theoretical questions arise exactly where they are most often taken to have fled, neopragmatism and the new historicism being most commonly believed to represent the moment of theory's demise as a pursuit central to literary studies as a discipline.

The Priority of Reference: Gottlob Frege's Influence on the Tradition of Analytic Philosophy

Underlying the analytic tradition's approach to language and philosophical problems generally is Gottlob Frege's work in logic, as is rather well-known today in part due to the contemporary British philosopher Michael Dummett. Frege himself, in fact, never truly made what has come to be called the "linguistic turn": the fixing of the starting point for philosophical inquiry in the study of actually existing languages or linguistics. Nevertheless, while not even as significant a figure as Frege can be responsible for a discipline as varied and as active as analytic philosophy in the twentieth century, his innovations did set the course for how philosophy subsequently was to be done, including how language was seen at the moment it became an explicit theme in this context.

Frege's work consists in a revolution in logic, with significant consequences for how language is to be understood. And, in part with an eye to Dummett, let me suggest the following three reference points as a way to sketch the scope of Frege's innovation, facets of his analysis which will introduce literary critics to a new way of viewing language, while also providing the basis upon which the rest of my argument builds. I will present this sketch of Frege's thought in light of its implications for (1) speech or discourse, (2) thought, and (3) signification—through its relation to the themes of the word, the concept, and language itself: how each appears in light of what I, following others, deem revolutionary in Frege's work.[6]

1. First, then, as to the word: Jacques Derrida now famously asserts that Saussure's linguistics implies a deconstruction of a language of words. In *Of Grammatology*, Derrida speaks of "a modern linguistics, a science of signification breaking the unity of the word," and by this he intends the undoing, at the hands of structural linguistics, of a model of language and signification arising at least as far back as Aristotle's *Peri Hermeneias*, which sees language as offering a set of *conventional* signs (*semeia*), themselves essentially names (*onomata*), each standing, in turn, for ideas and then things, both of the latter supposed nonconventional and universal (*OG* 21). Thus the word "dog" or "*Hund*" is believed to be a conventional sign for the thought of a dog as well as the animal, neither of which itself is anything like a sign or believed to have the conventional character of language. Good reasons exist, however, as we shall see, to think that the stance of Saussure's linguistics toward the word is more ambiguous than Derrida suggests, and in this respect, at least, the Fregean departure from the word would have to be deemed more radical.

Frege's departure takes place under the heading of what has come to be known as the "context principle." Frege first brought this principle forward in his *Die Grundlagen der Arithmetik* (*The Foundations of Arithmetic*). There it runs as follows: "never to ask for the meaning of a word in isolation, but only in the context of a proposition."[7]

Since Frege's aim in this work is to ground the basic concepts of arithmetic, what this principle amounts to is best seen in Frege's treatment of the word "*number*." For, the context principle demands that what the word "number" means be found by looking at *assertions* employing this term, by viewing the word "number" as it is *used in sentences*. The *meaning* of "number" for Frege, accordingly, does not simply flow from the *word* itself; it is not primarily to be found in a dictionary, or even by reflecting on the concept that the word might be thought immediately to express—by discovering what we believe the concept of number itself implies or by identifying an ideational content or representation that must accompany it. Rather, only by seeing this term used in sentences—here number statements, such as "the number of moons of Mercury is zero"— does its genuine meaning first appear.[8]

The context principle thus truly is a revolutionary dictum. All words, it indicates, primarily are meaningful only in sentences (or propositions).[9] So, too, the sentence or the statement would not consist of entirely independent, previously meaningful units, thanks to which, by juxtaposition or composition, it takes on its own sense. Such bits, what is usually meant by words (but also signifiers, morphemes, or monemes), would only be retroactive abstractions, at best secondary features of language corresponding to the circumstances surrounding the learning of it or related to communication more generally.

Not surprisingly, then, the context principle has had tremendous implications for all subsequent analytic philosophy of language. From here, for one, the emphasis on *use* in analytic philosophy starts to make itself felt.[10] With the priority given to the statement as the locus of meaning, every sentence begins to be seen as inherently individuated and its utterance happening for a "first time"; thus, the work the statement does in its assertion becomes primary. The context principle, accordingly, entails a rather radical break between the work of language and its overall appearance. Since a one-to-one correlation of words with things, even of words with meanings, here is no longer necessary, this principle renders questionable our usual way of thinking of language as a set of conventions that correlates meanings to words—a view still discernible, let me emphasize, even in Saussure's structuralism, where language remains a conventional articulation of *a total system of signifiers and signifieds*.[11] In fact, what language in its specificity at this moment might even *be* in analytic philosophy initially appears far from obvious.

Frege's context principle indeed renders doubtful our usual way of thinking of language as a set of conventions that correlates words with senses. Language in the tradition that he inaugurates, accordingly, becomes capable of functioning in a manner very different from what its surface suggests: a multiplicity of languages becomes possible, as well as a fracturing and repetition of the very entity known as "language." Frege opens the door to conceiving of languages at different levels explicating one another vertically, as well as to envisioning an internally differentiated linguistic surface consisting of a diverse layout of contiguous "linguistic" regions, neighborhoods, or zones.[12] Such a plurality of viewpoints proves to be inseparable from analytic philosophy's "linguistic turn"—a label that is thus something of a misnomer, since it suggests that a single, unitary view of language, rather than its inherent multiplication and fragmentation, is implied by this shift.[13]

2. The statement rather than the word thus receives priority as the unit of significance in Frege, and along with this emphasis on the sentence as a whole, a further important innovation of Frege's takes shape: one based on the notion that the reference of a sentence is its truth value. Frege thought a sentence as a whole finally named only one of two things, the true or the false, what was the case or what was not. This construal implies

that the meaning of a sentence, as well as the meaning of its components, consists preeminently in the part they play in allowing whether a sentence is true to be determined. As Barry Smith puts this in his article "On the Origins of Analytic Philosophy," "it turns out that the sense of a subsentential expression is identifiable as the contribution this makes to determining the truth value of the sentence in which it occurs."[14]

Frege was the first to suggest, then, that understanding the meaning of a sentence amounts to understanding those conditions under which it would be true or false, and this too has had enormous consequences for how language will be subsequently conceived in the analytic tradition, altering the very notion of meaning as it had been handed down.

More narrowly, Frege viewed the sentence, or the proposition, as composed of two heterogeneous aspects: (1) an empty or unfilled "concept," which Frege thought of as ultimately coincident with a function in mathematics; and (2) certain kinds of referring expressions (proper names and definite descriptions, between which he did not distinguish). Roughly, certain parts of sentences, what we would call subject terms ("Joe," "the baker from whom I bought the bread"), would have the job of referring to individuals and could be represented through a variable, and the rest of the sentence (e.g., "is a nice man") could be seen as a sort of function ranging over them—thus, when taken together (e.g., "Joe is a nice man") being capable of yielding or "equaling" one of two values ("the true" or "the false").[15]

Setting aside certain questions raised by this in regard to Frege's broader program, not only can a concept so construed not be identified with a concept *word* in important ways (a Fregean concept indeed being expressed by such phrases as "is a duck," or "has four sides"). Moreover, a possibility falls out of this that makes clearer the import of Frege's reconstrual of the concept and of meaning generally: namely, the possibility of defining concepts through what is called their extensions.

"Extension," a technical term in logic, is the range of instances in which a given concept turns out to be true (those instances thus being said to fall under this concept), and the meaning of a concept, on this view, is thus to be derived from all the true instances of its employment.[16] For example, the "meaning" of "is a red table" (an example of a Fregean concept) may be given through the class of cases—a, b, c, etc. ("Mark's table," "my dining room table," "the table near this door")—in which "x is a red table" happens to be true. It can be defined as what is common to, as the class of, all the valid instances of, its employment, as the notion that uniquely inventories the world in this way.

Not only, however, is this in itself a remarkable possibility—that the content of a concept would simply be derived from all the truths (or later, states of affairs or facts) which it helps to map or to give expression—but, even more importantly, understanding concepts in terms of their extensions illustrates that tight bond between truth and meaning that will come to be a hallmark of analytic philosophy and subsequently allow for much of its questioning of "essentialism about conceptual or linguistic items," as Samuel Wheeler puts this in a rather different context.[17]

This construal of the concept departs from what has traditionally been understood as the concept and its meaning in all previous philosophy, after all, including in Kant, Hegel, and even Husserl, for all of whom meaning is entirely independent of truth. With Frege, however, no longer would our use of language, our speech, imply a preexisting precomprehension of the meaning of the concepts that we use—a possibility often thought to require "essences" or "universals." To invoke a criterion of which deconstruction is fond, the sense or meaning of a concept, as well as the sentence generally, would by no means necessarily be "present" at the moment of utterance to the speaker, or to anyone else. Hence, rather than it being a puzzle, for example, how little Johnny can say and mean "Flipper is a fish," when he may not really know what "fish" means, there never would be a moment when the sense of a statement and how it relates to the world are radically separable.

Indeed, as the subsequent development of analytic philosophy shows, meaning construed in this fashion—the meaning of sentences being understood through their contribution to truth and the meaning of concepts construed through their extensions—ultimately holds the potential to render questionable *whether meaning genuinely exists at all*, as well as to radically individuate its work, making it doubtful whether meaning, if it does exist, would be of one sort, would correspond in any significant way to a single kind or genus. Meaning could be an empty, mobile cipher, an anthropocentric vestige, unable to be reckoned on with any rigor, thus to be entirely dispensed with in philosophy of language (which, famously, is W. V. O. Quine's position). Or, as always embedded in its individuated sentential work, found only in the vast array of the different instances of language's employment, "meanings" would not necessarily have anything in common with one another, even as meanings—just as a hammer, a color chart, and the frequency of light used in making silicon chips may really not have anything in common as tools. Meaning itself would thus cease to be conceivable as a single entity with a single sense, as in the work of the later Wittgenstein.[18]

3. Given all this, how do matters stand in the analytic tradition, then, when it comes to language? Is there here a single view of language? Is language itself even believed to be an entity that exists in its own right and that can be meaningfully investigated ?[19]

To the foregoing description of the fragmentation and multiplication that language here undergoes, which renders giving any single, straightforward answer to these questions nearly impossible, I would add only one further trait bearing on the analytic treatment of language, which, in the present context, will have to suffice as a clue to how language is there perceived. Frege's view of the concept, we now know, depends on finding those instances in which the attribution of the concept happens to be true, and it gives primacy to truth and, with that, to *reference* of some stripe, to the capacity of language to make statements about *particulars*.[20] Thanks to his claim that the reference of a sentence is a truth-value (and that the meaning of its parts may be derived from this), Frege's conception of language, in comparison with those that came before, indeed ends up stressing reference, giving priority to those paths by which the individual existents presumed to compose the world enter into language.[21]

Although this is a development not initially as clear in Frege himself as it will turn out to be in his successors,[22] Frege's starting point indeed ultimately allows meaning to depend on reference, and such considerations only grow larger as analytic philosophy develops. The mechanisms by which reference is to be achieved become the primary entry point to language as a whole in analytic philosophy, taking on the status of basic problems.[23] In great measure, in fact, they come to encompass those issues in philosophy more traditionally assigned to mind or consciousness (which, when invoked at all, are seen ever more in the context that the problem of reference provides).

By contrast, for so-called "Continental" philosophy, whether language is even capable of genuinely referring, of treating particulars (individual entities and circumstances) in their own right, remains a real question. On this alternative model of language, of a language of words (or, again, even that of Saussurean signifiers and signifieds), the *sense* of a sentence, such as "the red jar is on the table," may be understood wholly apart from its capacity to be true or to refer. Understanding the parts of which speech is composed—the word or the signifier—in itself already guarantees a sentence's comprehension. Language or discourse thus does not have to refer in order to have a meaning, a stance that obviously makes apparently non-referential uses of language like literature readily comprehensible (doubtless accounting for the prevalence of this model among literary critics).[24] In turn, however, with language so conceived, basically as a reservoir of meanings attached to signs and rules for combining them, the problem arises of whether language or speech ever *can* refer, at least to particulars. How can a sense presumed general in itself (thanks to the inherent generality of words and thoughts and concepts) ever reach out and arrive at and grasp particulars?[25]

Whatever else may be the case in analytic philosophy, this problem has ceased to be a live one. The restructuring or recasting of signification that Frege already brought about gives reference in some form a new privilege, making it an essential, not accidental, feature of language's functioning. Reference thus joins with the other two starting points already visible in Frege, the context principle and his treatment of the meaning of concepts, to present the defining traits of a view of language far different from the one with which many literary critics are familiar: a view in which the workings of language, or discourse, are different than their surface might lead us to expect (than any talk of words or even signifiers and signifieds would indicate); in which its unit of meaning, the sentence or proposition, is already keyed to those circumstances that would make it true; and in which language in its totality, along with becoming inherently multiplied and self-differentiated, is also caught in the facticity of the world, embedded in what permits speech (wordlessly and silently) to refer.[26]

Derrida or Foucault:
The Deconstructions of Sense or Reference

To this degree, and to this extent, the analytic view of language is indeed essentially decentering of the view of language many of us hold (of language as a reservoir of meanings and signs capable of being identified in their own right and standing apart from the world), and with this in mind, I would like to turn to more familiar precincts. Thanks to this alternative view of language having come forward, decisions as to how language is construed can indeed be seen to underlie various strategies in literary criticism and thus can differentiate schools or camps more usually seen as one. Not just unsuspected differences in approaches to language, however, divide more recent critical schools in novel ways, but also different approaches to questioning, or deconstructing, if one will, the self-evidences and reference points by which language is understood and made a theme. "Negative," deconstructive, or antifoundationalist strategies have had the largest impact when it comes to understanding language in literary studies, and our new-found grasp of this alternative version of language stemming from analytic philosophy permits a new view of these strategies as well.

More specifically still, more than one kind of deconstruction of language is indeed conceivable, a deconstruction of reference as well as a deconstruction of sense—and to bring forward these dual possibilities, which continue to lie behind much work undertaken in the humanities of late, I want briefly to turn to Jacques Derrida's early encounter with J. L. Austin's speech-act theory in "Signature Event Context" (SEC).

I do so, however, not to choose sides nor even to renew these debates, but because this discussion serves as a useful crossroads from which more general conclusions may be drawn about the analytic model just put forward, and its relation to those other models more familiar to most readers through Saussure or deconstruction. I do not intend to renew these old controversies, but rather to question the entire field anew, and thus only the broadest orientations toward language are of concern to me here: of the Derridean or deconstructive type and those that may be classified with it (let us continue to call them "Continental" for the moment), on the one hand, and those of speech acts and analytic philosophy more generally, on the other. From our present vantage point, I want to show the strengths and the weaknesses, the economies, some might say, of both approaches to language, and with that the different deconstruction each invites—from which significant questions concerning language again should arise, as well as a context enabling the mapping of some of the more recent developments and debates in literary criticism.

In the first place, let us recall that, though in many ways sympathetic to Austin's undertaking—in particular, as he would later emphasize, with its style—Derrida criticized Austin's notions of context, use, and the speech act, along with the values of the normal, the ordinary, and the serious that accompanied them, seeing in all of these a fealty to what Derrida calls logocentrism: a predisposition to view language through its capacity to do logical, or *logos*-related, work: i.e., to make statements and tell the truth. Austin's innovation, his emphasis on the *act* of speech in the total speech situation, which ultimately allied discourse with a theory of action more generally, was deemed by Derrida to be still too much in the thrall of the traditional conception of the work of language that philosophy had handed down, centered on telling the truth.

I want initially to suggest that in some important way Derrida is right here. The Fregean starting points do prove determinative for Austin in the ways I have begun to indicate; and these starting points are indeed indebted to a view of language that privileges its ability to refer and tell the truth—arguably, to an extent never before conceived possible.

At the same time, I must hasten to add, when Austin is approached within the context solely provided by other initiatives within analytic philosophy, Derrida's claims by no means appear obvious, and this may well be one reason Derrida's essay has caused so much controversy. Austin's debt to Frege is one of the least glaring, and much of the actual force of his speech-act theory indeed comes from questioning those same self-evidences upon which Derrida himself sets his sights.[27]

Austin's work as a whole clearly intends to be a corrective to the emphasis on truth that held sway in analytic philosophy (particularly in positivism) roughly up until the time that he wrote. Thus Austin, in his own way, wishes to question the superordinate privilege analytic philosophy gives to truth and to knowledge, in accord with Austin's own comment, near the end of his lectures, that he has "an inclination to play Old Harry with two fetishes, viz. fact / value and true / false";[28] a statement that Derrida also quotes). This devalorization by Austin can be seen most preeminently in the overall trajectory of his lectures. These start by distinguishing, and placing on equal footing, two classes of utterances: those that *tell the truth* (constatives) and those that *do* things (performatives). By the end, however, Austin subordinates the locution (the successor of the constative, now conceived as a function) to the illocutionary (the successor of the performative, also so conceived), thus privileging the latter.

Granting this departure from the reigning orthodoxy, nevertheless, Austin's very conception of a speech act remains intrinsically tied to the reconception of language and logic undertaken by Frege, in a way upon which Derrida indeed puts his finger. Thanks to our prior discussion, for both Frege and Austin, language, we can now see, is finally understood only through the work it does in *utterances* (a notion stemming from Frege's first innovation), and, along with that, through its *work* more generally in regard to the world, its functions in contact with particulars, with individual entities and circumstances—a view also owed to Frege. Both Frege and Austin, that is, assume that the various cantons of discourse indeed *go to work*; for both, such essentially factical or referential work and its success become an internal or defining possibility of language as such—in respect to truth in Frege, and with respect to all the other activities now believed to fall within language's employment in Austin. From this follows the dismissal by Austin of those supposedly empty, derivative, or citational instances concerning the status of which Derrida will inquire: instances of literature (or other "non-serious" cases) where such acts as saying "I do" no longer seem to perform their normal function. Language, understood as being at work in Austin, is thus an extension of the view of language found in Frege, even as Austin wishes to question some of those values Derrida also wants to bring into doubt. Derrida, accordingly, is within his rights, in seeing this emphasis on use, the entire development of the speech act, as stemming from an initial commitment of language to the *logos*, from an initial determination of language based on its vocation for referring and telling the truth.

Derrida indeed identifies and questions an important trait in Austin and the analytic tradition overall. At the same time, Derrida has perhaps also underestimated the scope of the resources of this tradition (with which he may not be altogether familiar), and this is of at least equal importance here. Another side of Austin's work, arguably also owed to Frege, eludes Derrida and, with this opacity, the presuppositions of the alternative tradition in which Derrida himself works become visible, as well as, arguably, certain unperceived limits of his own deconstructions.

Not only does Derrida accuse Austin of logocentrism, after all, but he locates the crux of this charge in the privilege Austin's theory gives to *consciousness*. Speaking of Austin's treatment of context and the speech act, Derrida claims "one of those essential elements—and not one among others—remains, classically, consciousness, the conscious presence of the intention of the speaking subject in the totality of the speech act" (SEC 14).

Derrida's denunciation of Austin on this point, however, is ill-advised, I believe, and thus more telling in respect to the models of language, meaning, and the concept at issue in Derrida's own work, and in the tradition in which he functions, than in regard to Austin's thought or even to analytic philosophy more generally.[29] Austin himself, after all, explicitly denies that of which Derrida seems to accuse him, denies in respect to performative utterances that "their being serious consists in their being uttered as the outward sign . . . of an inward and spiritual act."[30] As Frege before him, Austin in no way relies on any sort of introspection, or on the hypothesis of language-independent states of consciousness, to identify philosophically significant features of language's employment. Indeed, already in Frege, everything that privileges reference and truth also gives a remarkable independence, even opacity, to language and its functioning, decisively separating its surface from its depth. This opacity, this nonpresence to a speaker of her or his meaning as a whole, is also visible in Austin's way of working, which views concepts and their meanings only through their use, in their employment, rather than in some self-evident prior understanding of their idea, their essence, or of the definitions of the terms that express them.

Indeed, the distance of the analytic tradition generally from the sort of mentalism Derrida describes would in fact be hard to overestimate, as is most obvious in the issue of evidence; for, even when intentions are invoked, as they doubtless often are by Austin, access to them is always through linguistic and other public traits, never through any kind of private introspection. What counts as evidence for intentions radically distinguishes intention as used here from major currents in the phenomenological tradition; and when exceptions to this do occur, as in Searle's later thought, which I discuss below, such philosophies cease entirely to make the linguistic turn.

In fact, recourse to consciousness and present meaning remains implied far more by the way language is viewed in Derrida's own thought than anything to be found in Austin or most analytic philosophy. This is the second contrast that I want to bring forward between Derrida and Austin. The deconstructive critique of presence notwithstanding, deconstruction, structuralism, Continental philosophy, as well as all in literary studies that follows on these, are indebted to those presuppositions that cluster around the notion of "present meaning," including more traditional versions of the concept and the word, in a way that is simply not the case in the analytic tradition, largely due to the footing upon which Frege put it.

In particular, as I have argued in my previous chapters, Derrida begins from, and in certain respects upholds, Husserlian models of discourse and language (far more than has previously been explicitly recognized)—which models, as the context I am establishing also begins to make plain, on key points do not differ decisively from those of Saussure in some important respects. Such reliance can be seen within SEC itself near the end of its first section. There Derrida makes clear that Husserl's positions in respect to language and discourse embody a precursor position to his own, insofar as Husserl rigorously thinks the independence of meaning from reference. An initial, radically semantic orientation that takes the work of language as wholly separate from reference—"the absence of the referent" as a given in the face of "signifying form," as Derrida puts it—is, in fact, the ground shared by Husserl, Saussure, and Derrida.[31] The rigorous working out of this gesture, moreover, Derrida here assigns to Husserl ("Husserl investigated this possibility very rigorously" [SEC 10]), as he also does in *Speech and Phenomena*.

Thus for Derrida, for Saussure, as well as for Husserl, meaning exists securely in its own right, apart from reference; it is correlated with language as a clearly delimited and autonomous domain. Of course, Derrida's own interest finally goes in a direction different from Saussure's or Husserl's—here focusing on a possibility, which Husserl analyzed and dismissed, pertaining to what Husserl calls grammatico-syntactically impossible formations (such as "this green is either" [SEC 12]). Nevertheless, Derrida's characteristic gesture is to broaden out or radicalize that thought which he also contests—in this case, Husserl's. And in Husserl's own analysis, like those others that Derrida consistently targets, the concept and its supposedly preexisting meaning find expression in the word or the sign. Both meaning and concept take priority over reference and truth respectively, in a way very different from both Frege and Austin.

Consequently, a sort of substantialization or reification, as well as a homogenization of meaning in its own right—a positing of a realm of meanings as such, open to description and negotiation, and indeed self-present evidences—underlies Derridean deconstruction, at least up until the final moment, when it calls this entire matrix into question in a highly unexpected fashion, a move that Derrida, at least, would surely claim brings into question the totality of analytic philosophy as well.[32] Nevertheless, from the perspective brought forward here, from the reconstructed vantage point of analytic philosophy, such deconstruction may indeed look rather different than it appears to itself: it may well seem to retain a realm of meaning, models of the concept and the statement, that analytic philosophy has already surpassed.[33]

Derridean deconstruction thus finds its precursor, its object—something like the sublated to its sublating—as I have shown in Chapter 3, in determined models of language to which significant alternatives in fact exist, and this potentially sets limits to its own deconstructive work. My aim, however, is not to "deconstruct" deconstruction, or thereby to choose one of these models over the other. Rather, two very different starting points for thinking about language, it becomes evident, are possible, and thus two very different sorts of deconstructions of language are conceivable: a deconstruction of meaning (or sense), as well as a deconstruction of reference. Alongside the Derridean deconstruction of sense an alternative deconstruction exists that goes by way of reference, that privileges the referential functions of language, as Derridean deconstruction does language's capacity to mean, one that calls reference into question, by way of reference, as deconstruction does meaning by way of meaning.

Given the fracturing that language already receives within the analytic tradition, given that the function or presupposition of reference, opaque and silent, already draws language beyond itself—some might say beside the other or the "real"—what shape such a deconstruction of reference might take is not as immediately clear as it is in the case of sense. Leaving aside for now the extent to which such a deconstruction emerges within the analytic tradition itself (in particular, in Donald Davidson's undoing of Quine's scheme / content distinction, the so-called "third dogma" of empiricism), the works of Michel Foucault most notably have executed such an intention. Precisely as a deconstruction of reference in the sense specified—moving by way of reference to bring the stability and identity of reference into doubt—Foucault's alternative "deconstructions" focus on discourse and language in the context of the objects to which these refer (including at times those objects denoted by the terms "discourse" or "language" themselves).[34] More precisely, Foucault, as is well known, made the referents of the human sciences dissolve (along with the progressivist history of the disciplines that took these referents as endpoints), by rendering questionable the concepts and objects about which such discourses claimed to speak. Fashioning a kind of meta-pragmatic unit, in which objects, practices, and discourses functioned as a single item, Foucault put forward these totalities as the true, primary units of signification. Through these novel units (as well as their successors in his later writings), which Foucault called "epistemes," Foucault offered multiple scenarios on which reference ceased to function, in the sense that it ceased to appear as transparent, the capacity of these sciences to investigate their objects becoming something other than a result of the object or its truth. A previously unsuspected *Historie* (in German here, since closer to the early Heidegger's understanding of this term than any of its more common acceptations) was shown to be at work that rendered all the subject matter and the self-evidences belonging to these disciplines to be other than what they appeared. So doing, Foucault indeed performed a deconstruction in an objectivist tradition (a tradition initially carved out in France by such thinkers as Cavaillès, Canguilhem, and Bachelard),[35] a deconstruction focused on referents rather than meanings, and on truth rather than its conditions of possibility.

A deconstruction of reference, as well as one of sense or meaning, is thus conceivable, as this brief comparison of Foucault and Derrida makes clear. In turn, this distinction begins to provide a matrix against which many subsequent developments in the humanities may be mapped, particularly those in literary studies and literary theory. As Sedgwick's example already indicates, assumptions made as to the status of semantics—whether any treatment of meaning is *stricto sensu* possible—are often more decisive for understanding the variety of literary initiatives that proliferated in the '80s and '90s than many suspect. This distinction between the deconstruction of sense and reference has the potential, for example, to set off a Marxian initiative like that of Fredric Jameson's, which holds off reference to the last while compiling a novel and complex set of meanings, from others, such as those of Pierre Bourdieu or even, at times, that of Stuart Hall, in which reference plays a role alongside meaning from the very beginning. In these cases, as well as numerous others, however, to do justice to the positions in question requires a far more detailed analysis than I can here provide—in part because all critics now work in a highly sophisticated post-structuralist and post-theoretical context, which renders their treatment of these matters especially complex. Thus, in order to give a further concrete idea of the sort of work that might subsequently be undertaken on the basis of the distinctions I am laying out, I want to conclude by identifying the linguistic presuppositions of a single major movement in the last twenty years of literary studies in a fairly precise way, namely that of the new historicism and its heirs—the analysis of which forms a sort of bookend to the queer theory from which I started, the two supplying my central examples for a future, more comprehensive analysis.

Stanley Fish's Neopragmatist Deconstruction of Sense

Much of what was most powerful in the new historicism is bound up with this novel model of language it has tacitly employed, though I am by no means suggesting that any of the leading new historicists, such as Louis Montrose or Stephen Greenblatt, were aware of these developments in analytic philosophy and consciously applied them (albeit they may have tacitly gathered some of their import, taken on some of this baggage, by way of their close study of Foucault). In order to bring forward the alternative linguistic template that tacitly underlies the new historicism, it is necessary, however, first to focus on another specifically theoretical debate. This moment in literary theory may in any case appear to have gone too long unaddressed, since not only did the neopragmatist critics contribute to the demise of literary theory, but they were very much aware of the resources of analytic philosophy that I have begun to sketch. None of those points from which I began would be new to them, which is not to say that any one of these critics would endorse precisely the same formulations that I have offered.

This movement, however, not only was not as monolithic as it sometimes may seem in retrospect, despite its shared knowledge and goals; more crucially, the differences that came to the fore within it were not, in my view, the most important ones. Indeed, I have waited to treat this development in literary theory until now for this reason: so as to be able to put a framework in place through which the deeper differences among the neopragmatist critics might become visible. This new view, along with helping me determine the linguistic assumptions behind the new historicism, will prove central to my argument in a second way. For should it indeed become plain that a gap exists among the neopragmatists' own positions, that different models of language are at work among them, the future will be reopened to theory's questioning, since the neopragmatist's arguments against the sort of theory that I am trying to revive will have been undermined insofar as the divergence in their own positions itself demands renewed theoretical investigation.

I want to suggest, more specifically, that Stanley Fish's brand of neo-pragmatism, in particular, approximates what I am calling a deconstruction of sense, especially within the context of the analytic tradition as a whole, and that this fealty to meaning explains the deepest differences between his theoretical position and that of Steven Knapp and Walter Michaels.[36] The still-unexplained disagreement between these theorists in the *Against Theory* debate (still unexplained, since after being deemed the last of the literary theorists that Knapp and Michaels aimed to silence, Fish himself did not really take up Knapp and Michaels' initial criticisms, which centered on his understanding of belief, nor did they pursue these), is owed to Knapp and Michaels' own embrace of reference and their having mounted, accordingly, a deconstruction of reference over and against his deconstruction of sense.[37]

Fish's strategy, faced with the analytic model of language, which gives pride of place to reference and truth, and thus by definition appears to leave fictitious speech, like novels and poetry, out of the picture, was indeed to appeal to a latent semantic dimension of some versions of the analytic project, in particular that of John Searle and his version of speech act theory.[38] By insisting that the role of sense was greater and more unstable than Searle himself allowed, Fish in fact first forged his own stance as a theorist.

That a privilege of sense, that finally a version of what I am calling the deconstruction of sense, on Fish's part underlies his mature position, as well as a problem with that stance, can begin to be seen by turning to what arguably remains Fish's signature essay, his "Is There a Text in this Class?" Fish's focus in "Text," let us recall, is indeed on meaning—its stability, its normativity, as well as its relation to context and to a given situation. Already positioned among the arch-deconstructors of that time, Fish was at pains to deny that his teaching amounted to the claim that a text or a sentence could mean anything, and thus that his views had the potential to undermine the profession (a charge to which Fish would be especially sensitive, as we now know). Fish in "Text" thus retains the category of meaning and denies that his stance entails that an utterance, a text—in this case, a student's question from which his title comes—can mean *anything*, that it is somehow wholly indeterminate, or unintelligible in itself. Utterances indeed have determinate meanings; yet, Fish adds, *not the same ones.* Every sentence instead takes on a succession of stable meanings on different occasions, according to Fish, no one of which is authoritative in itself. As Fish himself puts it: "plurality of meanings would be a fear . . . if sentences existed in a state in which they were not already embedded in, and had come into view, in function of some situation or the other . . . but there is no such state: sentences emerge in situations and within those situations, the *normative meaning* of an utterance will always be obvious or at least accessible" (my emphasis).[39]

Fish's introduction of particular contexts and situations, as we shall soon see, clinched his mature views of theorist, which combine, as he says as late as 1999, formalism (an embrace of meanings, rules and norms) with antiformalism (context dependency and change of meaning in different situations).[40] Yet Fish's analysis also leads to an impasse, which proves to be telling in regard to Fish's semantic deconstruction as a whole and for the model of language that underlies it.

Fish's seemingly eminently reasonable claims in "Text" indeed leave one significant question unanswered (the very question that immediately receives a response in models like Saussure's, but which is far more vexed in a tradition that privileges reference): namely, how can Fish continue to identify and speak of sentences at all, of "sentences emerg[ing] in situations," and thus of sentences somehow distinct from those situations and able to be established in their own right? In part due to the underlying model implicit here, which separates language's surface from its depth and radically destabilizes the identity of all linguistic entities, how Fish can grant an identity to the sentence over time, even to deem it the same sentence, the meaning of which changes in different situations, demands clarification. After all, if what Fish says is true, if in each case the situation *immediately shapes the sentence* according to context, how is it still possible to speak of this sentence as the *same* in *different* situations or contexts?

Indeed, if pragmatic categories have already shaped utterances and no uninterpreted sentences exist, why compare "Is there a text in this class?$_1$," with "Is there a text in this class$_2$," as Fish does, rather than with "Is there a test in this class?$_1$," as uttered by someone with a speech impediment or by a speaker who has never encountered the word "text"? Indeed, why not just pick any sentence you like?[41] If all utterances are context-specific in the way that Fish suggests, and nothing to which rules are subsequently applied precedes this, such that it is inconceivable to imagine sentences apart from the situations that stabilize them and without their particular meanings, what, then, allows these different instances to be bound together as the same, and circumstances and norms asserted to be what also works upon them?

Nor is this a trivial concern. For without this claim, without maintaining that it is indeed meaningful to talk about a sentence *as well as* its interpretation within a given situation (even as he also denies that such uninterpreted sentences actually exist), Fish would indeed not be able to assert his most constant point in all these discussions: namely, that *conventional or institutional* rules and norms control *meanings* (of sentences, as well as larger portions of "text")—that the meanings, truths, or understandings that emerge in all of these situations are made rather than found, conventional, not natural; institutional, not brute.

Fish's most constant position (which embodies his main difference from Searle), never denies norms or rules altogether, but only their naturalness or absoluteness, as well as their universality, thus historicizing them.[42] Indeed, Fish consistently claims against more standard speech-act theory, especially the universalizing one of Searle, that, yes, there are rules, but these lead back to narrative, diachronic, local—and hence, necessarily contingent—contexts.

To make this argument, however, as we have begun to see, Fish must be able to affirm that rules and norms of some sort are at work in the first place (though these, along with the objects they are supposed to determine, at this moment seem ultimately to elude identification) and Fish here—in fact, like much cultural criticism, which also presupposes that there are such shared rules or norms defining of a culture's forms of making meaning—due to the broadest conclusions he wishes to draw, runs into trouble.[43]

I am interested less in this difficulty itself than I am interested in the latent semantic dimension, which, it should now be clear, informs all of Fish's thinking.[44] Without going into this too deeply, it is worth noting that in an essay prior to "Text" focused on Searle's *Speech Acts* (written after an even earlier essay in which Fish invoked both Austin and Searle in order to question alternative strains of analytic philosophy that he deemed "positivist" and focused on "referential theories"),[45] Fish took aim at Searle's own insistence on the difference between the serious and the nonserious, the normal and the conventional, and the concomitant universalization and naturalization of Searle's own findings, specifically, with an eye to the role reference played in Searle's account.

Over and against what Fish took to be an unwarranted fealty to what is called "the axiom of existence" on the part of Searle (the claim that for reference to occur, the object referred to must exist), Fish, more specifically, located reference in rules pertaining to a specifically illocutionary context, a "set of discourse agreements" allowing the mutual identification of the objects in question on the part of both speaker and hearer

(Fish, *Text* 242). Drawing on Searle's own findings that reference always occurs within "a universe of discourse" (a handy term Fish earlier employs: Fish, Text 237, 238), Fish thus concludes, against Searle, that no referent in itself exists able to provide an absolute stopping point to discourse. Thereby, thanks to demoting any ultimate referent to the work of a contingent frame of reference, Fish sets all knowledge back into an ultimately narrative, diachronic, and historical context.[46]

Reference, according to Searle's own presuppositions, Fish had already argued, depends on a larger situation of discourse able to render meaningful that to which it refers, and Fish himself gives even greater priority to meaning over reference than does Searle. Yet here also is where the problem pointed out earlier arises. For Fish in all his writings indeed has to give priority to language's capacity to mean over its ability to refer, to these semantical rules for illocution and the universes of discourse they posit over referents, in order for his wider-ranging deconstruction of natural, universal, or unmediatedly objective meanings to go forward, in order to give to culture and history the priority he assigns them. In turn, however, the basis of these claims becomes questionable when Fish in "Text" and thereafter apparently wants to step beyond Searle's framework entirely, and move to a more radically pragmatic posture, by claiming that not even the rules of the sort Searle previously discussed, upon which Fish depended, nor the sentences to which they apply, independently exist in the first place. Much like Quine's attack on Carnap, Fish's ongoing claim that no uninterpreted data exist clearly must and does refer back to another claim—in this particular case, Searle's—that both do exist; and Fish, again much like Quine, henceforth insisting on this negative semantic space, is forced to repeatedly shift back and forth between a perspective that wants to assert there are both rules and sentences (rules and utterances already situated and at work together), and one that denies that any such distinction between them may be drawn in the first place.

Fish's identification of sentences as the same across contexts, his talk of situated rules shaping sentences, thus shows how central this semantic space continues to be to his argument, even at the moment he wishes to step beyond it. For, again, without a commitment of some sort to something like Searle's principles, it becomes impossible to rigorously speak of rules of any sort, and thus impossible, of course, to claim that these rules and norms are conventional, or indeed have any other character. Fish's deconstruction, then, on one level at least (the level that has received the most attention), indeed remains an inherently semantic deconstruction—a deconstruction of sense—a deconstruction of Searle, speech-act theory, and "formalism" more generally, as Fish now puts this, relying on the implied semantic commitments of these positions in order to take a step beyond them. Fish's conventionalism and historicism are ultimately owed to a conception in which there are identifiable meanings and rules—universes of discourse able to be thematized and having priority over reference, and which are then said to have only a pragmatic and contingent rather than a universal or necessary basis, thus getting Fish into trouble when he wants to shed or question this framework still more radically.

"Against Theory's" Deconstruction of Reference: A Linguistic Template for the New Historicism

Fish's semantic commitments, then, permit the crucial difference between his positions and those of Knapp and Michaels in "Against Theory" to be grasped, and from this, the linguistic template underlying the new historicism and its offshoots may be gleaned. Steven Knapp and Walter Michaels' 1982 essay "Against Theory" in any case demands study in its own right. For this piece was indeed a bellwether for the direction in which literary studies was going at the time it appeared. Knapp and Michaels' essay perfectly captured the tectonic shift then underway from theoretical language-based literary criticism (also still often devoted to a narrow canon) to a much more diversified study of literature, which viewed its project as far more deeply implicated in culture and history than it had before.

Yet even as this essay has received an enormous amount of attention over the years, doubtless due to the feeling that it somehow encapsulated or captured this shift, what was most powerful in it, what let it function as the proverbial "bombshell," has never been pinpointed. The specific power of this work still eludes. And ultimately, I want to suggest, as the foregoing indicates, that Knapp and Michaels' essay had such an enormous impact, thanks to this mapping of language stemming from Frege, by drawing on the "subversive" possibilities already latent in the analytic modeling of language.

Of course neither this tradition, nor Frege, nor their essay was a direct cause of the changes then going on; Knapp and Michaels were as much influenced as influencing, if not more so. Yet their deployment of the analytic model and its privileging of reference indeed allowed them to put a finger on—to touch, shake, disturb—the most basic presuppositions about language that most theorists, as well as most critics up until that time, had held. They drove the final nail into the coffin of theory by rendering dubious, if not opaque, that very way of understanding, language, sense, meaning, and reference that had previously been the focus of a massive, albeit tacit consensus. In this fashion, in addition to anticipating one important novel trend in criticism, the new historicism (of which Michaels himself was a leading practitioner), their mini-revolution in theory, echoed the greater one that was taking place around them.

Of course, if we consider for a moment Knapp and Michaels' famous example of the wave poem (an example, as they remind us, they did not invent), my stress on their new modeling of language might at first well appear mistaken. Knapp and Michaels may themselves seem to be engaged in a sort of "retro" theory, offering arguments aimed at rehabilitating the long-lost rights of the author.[47]

Knapp and Michaels postulate that outlines in the sand putatively resembling one of Wordsworth's "Lucy poems" appear along a shoreline. Should these traces, these deformations in the beach, be recognized as caused by a natural occurrence, however, they argue, we would immediately know *not* to impart meaning (or interpretability) to what amounts to a natural event (like a volcanic eruption or a rainstorm). Knapp and Michaels thus conclude that the only thing any critic can interpret is an author's meaning—and that all debates in literary theory are correspondingly *strictu sensu* impossible, there being nothing here even conceivably left to discuss.

Despite their apparent stress on authorial intention, however, if we compare their argument to that of an actual proponent of authorial intentionality, and a more conventional and genuine speech-act literary theorist, namely, P. D. Juhl, it becomes evident that Knapp and Michaels are up to something far more radical than restoring the sovereign author, and that this something indeed concerns language. Juhl himself, after all, clearly endorses intention: he sees meaning residing in speech acts, and these in turn leading back to authors' intentions. As Knapp and Michaels themselves summarize his position: "Juhl recognizes that as soon as we think of a piece of language as literature, we already regard it as a speech act, and hence the product of intention."[48]

Accordingly, Knapp and Michaels' own difference from Juhl lies not in the role of intention (or of authors), but at the first stage of their description: with Juhl's recogniton of "language as literature," and thus with his initial conception of language as an entity. Indeed, what Knapp and Michaels criticize Juhl for here is simply that "Juhl can *imagine language* without speech acts."[49] Against this, they explicitly advocate their own radically innovative stance: a wholly unqualified "*identity* of language and speech act," and they thus enjoin us "to realize that Juhl's prescription—

when confronted with language read it as a speech act—can mean nothing more than: when confronted with language read it as language."[50]

The core claim of Knapp and Michaels in the first "Against Theory," then, is that language *just is* speech acts, and that, apart from this, in itself, it has no existence whatsoever.[51] None of those features believed to belong to a speech-independent language (grammatical rules, lexical norms, uninterpreted sentences, and so forth), they assert, are to be credited to it at all.[52]

In a Continental philosophical context, the novelty and radicality of their construal of language are probably most immediately evident in their treatment of the signifier, in these circles often thought to be the special provenance of language (*langue*). In this case, too, Knapp and Michaels explicitly contend, however, that the presumed signifier, or conventional sound, "Marion," as uttered by Rousseau, and glossed as being without any accompanying intention, is "not language either."[53] The linguistic signifier as such does not exist, since there is no language as a provenance separate from intentional speech.

Knapp and Michaels in the first "Against Theory" thus set forth a remarkable innovation concerning how language itself is to be understood—concerning, as they insist, its inherent ontological or structural character—one that asserts language *just is* speech acts (and that intentionality and authorship are present with language from the first), and which, as we can already see, is deeply indebted to the tradition that Frege founded. Indeed, their views might even seem bizarre, were it not for the familiarity already gained with the analytic starting point. The analytic model in itself, however, tends to diminish (if not entirely eliminate) conventional language's inherent identities, as we already saw with Frege, on account of the context principle (inaugurating the divergence of language's surface from its actual functioning), as well as the fracturing of language's identity and unity owing to concerns pertaining to reference.

Similarly, given our discussion of Fish, Knapp and Michaels in "Against Theory," it should be clear, have effectively embraced the position to which Fish inadvertently came, when he was left with nothing beyond the speech situation for his talk of emerging sentences to refer back to. The sentence in act, the pragmatic situation of discourse just *is* language in its own right, according to Knapp and Michaels: no knowable rules or norms govern it, no linguistic entities (sentences, rules, conventions) of any sort whatsoever preexist it.

Knapp and Michaels thus radicalize a tendency inherent in the analytic tradition, and in its prior appropriation in literary theory in their first

"Against Theory." Yet the novelty of their position ought not be underestimated, especially in regard to the key notion of intentionality—the intentionality that they assert, against Juhl, must already inhere within language, since, thanks to this, it can be seen to what their views more concretely amount for literary criticism.

After all, if language, according to Knapp and Michaels, just *is* speech acts, then speech acts, in the final analysis, themselves must and only can be language, intentionality itself having now become a wholly internal or *structural feature* of language's existence as such. As Knapp and Michaels continually state, intentionality is no longer to be conceived as "added" to something else (to uninterpreted sentences or texts). Rather, whenever a piece of language is encountered *as* language, intentionality will be there from the first—as a structural or ontological component, as already embedded and postulated—thus yielding what are finally bits of already intentionally invested (albeit otherwise free-floating) language . . . or *texts*, as others might call them.[54] Returning to the wave poem, Knapp and Michaels' argument, it must be emphasized, rests entirely on the negative case: the discovery, in the instance of natural causality, that what some might have thought to be a piece of language is not. Their point, then, so far from being that some actual knowledge of authorial intention precedes and really conditions our interpretations (that we have just witnessed some person writing in the sand, and thanks to this recognize language as language, text as text), is rather that the investment of intentionality *on our part* necessarily accompanies any identification of language as language. Such an investment, made in the absence of any known author, is indeed all our own doing (taking place in what can otherwise be a cognitive void). Language being recognized as language by *us*, intention (and author) automatically follows. "*We* must have already posited a speaker and hence an intention," as they state in this instance.[55]

The critic or reader, then, on Knapp and Michaels' model, simply by dint of recognizing language as language, co-posits both an intention and an author (each in an absolutely open and general sense). Indeed, only on this condition can it be understood how Knapp and Michaels in their essay can admit such an enormous range of candidates for *possible authorhood*. "Against Theory" and their first responses explicitly include, among acceptable authors, not only potentially computers, but entities as implausible, indeed as non-actual as "the living sea," "the haunting Wordsworth," or a "universal muse."[56] This striking ontological generosity, however, is a direct consequence of their unmitigated identification of language and speech-acts and their corresponding repositioning of intention. Whatever (no matter how nebulous, "the living sea") is taken as capable of intention here will be credited as an author—there being no limits set to this beforehand—just as whatever is taken as language just will be posited as embodying some otherwise equally nebulous intentionality.

Thus, by drawing on the resources offered by the analytic tradition, Knapp and Michaels have, in effect, fused the speech-act back into language, making everything start from the positing of language *as language*—the positing of an (otherwise wholly empty) intentionality and authorial identity following from there.[57] Yet what in Knapp and Michaels' world, then, will be decisive for the critic as she gets off the beach and heads back into the study with Lucy, given that intentionality and the author have here ceased to play any actual role? Granting their reconception of language in itself, bearing this new understanding of authors and intentions in its wake, how will the critic now go about her work?

To be sure, as Knapp and Michaels themselves insist in "Against Theory," they truly offer no prescriptions for criticism at all. Nevertheless, their reconstrual of language, pragmatically speaking, affects how the critic *can* function. Indeed, Knapp and Michaels leave only one moving part for criticism to get a hold on, and this part is, and indeed can only be, not speech acts, nor authors' intentions, nor any kind of meaning, but, rather, reference: a newly conceived, wild referentiality, itself coextensive with this new, wholly unlimited, structural or ontological authoriality and intentionality.

Still drawing on the deepest resources of the analytic model, Knapp and Michaels' account of language gives an utterly novel role to reference in literary theory. Reference emerges from their discussion as what is truly decisive for interpretation—something they themselves attest. Indeed, having asked how interpretation is to get under way, once a piece of language has been taken as language, they respond: by "adding information." "*Adding information* amounts to *adding* intention," they explicitly claim.[58]

"Adding information" here clearly precedes the identification of those entities (intentions, authors, meanings and so forth) such information is usually thought to be about. Accordingly, the practical import of their doctrine falls entirely on language's capacity to refer—on its ability to supply information in an absolutely novel and general sense. Coming before anything else, arising from the sheer recognition of language as language, finding information here can only mean tracking down any of the innumerable potential references implied by the texts from which the critic starts. As they themselves make clear, all sorts of references are possible; none have been ruled out (just as no authors, indeed not even any conceivable kinds of authors, have been excluded). Thus, as they put it in colloquy with an actual proponent of authorial intention, one who would gather a predelimited range of real historical evidence in the service of determining what the intention animating a piece may be—namely, E. D. Hirsch—"*nothing*," they insist in respect to their own views, "*tells us anything at all* about what should count as evidence" of this kind.[59]

In the first "Against Theory," then, Knapp and Michaels simultaneously privilege reference ("information") even as they reject limiting the range of reference to any previously known referents, thereby achieving an undoing or deconstruction of reference that proceeds by way of its privilege and indeed results in the proliferation of its work beyond all bounds. By contrast to Fish, who, in order to adapt the analytic model to literary theory and criticism, thought it necessary to reprivilege meaning and then efface the line between fact and fiction by showing them both ultimately to be the function of contingent, yet still authoritative, historical communities, Knapp and Michaels ultimately hollow this difference out. They expand factuality from within, removing all boundaries existing in advance between such reference and the work of language, or indeed the work of literature. Every instance of discourse is set back into that network of endlessly proliferating facts that pass through every piece of language, and this sweeping web of references now includes within itself, on a local level, without further differentiation, all those sites where fiction and fact, the true and the false, previously were thought to function.

Moreover, so doing, arriving at this novel model of language and the critic's work, one which exploits the deepest resources of the analytic tradition (its devalorization of our everyday intuitions concerning language, its incipient referential "bias"), Knapp and Michaels indeed sketched a theoretical template for the then nascent new historicism. The new historicism, after all, was an inherently referential approach to literature (since it was an historicism), yet it took for its work precisely the sort of wild referentiality, precisely the labor of producing novel referents by way of reference that Knapp and Michaels conceive—thereby, among other things, leading to those now familiar complaints that its historicism was not truly and genuinely historical enough.

The new historicism dispensed with all overt theoretical or semantic frameworks for interpreting literature in favor of a seemingly limitless referentiality that it produced rather than reproduced. The new historicism, just to be clear, did not undo reference historically, diachronically, as for example Foucault did. Instead, in line with Knapp and Michaels' interpretative model (which sets forth a wholly open-ended intentionality, yet one still pertaining to a putative discursive situation, an epoch, era, or period in the broadest sense), it multiplied reference beyond bounds within a synchronic frame: assembling an unexpectedly novel formation—including literature, its meanings, subjects, and authors, as well as numerous other facts, practices, and texts—that appears for the first time in the space of its own interpretation.

In "Against Theory," Knapp and Michaels, one could say, revived and further extended the radical power to disrupt our intuitions about language already implicit in Frege's modeling—its emphasis on reference, along with its latent particularization of language and discourse—and thereby broke the back of almost all earlier literary theory (which indeed owed a debt to one facet or another of the more traditional models), at the same time as they presented the latent linguistic template for this then-emergent critical genre.

Of course, again, my claim is not that new historicist critics were themselves aware of this novel linguistic template, that they were directly influenced by Knapp and Michaels' presentation, or even that Knapp and Michaels intended their work to function in this fashion, which they clearly did not. Nevertheless, it is indeed telling in respect to this linkage that Knapp and Michaels in the end not only deeply disagree with Fish as theorists, but that they do so in a way that maps precisely on to their stance as critics. Fish, as a theorist, argues for (localized, pragmatic) rules or norms that govern meaning; and what Fish, in his critical writings (on Milton and elsewhere) does is unearth just these sorts of meanings from texts. Similarly, Knapp and Michaels privilege a new wild reference, and this is indeed the style of criticism that Michaels especially came to practice. In their very own case, among the neopragmatists themselves, consequences thus do accrue to theory, over and against their joint claim to the contrary (since one thing about which all these theorists agree is that there is no point to pursuing theoretical questions). The deconstruction of language each pursues indeed casts light on, and jibes with (without necessarily determining), the kind of literary criticism each practices.

Yet, as the neopragmatists' own work attests, genuine doubts actually do exist as to just what professional rules and norms may be operative in any case (despite Fish's disclaimers), as well as opacities concerning what language and thus interpretation actually are (despite Knapp and Michaels' overly strenuous denials). Thus the sort of return to theory I am advocating seems relevant, indeed required, both in the case of the neopragmatists themselves (who turn out not to agree much), as well as generally. Numerous questions remain unsettled concerning the actual character of language, and with it, literature and literary criticism. Thanks to laying bare this alternative model at work in the analytic tradition, a plethora of such unanswered questions start to come forward in regard to the ability to isolate in or through language an autonomous realm of sense, as well as literature's relation to reference, including social and historical referents. Decisive questions for literary studies still congregate around issues related to language—not around the "ontology" of language, as Knapp and Michaels put it, but the relation of language to its "others" (meanings, referents, subjects, objects), as well as to those entities thought to comprise it: the word, the sentence, discourse itself, as well as other larger and smaller units, such as the phoneme, or the fabula, in the discursive field.

How these are construed, it should now be clear, do make, and always have made, a difference as to how critics go about their work—not only at these micro-moments just outlined, but at any moment when an account of literary studies is called for, including when critics talk to one another about what they do, and, perhaps most notably, when they speak about their discipline to the general public.[60]

Indeed, at present, depending on how these questions are answered, quite different versions of literary studies' relation to historical and perhaps all empirical research become available. Precision about literary studies' relation to empiricism, furthermore, proves especially critical at present, since literary studies today indeed faces a tipping point in respect to whether it is to become a truly empirical discipline or not: whether it shall or shall not turn into a subdiscipline of history or perhaps sociology. After all, once clarity about the specificity of language, and thus about the specificity of literature, has been lost—once how literature relates to other forms of speech has become obscure to the point that this relation disappears even as a question—what gives anyone the right to privilege those representations traditionally called literary or aesthetic? Indeed, the disciplines of history and sociology (not to mention sociobiology or cognitive neuroscience) as opposed to both cultural studies and the new and newer historicisms, are, in U.S. circles, at least, more and more turning into empirical disciplines, with many concepts crucial to literary-historical work, no longer being seen as acceptable within their purview. How then to fit literary studies and its current offshoots—cultural studies, postcolonialism, gender and race studies—all of which continue to privilege the signifier and its purported overdetermination into these frameworks?

In turn, should literary studies somehow continue to stand on its own how will it conceive those themes in its work that clearly *are* social and historical? Are we simply to settle for further isomorphisms—wholly contingent, often unpersuasive, connections between the literary text and the history that it embeds and in which it is embedded, too often based on a single word or a single historical coincidence taken apart from any larger context? Critiques of these tendencies in the initial new historicism notwithstanding, are we to settle for what remain largely formal connections, which are also somehow claimed to reveal decisive historical and social formations?

A need for a return to theory's fundamental questions concerning language and literature thus exists today.[61] For these issues with which we find ourselves are indeed genuine, no matter how inconvenient they may prove to be. And though there may well be no future for literary theory itself at present, literary studies must and will find a way to confront these questions, as it has repeatedly done, throughout its long history—that, or risk suffering the same fate as literary theory itself.

PART II

Jacques Derrida and the Problem of Philosophical and Political Modernity

Jacob Klein and Jacques Derrida

The Problem of Modernity

To bring together the work of Jacob Klein and Jacques Derrida may well seem unexpected. Jacob Klein was a friend of both Leo Strauss and Alexander Kojévè, and his philosophical sympathies clearly lay more with the former. Klein published a pioneering work in the history of mathematics in the 1930s, which is still largely unheralded and, apart from two studies on Plato, he was not heard from much thereafter, mainly spending his remaining time, after his emigration to the United States at the beginning of the Second World War, guiding a small institution of higher learning in Maryland.[1] Jacques Derrida, by contrast, even after his death, not only remains one of the most famous thinkers throughout the world, but his work, especially in the United States, is immediately associated with a rather different era than Klein's, that of post–World War II. Indeed, to many, Derrida's work seems equivalent on an intellectual level to the social, cultural, and political ferment so often associated with the sixties and seventies in the West.

Perhaps the most obvious reason to bring together these seemingly so different scholars is that both worked out and published extended interpretations of Husserl's late fragment *Die Ursprung der Geometrie*, "The Origin of Geometry."[2] They were some of the few to attend to this work in print during their own lifetimes, and for both, Husserl's late, vexed fragment was central to their own projects and self-understanding.

Why this coincidence takes on more than merely historical importance, and why it should inaugurate the sequence of chapters comprising Part II of the present work, only becomes plain, however, when another, less obvious reason for attending to Klein and Derrida in tandem is grasped. Jacob Klein assigns enormous importance to modernity as a philosophical category, as do a number of other twentieth-century thinkers—notably his friend Leo Strauss, but also Michel Foucault, Hans Blumenberg, Jurgen Habermas, and Niklas Luhmann. Klein was by no means an historicist, and the precise status of his inquiry will have to be examined further, some of the questions raised by it being ones Klein turned to Husserl's late fragment in order to answer. Nevertheless, Klein always took modernity as a category that thought had to confront.

By contrast, this category, modernity—roughly the shift in scientific, political, and other sorts of thinking that is commonly acknowledged to get under way in the early seventeenth century—precisely does *not* have this sort of central role in the work of Jacques Derrida. Though he early and late attends to authors comprising the modern canon—Descartes, Rousseau, Condillac, Kant—and assigns them a relative specificity, Derrida, thanks to a position that he in his own way gleans from Husserl, never sees these authors as representing a radical break, a real discontinuity in philosophy or in the character of knowledge.

Indeed, Derrida's downplaying of modernity is but the other side of the coin of what might be called, nonpejoratively, his presentism: his belief, announced as early as 1965 in the opening paragraphs of what became the first half of *Of Grammatology*,[3] that now, if any, is the time to herald an epoch of metaphysics and its coming to a close, now the unique time when a really radical discontinuity in conceptual, ontological, and semiotic reference points has begun to emerge.

Derrida's stance toward history and historicality consists in such a belief, and he does not seem significantly to alter it, only to expand, flesh out, and perhaps tweak it in his writings on ethics, politics, and religion in the eighties and nineties. This shift for Derrida is of a magnitude that eludes all concrete periodization and indeed draws into question the very terms—the now; a chronological, linear history; ultimately history itself—provisionally used to identify it as a phenomenon. Yet from here also stems the historicity of his own thought. One may only think forward into what is today coming to pass, Derrida insists. The leading edge of his thought—what calls it on or calls it forth—is to take responsibility for this event in all its dimensions (some of which are not themselves strictly historical) to take responsibility for this now worldwide movement, having no adequate or proper characterization in itself.[4]

Klein and Derrida thus give very different weight to modernity. And, given how many of those writers named a moment ago are, in some fashion, social, political, as well as specifically historical thinkers, part of what is at stake in this difference between Klein and Derrida will be Derrida's own stance toward politics, society, and history. Indeed, one prominent issue is whether, or to what extent, a standpoint that leaves modernity out, that does not credit this moment with its own perhaps radical specificity and discontinuity, can effectively overrun the borders of philosophy into these areas in the way Derrida has so long desired.[5] In addition, however, beyond wondering whether the present may really be addressed in the way Derrida wants, intervened in effectively, modernity being omitted, the question arises of whether Derrida has fully diagnosed what is now coming to pass: may not some part of the symptomatology that Derrida assigns to the totality of thought and knowledge, to philosophy both ancient and modern, better be seen as a result of the modern formation in its specificity?[6]

Raising these doubts concerning Derrida's stance toward the modern, this question will also have to be effectively turned around, and recognition given to what Derrida perhaps alone in this regard has managed to achieve (which will raise issues pertaining to Klein's project, just as Klein's characterizations of the modern question aspects of Derrida's endeavor). Derrida's own strategy, whatever its other limitations, by maintaining the historicity of his own thinking even as it avoids all historicism, manages to resolve or avoid a problem, the solution of which, it seems to me, we do not otherwise possess: namely, assuming modernity is central, whether and how it is to be engaged with philosophically. Modernity, in the first instance, after all, is an historical category. And just as it is not accidental that the thinkers mentioned above are all concerned with the political, social, and historical in its specificity, so, too, it is no accident that almost none of them pursue philosophy *strictu sensu*, pursue what would have once been called first philosophy in any sense.[7]

Indeed, perhaps most notably of all twentieth-century thinkers, Martin Heidegger was able to take up modernity philosophically, approach it as an event central to his thought; yet this was only because Heidegger had also transformed the practice of philosophy itself: transferring all that heretofore had been gathered under the name of reason or *theorein* into the domain of interpretation, *hermeneuin*—though, to be sure, Heidegger initially gave rational, or at least phenomenological, grounds for mounting this shift.[8] By contrast, Derrida never simply goes this route, even when moving closer to Heidegger in other respects. Despite the tenor of much of his reception, Derrida retains the difference made by theory, by what Husserl would call the theoretical attitude, and what other philosophers call the aim at the absolute—even as Derrida opens the way to transforming this idea—one result of this retention being Derrida's refusal to posit modernity as a radical break.

In turn, in light of this aspect of Derrida's project, the singularity of Jacob Klein's work on modernity, as well as certain questions accompanying it, emerge. For, among diagnoses of modernity, Klein's is one of the very few attempts to conceive this category on philosophical grounds—as a question concerning the status of knowledge as such, and in a way that ultimately keeps its distance from all historicism.[9] Klein describes the modern eruption primarily as an event of, and within, knowledge. Yet while Klein's characterizations of modernity from this vantage point may in large part be persuasive, whether Klein can successfully maintain the ultimately philosophical character of his own inquiry remains unclear; whether his genealogy or desedimentation of the modern scientific formation can function veridically, furnish an epistemology or some other sort of overarching philosophical evaluation of the origins of contemporary knowledge, emerges as questionable. Assigning the modern the status of a rupture, can Klein find for himself some sure footing beyond it from which to evaluate it—some vantage point safely other than that historiography and that "historical world view" he so deftly employs to describe it—these standpoints and the phenomenon of modernity itself ultimately being coincident for Klein?[10] These issues, at the very least, will be just the ones that Klein himself turned to Husserl's late thought in order to clarify.

Modernity as Radical Rupture: Jacob Klein

To begin, then, with Klein, and the overall status of modernity in his thought, first of all, it must further be made plain that Klein, in the second part of *Greek Mathematical Thought and the Origin of Algebra*, assigns to the modern standpoint a much greater force of rupture than either Husserl or Derrida. While Husserl's late work provides the background for both Klein's and Derrida's thinking about history, on this point Derrida, and not Klein, follows Husserl more closely.

For Husserl, the modern scientific attitude (which Husserl extrapolates through the figure of Galileo) represents a further unfolding of the ancient—a new wrinkle in knowledge, embodying a relatively novel but by no means discontinuous standpoint. Galileo, to be sure, takes for granted already existing sciences, like geometry; and, on this sedimented basis, his own knowledge falls into what Husserl calls "objectivism": the systematic neglect of those constitutive subjective acts responsible for the objects of a science that ultimately endow them with meaning and validity.[11] Nevertheless, for Husserl and, in a first move, for Derrida, the project of knowledge, the aim of *theorein*, remains one and the same across the tradition. The unfolding of a single idea, the Idea of reason, commands theoretical knowledge from its putative origin or eruption in Greece up until the present moment.[12] And though Derrida, who already questioned the evidence pertaining to this Idea in his "Introduction" to his translation of Husserl's *Die Ursprung* (*IOG* 139–41) will eventually come to contest this aspect of Husserl's thought in a unique manner, thereby launching his own complex understanding of an epoch of metaphysics and its closure; nevertheless, for him as well, all of philosophy and knowledge is ultimately to be conceived as a single, solidary tradition.

By contrast, Jacob Klein, in his first book, argues that with modernity the very project of *theorein* as such has undergone alteration, even rupture. At the foundation of the establishment of the modern sciences in the seventeenth and eighteenth centuries stands an essentially broken or ruptured conceptuality, "*ein gebrochenes Begrifflichkeit.*"[13] This riven conceptuality introduces a radical deviation between the modern approach to knowledge and that of the ancients in respect to both the objects and the contents of their knowledge. Most of all, it introduces a shift in what Klein takes to be the linchpin of *theorein* itself, the scientific-theoretical *concept*, the concept of the concept as such.

Klein deems the overall conceptuality, or *Begrifflichkeit*, of modern inquiry a ruptured one, thanks to two factors in particular, neither of which are to be found in Husserl's or Derrida's treatment. First, modern knowledge not only stands at a certain distance from its roots—Klein agreeing with Husserl that in modernity science ceases to directly originate from a lifeworld acquaintance with things—but this distance in large part derives from it having a positively different precursor for its own scientific standpoint and for its own theorizing than the ancient: namely, that of scholasticism. Another very different type of theoretical knowledge furnishes the backdrop for the modern theoretical attitude: that of the schools—one of which modern knowing is not fully aware.[14]

This precursor of its own thinking it never fully digests; this latent insertion into history only subsequent interpretation wholly discloses; and this lapse ultimately makes it impossible, on Klein's view, for modern knowledge in principle to come to those questions that oriented ancient inquiry. Proceeding by way of an adaptation, even deformation, of an already existing stock of theoretical concepts, assuming a theoretical attitude already at hand, the modern scientific standpoint cannot broach what the ancients understood to be the ultimate question for all *theorein*:

namely, those concerning the ontological status of theoretical and scientific concepts as such. Nor can it ask about the standing of the beings to which these concepts may apply.

A second factor widens this gap even further, shifting the orientation of modern inquiry away from the ancient all the more. This factor accounts for the self-understanding of the modern scientific viewpoint in its *positivity*, now that the ancient framework has been lost from sight; for, not only did modern knowledge turn *against* the schools, even as it incorporated their standpoint, according to Klein, but in doing so, ironically enough, the early moderns in fact believed that they were returning to the ancients, returning to the ancients' own so-called "natural" standpoint for philosophy and theory. Yet since knowledge as "natural," knowledge as the ancients practiced it, in the mistaken eyes of these early moderns, was inherently art, or technique, the early moderns actually construe their own knowledge and concepts in what today would be called an inherently functionalist or pragmatist manner.[15] The concepts of modern science, on this view, find validation only through the work they do in a larger network of scientific inquiry, through "the internal connection of all the concepts, their mutual relation," as Klein puts it (*GMT* 121). These concepts are legitimated by the ends they serve, the function they perform in relation to other concepts, in a total field of inquiry.

The rupture from which the "conceptuality" of modern science results for Klein thus consists in (1) a turn away from the scholastic understanding of *scientia* even as it takes this and the other scholastic concepts for granted, and (2) an identification, albeit mistaken, with ancient natural science; and it results in (a) the ongoing adaptation of received concepts in place of its own validation of theoretical concepts and the standpoint of *theorein* generally; justifying its knowledge instead by (b) a functionalism that sees the work of any single concept as grounded in the work of all the others and thus the total work of a given science, thanks to understanding knowing as "naturally" a type of art or technique.

Klein indeed understands the knowledge modern science pursues as of a radically different order than the ancient. Not one, but two steps removed from its origin, bereft of the ancient *terminus ad quem* in ontology and first philosophy, it has unknowingly, unconsciously, substituted a new aim and a new style of concept formation for the earlier, with the result that its own researches no longer can even conceivably culminate in any kind of ontological insight, nor, then, in knowledge definitive for individual or collective human life.

The radicality of this shift is confirmed by one last phenomenon depicted by Klein: the subsequent reorganization of the disciplines themselves that such new knowledge founds. With Descartes, as read by Klein, philosophy ceases to stand at the apex of an integrated, essentially hier-archized series of discourses, a ladder of sciences organized vertically. A new symbolic mathematics instead becomes the privileged basis, the single common root of all knowing. Mathematics in the narrow sense supplies a *mathesis universalis*, a universal learning, for a newly organized and soon to be burgeoning tree of knowledge, mathematics, at this moment, be-coming "the language of science," as some still say today (*GMT* 181–85).

Klein's account, replete with the most detailed scholarship, has enor-mous persuasive force. Given its power, it must be asked, however, what ultimate significance the depiction of such a rupture has in Klein's own eyes. Klein's description of this new scientific conceptuality, after all, is indeed remarkably prescient. Already in 1936, perhaps in part due to Pierre Duhem's influence, Klein sees modern scientific knowledge as es-sentially characterized by a kind of pragmatic holism.[16] As set forth by Klein, modern scientific concepts from the first find their justification solely in their *use*, in their function in relation to other concepts in the total undertaking of science as a whole, the aim of which is itself largely practical or technical. Klein's account thus accords remarkably well with that of someone like W. V. O. Quine, for whom any science, indeed all science, must be seen as a total field, none of whose concepts could not be swapped for others, each assuming their validity only thanks to their place and function in a total practice.[17]

Of course, for Quine himself, none of these features raise questions about the modern scientific standpoint as such, nor occasion an investiga-tion into its genealogy. Contrariwise, the very terms of Klein's sketch—his talk of rupture and forgetting—suggest Klein's account is intended to have a "critical" function. Moreover, not only can one wonder from what vantage point Klein depicts these developments due to the sharpness of the rupture that he presents, but further inquiry about his own stance becomes urgent, insofar as Klein in *Greek Mathematical Thought* also por-trays early modern knowledge as already giving some account of itself, as performing a structural, if not genetic, reflection on its own mode of inquiry.

Indeed, in the specific case of modern mathematics, in respect to the person Klein takes to be the inventor of the modern algebra, François Vieta, Klein acknowledges Vieta in effect invents the first formal axiom system. Arguing that "it is obviously impossible to see 'numbers' in the isolated letter signs [of Vieta] . . . except through the syntactical rules that Vieta states" (*GMT* 176), Klein himself concludes that these rules postulated by Vieta are "the first modern axiom system," and that "they create the systematic context which originally defines the object to which they apply" (*GMT* 176). Vieta thus arrived at a ground for his symbols in formal, syntactical rules, according to Klein, a claim which obviously dovetails with the new role given to concepts generally, these letter signs finally deriving their status as objects of calculation from a broader systemic or relational context.

Moreover, similarly, Klein asserts that Descartes is the sole thinker of this era who attempts to give a philosophical account of the cognitive or intellectual activity underlying the new mathematics that Vieta inaugurates. Vieta's invention ultimately rests on a symbol-making power, the source of which Descartes locates, according to Klein, in a new notion of intellect or mind: of mind now characterized "not so much [by] its 'incorporeality' as its unrelatedness" (*GMT* 202).[18] Mind conceived by Descartes will now be seen as radically autonomous, as essentially related only to itself. On the basis of this self-relation, moreover, it discovers a new power, to fashion symbols. Specifically, it assigns to its own imaginatively generated presentations self-grounded intelligible concepts and through these dictates to the phenomenal world—the imagination, on Klein's reading of Descartes, being at once the mind's bridge to the world as well as the measure of its radical isolation (*GMT* 199–201).

But in each of these cases, it can reasonably be asked in what consists the inadequacy of these accounts. Especially since Gödel's proof had only recently appeared, and it is not clear if Klein had yet read it, in light of what is Vieta's formal axiom system deemed insufficient? Alternatively, is there some other, truer epistemology or noology, thanks to which Descartes' symbol-making power, his philosophical grounding of Vieta's science in a radically autonomous intellect, comes into doubt?

Such questions, let me be immediately clear, are not intended to suggest that no conceivable responses to these problems emerge in Klein's writings. In respect to the contrast with Quine and the larger issues pertaining to Klein's own methodology, Klein indeed sought an account of his work's method in the writings of the late Husserl. In his discussion of Husserl's "Origin," Klein claims to find the possibility of disclosing the ultimate "aims which should control research in the history of science" (*Lectures* 65), and thus of showing how, without succumbing to historicism, history can be employed as a platform to reveal inherently philosophical problems.

Moreover, with regard to the more specific points just raised, flagging these issues to the degree that I do at this moment, my goal is by no means to contest Klein's descriptions as such. I do not at all wish to draw into doubt Klein's powerful mapping of the labyrinth of modern knowledge, if I may put it this way; but rather, precisely due to the strength of Klein's analysis, I am forced to wonder whether even Klein has finally found a wholly successful way out.

Indeed, to stay with Klein's depiction of this labyrinth a moment further, the central, positive contribution of Klein's genealogy, his demonstration of how Vieta's new symbolic mathematics originated from an ancient ground that it covered over and transformed, has not yet even been discussed. And before arriving at any broad conclusion, this development is due attention, not only because Klein's treatment of it is extraordinarily convincing in its own right, but also because this aspect of Klein's thought speaks directly to one of Jacques Derrida's most famous innovations. The invention of a specifically symbolic mathematics at the end of the sixteenth century, as described by Klein, is that to which, I will argue, Derrida's early project, above all his "signature" notion of *écriture*, is a response, even as this may also entail a partial misdiagnosis of this problematic on the part of Derrida himself

Alegbraic Numbers and Derrida's Writing

Thus, to take up again the details of Klein's analysis, at the core of Vieta's invention of algebra, of what makes this sixteenth-century mathematician the inventor for the first time of a truly symbolic mathematics, proves to be a new concept of the object of calculation as such, one which completely severs the notion of number from all ontological foundations, from any direct connection with beings in the world. The original life-world understanding of number, operative from the Greeks up through the late sixteenth century, essentially maintained a reference to entities, to real beings of some sort, proposed Klein in one of his most significant discoveries. Klein demonstrates in *Greek Mathematical Thought* through a massive labor of erudition that, from the Greeks forward, numbers (*arithmoi*) always designate definite multiplicities of objects, distinct aggregates of genuine things (six stars, two pupils, and so forth). Such concrete collections, are *arithmoi*, "numbers" in the primary sense for the Greeks; and this remains the case, though in a special way, even when, in theoretical arithmetic, pure numbers or *arithmoi* are in question, which are then taken to be comprised by pure monads or units.[19]

In turn, Vieta, according to Klein, on the way to inventing algebra and seeking a reference for his own mathematics, for his new, more general version of Diophantus' species notation, turns not to any actual *arithmoi*, or *Anzahl*, not to any genuine concrete multiplicity—thus not to any number in its former sense—but rather to the notion of such *arithmoi*, to an *Anzahl* in general, to the mere idea "of being a number of" (*GMT*

174). Vieta does not depend on any sort of concrete aggregates, any genuine numbers in his revamping of Diophantus, but instead to a new general notion of such aggregations.

Put otherwise, Vieta's new algebra is inherently symbolic, according to Klein. Vieta's signs can only refer, not to any actual multitudes—indeed, they in fact represent magnitudes or multitudes indifferently—but to what Klein, drawing on medieval logic, calls second intentions: concepts that inherently have other concepts as their objects. These concepts, these second intentions, moreover, thanks to their embodiment in a notation, will end up being treated as first intentions, as if what they conceptualized were indeed entities, objects, as genuine as any other. Thereby a symbolic mathematics arises, inherently lacking any reference to beings in the world.

Indeed, not only does Vieta invent a new, essentially symbolic mathematical entity—neither magnitude nor multitude, falling neither under arithmetic nor geometry, inherently more "universal" than them both—but Vieta's invention recoils on the original notion of number, which Klein identified. This double-tiered reference—to a general notion of an *arithmos*, to "a number of," itself referring to a concrete number of actual things—itself becoming occluded through its symbolization, redounds on, even the first-order "numbers" (*arithmoi*), with the result that all numbers start to be understood as mere symbols. "As soon as 'general number' is conceived and represented in the medium of species as an 'object' in itself, that is 'symbolically,' the modern concept of 'number' is born," writes Klein (*GMT* 175).

This new wholly formal object, the specifically modern notion of number, indeed replaces the original Greek concept, without this replacement even being noticed.[20] The aftermath of Vieta's transformation thus produces entities, the new "numbers," that exist, through the operation of symbolization itself. On this basis, the modern "intuition" of number as a kind of organizational schema appears, as well as the possibility of numbers (discontinuous multiplicities) being able to be coordinated with lines (continuous magnitudes) on a number line, for the first time numbering numbers being taken as stand-alone entities or objects—albeit entirely "mental" ones—without any inherent reference to things other than themselves.[21]

This eruption of the radically symbolic in modernity is that to which, in turn, I would like to suggest, Derrida's notion of *écriture* responds. Vieta's invention ultimately manifests the ability of a sign system, an innovation in notation, to reshape our most fundamental concepts and even reorganize the stock of beings taken to comprise the world. Just such a possibility, however, of a dissolution and reconfiguration of referents, itself stemming from a form of technique, indeed a technique of notation, Derrida has long invited us to think under the heading of *écriture*.

Derridean *écriture*, that is, grasps in its most comprehensive dimensions the ability of representation to produce the represented that signally emerges at this crossroads in the history of mathematics that Klein uniquely identifies. Moreover, thematizing such rootlessness, making it a permanent part of all thought, albeit one that the tradition as a whole necessarily had to suppress, Derrida can indeed be seen as attempting to find some response, some new footing for thought, as well as life, on the far side of this breakout of modern knowledge.

Derrida's *écriture*, without doubt, affirms and radicalizes the deracinating power of the symbol—a power that Klein, by contrast, attempts to reroot. Nevertheless, by generalizing this possibility around which modernity pivots and treating it as a structural as much as a genetic feature of all knowing, all speech, of every claim to truth, and thereby stripping it of any definite temporal horizon, Derrida proffers the possibility of some kind of fundamental thinking, of some not wholly implausible successor to philosophy, taking shape even now, in the wake of this development. Keeping at a distance from all positivism, yet thinking, even affirming something like the dispersal or dissemination of cognitive authority essential to the modern turn, Derrida, from his 1967 works forward, framed a new mode of thinking, a new way of working potentially able to incorporate, and perhaps thus ameliorate, modernity's novelty and radicality.

The aptness of Klein's own descriptions, then, to recur to a point raised earlier, by no means here come into doubt, since the entire interpretation of Derrida I am proposing is predicated upon them being right. Yet these descriptions themselves, especially seen in their coincidence with Derrida's preoccupations, raise concerns as to whether Klein's account can furnish us with an ultimately stable knowledge of its own. They force questions about what sort of truth Klein's own account may possess and from what perspective this insight into modernity becomes available.

Klein himself, after all, ultimately understands modernity as a twofold affair. Initially encountered as an historical event, as the object of historiography, inquiry into modernity ultimately leads back to essentially structural, systematic, or principled questions: concerning the nature of knowledge, of the beings, of number, and the true character and role of mind. Klein believed Husserl's late thought gave the explanation for how this shift occurs: how it was possible to move between factual history of science and the principled, ultimately philosophical problems behind these facts.[22] Husserl's last writings for Klein thus provide a way to tackle modernity as both an historical event and a philosophical problem at once.[23]

Yet Klein's own descriptions of modernity raise the possibility—without, by the way, deciding this matter—whether in this one unique case, insofar as modernity brings about a perhaps radical change in the character of knowledge, by presenting a wholly unanticipatable variation in the idea of *theorein* as such, whether it may itself prove a radically singular category: having one face turned toward the event, the other toward truth. Modernity may prove a unique hybrid of event and theory, of a sort that ultimately bars these dimensions (history and theory, truth and event) from being sorted out from one another. Indeed modernity, as presented by Klein, arguably overflows the borders of all such distinctions, outstrips all our existing conceptuality, while implicating within it all existing forms of knowledge, including what has always been thought to be knowledge's others (politics, history, society). Modernity may, then, represent a radically singular instance, a category finally eluding all proper historical and philosophical thematization, and thus one not far from what at other junctures and under other names Derrida has begun to teach us to think.

The Pivot: Husserl's Late History

At the very least, the ultimate status of modernity, it should now be clear, is what is most at stake in Klein's reading of Husserl, and even, as we have begun to see, in a different fashion, in Derrida's. For Derrida and Klein, although vastly different in so many other respects, each in his own way relies on Husserl's late thought, it turns out, to render modernity transparent: in Derrida's case, to avoid, by generalizing its disseminating power, the potentially radical singularity of this event; in Klein's, to render it accessible to a philosophical as well as an historical treatment such that the rights of both history and philosophy can be maintained.

To delve one step further into Klein's and Derrida's respective treatments of Husserl's late fragment, then, in Klein's case, more specifically, a way to articulate the factual developments with which the historian is concerned on to the principled questions addressed by philosophy is offered by a reading of Husserl's "Origin" that connects it closely to Husserl's genetic phenomenology program, specifically to the account of his thought that Husserl gives in *Formal and Transcendental Logic*.[24] Due to the fact that at the moment of the genuine historical inauguration of a science, such as geometry, the objects of this science must already be available to the protogeometer, a transcendental genetic constitution of these same objects, Klein argues, must be presupposed as having already taken place.[25] The actual historical development in real time of the objects of a science thus necessarily refers back to their development in what Klein intriguingly calls "eternal time,"[26] to their establishment through transcendental-genetic achievements, and this is what finally permits the back and forth between the work of the historian and that of the philosopher, which turns out to be a kind of cross-referencing of historical and transcendental-genetic roots.

Klein thus sees Husserl's construal of origin, more generally, as having pinpointed a moment in which transcendental-genetic accomplishments necessarily spill over into real historical ones. And it is worth noting that those structural features, such as linguistic and written expression, as well as the concomitant possibility of their sedimentation, that Husserl deems necessary for geometry's origin, Klein takes to be factors defining *only* of real history. For Klein, writing, documentation, sedimentation all belong to the real history of a science; these give to it its specifically historical character, and the ultimate aim of the historian of science for Klein is in fact determined by these—above all by sedimentation. Sedimentation, the departure from concepts and objects belonging to the current state of a science of a living meaning and intentionality, demands that the historian unearth these occluded meanings, restore their intentions to life, ultimately by tracing them back to originating principled or transcendental achievements.[27]

Husserl's last writings thus establish, for Klein, the true task of any history of science: the working back to roots that are ultimately suprahistorical. By contrast, Derrida interprets Husserl's fragment differently, in a way that proves, however, equally central to his own project. In Husserl's "Origin," notions like writing, language, and sedimentation, even that of history itself, all have a specifically transcendental connotation, according to Derrida.[28] All pertain to a history internal to transcendental intersubjectivity: a history itself ultimately governed by an idea in the Kantian sense.[29]

In Derrida's far different interpretation, Husserl's findings stand at an unbridgeable distance from all real history, and they inaugurate a specifically transcendental tradition and historicity. Derrida's interpretation, moreover, stems from an absolutely pivotal feature of Derrida's own intellectual development. Derrida himself first focused on the problem of genesis in Husserl, and he thus originally construed the relation of Husserl's late history writings to the rest of his corpus, much along the same lines as Klein—as following directly from Husserl's work on genesis. By the time Derrida wrote the "Introduction," however, Husserl's late turn to history represented a much more novel and relatively autonomous phase in Husserl's program for Derrida, and only on this basis emerged Derrida's own future relation to history—that "presentism," and his notion of a closure of the epoch of metaphysics, to which I allude above and have sketched in Chapter 4. Solely thanks to his new construal of Husserl's corpus and his rereading of the "Origin" as comprehending a specifically transcendental history and historicity does Derrida, by questioning the Husserlian framework so understood, arrive at his mature thought on these matters, as well as his mature conception of writing and language more generally.[30]

Yet despite these differences, doubtless significant in their own right, the parallel role Husserl's thought plays in these otherwise so different thinkers remains perhaps the most intriguing factor here. For both thinkers, it should now be clear, Husserl in the first place must be right about history if their respective projects are to go forward. For Derrida, Husserl's late work brings us to the limit of phenomenology's engagement with becoming and genesis, with history and historicity, ultimately to the limits of the entirety of philosophy's engagement with these themes. For Klein, Husserl's last work is significant first and foremost because it shows the way in which intellectual history leads beyond itself—including showing how historical and philosophical concerns with genesis may themselves give way to a more ancient ground, since Husserl, for Klein, is himself a philosopher on the threshold, an inquirer thinking his way beyond the modern from within it, and thus still marked as belonging to the modern moment by his starting point in mind and his fixation on roots.[31] Yet, though both Klein and Derrida ultimately want to leave behind Husserl's own framework, in accord with one reading or another, only Husserl's last phenomenological writings offer them a philosophically adequate way to engage with history in the first place.

Is just this, however, not what remains for us most in doubt today: that we dispose of any philosophically credible ways to deal with history, that philosophy can consort with genealogies and histories of any sort and still maintain its traditional relation to a more principled or a priori kind of knowledge? Indeed, the deep disagreement between Derrida and Klein about how to interpret Husserl's late fragment itself shows how difficult it is give an account of philosophy's intersection with history that ultimately can stand up to sustained philosophical scrutiny.

Moreover, modernity itself, arguably, is at the root of this demand that appears in both Klein and Derrida that philosophy now come to grips with history. The felt need of both Klein and Derrida for a philosophically adequate way to deal with history—as well as their perhaps not wholly successful recourse to Husserl in order to satisfy it—attests to this still untamed significance of modernity as so far described.

Doubtless, Klein engages with history ultimately only in the name of the uncertain possibility of returning to the potentially timeless wisdom of the past (above all, that of Plato); Derrida, by contrast, does so in the name of a radical alterity and an absolutely unthinkable, eventually quasi-messianic, future. Yet both pass through Husserl's last writings in order to take a first faltering step beyond our own epoch, and what demands they do so may well be modernity itself, and what still remains not understood concerning it. Especially when taken together, the thought of Derrida and of Klein thus stands as unique witnesses and warning signs of this category or event even now continuing to unfold itself invisibly around us.

Jacob Klein and Jacques Derrida

Historicism and History in
Two Interpretations of
Husserl's Late Writings

As I began to suggest in Chapter 5, modernity as a problem—a philosophical problem or a problem for thought—has still not been fully plumbed. This is so perhaps in an especially vexed fashion when it comes to the project of Jacob Klein. Klein, as earlier indicated, was at once a working historian and a proponent of a view of modern science that ultimately saw it as a product of a rupture or break—thus as embedded in history. In sum, Klein is a thinker of modernity.

Yet historical work, this same conceptuality and method that Klein himself uses, Klein also deemed a symptom of that modernity which he diagnosed by these same means. Ultimately, Klein sought to distance himself from any historical framework and put behind him what amounts to a first or opening stage of his meditation. Consequently, Klein's work, in its first phase, embodies a sort of paradox: a position I call antihistoricist historicism. For Klein, modernity, even to be identified as a category, requires recourse to history, some species of historical self-awareness. Yet this very awareness eventually leads to the rejection of history as thought's final horizon, owing to the discovery that historical thinking is itself an historically conditioned phenomenon.

Klein throughout his writings indeed repeatedly stresses that the proper understanding of modernity shows that the historical attitude as such, the belief that recourse to history is a necessary and ultimate horizon of thought (in a word, historicism), is itself a product of this very rupture, itself a specifically modern phenomenon—as are also the techniques of historiographical research that Klein himself employs. Thus, in his early article "Phenomenology and the History of Science"—and he will echo these sentiments in his 1953 lecture "History and the Liberal Arts," in which he returns to some of these themes—Klein claims that "the discovery and description of man as a specifically historic being" is modern;[1] and in both works Klein argues, on the basis of a reading of Vico, that historical self-consciousness, the historical attitude, is the complement to that very mathematical physics that Klein identifies as defining of modernity.

Thanks to having recourse to modernity as an historical category, then, the rights of the category of history itself end up being demoted. Historical self-consciousness ultimately has a kind of self-canceling quality—Klein, one might say, having historicized historicism. Yet, treating historical consciousness thus, as a product of modernity, Klein also takes a further step—and must do so, if his work is not to fall into the trap, more common than one might think, of rejecting historicism on purely historicist grounds.

Accordingly, Klein, even as he historicizes historicism, ultimately also dehistoricizes modernity itself. Klein, that is, takes modernity, understood as an historical category, as but a foreground effect, as a threshold phenomenon. Its deepest roots, Klein repeatedly insists, are not themselves historical, not finally addressable within this branch of inquiry—with the result that the consideration of modernity as a moment in real history ultimately must give way to an inquiry of a wholly different type, to questions and problems of a principled, not a factual, nature. Modernity as an historical occurrence represents, for Klein, a bridge, a steppingstone toward another set of issues—the nature of knowledge, of the true good for human life, of the genuine character and being of mind, the consideration of which is intrinsically nonhistorical.

How precisely this works shall become clearer in my discussion of Klein's Husserl interpretation, since Klein's second stance toward modernity and history, his dehistoricization of the modern, rests explicitly on Husserl's late thought. Klein turned to Husserl's late work in order to articulate conceptually the possibility of passing from an historical to a nonhistorical plane, of moving from modernity, and the modern rupture, to a more philosophical framework. Even in his first writings, as we shall see, Klein by no means wholly endorses Husserl's thinking. Yet Klein believes that Husserl provides an inherently nonhistoricist account of beginnings, of working with roots and origins, that permits Klein to clarify the step his own work takes from modernity, initially engaged as an historical fact, back to its understanding in terms of problems and evidences of a principled order.

Before pursuing Klein's interpretation of the late Husserl further—the exposition of which will eventually bring us to Jacques Derrida's very different appraisal of these same texts—a second set of questions must first be raised, since these furnish the broadest horizons of this chapter. Klein's dehistoricization of modernity, in whatever way it may finally be established and conceived, his point that modernity in some respect must reach beyond history—that it includes a dimension different from the merely historical—is a cogent one, I believe, and, taken in a certain way, it returns me to those conclusions concerning the singular, hybrid character of modernity that appeared at the end of Chapter 5.

The category or occurrence called "modernity" cannot simply be one self-evident historical fact or category, as Klein asserts, first and foremost, because, by altering the very operation of cognition, it represents a variation in how truth is understood and conceived. Modernity proposes something wholly unexpected: a reorientation of the very parameters of truth and knowledge, including the versions of these upon which history relies. Moreover, in tandem with this, as part of the same phenomenon, as Klein shows, historicism as such, the view of history as itself authoritative for thought, is indeed a modern product. With modernity, radical historical self-consciousness originates; modernity brings with it the imperative to historicize, the injunction to understand oneself historically. Such a requirement *as a requirement*, however, could never emerge merely from history taken simply on its own (necessity of all sorts, any imperative for thought, there being absent). The demand that one historicize in fact can only emerge thanks to a transformation, an event that implicates a dimension not wholly historical. Accordingly, modernity cannot be folded fully back into the work of historicization and be deemed a transformation residing entirely on the historical plane.

Such a suprahistorical facet of the modern further attests, then, to what was suggested at the conclusion of Chapter 5: that the advent of modernity belongs to a wholly *singular* category or occurrence, at once history *and not*, simultaneously event and *a priori*, of a still unknown and unmastered, and perhaps even unmasterable, type.[2] Modernity would indeed necessarily be hybrid—at once an event as well as an *arche*, intrinsically an occurrence within history and also of a distinct order. As such, altering the self-consciousness and conceptuality—the very reference points—of the being undergoing it, it would challenge all existing techniques for its categorization and conceptualization, the bulk of which, in any case, it has itself spawned.

Jacob Klein's Genetic-Historical Interpretation of Husserl's Late Writings

Klein, of course, just to be clear, did not himself set forth modernity as such a hybrid. Instead, again, he sees modernity, as well as the historical awareness it enjoins, as steppingstones to an entirely different set of questions of a decidedly nonhistorical nature. For him, the conceptual or principled dimension finally stands wholly apart from the historical one—just as is the case for the true historicist, though for opposite reasons.

In order to clarify how Klein himself understands this complex articulation of historical and ahistorical thinking, it is necessary to examine Klein's sole extended, published treatment of Husserl, his 1940 essay "Phenomenology and the History of Science."[3] The intricate structure of this essay, in which Klein's own historiographical work and Husserl's conceptual treatment swap places, maps the multiple dimensions of Klein's interaction with Husserl.

At the beginning of his essay, Klein indeed indicates what has already just been emphasized: Husserl's late thought furnishes the philosophical context for his own historical work. Klein speaks of the connection of the project that he had already undertaken in *Greek Mathematical Thought and the Origins of Algebra* (*GMT*), of those aims "which should control research in the history of science," to Husserl's own broader philosophical interest in questions of origins and beginnings.[4] Husserl's philosophy should elucidate the presuppositions that control Klein's own historical work on the development of the modern scientific standpoint, findings that Klein had previously laid out in *Greek Mathematical Thought*, and that he reprises at the end of his essay.

Contrariwise, in Part 4 of his essay, when Klein arrives at his own historical treatment of the development of modernity, his treatment is explicitly said to supersede Husserl's treatment of this same theme in the *Crisis*. There Klein refers to what he calls "the actual historical development,"[5] by which Klein clearly means his own work in the second half of *Greek Mathematical Thought*.

Husserl's conceptual work and Klein's historical findings thus trade positions: Husserl's concepts furnish the basis for Klein's history, which itself subtends Husserl's own historical reconstruction. This "crisscross" not only again raises those questions brought out above concerning which, philosophy or history, has priority in Klein's thought, it also makes clear the centrality of Husserl's project for Klein's own. Indeed, the trajectory of Klein's essay, as just sketched, itself *enacts* that possibility, which Husserl alone *conceptualizes*, of moving back and forth between conceptual and historical material.

Thus interweaving his project with that of the late Husserl, Klein, it should be noted, does not, however, endorse Husserl's philosophical standpoint in toto, something that adds to the uncertainty as to how history and philosophy here finally relate.[6] Throughout his text, but especially at its beginning, Klein gently insinuates a criticism of Husserl, even as Klein is in the midst of identifying his thought with that of the phenomenologist.

Klein, as already touched on in Chapter 5, indeed contrasts Husserl's interest in roots, *rizomata* (defined as that from which other things grow to perfection), to an interest in *archai* (which pertains directly to the perfections these things putatively attain).[7] Despite the many breakthroughs Husserl made in establishing that scientific knowledge can never be reduced to its origins in a real genesis—neither a genesis in the soul or the mind, the reduction of knowledge to which is called psychologism; nor a genesis in real history, which is called historicism; nor one in the natural history of the human organism or species, which is termed naturalism (Husserl having discovered a nonhistoricist, nonpsychologist, nonnaturalist way of working with roots and genesis generally)—nevertheless, Klein notes, the very fact that Husserl focuses on beginnings, on genesis, and on roots marks him as modern, as indebted to the modern viewpoint.

Klein's article represents only a limited or partial endorsement of Husserl's program, thanks to its structure and its opening section, as well as owing to a number of other hints discreetly deposited here and there. Husserl's work for Klein is finally liminal. It opens a way beyond the hitherto closed character of modern thought, yet it is itself ultimately affiliated with that very same modern starting point that it helps to overcome. Husserl does discover a way of working with origins, with beginnings and roots, that takes us beyond historicism, Klein believes. Yet, on account of its focus on beginnings and genealogy, this work exhibits an identifiably modern profile, and its overall philosophical pertinence in Klein's eyes is finally limited.[8]

This threshold position that Klein assigns to Husserl's thought overall, moreover, as well as a second point about to be raised, establish some of the most important differences between his treatment of Husserl's late thought and Jacques Derrida's. Derrida, in what is really the second of three confrontations with Husserl's thinking as a whole, in his 1962 commentary on Husserl's "Origin of Geometry," the work also at the center of Klein's account, understands Husserl's last work as the capstone of all his other philosophical writings. So construed, for Derrida, the late writings bear on Husserl's total enterprise of a transcendental phenomenology, however, not primarily on the history of science or even modernity.

Derrida thus engages much more broadly with Husserl's project than does Klein. His passage through the late Husserl engages the entirety of Husserl's philosophy, and Derrida's own philosophical orientation, no matter how far afield he may subsequently venture, in fact stands closer to Husserl's than does Klein's.

This difference reflects another significant deviation, pertaining to what Husserl's late thought accomplishes. For Klein, Husserl's last works not only involve a nonhistoricist genealogy, an intentional history, but they permit the explicit articulation of this history with real history—the articulation of (1) an *actual*, with (2) a *conceptual* historical treatment. Understood in this fashion, Husserl's last work buttresses the research that Klein himself did as an historian, and this interpretation, with its focus on real history, also decisively separates Klein's treatment of Husserl's late thought from Derrida's.

Klein and Derrida thus part company in these two ways (merely in the restricted area of the interpretation of Husserl), and these two points must now be explored further, initially exclusively in respect to Klein's own work.

Klein's essay, including its very structure, makes clear that, in the limited form in which Klein endorses Husserl's program, Klein turns to it, first, to discover a nonhistoricist way of working with roots, a nonrelativist notion of genealogy and development (in sum, an intentional history), and, second, in order to work out the status of actual history, to articulate how intentional and real history relate, thus elucidating those goals "which should control research in the history of science," as we have already seen Klein stipulate.[9]

Concerning the first topic, in order to orient his approach to Husserl's thought and lay out Husserl's general philosophical stance toward beginnings and origins, Klein draws extensively on one of the few late works of Husserl's that was actually published in his lifetime, *Formal and Transcendental Logic*.[10] *Formal and Transcendental Logic*, along with the *Cartesian Meditations*, belongs to a phase of Husserl's thought often labeled genetic phenomenology, as opposed to an earlier so-called "static" phase. And, as has already been suggested and shall be shown below in more detail, the greatest differences between Klein's treatment of Husserl's thought and Derrida's ultimately are owed to this decision; they are due to Klein's taking Husserl's late historical phase very much as an extension of his prior researches into genesis, into egological genesis. By contrast, though Derrida himself had previously taken genesis as Husserl's most constant theme, in his "Introduction" Derrida argues that the last historical work transcends or transgresses the limits that had previously governed all of

Husserl's work, including this thematic of genesis. For Derrida, Husserl's final historical writings represent a breakthrough in respect to phenomenology as a whole, and this way of viewing Husserl's corpus will prove as definitive for Derrida's mature thought as Klein's opposed understanding does for his.

To remain for the moment solely with Klein's interpretation, however, the crux of what Husserl's genetic researches bring to light, what Klein above all gets from *Formal and Transcendental Logic*, is first and foremost a kind of philosophically valid *sequencing*, a style of *serial* development, which nevertheless is able to be thought of as necessary or *a priori*, insofar as it appears wholly within Husserl's own absolute. Thus, in what is only an apparent paradox, Klein starts to make his way toward this standpoint, toward Husserl's intentional history, in Section 1 of his piece, by bringing forward Husserl's critique of all hitherto known genetic accounts of knowledge, a critique that Klein himself unequivocally endorses. Klein asserts that Husserl "show[s] irrefutably that logical, mathematical, and scientific propositions could never be fundamentally . . . determined" by any sort of real genesis.[11] By contrast, what *can* play a validating role in knowledge and furnish the subject matter of philosophy, Klein states immediately afterward, is Husserl's discovery of essences and invariants in the flow of conscious everyday life. "First in the actual development of Husserl's thought and first in any phenomenological analysis," Klein declares, is the isolation of a "common essence," an *eidos*.[12]

Step one in all phenomenology is thus this discovery of invariants and essences; yet, as Klein rightly states, this is but a first step, belonging to the first phase of Husserl's phenomenology. Phenomenological inquiry subsequently deepens when it is recognized that these essences and invariants themselves presuppose a new, special kind of thinking, which also turns out to have built within it a new kind of sequential or genetic order. Thus Klein writes: "Whatever we discover as having a definite significance . . . has also a backward reference to a more original significant formation." And "each 'significant' formation," he goes on, "has its own essential 'history of significance,' which describes the 'genesis' of the mental product."[13]

There are in fact two different, critical, albeit related points implied here (in part due to where in Husserl Klein has situated himself, owed to his reliance on *Formal and Transcendental Logic*), which, when understood, furnish the outlines of Husserl's intentional history, and thus sketch the possibility of a nonhistoricist genealogy or history as understood by Klein. The first point concerns what Husserl means by transcendental constitution generally. As Klein states later, recurring to these essences and invariants just mentioned, such "an invariant, as identically the same . . . seems to transcend any possible limits. Its 'eternity,' however, is but a mode of 'eternal' time: its identity is an intentional product of the *transcendental subjectivity* which is at work through all the categorical determinations that constitute a significant unit."[14]

Transcendental constitution refers to transcendental subjectivity at work establishing essences and their significance. Husserl believes that the validating *objects* of theoretical knowledge, such as geometry—and for Husserl the geometrical triangle, as opposed to a wooden one, is an essence, an *eidos*—while maintaining their validity, could not ultimately be understood apart from the possibility of a special kind of thinking, ultimately a unique sort of subjectivity, standing over against them. This kind of thinking, transcendental thinking, nevertheless preserves the authority of *objectivity*, of the truths of geometry, and is thus thinking of a wholly special type, belonging to no worldly being or even real substance. (It *can* belong to no worldly being or real substance, in part because this thinking is itself responsible for all substances and worldly entities being able to appear, being able to be identified and known as what they are.)

To be stressed here, however, is that this possibility of subjectivity opens the door to an activity of thought that takes place in " 'eternal' time," according to Klein—Klein himself putting "eternal" in scare quotes. For Husserl, this kind of thinking—transcendental constitutive work—is indeed a lived phenomenon, which intrinsically has time, temporality, in fact lived temporality, as its basis. Due to the special status of all transcendental achievements, however, while these are temporal through and through, their work does not take place in the time of physics or cosmology, in any worldly time, and, on this account, Klein here deems it "eternal."

Husserl himself, of course, devoted an enormous amount of work to specifying of what sort was the thinking that operated in this unique way—at once temporal and absolute—and how it was to be arrived at and described. Klein, identifying this as a temporalized yet somehow eternal production, *Leistung*, sidesteps much of this. Though giving an apt description of transcendental constitution, as far as it goes, Klein avoids the issue of how this thinking can be authoritatively accessed so as to form the basis of a philosophical science or knowledge. This lacuna, which appears to be one with the limits that Klein sets to Husserl's enterprise generally, contrasts with the stature of this problem in both Husserl and Derrida. The status of transcendental subjectivity not only furnishes the focus of the bulk of Husserl's work, certainly his published work after

1910, but also looms foremost in Derrida's engagement with Husserl from the beginning.

Transcendental syntheses taking place in lived time, as just discussed, are one important feature implied in Klein's claims. At this moment, however, not only has transcendental constitution made its way into Klein's discussion, but genetic transcendental constitution in its specificity has appeared as well. All essences, every significant formation, Klein declares, in fact can be known *a priori* to be the product of a very special kind of genesis, which takes place in just this same "eternal time" that has been brought forward. Not just the surface work of constitution finds its place in an eternal, as opposed to a natural, or real historical, time. Transcendental activity turns out to have a dimension belonging to a still deeper past and future and, in this way, it becomes subject to "history" in a new and special sense.

This notion of a "history," of an intentional history inherently belonging to the transcendental ego, emerges when Klein follows Husserl as Husserl steps through a synthesis in which "the object is constituted as persisting, as one and the same (identical, 'invariant') object."[15] In such a synthesis, according to Klein, specifically in "the continuous modification of the retentional consciousness" (the immediate awareness of the past, say, the beginning of a note that is continuing to sound), a "limit" will be reached, at the moment "when the 'prominence of the object' flows away into the general substratum of consciousness" (when the note as a whole has gone and ceased to be an object of attention). All actual activity of apprehension and constitution thus flows into a past deeper than that being constituted in the present, and it also itself has such a past: a past that precedes and conditions "the 'evidence' experienced in [any] . . . immediate presentation."[16]

Such experience of the past disappearing beyond any conscious bounds makes possible the assertion that the evidences that the ego makes manifest in constitution themselves have a past. Accordingly, the ego, the transcendental subject, defined as what is responsible for all such evidence, turns out not only to be temporal in the sense of being at work in eternal time, but also "historical" in this precise fashion. A prior, not currently conscious, phase necessarily belongs to all its present constitutive experiences and achievements. This yields genuine seriality or sequencing within the ego, a true transverse dimension. Some acts and objects necessarily have other objects and other sorts of acts as their precursors, with the result that Husserl's absolute indeed knows a history or genesis internal to itself. As Klein puts this, focusing first on the transcendental feature, "it is here, that the intrinsic 'possibility' of the identity of an object is revealed out of its 'categorial' constituents." And it is here, he continues, "that the 'intentional genesis' leads back to constitutive 'origins,' that the 'sedimented history' is reactivated back into the 'intentional history.'"[17]

Klein thus discovers a philosophically valid, wholly nonhistoricist and nonrelativist way of conceiving development, genealogy, and origins in Husserl. Husserl's transcendental ego, defined by its ability to produce the objects of knowledge—to produce all significant formations, with the validity and meaning they have—turns out necessarily to have a genetic or developmental vector running through its own thinking and intentionality. Talk of an intentional history and a certain kind of "historical" work thereby becomes possible. Specifically, the disclosure of the various strata underlying the transcendental ego's present accomplishments will comprise this new, special sort of history.

This genesis only shows its deepest implications as history, however, when Klein, in a second phase, connects it to real, factual, history: the real history of the sciences or of theoretical knowledge. Klein first addresses the relation between intentional and real history in Section 2 of his essay. Klein's focus there falls largely on what Husserl calls *ideal objects*—things like a theorem, or a number (*Zahl*), or, again, a geometrical triangle— objects that do not themselves exist as spatiotemporally individuated particulars and that are thus treated by a purely theoretical knowledge. In regard to these objects, "if the object is in itself an ideal formation," Klein strikingly announces, "a transcendental inquiry . . . reveal[s] the essential necessity of its being subjected to a history in the usual sense of the term . . . the necessity of a historical development within *natural time*."[18]

Klein thus discovers in Husserl a lesson pertaining not only to transcendental, but to real history. In respect to ideal objects, like those of geometry and other theoretical sciences, precisely because they are not of a natural type, and in principle must undergo constitution, the one who first invents or discovers them, to whom they first appear, the so-called "proto-geometer" in the case of geometry, can and indeed must be understood as having translated what are a set of transcendental-genetic accomplishments into real historical ones.

Specifically, for Klein, *Vorhaben*, forehaving or anticipation, establishes this relation between an intentional or transcendental history and an actual historical development. At the moment the first geometer makes these ideal objects (such as a geometrical triangle or a given theorem) first appear in real history, at the moment of his or her science's invention or discovery, s/he must already, anticipatorily, possess these objects. Accordingly, their specifically transcendental genesis must have already taken place (in a sense of "already" that is of course logical, not itself temporal or historical).[19] These objects indeed necessarily know a kind of sequence, development, or genesis within the "eternal" time of transcendental consciousness. And appearing to the protogeometer in some fashion, in advance of their actual historical emergence, the geometer at this moment necessarily serves as a crossover point from their transcendental constitution in "eternal time" to their real genesis and eventual existence in the world.

The first real geometer thus "*translate*[s]," and this is Klein's own word and emphasis, "into terms of 'reality' what actually takes place within the realm of 'transcendental subjectivity.'"[20] This translation of the transcendental into the real by the protogeometer provides the first of two *a priori* frameworks laid down by Husserl's late thought for the operation of real history and thus for the historian—specifically, for histories and historians of science, which have such ideal objects as their subject matter.

Transcendental genesis, as Klein interprets Husserl, indeed gives a necessary content to what Husserl understands in the *Origin of Geometry* as "first-timeliness," or *Erstmaligkeit*[21]: the moment when geometry or any other science is factually invented or discovered. Since geometry's actual invention by dint of forehaving, of anticipation, implies a "prior" transcendental genesis, a knowledge of what this first time actually entails must also be possible, according to Klein, even if the actual historical advent of a science, in this case geometry, is not otherwise known to real historians. Only in a situation, after all, in which all the transcendental preconditions of the geometrical object have actually been met, in which all the formations and meanings that prove transcendental precursors to the genesis of the geometrical object are themselves genuinely historically available, can geometry really be invented or discovered. An essential content thus belongs to the first time of geometry's invention, and an essential knowledge of this event becomes possible, even in its facticity, even in that case where every other historical circumstance, such as who the first geometer really was, remains unknown. Husserl's intentional researches, as read by Klein, give to the historical beginning or inauguration of a science such a content. They provide an *a priori* subject matter that necessarily informs any already constituted knowledge.

Secondly, Husserl's late work establishes an essential *form* for the ongoing character of this real history itself, a form of real history as such. With this establishment of an *a priori* form, Husserl's work lays down what was sought above in respect to Klein's own labors: the ultimate aims of all work in the history of science—or, put otherwise, the methodological orientation for any authentic history of science.

For Klein, actual history only comes about, in fact, when the founding insights of this so-called protogeometer are put into words: into real speech and language, and, above all, writing—this last being a factor of which Derrida, of course, will make much (though he understands writing's role here significantly differently than does Klein).[22] Only when thought comes to speech, only when the protogeometer's anticipations and insights are put into words—above all, when they are deposited in writing—does "the *real* history of a science . . . begin," according to Klein.[23] Verbalization, linguisticization, inscription, for Klein thus give birth to real history, and they do so especially insofar as they make possible the loss, the disappearance, or concealment of these founding intentions, of the meanings and experiences from which a science such as geometry originates, as well as those which establish each subsequent stage of a science's progress.

Every ongoing science, every living scientific tradition, Klein avers, cannot avoid taking many of its most important insights and discoveries as given—in fact, all those not in question at the current stage of research. It cannot help but view their meanings and truth as a self-evident stock or resource to be drawn on as needed in the way that the presentation of these findings in speech and, above all, writing uniquely appears to make possible: as something already accomplished, still at hand, and without need for further thought or questioning. As Klein more tendentiously puts it, "no science in its actual progress can escape the 'seduction' emanating from the spoken and written word."[24]

The expression of foundational, inaugurative insights in words, in spoken and written language, makes possible, indeed requires, at every stage of a science the treating of its inherited stock of concepts and truths as finished products. It thus necessarily entails, in Husserl's language, "sedimentation": the covering over of the intentionality that enlivened these meanings and truths when they were first deposited at an earlier phase of research. Such depositing of present meaning in verbal and linguistic "bodies," and the subsequent occlusion of their once-animating intentions, structures scientific development as such, according to Klein; it fashions the internal framework of a scientific tradition establishing the present stage of a science, whether consciously or no, as necessarily the development of an earlier one and as bearing an intrinsic connection to it. A scientific discourse has history as an inherent feature of its present cognitive products, insofar as all "the previous steps leading to a given stage" are necessarily found sedimented within it—its latest developments, its newest discoveries necessarily taking place on an inherently stratified platform. Sedimented meanings, insights, and truths—deposits from an earlier moment—internally connect the various phases of a science to one another, so that the history of any science simply is, as Klein puts it, the "interlacement of original production and 'sedimentation' of significance."[25]

These features, sedimentation and development, in turn define the authentic historian's task. From these essential characters of real history—stemming from all science's recourse to language and writing—emerge Klein's own understanding of the work to be done by the historian of science. "The signifying function of the spoken [and written] word . . . by its very nature," has "the tendency to lose its revealing character," Klein writes. Nevertheless, Klein insists that this revealing character also "is there in every word, somehow forgotten but still at the bottom of our speaking and our understanding however vague the meaning conveyed by our speech might be."[26] The historian's true task, then, the goal able to be gleaned uniquely from Husserl, is to get back to these originary meanings that have been forgotten and obscured through linguistic externalization, yet always in principle remain able to be recovered. In a word, the historian aims to *reactivate*, as Husserl calls it, these meanings corresponding to various stages of a science's development, in order to find what is at present unknowingly presupposed and return it to light. "The main problem of any historical research," thus states Klein, is "precisely the disentanglement of all these strata of sedimentation," with the goal of "reactivating 'the original foundations.'"[27]

This work, moreover, as conceived by Klein, and here we come to the crux of the matter, will ultimately be at once intentional and historical, on account of the transcendental component set out above. Insofar as the historian unearths earlier strata of a science—the previous layers on which it has been built—he or she in fact also necessarily works back across the principled stages of the transcendental-genetic or historical-intentional development of that science and its objects. Though perhaps not every stage of the one necessarily maps onto the other, for the largest articulations, such as those at work in the reinvention of the sciences in modernity, these movements through real history and through the scientific object's transcendental development for Klein are necessarily one and the same. The regression through a science's history ultimately orients itself by a confrontation with the same developments that alone could originally bring about the transcendental constitution of its subject matter.

Concluding this section, Klein himself, accordingly, affirms a specifically Husserlian nonhistoricist form of history or genealogy, siding with some of Husserl's own most radical and novel claims concerning history. Klein declares "from that point of view," namely, Husserl's, "there is only one legitimate form of history: the history of human thought."[28] And, he goes on to state, apparently in his own voice, even as he is again echoing Husserl, that "a history of this kind," of the sort that Husserl laid out, is the only legitimate form of epistemology."[29]

Klein endorses Husserlian history as the only legitimate history—a history, in turn, at once the only legitimate epistemology. Moreover, he embraces Husserl's standpoint as an account of his own work on the origins of modern scientific. Tellingly enough, Klein ends his piece by presenting these, his own historical or quasi-historical findings, in Husserl's own terms: explicitly in the form of *sedimentations*. Klein mentions three such sedimentations—concerning number, geometry, and the prescientific world, two of which are owed to Husserl, one of which is his own—all at once historical and intentional and unknowingly at work at the moment of the real historical inception of modern mathematical physics.

In Husserl's late writings, Klein, in sum, found a way to make more explicit, and conceptually transparent, the nature of his earlier historical researches: to make clear how his inquiries, starting from history, were able to reach beyond it and take up questions that were more than historical in the historian's usual sense. The aims that Klein himself had assumed all along for his own history of science, including the key question of how such history could function philosophically, are rendered transparent by Husserl's last writings in Klein's eyes, even as Klein in this essay also maintains a further significant distance, not from Husserl's history, but from the standpoint of his philosophy as a whole.

Jacques Derrida's Transcendental Historicity and the Deconstruction of an Infinite Teleology of Truth

Having thus reviewed Jacob Klein's engagement with Husserl's late thought—having showed its importance to Klein, and explored Klein's specific interpretation of it—it is time now to turn to Jacques Derrida's treatment of these same themes, his interpretation of the very same text that proved pivotal to my discussion of Klein, Husserl's *Origin of Geometry*. After examining Derrida's interpretation, and pursuing the role it plays in Derrida's first mature deconstructions,[30] I will work my way back to the subjects broached at the beginning of this chapter: modernity, history, and the clues that Derrida's and Klein's projects offer us for thinking their relation.

The central difference between Klein's and Derrida's reading of Husserl's *Origin*, as previously noted, ultimately concerns the status of factual history. Derrida takes Husserl's approach to history as more discontinuous with history as it is usually understood than Klein—as more of a transformation of what is meant by history. In addition, Derrida does this because, Derrida reads Husserl's late work as presenting a transformation or expansion of Husserl's own core notion of transcendental subjectivity.

Derrida's emphasis on the theme of transcendental subjectivity furnishes another central difference between Derrida and Klein, one already mentioned, but only sparsely discussed until now. Derrida, in all his writings on Husserl's phenomenology, asks how transcendental subjectivity, Husserl's philosophical absolute, is to be conceived—a concern that Derrida clearly shares with Husserl himself, who devoted much of his writings, especially his published writings, to what are called the phenomenological, transcendental, and eidetic reductions: the steps by which the transcendental subject is to be arrived at in a philosophically and epistemically authoritative manner.[31]

Derrida views Husserl's talk of an intentional history also in this light. For him, a new view or dimension of transcendental subjectivity emerges in the *Origin* that exceeds the confines of all of Husserl's previous explorations of this topic, including his genetic phenomenology, that same model of transcendental functioning central to Klein's interpretation of the late work. Derrida stresses this new status of Husserl's central theme at the end of Section I of the "Introduction": "By a spiraling movement *which is the major find of our text*," he states, "a bold clearing is brought about within the regional limits of the investigation and transgresses them toward a new form of radicality" (*IOG* 33–34, my emphasis).

The core issues in Husserl's last writings for Derrida do not, then, pertain to a transcendental genesis within the ego. Rather, a genuine, specifically transcendental history emerges in these very late works. Transcendental intentionality, the activity of the transcendental subject, implies a transcendental community of subjects, a so-called transcendental intersubjectivity, and across this community a more profoundly transcendental history unfolds than any that Husserl had previously disclosed or that Klein discusses.

This difference can be made more concrete by returning to the issue of essences, and of ideal formations, from which Derrida's discussion starts, as did Klein's. For Derrida, unlike Klein, it will not be sufficient to arrive at an eternal kind of thinking and posit such essences and invariants as standing over against it. The tracing back of significant formations to earlier ones, upon which Klein insists, still assumes, after all, that these essences are known and given in their own right. Other acts may have to be acccomplished and other objects apprehended before such essences can come to light; nevertheless, these essences themselves, for Klein, are time-less, eternal. In particular, they do not know a first time within transcendental thinking itself, a genuine moment of transcendental inauguration or institution.[32]

By contrast, Derrida indeed understands the Husserlian *Erstmaligkeit*, that first-timeliness that I discussed earlier, as pertaining to a specifically transcendental history (*IOG* 47–48). For him, the central question investigated by Husserl in the *Origin of Geometry* is how essences and other sorts of ideal formations first arise and then perdure in a novel, historico-transcendental sense. The last phase of Husserl's writings proves critical for Derrida, precisely because in it alone Husserl talks about the radical origination, the genuinely transcendental-historical emergence, of essences—still, however, without calling their validity into doubt. Geometrical science is made up of essences—of pure essences, in Husserl's lingo—and insofar as Husserl now explores their origins, Derrida sees Husserl as ultimately also venturing a reconception of the origins of transcendental thinking, one that places it on a profoundly reconceived, newly understood, "historical" ground.

Derrida thus takes much more seriously than Klein the possibility of a transcendental history, which would include a moment of invention and discovery with its own "first time." Two subsidiary points derive from this, which further differentiate Derrida's reading from Klein's, and thus define Derrida's reading on its own terms.

First, Derrida's account of the roles of writing, speech, and language in Husserl's last works crucially differs from Klein's. For Klein, as brought out above, language, speech, and writing essentially condition real history, a history that takes place subsequently, speaking logically, to the solitary transcendental genesis eventually captured therein. At the moment such actual, and not transcendental, history begins, for Klein, it relies on language and writing, which are themselves also factual and worldly entities. For Derrida, however, language and writing condition, and thus belong to, this new transcendental history itself. They are structural possibilities of a new, transcendental historicity. Taking on such a transcendental function, they, too, are to be conceived as pure transcendental possibilities, as having a specifically transcendental meaning. Derrida's own mature thought, as will become clearer below, directly follows from this unique interpretation of Husserl's late work: from the openings, as well as the aporias, presented by the notions of a specifically transcendental writing and language.

Returning again to this theme of essences just discussed permits the transcendental work done by writing, what it means to talk of a transcendental writing or language, to be more concretely grasped. For Husserl, read the way that Derrida reads him, writing conditions the transcendental emergence of essences. Doubtless essences in Derrida's eyes, too, appear to exist once and for all; they are not spatiotemporally individuated and they announce themselves as eternally valid, as apparently timeless modes of meaning, being, and truth. Understood from a transcendental perspective, however, this eternal character of essential truth, Derrida argues, must be seen in terms of what Husserl himself calls "omnitemporality," or all-timeness—not as simple timelessness or *eternality*, but as the ability to be grasped *across* time, at any time, by a constituting transcendental subjectivity.[33] The eternity of essences, in a transcendental context, amounts to the possibility of their being continuously available to a transcendental intentionality: the ability, without restriction, for them to be intended, and intended as valid by transcendental subjectivity. And the question thus arises, for which writing eventually provides the answer, of how such a possibility itself may be given to an instituting consciousness at the moment of an essence's transcendental-historical inauguration. What makes present to the originally constituting consciousness this capacity to be ongoingly intended, upon which the timeless validity of an essence transcendentally rests?

Writing's role in Husserl's last work takes shape in response to this question. The original intention of the transcendental instituter, Derrida argues, must itself be able to be repeated ad infinitum for the possibility of the "timelessness" or "omnitemporality" of an essence to be grasped at the moment of geometrical or essential inauguration. A noetic stratum must thus already be in place that permits the initial *act* of intending to be repeated and transmitted without end, if the potential omnitemporality of the *object* at which this intention aims is to be meaningfully available to other transcendental subjects at the moment of its transcendental inception.

Writing alone makes such repetition or transmission available, according to Derrida. Only it furnishes such a stratum. Writing extends the power of transcendental consciousness generally to transmit and repeat its original intention out to infinity, thus providing a subjective intentional correlate to the essential object's transcendental capacity to be continuously accessed as true throughout all times. In this way, writing as a medium supplies the transcendental-historical subjective and communal ground for the omnitemporal validity belonging to all ideal, essential, and theoretical truth at the moment of that truth's inauguration.[34]

Derrida perhaps makes this most plain, he encapsulates this new interpretation of a specifically transcendental writing, when reversing a claim Eugen Fink had previously made about writing's role, as well as that of language more generally. Fink, who was Husserl's last research assistant and a virtual collaborator during Husserl's last years, had asserted that "in sensible embodiment occurs the 'localization' and the temporalization of what is, by its being sense, unlocated and untemporalized" (*IOG* 89). Writing and speech for Husserl, Fink thus claims, give a sensible location, a "sensible embodiment" to the otherwise unlocatable and timeless sort of ideal existence belonging to essences and all theoretical truths. By contrast, Derrida insists that "non-spatio-temporality" "only arrives at its sense thanks to linguistic incorpor*ability*" (*IOG* 90 / *LOG* 88, trans. altered). The mode of being specific to essences (and other theoretically validating objects such as the truths of geometry), Derrida asserts, can only have the kind of objectivity proper to them, can only attain to nonspatiotemporality, thanks to the possibility of their being incorporated in (transcendental) writing and language. The transcendental possibility of linguistic inscription initially grants these objectivities their nonspatiotemporal mode of being, rather than itself simply providing a mere location, a sensible locus, for a mode of existence already otherwise achieved in its own right.[35]

Accordingly, writing and language as pure transcendental possibilities must be available, according to Derrida, at the inception of a science like geometry, at its transcendental-historical inauguration, in order for the objects appropriate to theoretical truth to emerge. That is the meaning of giving to writing and language a specifically transcendental role.

Before proceeding to the next major difference between Derrida's and Klein's interpretation, a corollary of this one should first be cashed out, among other things, since it leads to this latter development. This corollary concerns the notion, so crucial for Klein, of sedimentation. Sedimentation, for Derrida, like writing and language, concerns a specifically transcendental history; and it must do so, now that writing and language have taken on a specifically transcendental acceptation. In fact, this is another reason—in addition to the inclusion of a first-timeliness, an *Erstmaligkeit*—that a specifically transcendental history can be spoken about it.

The grounds Klein gave for seeing tradition and development as intrinsic to factual history themselves, after all, now exist on a transcendental level, given the inclusion of language and writing. The transcendental work of writing, speech, and language, that is, now impart to a specifically transcendental intention or experience the possibility of being deposited and covered over, i.e., sedimented, thereby, establishing a genuinely transcendental history. Tradition and development indeed are installed on the transcendental plane and take on a transcendental pertinence, once transcendental writing and language are posited.

Such sedimentation, moreover, poses a far graver danger, a far more profound threat to meaning and truth for Derrida, than it does on Klein's reading.[36] A potentially infinite sedimentation now becomes possible, thanks to the transcendental role of writing. For Derrida, writing makes possible an infinite traditionality, a potentially infinite passing on of meanings, a virtually infinite transcendental community, correlative to the kind of objectivity belonging to essences and to scientific truth. Such a possibility of infinite transmissibility, however, can also *infinitely* distance a science, its meanings, and achievements, from its origins, from its founding acts and experiences. It can imply a now-infinite removal from its roots, *seemingly* making possible the loss or disappearance of truth in a radical sense.[37] Writing, a condition of essential truth, on Derrida's reading, also makes possible the potential disappearance of this truth, since it opens the door to a now potentially infinite sedimentation.

Writing is thus the moment of any and every crisis of the sciences, in Derrida's eyes, and the distinction, central to Husserl and Klein, between genuine science and merely technical or instrumental achievements, for Derrida on these grounds already comes into doubt in the "Introduction." That science, or *theorein*, becomes the kind of merely symbolic and instrumental inquiry that Klein takes to be characteristic of modernity, a development that both he and Husserl believe is corrigible, for Derrida is a possibility inherent in all scientific knowledge and theoretical truth from the first. It is one with what permits genuinely validating theoretical objects originally to emerge: namely, the transcendental work of writing and language. This transcendental contribution of language and writing already may lead at least to a partial disappearance of the meaning and truth of scientific insights in the ever-extending recursivity of research, in the ever-ongoing progress of a scientific tradition.

Now, even the foregoing, let me be clear, at least in Derrida's 1962 "Introduction," does not imply that truth and truth's disappearance stand on entirely the same footing. As discussed in Chapter 3, the transcendental-historical inauguration of a scientific theory and the sedimentary concealment of that theory's foundations do not have an identical status for Derrida in 1962. And seeing why this is brings forward the second major difference between Derrida's and Klein's interpretation of Husserl's late thought.

Writing, as conceived by Derrida, may indeed function as a structural possibility of both truth and its forgetting. Yet, as I have previously indicated, a teleology of truth, bearing a transcendental presupposition in favor of theory and its rights, from the first governs both these moments.

"If the univocity investigated by Husserl and the equivocation investigated by Joyce are in fact *relative*," Derrida declares in a noteworthy formulation, "they are, therefore, not so *symmetrically*. For their common telos, the positive value of univocity, is *immediately* revealed only within the relativity that Husserl defined" (*IOG* 104).

Truth, posited as an overrriding transcendental aim, as the goal of Husserl's own philosophy, thus commands the possibility of the first appearance of theoretical objects, such as those of geometry, as well as any possibility of their disappearance. And this *telos*, ultimately of reason as such, of pure thought itself, necessarily prevents these opposite outcomes—revelation and forgetting, disclosure and occlusion—from being wholly symmetrical, from simply being equipotent possibilities.

This must clearly be the case, truth must indeed receive some kind of privilege, since, after all, what puts this whole machinery of transcendental history and historicity in motion, including infinite sedimentation, are writing and language conceived as pure transcendental possibilities, something only thinkable on the basis of Husserl's transcendental phenomenology and its aim at truth. Though Husserl's analysis of the transcendental historicity of the sciences may disclose the possibility of an infinite forgetfulness of origins, this very analysis still presupposes the veridicality of Husserl's own philosophy, and it would collapse without its own aim at truth being valid.

The latter, however, the truth of Husserl's philosophy, in fact the truth at which all philosophy aims, undergoes a novel thematization in Husserl's last writings, where it indeed first becomes understood as a *telos*, as an infinite Idea. This development in the articulation of Husserl's philosophy furnishes a second major point of contrast between Derrida's and Klein's accounts, since such teleology receives virtually no attention in Klein's discussion, though prominent in all of Husserl's late texts.

Because, however, Derrida's focus in the first place falls on this transcendental-historical stratum that he believes Husserl has newly disclosed, this teleology does prove central for Derrida. The notion of an infinite idea plays a crucial role in Derrida's interpretation of the *Origin*, as well as for his subsequent work, in which, by dint of further distancing himself from the position he believes Husserl takes here, Derrida arrives at his own mature stance with respect to history and its relation to philosophy.

Of course, the status of this teleology in Husserl's last works is itself notoriously complex, even vexed. Such teleology concerns the development of philosophy in its entirety, including the place of Husserl's own transcendental phenomenology in the history of philosophy and the tradition of knowledge as a whole. The final phase of Husserl's thinking, more specifically, entails that the history of philosophy itself knows a sort of transcendental counterpart or interpretation—its own transcendental or intentional history—in which Husserl's transcendental phenomenology represents the final (specifically infinite phase) of the unfolding and coming to itself of reason in general, of what Husserl also sometimes calls the absolute *logos*.[38]

Not only does the insertion of Husserl's thinking into the broader context of the history of philosophy raise questions as to how these claims comport with earlier phases of his thinking, however—since in prior phases Husserl seemed to hold his project back from all contact with history—but it complicates the situation of the piece of writing today known as the *Origin of Geometry*. In works just prior to this fragment, in the *Crisis of the European Sciences* above all, Husserl had sketched an historical-intentional account of the movement of objective knowledge, of the unfolding of *theorein* as such, with philosophy standing at both the origin (ancient philosophy) and at the end (Husserlian phenomenology). In light of this treatment, all that Husserl accomplishes in the *Origin* appears as a subset of what Husserl had previously laid out, a part of this late phase of his own thinking, itself embedded in that intentional history of *theorein* the *Crisis* offers, wherein Husserl's own thought emerges as the final fulfillment (the *Endstiftung*) of reason and philosophy.

At the same time, the *Origin* alone, especially as read by Derrida, accounts for the *methodology*, thanks to which Husserl mounts the *Crisis*'s discussion in the first place. Only the *Origin* seems to explain how such a historicizing of knowledge, reason, philosophy, and Husserl's own project are possible. Husserl's analysis in the *Origin* elucidates the methodology specific to historical-transcendental or historical-intentional work generally, clarifying what permits Husserl to speak of a crisis of reason, even as this analysis of the founding of geometry, and its clarification of intentional history, also appear as but a portion of the philosophical-historical response that Husserl had already begun to mount to the crisis named in that work's title. The *Origin*'s ultimate context remains Husserl's interpretation of transcendental phenomenology as representing the final stage of reason's coming to itself on a transcendental historical plane, yet only the *Origin* rigorously shows how access to this plane is possible.

This is one reason, to return to the point above, it would indeed be impossible, absurd, an *Unsinn*, in Husserl's eyes, for meaning and truth to be permanently lost, to utterly disappear at the hands of infinite sedimentation, since such an idea, such a *telos* of reason, in its final phase is the source of even Husserl's own transcendental inquiry. More specifically still, faced with such potentially infinite sedimentation, Husserl tells us, an idealization is indeed possible, which allows even this sort of seemingly infinite sedimentation in principle to be overcome, thereby permitting a scientific tradition, here that of geometry, to be returned to its origins, and to recover its founding meanings and acts. Such an idealization, in which an infinite sense shows through and lets itself be grasped across a practical finitude—a finitude in the actual power of recovery of the potentially infinite mediations comprising geometry's history—allows the possibly infinite sedimentation of this or any scientific tradition in principle to be removed.[39]

Taking note of Husserl's appeal in the *Origin* to such a teleology and idealization, a further complexity, another nuance or fold within this same text, corresponding to the broader one concerning its position within the late writings generally, begins to emerge. For this idealization, this infinite movement of thought, by which sedimentation is to be overcome, itself a part of Husserl's own reflection on the transcendental history of science, also turns out to be the crucial component at work in the *Urstiftung*, the original founding, of geometrical science itself. The same sort of idealization that guarantees the recovery of meaning of any scientific formation, its continuity as a tradition, brought forward by Husserl on a transcendental plane, is also what has made possible the coming into being or advent of the objects of geometry in the first place in the analysis that Husserl sets forth within the *Origin*.[40]

For Husserl, geometry's objects, things like a geometrical triangle, indeed arise through an infinite passage to the limit that refashions the pregiven, essentially vague shapes of the everyday world into the exact figures of geometrical science. The geometrical circle, for example, comes to light for Husserl at the moment when a vague morphological shape drawn from everyday life—say, the roundness common to the moon, a plate, and a bowl—is reconceived as an ideal limit shape. This takes place thanks to a movement of what Husserl calls pure thought, in which an idea in the Kantian sense, an idea of an infinite task, intervenes to permit all the real, practical limits to the sort of perfection or precision found in a geometrical circle to be overcome. Though, as Derrida says, such passages to the limit are not to be done randomly—an essence or an *eidos* in some sense is waiting there to be exposed—this essence, the geometrical circle or triangle, is indeed constituted for the first time only thanks to an infinite idealization operated on the vague shape, which ultimately takes place under the rubric of an infinite idea.

For Husserl, the origin of geometry is thus necessarily concurrent with *the origin of philosophy itself*, though the facts of the matter may otherwise not be actually known.[41] An act of pure thinking—the general possibility of such an idealization—must already be at hand for these sorts of objects, the theoretical objects of geometrical science, to appear. Correspondingly, the protogeometer must already have in his or her possession the *idea* of pure theory as such, he or she must have something like an infinite theoretical labor at his or her disposal, to be able to accomplish this anticipation, this passage to the limit, by way of which the inauguration of geometrical objects takes place—Derrida himself focusing on that same role of anticipation, of the *Vorhaben*, that we have already seen to be crucial for Klein, while construing it quite differently. In order to pass to the limit, to overcome a practical finitude and a limited anticipation and produce an ideal limit shape, the possibility of such pure theorizing—producing objects with an infinite or unlimited validity—must itself be at hand, and, on these grounds, philosophy itself, the possibility and unique opening of pure thinking in general, must already have come on the scene.[42]

Derrida, then, reads Husserl not only (1) as fashioning a genuinely transcendental history, leading him to conceive of specifically transcendental writing and sedimentation; but Derrida also highlights, especially at the end of his work, (2) this notion of philosophy and its inaugural idea, a notion central to Husserl's late understanding of the very possibility and meaning of all philosophy, as well as the truths of geometry and all "theory." What above all excites Derrida's interests is the Idea, the status of the Idea in a Kantian sense—the condition of such theoretical labor—and the question of its relation to the rest of Husserl's thought. The deepest probing of Husserl's philosophy on Derrida's part in the entire "Introduction" emerges thanks to this questioning, which, along with that concerning writing, will indeed have the greatest influence on Derrida's later standpoint.

The problem that Derrida raises in respect to Husserl's claim, that an Idea has already been given and is at work at geometry's origin concerns, more specifically, the evidence that pertains to this *telos* as such: how such evidence relates to what Husserl calls phenomenology's principle of principles. Near the beginning of *Ideas* I, perhaps Husserl's single most comprehensive statement of his thought (though one that is provisional and may even be flawed), Husserl famously states that phenomenology as a science can only admit as true what is given to it "in person"—i.e., what genuinely presents itself to consciousness, what emerges within its own self-presence.[43] Phenomenology's principle of principles thus requires that no hypotheses (such as those concerning the workings of our neurons or what must have been in God's mind at the creation of the world), be admitted as philosophically authoritative, but instead only "self-giving evidences," as Husserl sometimes calls them.

An idea in a Kantian sense, however, precisely because it is an idea *of* infinity, can never be conceived as presenting its subject matter in this way, argues Derrida. As an idea of infinity, the object at which this idea aims necessarily overflows the consciousness of this idea (*IOG* 139). Indeed, only this object's nonappearance and nonpresentation in its idea, only a nonadequation between them, can allow the infinite to come forward in any fashion. Accordingly, only such nonadequation can be envisioned as establishing the opening of all theoretical knowledge: an opening that takes place within the difference between this thinking of the idea of infinity and that which it thinks about. The idea that opens philosophy, that makes possible pure thought in the first place, on Husserl's own construal, must itself violate phenomenology's cardinal principle in respect to evidence and philosophical knowledge.

This analysis obviously has enormous implications for Husserl's thought as a whole. In the final phase of his thinking, Husserl's self-understanding of his own transcendental phenomenology rests precisely on this idea and its givenness. Husserl's own thought supposedly represents the ongoing taking up of this idea: indeed, this idea's fulfillment in a final stage, or final founding, its so-called *Endstiftung*. Thus, Derrida, on this basis, concludes that phenomenology can never establish within itself its own meaning and possibility. From the first, it lives off of a difference between an awareness and what it is an awareness of; it exists thanks to this difference between the idea as such and that at which it aims. This idea—nothing other than the idea of objectivity as such, presenting to thought the difference between itself and its other, opening the task of absolute theoretical truth—conditions phenomenology's project from a transcendental-historical, as well as a principled, perspective. It represents the origination, the founding, the *Urstiftung* of all philosophy as well as being at work in Husserl's treatment of what structures the transcendental history of thought, knowledge, and truth themselves. For both transcendental-historical and structural reasons, then, there can never be, as Derrida puts it, a "phenomenology of phenomenology," an entirely phenomenological treatment of the aims and possibility of phenomenological inquiry itself (*IOG* 141).

Now, none of this, let me again emphasize, simply blots out, reduces to zero, Husserl's phenomenology, since the non-givenness of the Idea only has any sort of weight, has any significance at all, if there is such an Idea and it operates in the fashion that Husserl uniquely identifies. Nevertheless, Derrida does put his finger on possibly decisive, albeit non-disqualifying, limits of Husserl's enterprise in the final pages of his "Introduction to the *Origin of Geometry.*" The significance of these limits for

Derrida's own thinking changes, however, as his thought matures.[44] In the "Introduction," as others have also recognized, Derrida seems to present this entire problematic more as a kind of appendix, an addendum or supplement, to Husserl's own thought and labors, rather than as a break with this project in its entirety.[45] Insisting that the ultimate meaning and goal of phenomenology can only be thought even as a problem by starting from within phenomenology, by accepting its premises as presented by Husserl—something which is clearly the case, since the principle of principles, as well as the notion of philosophical reason as an infinite idea are themselves entirely Husserlian conceptions—Derrida presents his own concerns as furthering, even as they refashion, the totality of Husserl's project. Entailing this retention of Husserl's philosophical itinerary, Derrida's critique in the "Introduction" thus ends up being part of a broadening out or reconception of phenomenology, supplying that "phenomenology of phenomenology," or, better, that meta-phenomenology, that Husserl himself cannot finally fully provide. Working from what Husserl has given him, Derrida's reconception takes account of this factor, this infinite opening that eludes all proper self-appearing, all phenomenologically sound self-evidence, as well as including, it is worth noting, a more radical finitude, a thought of an absolute particularity or absolute facticity, of the thing or the event.

Thus Derrida at the close of the "Introduction" now famously speaks of an "ontological question . . . in the non-Husserlian sense." This question, Derrida goes on to make plain, asks about the fact, history, and the event in respect to their existence, above and beyond their sense. It asks: "is there and *why is there* any historical factuality?" (*IOG* 150). Bringing to bear a thought of radical facticity, Derrida's concerns at this moment are self-avowedly close to Heidegger's.[46] At the same time, as Derrida himself emphasizes, for him, unlike Heidegger, such questions may only be responsibly posed at the end, not the beginning, of phenomenological inquiry (understood as Husserl understands it). Thus he concludes: "on the condition that the taking seriously of pure factuality *follows after* the possibility of phenomenology and assumes its [phenomenology's] juridical priority, to take factuality seriously as such is no longer to return to empiricism and nonphilosophy; on the contrary, it completes philosophy" (*IOG* 151).

Derrida, to this degree and in this precise fashion, in the "Introduction" thinks both moments of infinity and finitude ultimately as coincident, thereby sketching a thought at once more and less radically finite than Husserl's own, and which, in this manner, anticipates many of Derrida's later key concepts, such as *différance*, or the trace. Nevertheless, in his later writings, Derrida also puts a much greater distance between himself and Husserl in respect to these matters, as he further expands the other thematic reviewed here, of writing and its role. This is a coordinated movement. The idea, truth as an infinite aim, in addition to being the focal point for these questions about the evidence opening the project of phenomenology and all philosophy, plays a determinative role at the moment that the sedimentary powers of writing threaten to call into doubt the project of the reactivation of the founding meaning of theoretical knowledge and truth. Calling Husserl's project still further into question in respect to the workings of the Idea, Derrida can also lay claim, then, to a more radical notion of writing than any he put forward in the *Origin*: one that really is equally at once the possibility of truth and its disappearance. Though how this works in detail remains the subject of a very long discussion,[47] writing—no longer held within the parameters of Husserl's transcendental inquiry, though still not able to be identified with writing as it is usually understood—standing at the borders of, or even beyond, all idealization and the infinite recovery of meaning, will be thought by Derrida as a genuinely radical condition of truth, one indeed able to make it and its now radical disappearance possible. What emerges from this development, Derrida's signature notion of *écriture*, is thus a wholly new, entirely unprecedented conception of what has previously been known as writing—one that has Husserl's own transcendental acceptation at its semantic core, even as it is precisely this at which it takes aim, and by dint of departing from which it fashions itself.

So, too, in line with this, Derrida, in the first phase of his mature thought, in his first deconstructions, now views Husserl's treatment of history as assimilable to other treatments of the history of philosophy, all of which, Derrida believes, function thanks to an illicit teleology of presence. For Derrida, all philosophy hitherto finds itself in the position we have run across in the treatment of Husserl—though Hegel has perhaps more self-consciously known and embraced this than anyone else—in which the supposedly infinite powers of presence, as embodied in theoretical knowledge aiming at an infinite meaningfulness and truth, turn out to depend on a *différance* that thought and theory as such cannot themselves include. The difference between the theory and practice of pure thinking is itself determined by an infinite idea, and thus rests on a difference, or differentiation (including both this idea and that practice), at once more and less finite than any philosophy can recognize. Accordingly, Derrida will insist in his mature writings, at the moment when this dependence becomes explicit, at the moment when philosophical truth and knowledge are known to live off a difference at once more and less finite than them-selves—presumably, the present moment—that the history of philosophy, the history of metaphysics, as Derrida now calls it, is closed. Not ended, he insists, but closed: its limits, both structural and genetic—which turn out to be the same, to be a certain structure of genesis—having in princi-ple been sketched.

Finally, Derrida's own mature thought, having clearly moved closer to Heidegger's, understands its own possibility, its own vocation and self-historicization, on the far side of this formation of the metaphysics of presence, and thus as at once more and less historical than any prior thinking. Inserting itself into becoming, into what would otherwise per-haps be called history—albeit achronologically, and in a self-avowedly more open-ended fashion than all previous thinking—it keeps its distance from historicism, something that differentiates Derrida from Heidegger, and even now is owed to Derrida's continuing to have Husserl's thought as the starting point for his own.[48] Indeed, it is only thanks to Derrida's having readapted Husserlian models of consciousness and transcendental-ity, rather than dismissing them and substituting others à la Heidegger himself or even Merleau-Ponty (thus owing to what some would call a residual Cartesianism),[49] that the mature Derrida can lay claim to a new, more radical historicity—a hypertranscendental historicity including a radical facticity—which nonetheless keeps a distance for all and every his-toricism and relativism.[50]

Indeed, Derrida, having seen rationality thought by Husserl ultimately in the form of an infinite idea, and seen this conflict with Husserl's own principle of principles, eventually, thanks to this tension, concocts his own nonhistoricist, yet radically historicizing or temporalizing, stance toward thought and the history of philosophy generally. Building on what Husserl had done, or indeed failed to do, building on a fault-line in Hus-serl's systematic thinking—which is what is meant by de-con-struction—Derrida, in his mature work, conceives of a project that starts on the far side of, as well as within, this closure of metaphysics: at once radically historicized or temporalized, yet not neglecting the seemingly infinite rights of reason, and whose relation to the future, according to him, at least early on, must thus necessarily be one of monstrous unthinkability, and take place under the sign of the unanticipatable.

Derrida and Klein In and On History

Very briefly, let me take one final step back, in order to achieve a view of Derrida's and Klein's projects as a whole. Their stances, as we have seen, are above all differentiated by the role of history. Klein sees Husserl as offering a new way to approach real history and the historian's work, while Derrida sees Husserl as reconceiving history's relation to philosophy—history's relation to Husserl's own transcendental phenomenology first and foremost. In Husserl's last writings, the young Derrida finds a new way of conceiving transcendentality, and this subsequently opens the door to this standpoint's further transformation—both a radical contestation and an expansion—in his mature work. By contrast, Klein finds in Husserl a launching pad, a jumping-off point, that will let history be left behind entirely, including, finally, Husserl's own perhaps too-historical philosophy. For the mature Derrida, however, the very feature of Husserl's late thought so important to Klein—namely, that inquiries into history and knowledge ultimately merge into one—instead shows that history has never been as far from knowledge and philosophy as historicism and empiricism would like to think.

Yet, it is at least suggestive that for both Klein and Derrida Husserl's work must be philosophically authoritative, in a strangely similar, albeit limited and even finally provisional manner, for them to go on and construe their very different total positions within contemporary thought. For each thinker, Husserl proves an indispensable, albeit finally liminal, philosopher.

Indeed, even as both Derrida and Klein find Husserl's philosophy to be only provisionally convincing, both turn to Husserl, ultimately to take their bearings in respect to history: in their quest for an adequate account of history and philosophy's relation to one another. Even as each author in his own way also senses limits to, and problems with, this phase of Husserl's project, a passage through Husserl's work proves necessary to grapple with thought's fate in our "historical" age.

And both the felt need of some authoritative articulation of philosophy and history, as well as Klein's and Derrida's partial, yet perhaps not wholly, successful recourse to Husserl in order to satisfy it, let me refer back to the still-unresolved question of modernity.[51] It is modernity, after all, as I argued at the outset, that requires philosophy initially to turn to history at all, no matter how this turn may be subsequently negotiated, whether in Klein's or in Derrida's very different fashions. The similar role that Husserl's thought plays for these otherwise enormously disparate thinkers—that of providing some kind of decisive treatment of history and philosophy together—indeed demonstrates how the problem of modernity, despite themselves, fundamentally and irresolvably haunts each of their endeavors.

Modernity's welling up at the intersection of Klein's and Derrida's programs allows this problematic itself, moreover, to be further fine-tuned. Though already described as a kind of rupture, shock, and hybrid, modernity is perhaps most fully comprehended in terms of the impossibility of knowing whether with it everything has indeed changed—whether as a break it represents a transformation of both the historical and the conceptual at once (and thus a formation that itself stands beyond either, embodying a radical singularity)—or whether it indeed can be resolved into either a factual and / or a principled comprehension, the current impossibility of doing so being a function of our still living within what is perhaps its merely historical shadow. Modernity, as "lived," one might say, is precisely the experience of not knowing whether one is passing through an absolute singularity or instead embedded in an assemblage, doubtless of unexpected, even unknowable consequences, yet hewn from pieces each of which could be identified with categories, by concepts, that in some fashion already exist.

And it is just this nonknowledge, this ambiguity, finally, that perhaps both Klein and Derrida refuse to tolerate. Klein ultimately seeks a radically timeless standpoint beyond its viscissitudes, to which modernity itself would be able to be led back, in order to ensure such a standpoint's power. Derrida, alternatively, wishes to make this possibility that modernity may represent, of a radical intermixing of thought and event, of a contamination of one by the other a necessary structural feature of all thinking. Yet, Derrida, too, thereby renders modernity a quasi-timeless affair, on the far side of which thought can and will resume, albeit in a new, and hitherto unknown, register. Perhaps all that may truly be affirmed, however, even in the wake of these two looming thinkers, is that modernity, now more than ever, remains a conundrum to which no one today has an adequate response.

Derrida's Contribution to Phenomenology

A Problem of No Species?

For Bernie Rhie

Edmund Husserl, in some tentative, exploratory pages, now an appendix to *Ideas* II, already looking toward the last phase of his work, avers that his own research furnishes the *"absolute human science."*[1] And phenomenology indeed does aim at such a science. In the midst of a world and a nature undergoing radical revision at the hands of those beings we are accustomed to assign to the human species, Husserl's work attempts to think some adequate, orienting version of the human as such, to lay bare an authoritative semantic core, a newly conceived meaning for this being (one also but a further unfolding or making explicit of what it already is). Husserl's ultimate understanding of his own philosophical responsibility entailed allowing humanity as such to appear, thus permitting it to gather itself up to undertake, responsibly and self-consciously, a new, nearly unlimited global phase of its own existence.

Moreover, it is not unreasonable to claim that many of those who followed after Husserl in the phenomenological tradition—Jean-Paul Sartre, Emmanuel Levinas, Maurice Merleau-Ponty, Hans Georg Gadamer, and even Martin Heidegger (though his is clearly the most complicated case)—shared this goal. They desired to refound, by radically disclosing, the being of human being, at a moment when this presumptive entity and its conceptualization—undergoing an unprecedented self-manifestation—appeared at once as more central to everyday life (e.g., in liberal republican government, the achievements of science and technology) and more unstable than it had ever appeared before.[2]

Yet characterizing phenomenology's contribution as an aim at an absolute science of human nature—and in this light, I will eventually turn to Derrida's endeavors and examine his contribution to the phenomenological traditions—problems also immediately arise. The present proliferation of efforts to parcel out and master human being at the hands of what Husserl would call "regional sciences" (cognitive neuroscience, genomics, and sociobiology today being the most notable) fulfills a research program already identifiable in Descartes, for whom reckoning with the human subject (as the means or medium of all other knowledge) came first, only to give way to real knowledge of it at the last—the human subject as object being the most complex of all possible areas of scientific inquiry.[3] The ever-burgeoning scope of this attempt at mastery today raises the question, however, of phenomenology's own standpoint as a science, and especially as "absolute human science." How does phenomenology approach the subject of the human, such that it can claim that its own knowledge and enterprise reach beyond all other existing and nascent disciplines devoted to the study of the human?[4]

To be sure, Husserl never ceased to attempt to resolve this issue—an "external" issue, if you will, first posed by the proliferation of modern knowledge, which philosophy has confronted since at least as far back as Kant. Especially in *Ideas* II, Husserl preferred a multilayered account of human being and human dwelling, one that provided a perspective from which the findings of the modern natural sciences could be deemed true, along with the insights of the humanities, thanks to embracing them both in a still more comprehensive understanding, a realm more primordial than they—this, Husserl's own area of investigation, being what his "absolute science" specifically names.

Taking up the ways of framing their objects defining of the natural sciences and the humanities (which in their totality Husserl dubs "attitudes") within his own inquiries, whether Husserl can wholly successfully coordinate these various manifestations and registers of the human, both among themselves and with his own absolute standpoint, however, remains unclear.

Not only does a well-known set of problems exist concerning how to distinguish between Husserl's absolute, the transcendental-phenomenologically reduced ego and human being as such authoritatively enough to establish a genuinely philosophical science—a set of problems pertaining to the various reductions (eidetic, phenomenological, and transcendental), and their meaning, possibility, and the language in which they are described, but, in Husserl's later writings, a related constellation of issues emerges pertaining to the constitution of aspects of the human within Husserl's transcendental perspective, which render even more problematic this intertwining of the human standpoint and Husserl's own. As Husserl's analyses, leaving in abeyance his earlier logical preoccupations, come closer to the phenomena in their individuality—particularly with the advent of the world-horizon and his description of the givenness of the existent as existing—they more and more draw on formations seemingly specific to human being (such as intersubjectivity and the human body, or, later, history and language), which thematics, though provocative in themselves, render problematic whether Husserl can separate out, in any philosophically respectable way, his constitutive standpoint and what it implies from an actually existing humanity.[5]

Indeed, the constitution of the human (of the human body, as well as the realm of society, culture, or spirit) being the constitution of what in other registers now plays a constituting role (as transcendental history, or intersubjectivity, transcendental language, or writing), Husserl's descriptions, at critical points, seem either to refer back to an irreducible facticity (in an analysis that claims finally to be a form of essential knowledge), or to offer an incomplete or intrinsically unsatisfying treatment of those referents, the constitution of which it does present. Husserl's inquiry thus seems at times to find itself at once ahead of itself (already presupposing matters that are only to be later constituted on its basis, as may be the case with some of his treatments of the body) and lagging itself (not fully capturing those phenomena it treats at the moment they are in question, such as those pertaining to the Other, to intersubjectivity) with the result that multiple, shifting, seemingly unstable instantiations of the human—as biological life, as psyche, as person in a world with others, as well as bodying forth the pure ego or absolute subject—arise and recede within it.

Accordingly, the problem of the human, the problem of knowing what content is to be given this notion today, politically, publicly, and in the midst of the proliferating sciences devoted to mastering it, as well as in Husserl's own thought, even now stands as an axial issue for phenomenology as a whole. It proves inseparable from Husserl's project's own self-understanding, as well the novelty and explanatory power of his unique conception of the absolute subject.

And, as noted, the vast bulk of Husserl's successors have joined him in the attempt to refound or rethink the human—in trying to restore an integrity to the notion of humanity at the moment this notion and its presumed referent seems to be taking on global significance. To be sure, few have maintained all the different phases of his own project, all the different registers and acceptations in which the subject there comes to manifest itself. Most "heterodox" phenomenologists—Sartre, Merleau-Ponty, Levinas, Heidegger (again, as always, the most difficult case), but also others such as Roman Ingarden, Alfred Schutz, or Max Scheler—ultimately privileged the human, factical, and phenomenological, rather than the purely transcendental, side of Husserl's endeavor. Faced with the deepening entanglement, especially in the later work, of Husserl's transcendental-phenomenological-eidetic standpoint with human being, they have opted for raising the latter (in its facticity, yet still as disclosed through phenomenological description), to a kind of absolute. So proceeding, they retain the vocation of Husserl's endeavor, its claim to furnish an "absolute human science," even as they have understood in a different way than Husserl the status of phenomenological inquiry and its own standing as knowledge.

The contribution of Derrida's thought to the phenomenological tradition stands out sharply in the context of phenomenology's ongoing concern with the human, and these debates over phenomenological method. As to the latter, Derrida perhaps surprisingly differs from every other heterodox phenomenologist, in that he wholly sides with Husserl's own transcendental and eidetic version of phenomenology, entirely embracing the project of transcendental phenomenology on Husserl's own terms. Thus wherever he subsequently goes, in the interchange with Husserl's thought that Derrida mounts, he retains the reductions and their various stipulations; he supports Husserl's philosophy's claim to being knowledge and its "Cartesian" model of consciousness (as it is sometimes put) over against all (transcendental) empiricism as well as all wholism—of the sort practiced by almost every post-Husserlian phenomenological thinker (in the case of empiricism especially), as well as many other contemporary philosophers, such as Ludwig Wittgenstein, W. V. O. Quine, or Richard Rorty.

To be sure, in line with a schema that he first avowed in 1954, Derrida also appends to Husserl's framework certain dialectical or later, supplementary considerations, which alter it radically in a way uniquely different from all these just named. On account of these considerations, Derrida claims that he also departs from Husserlian phenomenology and its self-evidences in a more fundamental manner than anyone else working in this tradition (including Heidegger). Nevertheless, even this gesture, as we shall see, presupposes that Husserl's philosophy is in some sense true, that the Husserlian framework, philosophically speaking, is authoritative. The unique character of a Derridean "deconstruction" actually depends on there being no philosophically conceivable alternative to the position being deconstructed (it is thus not a counter-argument or "critique"). And such a standpoint, assuming the irrefutability or irretractability of the position in question was itself first developed through Derrida's repeated encounters with Husserl's thought.[6]

At the same time, even as he transformatively, perhaps transgressively, appropriates Husserl's project in this fashion, Derrida contests the very concern or aim linking Husserl to his successors: namely, the focus on the human—this shared commitment to redisclosing the meaning and status of human being and dwelling as such. Under the headings of the "ends of man," "*Geschlecht*," "the hands of man," "phenomenological anthropology," and "hominisation," Derrida has made it clear that he wishes to break with this theme and the animating impulse it gives to Husserl's thought, as well as to phenomenology as a whole.[7]

Now, the coincidence of these two traits (if not the existence of the gestures themselves, especially the first) will be no surprise to Husserlians. "Anthropologism," after all, was the charge first leveled by Husserl himself against Heidegger's (anti-Cartesian) reworking of his phenomenology. Yet each of these gestures raises questions in its own right, ones that I will now review and that this chapter will subsequently canvass in more detail.

First, the question arises of Derrida's (deconstructive) reappropriation of the Husserlian transcendental standpoint, especially with an eye for what his (perhaps only strategic) loyalty to Husserl entails for a host of alternatives that percolate throughout contemporary philosophy: pragmatisms of all stripes, various holisms, the critique of Cartesianism, as well as the linguistic turn. Derrida's own aims, his proximity to some kind of transcendental thinking, have long been examined in the literature (most notably by Rodolphe Gasché, Rudolf Bernet, Geoff Bennington, and, more recently, by Paola Marrati and Leonard Lawlor). Yet the extent of Derrida's proximity to Husserl and its implications for the arguments Derrida makes, for his deconstructive operation (as well as for his relation to alternative philosophical or "post-philosophical" approaches), even now have not been grasped in their full concreteness. The first thing I wish to do, then, in what follows, taking Merleau-Ponty's thought as an exemplary counterinstance, is to make clearer still in what Derrida's own program consists: by showing through what specific means Derrida fashions his unique proximity to, and departure from, transcendental phenomenology.

In the second place, however, along with inquiring into what Derrida concretely does, the question of *why* Derrida does what he does must be pursued. Subscribing perhaps finally only in a "strategic" fashion to transcendental phenomenology's absolute, Derrida also breaks with it—expands and goes beyond it—in a word, delimits it. Doing so, he asks specifically about the residue of the privilege of the human that resides within it, about phenomenology's adherence to the human in preference to other animals, as well as finally to life over the technical or machinal, thereby fraying the borders of the human species itself (across the animal realm, as well as dividing it within itself), and finally breaching the limit between the living and dead.

Yet, granting Derrida does something like this, what is less clear is *why* one might do this, why should one want what Derrida wants—especially given that, as we shall see, Derrida's grounds for breaking down these distinctions by no means are the usual ones? Derrida does not, for example, in the case of the animal, privilege those facets of human being usually taken as common with animal existence—the body, feeling, sensibility, so forth—but rather, almost nearly the opposite. What, then, motivates this almost uniquely Derridean desire? In light of what, in the name of what, does Derrida believe that the project, common to almost all phenomenology, of refounding or redisclosing the being of human being, is no longer desirable (or viable)?

Of course, Derrida in his own way attempts to respond to those same developments in contemporary life as do Husserl and the rest of phenomenology. He believes, however, that his predecessors have misdiagnosed the magnitude of our actual situation (the enormous dimensions of the "event" or "transformation" taking place around us), and the true depth of our current need, as well as the radical and unexpected innovations that are demanded or commanded today by responsible thinking.

Yet, do not these very claims—what Derrida once called his radical empiricism, along with his diagnosis of the situation itself—raise the possibility that a still-concealed ground is at work informing Derrida's decisions concerning the human and what the present requires, one that finally brings him back into contact with that very same phenomenological diagnosis that he rejects? After all, the fact that Derrida believes that where we are is such that the conception of humanity has emerged, and that he believes, accordingly, that *contesting* this is what needs to be done, and that doing so will indeed have significant political and historical effects—does not all this indicate that Derrida himself credits the same basic diagnosis of our present as phenomenology (albeit now in the form of something to be spoken against)?

Derrida, that is, also believes the conception of the human is the central issue for our time, with the twist that the surpassing or delimiting of it, not its clarification, offers hope for a new (and perhaps more just) world. Yet is it not at least conceivable that the human has still really not arrived in its own guise, and thus, not the future, but the past, has already brought with it that monstrousness and unthinkability that Derrida declares is still to come? May not a radical shift in terrain akin to the one Derrida believes now underway perhaps have *already taken place*, having as its consequence this proliferation of figures of the human, even as the identity of this being comes to be ever more greatly eroded? Husserl and the rest of phenomenology, as well as Derrida himself, would have thus striven, and necessarily failed, to master this prior emergence: of an inherently monstrous, unresolvable figure of the human, putatively defined by itself alone, one ascendant already with Descartes and Hobbes, Bacon, and Shakespeare?[8]

The past, not the future, may indeed already be marked by a monstrous rupture within the figure of the human, a break emerging under this heading. And Derrida, believing that this is to come, would thus join much of the rest of phenomenology in taking modernity itself essentially for granted, viewing it as distinct from, yet ultimately continuous with, the development of the so-called "European" tradition.[9]

Nevertheless, however this may be—for these are but provisional perspectives—with such questions in mind, I now turn to Derrida's last published treatment of Husserlian phenomenology, *Le Toucher: Jean-Luc Nancy*.[10]

Otherness: Jacques Derrida and Maurice Merleau-Ponty on Touch

In this volume, Derrida, some thirty-three years after he had last made public work devoted to the interpretation of Husserl, returns to the milieu of Husserlian phenomenology, perhaps in part with his own legacy in mind. In the middle sections of this book, Derrida once again mounts a hand-off or interchange between phenomenology and his own project. Thus a chance exists in these pages to see more clearly what operations Derrida performs, what maneuvers he undertakes, in the neighborhood of phenomenological thinking: the character of his specific (and perhaps limit) variation of the phenomenological absolute and how this stands in respect to such thinkers as Merleau-Ponty, as well as Husserl himself. This will eventually permit the deeper question to be pondered: *why* Derrida does what he does, what particular consequences he believes it to have, and what relation he wishes it to bear to the still-unresolved problem of our species, which may finally turn out to be a problem of no species, a problem of no previously known type.

Derrida's 2000 work is primarily devoted to the thought of Jean-Luc Nancy (and particularly to what touches on touch in it). At the center of *Le Toucher: Jean-Luc Nancy* stand five self-proclaimed tangents, gathered under the heading of an "Exemplary History of the Flesh." Derrida, before turning to Husserl's and other specific treatments of touch in the philosophical and phenomenological tradition, at the very outset of this development, characteristically begins by laying out a history and system of (presumably illicit) privilege given to the sense of touch. Derrida—here perhaps oddly, given how many have preceded it—indeed inaugurates a new *centrism*: not that of the voice, nor of sight, nor of hearing (-oneself), but of touch: haptocentrism, from the Greek *haptos*, touch.[11] The supposed immediacy of this sense, the directness of the feelings associated with it (thanks to which the subject is believed inserted into the world), allegedly betray a fealty to the value of presence generally, and also to the notion of the human, to a certain anthropocentrism, especially when touch is associated with the example of the hand.

Indeed, the singling out of touch as bound up with the exemplarity of the hand ultimately returns, Derrida claims, to notions of effort and the will and thus to the personhood of the person. Derrida, accordingly, on this basis further declares that "touch signifies 'being in the world,'" and that implicit in it is "a phenomenology of finitude" (*LT* 161). From the very first, then, Derrida associates themes such as finitude and being-in-the world with an illicit, even if at times concealed, anthropocentrism. From the opening pages of this section, Derrida questions the privilege of touch and the hand of man (and its role in phenomenology), thereby distancing himself from all phenomenological humanism.

Just to give a very brief overview of this section as a whole (before proceeding to Tangents II and III, which are my primary concern): in the remainder of Tangent I, Derrida sketches this tradition of haptocentrism from an historical, rather than a systematic, perspective. Such haptocentrism, he asserts, is traceable back to some of the eighteenth-century *philosophes* (most notably Diderot) up through Maine de Biran, Ravaisson, Bergson, and, more recently, Husserl and Merleau-Ponty, as well as Gilles Deleuze. In turn, Derrida's last two tangents treat contemporary accounts of the theme of touch: they concern, respectively, the quasi-phenomenological approach to touch (and the body) of Didier Franck and the neo-Thomist approach of Jean-Louis Chretien.

With an eye eventually to asking why, in every one of these cases, Derrida wants to question the privilege given touch, the hand, and ultimately humanity itself, I want to first lay out what Derrida puts in its place: that formation, that sort of absolute or quasi-transcendental that his own thought sketches, as well as this formation's relation to Husserlian phenomenology. I will begin with Tangent III, with Derrida's discussion of Merleau-Ponty (to whom Derrida has already referred in Tangent I), since in Merleau-Ponty's work most clearly is found the sort of personalistic or humanistic absolute from which Derrida has always distanced himself: a species of "being in the world" immediately identified with the body, its effort and praxis, and thus one ultimately traceable back to factical human being.

Merleau-Ponty, in passages, some of which are cited by Derrida (*LT* 238), at times denies that his own thought is primarily anthropological, and I am not suggesting that his program presents itself primarily as a description of human being. Nevertheless, as Merleau-Ponty's discussion in *Phenomenology of Perception* of the role of "the spatial level" in perception makes plain,[12] his thought everywhere presupposes a reference back to what he calls the "organic relation of the subject and space"[13] and thus to human being in its bodily facticity, albeit this is not the only, or even primary, characterization that Merleau-Ponty would give to these findings.

Now, Tangent III is the sole place in Derrida's published corpus, at least as far as I am aware, where Derrida makes Merleau-Ponty's thought his primary focus; yet, by directly discussing Merleau-Ponty at this late date, Derrida closes a chapter in his oeuvre, which begins in 1962 in his commentary on Husserl's *Origin of Geometry*. There, it becomes clear, both in his text and in its footnotes, Derrida already had grave doubts about Merleau-Ponty's interpretation of Husserlian phenomenology as a whole, and he also, though less obviously, stood at some remove from Merleau-Ponty's own project.[14]

In 2000 Derrida thus makes explicit a frustration with Merleau-Ponty's thought that careful reading could show to have been at work from the very beginning of his career. And to begin the comparison of Derrida's and Merleau-Ponty's stances, I want to draw attention to an apparent oddity in Derrida's treatment of Merleau-Ponty's Husserl reading. Derrida, before turning to Merleau-Ponty, when speaking of Husserl's own text, contests the privilege that Derrida believes Husserl gives to touch over all the other senses. Husserl, in the course of bringing forth for the first time the Body proper (*Leib*, "animate matter," or "flesh") and a specifically animal nature, distinguishes touch from the rest of the senses, insofar as touch alone seems to supply at once a reference to the subject's own body as a physical, material thing, while also presenting this entity as one in which sensations (of a unique type) are found and lived.

This is the well-known "double apprehension,"[15] as it is called, of my body as both a thing and as itself a locus of experiencings, of sensings—a double apprehension that Husserl claims is absent from sight (where my sensing and a thing sensed—even the eye, my bodily sensory apparatus—are never grasped simultaneously), and which paves the way to the emergence of Body as such, of a new type of entity in nature: Body, *Leib*, itself a spatiotemporally individuated *thing*, yet one that has localized feelings and sensings uniquely providing some of its attributes.

More specifically still, when one of my hands touches the other (which is indeed Husserl's example), the touched hand, Husserl asserts, is disclosed as both a thing experienced like other bodies, but also as itself a site of sensations wholly different from the sensory qualities pertaining to things belonging to a simply material nature. The feelings that I find in my hand at this moment are not given through adumbrations or profiles (*Abschattungen*), as are the properties or qualities of material things. Instead, they manifest themselves as absolutely present and localized, as immediately belonging to the hand, as being the "hand itself," thereby giving birth to this wholly new sort of entity: a living body (*Leib* or Body) as opposed to a merely material or physical body (or *Körper*).[16]

Of course, as Derrida points out in passing (*LT* 200), no sensing of any sort is ever given through adumbrations: no seeing is given as something experienced through profiles, as are the colors and extensions seen belonging to a surface of a material thing. Yet the privilege given to touch consists, then, in such sensing also being somehow *immediately referred to a body*, experienced as *spread across it*, thus at this moment allowing for constitution of the Body proper (*Leib*) in its specificity. And at issue in Derrida's own reading will be the form this reference takes, under what conditions this discovery or disclosure of the lived and hence living body is conceivable. How is body of any sort to be integrated into that immediate self-awareness characteristic of lived experience as such? Does the inclusion of the body draw into doubt the purity of such awareness? Does it show this awareness, this consciousness to be always already affected by an other, its seeming unicity and privilege thereby becoming questionable?[17]

Now Derrida, in the face of this analysis, perhaps somewhat unexpectedly, insists on the role sight must play at this juncture. In an argument that will be rehearsed further below, sight (or at least the access to the non-egoic exteriority it implies), must already be at work, Derrida claims, for these localized sensations in their singularity to be discovered—in part since without this reference to exteriority, to something other than myself, there could be no grasping of my Body as a body in the first place, and thus no double apprehension. My Body (*Leib*), according to Derrida, has reference back to body (*Körper*, matter), and thus presupposes sight, as the sense that here correlates with access to the externality of the world (ultimately making available a pure difference or hetero-affection). Derrida thus contests the haptocentrism that he believes informs Husserl's text at this moment (*LT* 200).

What proves odd, however, the puzzle to which I wish to point, is this. When Derrida turns to Merleau-Ponty's account of this same analysis, Derrida appears to criticize Merleau-Ponty for insisting on the very same thing: for bringing in sight, for making it coeval with touch, at the moment that the lived body first comes to be constituted. Discussing Merleau-Ponty's article "The Philosopher and his Shadow," Derrida states "although, following *Ideas* II, Merleau-Ponty seems to start from it [touch], he has already made associated with it, upon the same plane . . . the example of sight" (*LT* 212). Compare this to Derrida's own refusal a little earlier to sanction any "limit" "between a pure auto-affection of the body proper . . . of touching-touched and, on the other side, a hetero-affection of the sight or of the eye" (*LT* 205).

To be sure, there exists a hermeneutic aspect of this problem. To restore the whole end of his sentence, Derrida, when criticizing Merleau-Ponty, speaks of Merleau-Ponty's inclusion of "the example of sight" as something "Husserl would have never judged legitimate." Part of Derrida's concern, clearly, is that Merleau-Ponty has misconstrued Husserl's text—a claim that, within certain limits, is probably true, though perhaps not as simple as Derrida makes it out to be. Yet, beyond this, a difference in the stance of both authors toward the role of touch and the body, toward being in the world—finally, toward Husserlian phenomenology as such—also makes itself manifest at this moment of what is perhaps a merely apparent symmetry.[18]

To see why this is so, however—why Derrida criticizes Merleau-Ponty for putting touch and sight on the same plane, even as he appears to do so himself, and thus to see the very different ways in which each of these authors appropriates Husserl's legacy—it is necessary to grasp in more detail Derrida's difference from Husserl when it comes to the role of this sense. Derrida specifically targets Husserl's claim that the sensed qualities that I experience at this moment (when one of my hands touches the other) are radically different in kind from those qualities that refer to states of real, worldly things. The sensations I find in my hand (and that, insofar as my hand is also itself given as a thing, present "properties" or "qualities" of this thing), Husserl insists, are not given through adumbrations or profiles (*Abschattungen*), nor will they eventually come to stand in the larger causal nexus of material nature.

Derrida, in turn, contests the singularity that Husserl imputes to these sensations belonging to my body at this moment. Yet he does not, it must be emphasized, claim that there is no difference between those sensations immediately given as belonging to my Body, and those sensed qualities that present properties of a material thing. He does not deny altogether the validity of Husserl's distinction. After all, the difference between the nonadumbrated, yet localized, sensations (say, those in my hand), from those giving qualities like color (or smoothness) across the surface of a putatively transcendent, material thing, as Derrida recognizes, is finally tantamount to the difference between the experiences of a subject and everything given through these experiences: it is the difference between the subject as such and transcendent being generally. Were this difference simply jettisoned, then, with it would go the entirety of Husserl's philosophical framework.

Derrida argues instead that if the former (the sensations in my hand) are to attain to this immediate self-givenness (upon which Husserl insists), this other system or matrix of sensation (pertaining to the real thing) must continue to be at work at this same moment, at least evanescently, as a pure difference. Not only does the possibility of an object (of a thing that at least gives itself as real and other than myself) necessarily play a role in the initial recognition of my Body *as a body*, as itself in some sense a material thing, but this real thing, and the sensing of it, makes possible the recognition of Bodily sensing *as immediate*, according to Derrida. It makes possible the grasping of the Body in its specific difference from that apprehension which pertains to transcendent things.

More specifically still, at the moment that I discover these lived sensations as immediately mine, Derrida argues, the possibility of some (transcendent) exteriority must already be announced, since these sensations (even those of touch), just *to be* sensations in the first place must be sensations *of* something, of something other than themselves (even if they are also sensations of oneself). The intentional structure of feeling or sensation (and thus of myself as feeling or sensing something else) must already be at work at the moment feeling becomes localized, and this would not be possible were not a thing other than myself at least available in principle, some (transcendent) real at least virtually in play, with its different adumbrative qualities (which, again, is what the work of sight, as opposed to touch, delivers). This difference, this intention toward an other, thus ultimately allows me simultaneously to recognize my own sensations as sensations (insofar as they intend some other generally), and lets appear their difference from those that give transcendent, material things. The relation to an outside in general is what permits me to register my sensations of myself as sensations and as mine, at a moment when my own sort of embodied immediate self-awareness (and eventually embodiedness as such) are in the course of being disclosed.

As Derrida himself writes: "As subtle, furtive, unseizable as it may be, this detour through the foreign outside is at the same time what permits speaking of 'double' apprehension . . . and what permits me, thanks to the test of this singular experience, to distinguish between me and the non-me. . . . For that, it is necessary that the space of the material thing insinuate itself (*se glisse*) as a difference, as the heterogeneity of a spacing, between the touching and the touched" (*LT* 200).

"The space of a material thing," "a difference," "the heterogeneity of a spacing," will thus already have been at work, according to Derrida, at the moment when I discover these sensations in their immediacy as belonging to my body. And this manner of proceeding, which retains Husserl's analysis (the distinction "between me and non-me"), even as it contests it in a unique style, is characteristic of Derrida's way of working generally, especially when it comes to Husserl's phenomenology. However, even as fine a reader as Dan Zahavi has overlooked this feature, objecting to Derrida's interpretation of Husserl, though Zahavi himself otherwise often exhibits a great deal of generosity and sympathy toward Derrida's positions.

Indeed, in *Self-Awareness and Alterity*, Zahavi claims that Derrida, introducing the work of hetero-affection into auto-affection, goes too far and "dissolves and eradicates the very phenomenon being investigated."[19] Derrida, however, never frontally disputes or unequivocally cancels the truth of Husserl's standpoint, to the extent that this very phenomenon of self-awareness would be effaced. Instead, Derrida deploys something like the conceptual equivalent of the "split screen" in cinema. Taking the truth of Husserl's analysis in fact for granted (the truth of "this singular experience [that permits] distinguish[ing] between me and non-me" [*LT* 200]), Derrida asserts a further condition of this insight's being true, a condition only relevant if Husserl's own thought is valid (though also a condition that the structure of Husserl's thought, at least on Derrida's reading, seems not to allow)—this difference and heterogeneity (of a spacing) correlative to the work of sight. Derrida's gesture—deconstruction's operation in its unique specificity—is thus finally as much, perhaps even more, globalizing or expansive than it is limiting or critical. It expands the context, here, of Husserl's remarks to the point of delimiting, undoing, this standpoint, with respect to the privilege that Derrida believes Husserl gives to one possibility rather than the other (here, self-awareness over other-awareness) even as these remarks' *local truth*, their validity in Husserl's own text, is also maintained, and in fact presupposed.

And lest questions about the exemplarity of this instance be raised, lest worries arise about these remarks applying only to Derrida's treatment of Husserl in 2000, it is easy to show that Derrida is in fact reprising an argument that he made in Chapter 6 of *Speech and Phenomena* (the work on which Zahavi focuses), some 33 years ago, albeit now in a different register.[20] There, just as here, Derrida never denies, it is worth underscoring, the singular self-relation at the basis of the Husserlian transcendental subject. In fact, he insists on such auto-affection having priority over any ontological dimension, any subject-substance as such. Nevertheless, such auto-affection must also necessarily have "preceding" it, Derrida argues, just by dint of being, originarily, a relation,[21] a difference—again a radical heterogeneity, or spacing (here keyed to themes of language rather than the body)—that virtually reintroduces the possibility of all that Husserl claimed was excluded, and only subsequently constituted on this subject's basis: namely, things, the real human voice, the words of an empirical language, the indicative work of discourse and so forth. A hetero-affection thus conditions auto-affection without ever canceling it out. And Derrida, accordingly, has always claimed that a previously unidentifiable, wholly radical alterity must have been at work at the heart of Husserl's transcendental constituting subject—an alterity "radical" and "previously unidentifiable," now identified or indicated, however, only thanks to this passage through Husserl's phenomenology (including all its corresponding strictures and stipulations), thus ultimately thanks to Derrida's maintenance of the Husserlian perspective in the unique form that has just been set out.

To return, then, to the above debate, with this outline of Derrida's approach in tow, let me ask in what way Derrida's stance differs from that of Merleau-Ponty, who, as we have already seen, would also introduce the workings of sight and a certain exteriority into Husserl's discussion at this moment. In what way does the Derridean invocation of these themes diverge from Merleau-Ponty's introduction of these seemingly same features?

Derrida differentiates himself from Merleau-Ponty (and to the extent that Derrida sets out Merleau-Ponty's own position, *not* Merleau-Ponty's *interpretation* of Husserl, Derrida's account seems to me accurate and can stand in for Merleau-Ponty's own text), insofar as Derrida rejects the equivalence between other and same that underlies Merleau-Ponty's entire analysis, indeed the *equiprimordiality* that Merleau-Ponty gives to these two moments of sight and touch. Derrida contests Merleau-Ponty's putting sight and touch—and thus the relation to otherness and the relation to self—on exactly the same footing: this gesture in Derrida's eyes including, perhaps finally even enclosing, difference or heterogeneity in the realm of immediacy and identity.

To be sure, one must go slowly here. Just as it was previously stressed that Derrida does not deny all the rights of the immediacy of lived sensing in its own realm, so, too, Merleau-Ponty is not saying that immediacy (and thus identity) is all there is, nor is Derrida suggesting this. As is well known, Merleau-Ponty by no means denies altogether the dimension of difference, exteriority, or of noncoincidence. Instead, as Derrida himself puts it near the end of his discussion, with specific reference to the last section of Merleau-Ponty's *The Visible and the Invisible*, Merleau-Ponty, when laying bare the sphere that he calls "primary being," invites us to think "the coincidence of coincidence and non-coincidence as well as the non-coincidence of coincidence and non-coincidence" (*LT* 239).

Merleau-Ponty does include difference or otherness (here the otherness of precisely those things to which the visible gives access), yet he includes it in a realm characterized by immediacy and thus identity overall. For, alternatively, it could be said: Merleau-Ponty, generally speaking, thinks the identical, but thinks it as what it is only thanks to its immediately opening on to otherness, difference, radical noncoincidence, and heterogeneity. Difference thus has not been eliminated in his notion of a flesh of the world, through which Merleau-Ponty brings about his self-proclaimed "ontological rehabilitation of the sensible." Rather flesh and bodies, Body and bodies are seen as already having interpenetrated one another, as referring to each other in advance, and forming a single, albeit differentiated, even differential, whole—a single, although internally mobile, surface.

And from this very bare outline of Merleau-Ponty's project—his work, his interpretation of Husserl in particular, will be returned to in my next section—I want to take what this indicates about the workings of Derrida's standpoint as well as Merleau-Ponty's, and what it tells us about the different relations of Derrida and Merleau-Ponty to Husserl's transcendental phenomenology in its specificity.

Above all, two comparisons, embracing two distinct, though related reference points, are to be gleaned from this rather surprising intersection of Merleau-Ponty's and Derrida's departures from this same Husserlian text. For, Derrida—to come to the full solution to our conundrum—on the one hand, criticizes Merleau-Ponty's reliance on the very same possibility (sight and exteriority) that he himself invokes, to the extent that Derrida resists making difference, or heterogeneity, in any way present themselves *alongside* the same or the identical. By denying Merleau-Ponty's claim that sight and touch, interiority and exteriority, ultimately the same and the other, are cofounding, Derrida installs a more radically unstable otherness, a more unreliable difference than Merleau-Ponty, without an established identity of its own, and which, in principle, never presents itself as such. Derrida's "spacing" (the placeholder for which is here the work of sight) is at once more primary and more elusive than the otherness, the invisibility, inherent to, and coeval with, visibility in Merleau-Ponty.

But this means, as the foregoing begins to let us grasp, that Derrida's own thought of difference is finally more indebted to the specifically transcendental side of Husserl's phenomenological project than Merleau-Ponty's thinking. Indeed, Derrida's difference is of this privileged sort only because it plays a uniquely *constituting* role. Derrida's retaining of the framework of transcendental constitution permits the production of his so-called "absolute otherness." His radical difference's resistance to presenting itself to, or beside, the same is owed to its position as constituting: as constitutive of what on other terms would be constitutive for it (the transcendent thing in Husserl finally having its own constitution through an embodied self-awareness). Derridean otherness or spacing—here taken from the visual field, with its transcendent or empirical sign subtracted—finally sheds all (empiricist) self-identity by virtue of functioning constitutively, and thus through the retention (and adaptation) of that attitude uniquely achieved through Husserl's own reductions.

By contrast, Merleau-Ponty's thought, as has been clear as early as *Phenomenology of Perception*, ultimately aims at the disclosure of a single, albeit complex, *Ur-phenomenon*, if you will—a radical, internally differentiated and articulated *Urgrund* (supplied through sensibility and tied to the Body as such)—a "primary *being*," which includes at once things ("in their innocence," one might say) along with (our) originary access to them. Merleau-Ponty aims at the revelation of a primordial phenomenon, characterized by a radical facticity, which dispenses with any privilege for intentional or noetic achievement. The possibility of the things and of the taking hold of these things are one and the same; self- and other-awareness at this primary level are equiprimordial—as encapsulated in Merleau-Ponty's talk of "a flesh of the world." Individual consciousness at best only emerges at a later stage and plays only a secondary role, and, in this way, too, Merleau-Ponty's standpoint differs from all transcendental-constitutive (not to mention eidetic) analysis.[22]

Merleau-Ponty's thought, more broadly still, accordingly, implicitly (and in fact explicitly) simply rejects Husserl's attainment of a constitutive transcendental standpoint in its specificity.[23] Replacing, as it does, Husserl's more elaborate, logically oriented methodological schemas, with considerations stemming from the (human) body and sensibility, Merleau-Ponty clearly doubts that Husserl's thinking *can* free itself from the human dimension, from the facticity of our embodied being in the world. Merleau-Ponty's own understanding of the absolute, especially in his late thought, thus quietly sets aside Husserl's fulfillment of the age-old aim of philosophy to obtain a standpoint other than the human as articulated through the transcendental reduction (even if this possibility, the reduction, for Husserl proves immanent to this being). Despite its other achievements, which doubtless are vast, Merleau-Ponty's is finally but a quasi-absolute: the facticity of human existence in its phenomenal manifestation turning up as a last (or first), instance behind which we cannot get, rather than a standpoint of genuine, comprehensive clarity.

And this may well be at least one motive for Derrida's critique of phenomenological humanism (especially in the shape it takes in Merleau-Ponty). Derrida's own thought, as we have seen, explicitly retains just this side of Husserl's project, its transcendental (and a-human) dimension. Thus at least a part of Derrida's own desire, of the erotic that drives his thought, ultimately is comprised by the most traditional of all philosophical urges: namely, to obtain a standpoint more, or other, than the human one (one no longer entirely conditioned by our biology, the societies in which we live, the rest of our all-too-human starting points). Though Derrida would also make this standpoint open outward without limits, nevertheless, the fact remains that Derrida, more than many other post-Husserlian thinkers, has remained loyal to this trans-human feature of all philosophy.

Of course, such a characterization of Derrida's endeavor is highly provocative, Derrida being thought most of all to have abandoned—or at least sketched the closure of—philosophy's project. In addition to Derrida's own repeated insistence that he is responsible to philosophy and wants to "remain a philosopher,"[24] as well as the problems raised by the ultra-skeptical side of his project as set out in Chapter 1, numerous ways of exiting or departing from supposedly more authoritative or even authoritarian modes of thought exist, however. Different economies with different commitments necessarily accompany these various departures;

and indeed, why assemble the enormously elaborate apparatus that Derrida brings to these questions, if at stake is simply the rejection of reason, the abandonment of any attempt to engage in fundamental reflection? Especially today, are not many more simple egresses from philosophy available than that mounted by deconstruction: from positivism to scientism, from historicism to empiricism, from decisionism to faith?

One thread of Derrida's work thus always insists on retaining philosophy's most traditional aim, as has been made manifest by the comparison of his appropriation of Husserl's legacy with that of Merleau-Ponty's, who in other ways is certainly the more traditional, cautious, or even reasonable thinker. Yet this claim raises a new question, along with the standing one concerning Derrida's motives overall (since further motives doubtless exist for why Derrida takes this stance toward the human and the more-than-human—especially in the unique form that we find it here—some of which have already been mentioned and to which I shall return): namely, whether Derrida *can* do what he wants, whether he *can* achieve the kind of program that has so far been sketched. Does Husserl himself successfully arrive at a radically transcendental dimension, beginning from human experience, and the phenomenological reduction, such that Derrida *can* build upon (and unbuild) it in the unique fashion that has been reviewed here? Now that the singular form of departure from Husserl that Derrida envisions—so different from that of Merleau-Ponty and almost everyone else in the phenomenological tradition—has emerged, the question can be posed as to whether the human and the transcendental sides of experience really are able to be satisfactorily distinguished from one another in Husserl's phenomenology, and subsequently put in a still-more-complex relation in Derrida's deconstruction, such that Derrida's own undertaking is truly possible.

Other Others: Derrida, Merleau-Ponty, and Husserl on Intersubjectivity

To sketch an answer to these questions (in respect to Husserl's thought, solely as taken up within the confines of *Ideas* II, which may well not be where *Husserl's* final answers are to be found),[25] I want to continue my reconstruction of Derrida's criticisms of Merleau-Ponty, now returning to the issue, postponed above, of the correctness of Merleau-Ponty's Husserl interpretation. Granting that both Derrida and Merleau-Ponty add sight to touch at the moment of the lived body's constitution, thereby inflecting Husserl's descriptions toward their own thinking, who is actually right about Husserl's intentions at this juncture? This is an especially pressing issue, as it concerns the moment when Husserl sketches the constitution of the human being as such—which is here necessarily the embodied human being. For, were Husserl himself successfully able to achieve this, the status of his transcendental-constitutive perspective would indeed be secure. In order to capture the meaning-achievements constitutive of humanity in the totality of its aspects, after all, Husserl necessarily must occupy a standpoint beyond the human itself; he must have discovered a site for his own thinking no longer bound to humanity in its facticity, to its accidents and predicaments, and thus be able to survey the structural and genetic principles of these traits.

Indeed, the importance of this development for Husserl's own thought and for phenomenology generally—and with that, the broader context for Derrida's and Merleau-Ponty's interpretative dispute—can be further gleaned from the claims made by Merleau-Ponty about this moment in his essay "The Philosopher and His Shadow." Merleau-Ponty stresses the factical and human side of Husserl's analysis, and for him *Ideas* II thus signals a deep shift, almost a revolution in Husserl's thinking—one supporting Merleau-Ponty's own understanding of phenomenological practice.

Ideas II, more specifically, Merleau-Ponty declares, represents a significant departure or break from Husserl's earlier standpoint in respect to just this theme of constitution that has so far already proved critical. "*Ideen* II brings to light a network of implications," Merleau-Ponty explicitly states, "in which we no longer sense the pulsation of a *constituting consciousness.*"[26]

Husserl, for Merleau-Ponty, inaugurates something close to a new methodology at this moment in *Ideas* II, or at least significantly alters his old one. Husserl breaks with his earlier concern with constitution, and moves much closer to Merleau-Ponty and his own "Urphenomenology," his disclosure of "primary being," as already characterized above. Merleau-Ponty in part telegraphs this shift when, speaking of certain "pre-givens" that putatively "could not possibly reach completion in the intellectual possession of a noema," he asserts that "Husserl's thought is as much attracted by the haecceity of nature as by the vortex of absolute consciousness."[27]

The test case for this, however, the crux of Merleau-Ponty's assertion that Husserl has abandoned or exceeded constitution for a different type of description and concern, rests on Husserl's treatment of intersubjectivity, of the givenness of others to me in *Ideas* II. My body "as a universal," Merleau-Ponty argues, here furnishes a hitherto unrecognized "aesthesiological dimension." This dimension, in turn, permits the Other to present itself to me within my immediate *co-presence* (at once presence to myself *and* to things other than myself), in a way that gives the other to me with the same *immediacy* as myself—within this same co-presence, this same "coincidence of coincidence and non-coincidence," as it was put by Derrida above. Accordingly, glossing Husserl's own statement at the end of section 46 of *Ideas* II that the other presents itself at this moment "without introjection," "*ohne 'Introjecktion,'*" Merleau-Ponty takes this as saying that for Husserl others are given to me exactly as I am given to myself: i.e., in an *immediate* manifestation without further intervention.[28]

In turn, to come directly to Derrida's specific objection to Merleau-Ponty's gloss, Husserl, on Derrida's view, at this moment is really describing how the other is *given to herself* or himself. Merleau-Ponty, according to Derrida, has indeed misread, or is intentionally misrepresenting, Husserl's analysis of intersubjectivity—in particular, Husserl's phrase "without introjection." What Husserl really means, Derrida insists, is that the other is given to her- or himself, just as I am given to myself, without introjection. Moreover, such givenness is owed precisely to the work of analogy (which Merleau-Ponty explicitly discredits[29]) and to the labor of introjection on the part of the self—precisely on account of those specifically constitutive operations that Merleau-Ponty claims have been excluded or superseded in this version of Husserl's account of intersubjectivity.

For Merleau-Ponty indeed views Husserl's *Ideas* II discussion of intersubjectivity not only as signaling a relatively novel methodological standpoint, but also as a way out of those problems long associated with Husserl's better-known treatment of intersubjectivity in *Cartesian Meditations* V.[30] Such a readaptation of his treatment of intersubjectivity is part of the reformation of Husserl's thinking that Merleau-Ponty believes he discerns here. In Merleau-Ponty's reading, the account of intersubjectivity in *Ideas* II specifically resolves those dilemmas concerning the ego's relation to the other, the alter ego, in Husserl's thought that at one time were famous—problems that Heidegger broadly implied at the outset of *Being and Time* (in the course of arguing for an alternative starting point for all phenomenology), and which, with rather different aims in mind, were famously set out in greater detail with reference to Husserl's own discussion in *Cartesian Meditations*, by Alfred Schutz, in his well-known 1950 essay "The Problem of Transcendental Intersubjectivity in Husserl."

In these instances, as well as in other related ones (as we are about to see, Derrida aptly calls Merleau-Ponty's position "typical"), no constitution, indeed no genuine experience, of the other is really possible, it is maintained, if one starts from Husserl's transcendental perspective.

Rather, for an other to genuinely appear, he or she, in effect, must have *already* appeared: some common ground must already be at work (back behind which the subject cannot get—here provided by the facticity of the human body), which makes possible his or her appearance along with my own. A more radical (but also common, and thus necessarily non-apodictic) starting point must precede both the other and the I, thereby permitting us to encounter one another on the same "playing field," allowing for an existential symmetry between I and other, thanks to which alone the other genuinely manifests itself as another person or self.

The question of the other, of Husserl's treatment of intersubjectivity, has indeed perennially been a touchstone for the viability of Husserl's constitution project as a whole, for the validity of the specific form that transcendental inquiry takes in Husserl's hands, at the center of which stands the putatively unique access of a solitary subject to apodictically evidentiary experiences. And due to the overarching significance of this question for Husserl's own project, Derrida's response to Merleau-Ponty's interpretation proves as telling about his own project and his relation to Husserlian phenomenology generally, as well as to the theme of intersubjectivity in particular, as Merleau-Ponty's does about his.

To further pursue, then, Derrida's response: after deeming Merleau-Ponty's standpoint "paradoxical and typical" ("typical, because [it has] often given rise to similar gestures, notably in France. . . ." [*LT* 218]), and now laying out this paradoxical side, Derrida, doubtless to the surprise of many, explicitly affirms the rights of "a Husserl more classical, more egocentric" than any Merleau-Ponty presents (and than the one that most other heterodox phenomenologists would embrace). To be sure, Derrida's specific claim—and this is the "paradox" in his view—is that pursuing a different, supposedly more authentic version of the other than Husserl's (especially as presented in *Cartesian Meditations* V), going the way of Merleau-Ponty, Schutz, Heidegger, and so many others "risks . . . re-appropriating the alterity of the other more surely, more blindly, more violently than ever" (*LT* 218). Derrida himself thus affirms the "Husserlian prudence [which] always remains ahead of us," while aiming, he claims, at a still-more-dissymmetrical otherness of the Other, a more radical foreignness of other selves than that at which these authors arrive (*LT* 218).

Nevertheless, whatever one makes of Derrida's construal of intersubjectivity as such (I tend to disagree with Derrida about which scenario more genuinely allows for the other to appear as other), his decision clearly stands or falls with the rest of Husserl's approach to phenomenology. Husserl's analysis indeed begins from the other's *appearing to me* (the transcendental ego) as an *other*, from the apodictic experiences that *constitute* another (transcendental) self for the Ego (constitute it through meanings and as meaningful, of course, not create it out of nothing). Affirming this approach, against an entire tradition of dissenters, Derrida thus sides with Husserl in a debate whose scope finally takes in Husserl's philosophy as a whole. Derrida affirms Husserl's approach resting on a pure transcendental self (something he has always done, with the exception of his singular style of contestation set out above, as we have seen, when it comes to intraphilosophical questions). In particular, Derrida explicitly affirms the "classical," "egocentric," Cartesian side of Husserl's thought—and whatever Derrida may subsequently make of this, he cannot produce anything still more novel or radical without having first endorsed Husserl's stance on the constitution of intersubjectivity (and thus toward transcendental phenomenology in its totality) over and against a range of alternative, competing positions.[31]

Broaching the themes of the Other and intersubjectivity in a Husserlian and phenomenological context, it is impossible today not to refer to the thought of Emmanuel Levinas and his vast contribution to this topic. A review of Derrida's tangled, shifting stance toward Levinas and the latter's treatment of this very theme would, unfortunately, take me too far from my present concerns. Suffice it to note, however, that Levinas's own teaching appears to fall between the two stools so far set out (and thus perhaps also exceeds them both): namely, one position in which an other who has the same priority as the I, arrives as soon as the I, and accordingly is understood through the category of immediacy and, perhaps necessarily, some kind of presence (*pace* Merleau-Ponty); and a second approach, in which the other is not simply symmetrical, not thought as immediate and thus not as present or copresent, yet this is accomplished only thanks to some trace of its having been constituted by an absolute transcendental ego. By contrast, Levinas's understanding of the other views her or him as immediate, as already there alongside the self, in fact as preceding any securely self-identical egological stratum (as in the first scenario); yet, like the second, Levinas takes the other as not fully present or given in presence, as infinitely other, different, and thus escaping the hegemony of the same. Accordingly, Derrida, in his later writings, was able to side with this last aspect of Levinas's thinking that emphasizes the other's alterity, while staying relatively silent about the former aspect and the dismantling of the authentic constitutive transcendental-phenomenological perspective that it entails. Nevertheless, it is worth recalling that in "Violence and Metaphysics" the analysis that has just been in question, Husserl's account of the constitution of the other through analogy and appresentation in

Cartesian Meditations V, was brought forward by Derrida explicitly to contest what he then took to be Levinas's critique of Husserl—Levinas indeed taking Husserl himself still to be too closely tied to a theoretism and a model of intuition based on sight that ultimately rendered persons and things equivalent, despite all in Husserl's own thinking that mitigated against this analysis.[32]

However this may be, staying now exclusively with Derrida's and Merleau-Ponty's Husserl interpretations, and having noted their profoundly different understanding of Husserl's account of intersubjectivity in *Ideas* II, who is in fact correct, at least about this passage: Derrida or Merleau-Ponty? Does Husserl here broach a new, or at least an alternative, account of intersubjectivity, and thereby take at least a step toward a renunciation, or alteration, of his founding methodological precepts—a step many other interpreters, some perhaps more cautious than Merleau-Ponty, have in some form also believed Husserl took around this time?[33] Or does Husserl, *pace* Derrida, offer essentially the same account of intersubjectivity at this moment in *Ideas* II as he does in *Cartesian Meditations* V—a claim not unlikely on its face, since this latter work was written some fifteen or twenty years after the text that currently concerns us?

Recourse to Husserl's own text must be had to answer these questions, a recourse that should resolve the issue of the status of Husserl's project in its own right—a recourse especially necessary, since Husserl's treatment of intersubjectivity is decisively more complex at this moment in *Ideas* II, I would suggest, than either Merleau-Ponty or Derrida credits it with being.

To be sure, in *Ideas* II Husserl doubtless does invoke those aspects of his approach to intersubjectivity that Merleau-Ponty denegates and that Derrida stresses—namely, analogy, appresentation, and introjection (which, for Derrida, at least, point the way toward a still more radical alterity or otherness of the Other). With this theme of other subjects in mind, Husserl thus begins this section by stating outright that certain kinds of beings cannot themselves be given in the sort of "primal presence" that characterizes straightforward thing-perception.[34] Accordingly, he goes on to sketch how the solipsistic, yet partially embodied ego—its sensibility first localized through touch and its Body disclosed in the fashion canvassed above—encountering another material thing apparently akin to its Body, will transfer over to it the localization that it experiences of its own various sense-fields.[35]

Husserl is not, then, so far from that schema of the constitution of other subjects that he lays out elsewhere (which is, again, no surprise, given the order of Husserl's treatments of these themes). Nevertheless, matters are further complicated (especially when it comes to the citation in question) because, as Merleau-Ponty rightfully stresses, it is the constitution of other *embodied* subjects, eventually of the *embodied human being* as such, that is under discussion. At issue is really the constitution of what Husserl clearly identifies (though neither of his interpreters do explicitly) as mundane, not transcendental, intersubjectivity.

To be sure, "the point of departure" for imputing to the other not only my own sensory experiential capacity but what is described as an "interiority of psychic acts" remains, as Derrida insists, "a transferred co-presence" of psyche and Body.[36] Yet, having already spoken of the contribution that the other makes to my experience even of my Body (I would not have a grasp of all of it, e.g. of my back, without the other), Husserl now takes a further step and next describes an open-ended network of experiences whereby what he sometimes calls "spiritual interiority" comes to be *fused* with the other's bodiliness. A "system of indications" takes shape (however initiated, including, here, indeed in part by introjection),[37] which eventually presents the psychic life of the other in its *immediacy*, according to Husserl, through (a special kind of) corporeality. The other's Body ultimately functions—as will eventually also its words—as an *immediate* expression, a direct manifestation, of its personhood or subjectivity. Husserl thus concludes this section by stating that the other confronts me (as a spiritual or psychic being) just as I manifest myself: i.e., immediately and "*without introjection*," as *Merleau-Ponty* indeed suggests.[38]

When it comes to the passage in question, Merleau-Ponty appears right, though how this relates to the larger issues, to the question of whether Husserl thereby has abandoned or deeply modified his doctrine of (transcendental) constitution, is still not clear. Does Husserl's emphasis on the Body, the person, and a coequal or symmetrical plurality of subjects in some fashion signal the opening of a new path in Husserl's thought generally, as Merleau-Ponty also claims? Or, on the contrary, does Husserl maintain his original transcendental constitution perspective throughout—and indeed *can* he maintain it throughout—in the form that Derrida identifies it, and which Derrida's own project both further radicalizes and uniquely contests?

The key to these issues finally proves to be the rather startling role played in Husserl's thought by the fusion of the other's psyche and his or her Body (giving to me other embodied persons or human subjects in a perhaps novel kind of immediacy); for, on Husserl's account, this fusion makes possible even the awareness of my own self as fully embodied. It founds the constitution of my own psychic life as bound up with a Body, ultimately the constitution of "myself" as a *human* being, *a human person*. Only in the face of fully embodied *others*, Husserl insists, only by confronting true human subjects localized in every respect, does the partially embodied solipsistic ego (from the vantage point of which Husserl's own analysis has been proceeding) first also conceive of itself, indeed constitute itself, in this manner.

The experience of the other is thus founding of the self in the case of what Husserl calls "the embodied subject," in respect to a specifically human subjectivity, and this result, it should be noted, is necessary for the broader aims of this section and of Part 2 of *Ideas* II as a whole.

Section 46 of *Ideas* II, which is the focus of Merleau-Ponty and Derrida's dispute, is intended to show, after all, how embodied "souls," true persons (both selves and others) first emerge. In turn, this prepares the work of the next section, 47, the final section of Part 2. This section, bringing to completion Part 2 as a whole, sets out the constitution of the human animal, of the biological human species as such—the psychophysical unity "man," as studied by the natural sciences.

Now, the nuance not to be overlooked in Husserl's analysis with regard to his own intentions in *Ideas* II is that the constitution of *embodied* persons (of the embodied self by way of other selves) in the order of his argument *precedes* the constitution of the biological species, of the human animal as such. It is on account of this, because the constitution of "our" biological species comes about on the basis just set forth, because it is owed to the emergence of *persons* in their specificity—finally to expression, and to the ability of "cultural" objects to present "personalistic" significances in a special kind of embodied immediacy[39]—that Husserl can (or at least can attempt) to balance and coordinate the sphere of persons (and society and culture) with that of the naturalistic sciences, which is indeed one central task of *Ideas* II as a whole.

The overarching aim of *Ideas* II is, in fact, to clarify the scope of the various disciplines by presenting the essential insights and constitutive achievements underlying each broad region (material nature, animal nature, the personal world) to which they appertain. And thus at stake at the above moment in Husserl's own text is the possibility of giving the natural sciences and their intrinsically deterministic view of human being their due with respect to life and the human, even as the rights of the person (and the humanistic disciplines, the *Geisteswissenschaften*, devoted to the study of this theme) are preserved.

More specifically still, because the constitution of the person, my Body, as giving myself and others in (expressive) immediacy *precedes* (and makes possible) the biological unity of the human being, of the so-called psycho-physical subject, Husserl *can treat as legitimate* explicitly causal hypotheses pertaining to human being as a part of nature (of the neurophysiological, genetic, and evolutionary type—so much more powerful in our own day than in his), while still preserving the descriptions and evidences pertaining to the personal, or social (or the everyday) world, including that imputation of freedom and agency that phenomenally appears to characterize this latter domain. For Husserl indeed wishes to grant a latitude to empirical inquiry, to natural scientific inquiry into neurophysiology, brain chemistry, and so forth, even as he retains, in one sense as more fundamental, the true contours of everyday social life (including the intrinsic meaningfulness and value of Others, of actions, as well as equipment and artifacts of all sorts). And he is able to do this precisely because the constitution of the natural subject, of the human as a biological or animal species, depends on the person, and, because, as we have just seen, the Body as a fully human body appears first as an expression.

To this extent, moreover, there is a way in which Merleau-Ponty's larger claims are not simply wrong: Husserl does present the Body and the meanings it brings with it, myself and other persons, as a new kind of phenomenological absolute, at least in respect to the other so-called regional disciplines. The sphere of persons, of others and myself—our identities fused with, and manifested by, our Bodies—is presented by Husserl as a sphere of phenomenal freedom that precedes, even as it does not cancel, the rights of all scientific investigations and hypotheses.

Yet this same anticipation at work here, the upsurgence or emergence of the person and her realm prior to the constitution of animal nature as such, also poses problems for Husserl's transcendental constitutive perspective overall, a perspective that, as far as I can tell, contra Merleau-Ponty, Husserl does (and, as we shall see, must) continue to maintain. Despite Merleau-Ponty's suggestion (and here Derrida's broader criticism of Merleau-Ponty's interpretation is on target), Husserl by no means gives up his transcendental constitutive standpoint in this work, renounces the ego and its privileges, and the subject solipsistically conceived as a privileged sphere of evidence. Subtending this vantage point—to which the foregoing analyses are in fact owed, including those that Merleau-Ponty appropriates—is a concern, noted at the outset of this piece, that runs like a fault line, or at least a question mark, across the architecture of *Ideas* II: namely, whether and how the human, the embodied person, and the biological species *can* finally be coordinated with Husserl's own transcendental perspective.

The order of presentation, the *Darstellung* of Husserl's entire analysis in respect to this problem, indeed appears odd or skewed. Three major regions (again, material nature, animal nature, the personal world) are studied by Husserl in *Ideas* II, yet the relation among them—which region is constitutive, or founding, of which—is never made fully clear. As we have just witnessed, the person in its specificity (myself and others in the cultural or social world) emerges before the human animal, raising questions (no matter how salutary this otherwise may be) not only about the order of Husserl's own analysis (since this appearance runs contrary to the order of *Ideas* II as a whole, in which the constitution of the species precedes the person), but, also, more profoundly, concerning what a human person is and how it is related to the human species and its own body. Can personal identity and personhood truly be independent of these last, of the *body* and the species? Is the Body a fully formed social or cultural phenomenon *before* being a biological one, such that the latter, the biological may indeed be constituted on the former's basis? Husserl, it should be noted, claims more than once in *Ideas* II that the Body itself as found in the personal world, as specifically belonging to a person, could as well be a phantom—a spatial presentation wholly without any of the causal linkages constitutive of our experience of natural things.[40] Is the personal, social, and political sphere, even in its mere meaningfulness, however, really as free from material or natural necessity as such an account suggests?

Moreover, a related concern pertaining to the architectonic of Husserl's text surfaces in Part 1 of *Ideas* II (the part devoted to the constitution of material nature). There, again, the human animal (or at least this same embodied community of mundane subjects, as constituted at the end of Part 2) plays a critical role.[41] Indeed, in an extraordinary development, which, perhaps surprisingly, resonates with the approach that positivism would soon be taking to these same issues, Husserl argues that physicalistic nature, a nature true in itself, subject to laws, and stripped of all sensuous properties, only emerges thanks to jumping off from an awareness of others like me and of our shared Bodily constitution.[42]

The awareness of our common mutual embodiment, of something like ourselves as a species, more specifically, according to Husserl, permits our own factical constitution *to be varied*, to be imagined otherwise—thereby yielding a nature in itself, conceived apart from all sensuous predicates. The subject's recognition of its shared embodied being, Husserl claims, allows its normed, and normally, functioning senses to be viewed as but one *possible* mode of relating to things. Thanks to this self-variation, the possibility and project of an entirely nonsensuous, mathematized description of true being (based only on primary qualities) emerges, itself having reference back to the embodied or human subject in the entirely singular form of explicitly dispensing with it and going beyond it.[43]

Yet this highly provocative analysis nevertheless raises problems (akin to the ones set out above), since, up to this moment, the reference point for Husserl's own discussion has indeed been the subject solipsistically conceived, the *solus ipse* (a prototype of what he will later call the monad, the subject reduced to its sphere of ownness). As we already know, this subject in its specificity is not, as such, embodied: it is not even, properly speaking, a human being. Husserl himself in Part 1, emphasizing this difference from any actual, embodied human subject, in fact claims, in some rather stark and haunting language, that the abstraction carried out to reach it does not "consist in the mass murder of the people and the animals of our surrounding world, sparing one human subject alone,"[44] thereby driving home the point that this perspective is not equivalent to that arrived at by starting from a real human being or human subject that is somehow subsequently isolated from all others.

Yet, and here emerges the difficulty, insofar as this analysis of physicalistic nature at the end of Section 1 makes reference *to the human body in its facticity* and an interpersonal awareness of ourselves as a species, and since it is only thanks to this that there is (physicalistic) nature in the first place, will Husserl, coming to *the Body (Leib)* later (in the sections that we have already discussed above), not be turning to the constitution of an entity that has already here been at work in a *constitutive* capacity, insofar it founds such a nature? Will he not now be attempting to set forth the constitution of the embodied person (ultimately, humanity), on the basis of a nature to the constitution of which it has at least partially already contributed in some fashion?[45] And does not this, along with the analogous development just reviewed (in which the human person came before the human animal and thus contributed to the constitution of what precedes it) bring into question the stability of Husserl's constitutive perspective here? Does it not shake one's confidence that Husserl *can* successfully separate out his transcendental-constitutive perspective from a human one (here at the point of maximum pertinence, when the constitution of the human as such is in question)—disturb our belief that the human as such can have its constitution traced out from a perspective necessarily other than its own, from a solitary, ego-centered, ultimately transcendental vantage point?

Serious difficulties seem to accompany Husserl's attempt to separate his transcendental constitutive standpoint from the human, as well as relate them, though this is by no means a reason, let me emphasize, to cease investigating Husserl's own deepest intentions (which again these pages may not fully reflect).[46] Nevertheless, contra Merleau-Ponty's implied view, within the covers of this volume itself, the task that Husserl set himself throughout *Ideas* II, the setting of the limits to the disciplines and the establishment of their compatible yet distinct meanings, seems to me to stand or fall with the status of this transcendental perspective as such and its claim to lay bare a more primordial fundamental dimension of an absolute ego, to found an absolute science (of the human), as well as this work's ability to furnish *eide* or essential descriptions pertaining to these.

In terms of the stage of Husserl's description that has just been reached, Husserl himself concedes that the extent to which psychophysical causality does hold sway over the personal—to which mind and intellect may be accounted for from a naturalistic perspective—is itself an empirical question.[47] Thus, the sole limit set here to the final incorporation of the one by the other, of the realm of "spirit," as Husserl calls it, or that of the person by physicalistic science, depends on the ultimate validity of Husserl's own philosophical standpoint, specifically its transcendental-constitutive dimension over and beyond any merely phenomenological description. The personalistic attitude only permanently retains the priority that Husserl so resoundingly assigns it insofar as it is finally traceable back to the working of the cogito, itself secured as a realm of freedom and the root of all meaning (including that of the thinking human subject) by the transcendental-phenomenological reductions.

Merleau-Ponty's alternative stance (and this seems to possibly hold for all appeals to the lifeworld, including for all pragmatisms), itself lacks any real force, apart from the further "vertical" structure that Husserl imparted to his own findings (or believed he was able to reveal there) over and against that "horizontal" one, that Ur-phenomenal surface of "primary being" that Merleau-Ponty privileges. What is in question in those analyses with which Merleau-Ponty is so remarkably in tune (and I by no means wish to cancel the enormous contribution that he has made to grasping aspects of Husserl's thought, nor the depth, sincerity, and intensity of his own vocation to thought) is indeed mundane intersubjectivity, the constitution of embodied human being and dwelling. Yet all appeals to the human, without the transcendental and eidetic dimension, seem finally to lapse into something like tautology in the face of the contemporary disciplines and their knowledges. Is such facticity not everywhere a mere starting point, in fact acknowledged by all, yet not a *result* able to stand up to the more definitive knowledge of what truly is (and who we truly are) that the sciences claim to supply? At best, the facticity of the one (the lifeworld) is simply confronted by the alternate and explicitly more authoritatve facticity of the truths of other. That all scientific achievements are in some way owed to this beginning in fact (at least as long as research is exclusively undertaken by human persons), after all, is certainly true; yet this fact lacks any weight, any final critical or determinative power, without something like the genuinely absolute (and a-human) dimension of Husserl's own project, especially since science itself in its modern form, has arguably taken just this human beginning explicitly into account: its methods and institutions, unlike ancient science, having been designed to approximate an infinite certainty through the common labor of an endless number of essentially finite human beings.

Derrida's Contribution to Phenomenology

Having followed Merleau-Ponty into this aporia, and having seen the unsteadiness of Husserl's own enterprise (at least within the confines of *Ideas* II), Derrida's project and its aims arguably look different. A fuller answer thus may be forthcoming to the question of *why* Derrida wants to do what he does—why, swimming against the currents of the phenomenological tradition, he insists on extirpating the human from phenomenology, while hewing (albeit in a remarkably novel way) to Husserl's specifically transcendental perspective.

To begin with, Derrida's stance clearly comprises a rescue operation of sorts. Derrida's resistance to this stratum of Husserl's discourse (and of the human within phenomenology), whatever else it does, in fact distances him, at least at points, from the very problems just encountered in regard to how the human and the transcendental mix. Taking up the transcendental vector of Husserl's thinking over and against the phenomenological one, Derrida oddly enough effectively purifies Husserl's project of this prior dimension. Making the other, exteriority, alterity, in principle coeval with Husserl's transcendental attempt (without making the latter simply disappear)—making "contamination" a structural-genetic feature of Husserl's absolute—Derrida in a unique fashion actually counters the problem posed by Husserl's own approach to the human in its specificity—namely, the manner in which this referent arguably weighs down and perhaps even threatens to sink Husserl's philosophical enterprise. By deconstructing him, by making this mix-up a necessary feature of all thought, not only does Derrida account for the entanglements of the factical and transcendental that arguably emerge in that work, but Derrida frees Husserl's thought, by further "formalizing" it, from this specific referent (the human), thereby in part preserving Husserl's own radically philosophical, more than human standpoint—this, at a time when such a possibility has indeed come gravely in doubt.

Yet beyond his singular loyalty to a transcendental dimension in a Husserlian sense (to the difference, the nothing, specific to the transcendental reduction), the character of Derrida's alternative intervention, and indeed the aims of deconstruction as a whole, can be more concretely determined, thanks to the larger context that has been restored. As attested by the well-known theme of the transcendental and the empirical, Derrida's own enterprise can also be seen, more broadly still, as an attempt to regain Husserl's working attitude toward the other disciplines. Across his enormously wide-ranging corpus, Derrida has effectively forged for himself a footing akin to Husserl's own modern, open, mobile, one toward contemporary research in its diversity (a posture exemplified, in Husserl's case, by his thinking in *Ideas* II). Such an ability to interact openly and fruitfully with the ever-more-burgeoning empirical disciplines, including the "sciences of man," by contrast, is notably lacking, for example, from Heidegger's thought and his reposing of the question of Being and repetition of its history, which furnishes a far different version of Husserl's transcendental posture.

Of course, it remains doubtful in the present configuration of the disciplines that a purchase may be gotten on them in Husserl's style, simply from above, an overview found from which to coordinate their endeavors in the way that Husserl himself believed (nor even, perhaps, a point below, a fundament or firmament, more radical than them all, revealing a still more radical human truth, à la Merleau-Ponty). The project of deconstruction thus appears as Derrida's own means of attaining a standpoint (on knowledge, its objects, and its ramifications) not belonging to any regional research, one faithfully more or other than human, yet with a sympathetic, healthy, explorative, tenor, consonant with modern knowledge and modern empiricism generally—the latter being an endeavor to which Derrida has always declared himself attracted (even as he holds back from it).

Derrida's relation to empiricism, his specific mode of departure from "phenomenological humanism," exhibits a further, associated motivation, which admittedly has not yet been taken sufficiently into account—Derrida, for example, claiming that he goes this empiricism one better, even as he retains this more than human standpoint allied to Husserl's and the rest of philosophy. While maintaining thought's status, and wishing to intervene in the burgeoning multiplication of the disciplines and technosciences from a standpoint unable to be identified with any single one of them, Derrida also at times embraces those *values* that today seem to command these developments (unfreedom, the machinal, a death greater than life that would not simply be the pinnacle of an exclusively human existence). Derrida, that is, rejects the ethical framework of phenomonological humanism, along with some of its techniques and operations, and what he affirms in its place is, of course, foreign to Husserl himself, as well as to much of the rest of the tradition.

Whether because of his belief that thought cannot withstand the increasing power of this same technoscience, whether in the name of a justice without bounds, or whether for some other reason, Derrida's departure from phenomenological humanism indeed has never been solely tactical. This is most noticeable in his relation to language and writing. For, nearly from the first (after 1957 or perhaps 1962), Derrida has doubted the adequacy of any description of language based on the notion of expression, grounded in a phenomenally free human activity, including the values orienting such a treatment. He has thus particularly (albeit still uniquely) distanced himself from just those reference points that proved pivotal in Husserl's and Merleau-Ponty's analysis of embodied others and selves: expression (and all expressionism), and the power of immediate self-manifestation (of thought or meaning), especially when conceived as emanating from persons and as definitive of the realms of culture, society, and finally spirit.

The exact form of this contestation I will not pursue here, since I have analyzed it elsewhere in depth.[48] Nor do I wish to dwell on what some might see as a suspicious confluence of these last two mentioned traits: the fact that Derrida, insofar as he does maintain the rights of thought in some form, practically speaking continues to assign an enormous privilege to the concrete work undertaken by the extant humanistic disciplines—the work of interpretation, as applied to philosophy, as well as "literary criticism," "philology," and even "rhetoric"—even as, thanks to his rejection of phenomenological and humanistic values, his and related labors are able to appear almost nihilistically ascetic, and thus more "cutting edge," more "rigorous," and more "demystified" than any of even the supposed "hard" sciences.

Instead, having restored this partial lacuna in Derrida's Husserl interpretation, having situated his critique of humanism at this juncture within phenomenology and its debates more generally, and faced with what might seem to some Derrida's restoring with one (transcendental) hand what he removes with the other (human) one—namely, freedom—let me ask, recurring to my introductory remarks, by way of conclusion, whether, in this one instance, when it comes to phenomenology and its humanism, Derrida's doubts are finally radical enough.

Given the foregoing, Derrida's confidence that some actual alternative exists to either embracing a wholly phenomenal and perhaps finally superficial realm of freedom (the lifeworld given in its facticity), or affirming the ever-spiraling work of the empirical sciences—might this not itself be a sign of how deeply Derrida shares this same terrain, that, in his own way, he, too, stands on the same specifically modern ground as the rest of phenomenology, continuing somehow to speak the language of the (Husserlian and Kantian) transcendental (even if, within this setting, he has perhaps gone furthest in calling this ground into question)? Is Derrida's thinking not itself so steeped in the phenomenological tradition as a whole and all that it shares with modern knowing—its starting point in freedom, the subject, the human being—that even he never breaks with this sphere entirely? Perhaps this is one reason Derrida never really worries that a retraction of the human, and the values accompanying it, in their totality, could prevail or be wholly embraced (at least he took ever-fewer safeguards against this as time went on), an outcome that he himself designates from time to time under the heading of the "worst violence."

Over and against Derrida's modern attempt to think our current situation otherwise, still so deeply indebted to Husserl's, is not another more, or other, than human knowledge, today again at least conceivable: one perhaps more ancient and even more "brutal" than anything Derrida himself conceived—that has done with all talk of the subject, and that bears an insight that would not refer back to human life and human ends in any way? Such a standpoint would thus be thoroughly rebarbitive to (1) the transcendental meaningfulness and intentionality that Derrida still shares with Husserl; (2) the revamped historiality and historicity, visible in his talk of an epoch of metaphysics and its closure, abutting on Heidegger's central concerns; and (3) the call for justice that Derrida embraces along with Levinas, Benjamin, and Marx (while Derrida himself, of course, also tweaks all three of these formations and turns them to his own ends)? A thoroughly inhuman knowledge—in the sense of finally having no reference point in human beings at all and whose only insight into human ends would be the impossibility of their being any such—may (again) be thinkable today. Indeed, was not perhaps such knowledge once called metaphysics at certain times and places?[49]

However this may be, however such matters may finally play out (for if possible, it is not clear that such knowledge is true, and if true, desirable), Derrida's overall project at least attempts from one side to bring the phenomenological tradition (perhaps an entire swath of modernity itself) into the greatest proximity (if not total contact) with what is essentially foreign to it, to an unthought that potentially calls it into question as a whole. At the same time, it should now be clear, Derrida has also sought to preserve, even as he transforms, this tradition's specifically transcendental legacy, which is itself the distillation of philosophy's founding hope of a standpoint other, or greater, than a merely human one.

Especially when taken together, then, both of these things seem genuinely to warrant the title of "Derrida's contribution to phenomenology," even his contribution to "thought," or to "philosophy," as a whole. And because this is so, because of the profundity and complexity of Derrida's engagement with this tradition, to what this contribution amounts, Derrida's ultimate legacy, is not only up to us who survive him, who attempt to read his works (and to read faithfully those works, I might add, through which his own thought was formed and which he himself never ceased to read), but is also bound up with what in the future will happen in the humanities, in the disciplines generally, and, indeed, in this strange, new world (of which so many speak), which even now perhaps is ever so slowly aborning. For Derrida was in truth one of those rarest of scholars or writers, of the sort that Heidegger or Nietzsche would have called thinkers: one who articulates problems at such a fundamental level, and in such a comprehensive way, that the fate of his or her reflection remains tied to the continuing enigma of the identity of what we call "human being," and perhaps also even the latter's fate.

Foretellese

Futures of Derrida and Marx

The near-term context of Jacques Derrida's engagement with Marxism in *Specters of Marx* is provided by Francis Fukuyama's *The Ends of History*. This strange, yet provocative book declares—in part on the basis of what was then called the collapse of the Soviet experiment—that the end of history in a Hegelian sense has arrived: that in principle the best form of human governance and the best life for human beings is now known. Fukuyama thus projects the present historical moment (at least in 1992 in a large portion of the West) out onto an eternal or supratemporal plane.[1] The circumstances surrounding us now, the absence of a comprehensive alternative to republican government and liberal economics, Fukuyama argues, are determinative for the future, indeed for all time. In this sense, the end of history has been reached.

The timeless dimension of Fukuyama's analysis bears emphasizing, first of all, since Derrida, in his discussion of Fukuyama in his 1993 *Specters of Marx* (*SM*), surprisingly does almost, if not quite, the same thing. Over and against Fukuyama's claim that Marxism is over, Marxist thought gone by the wayside, Derrida insists that Marxism is as relevant as ever, that it has informed, still informs, and indeed *will* inform all political discussion henceforth, all future politics. Though Derrida's treatment of temporality, Marxism, and Marxism's futures takes place in a number of registers, in at least one of these Derrida as resoundingly casts Marx in a permanent role (albeit as *revenant*, or ghost) as Fukuyama denies this status to him.

For both authors, accordingly, the only significant alternatives appear to be either Marxism or the current order; they omit the fact that the demise of Marxism as a viable political outlook might well someday take place and Fukuyama's conclusion still not be true: other forms of government, novel political and social institutions and arrangements might arise, really owing nothing to Marx, but which would not necessarily be liberal, neoliberal, republican, or even parliamentary-democratic.[2] This possibility of genuinely unforeseen political inventions and arrangements, of discontinuous political and social change (whether desirable or no) thus plays no role in at least this phase of Derrida's rejoinder (there are others where it does), and the absence of this alternative is even more glaring in others' discussions of *Specters*, a work to which a good deal of critical ink has already been devoted.[3]

A number of Derrida's critics, sympathetic to Marx, indeed went even further than Derrida. Not only did they assume the present (and continuing) relevance of Marxism, but, in order to brandish a supposedly more potent, radical, activist Marxism over what they saw as the more milquetoastish, liberal, reformist Derridean alternative, they acted as if Marxism still exists today in the West as an ongoing political struggle, as an active political movement—that, in this sense, Marxism today is no different from what it was when the *Manifesto* was written, when Marx and Engels were alive, or in the nineteen-tens and -twenties in Europe and the U.S.: namely, an organized revolutionary movement aimed at seizing state power in the name of the working class by whatever means necessary.[4] So doing, these writers did as great a disservice to themselves and the Marxist tradition as they did to Derrida's thought, since this tradition, at least since the '50s, has for the most part consistently strived to take into account major changes in historical circumstances and new political experience. In the meantime, many "defenders" of Derrida were guilty of the symmetrically opposite error: basically, they wished to assure us that in some sense Derrida was a Marxist after all—deconstruction a more subtle version of Marxist / post-Marxism—thereby, as we shall see, themselves losing sight of just what is most novel and difficult in Derrida's late political writings, including *Specters*.[5]

To focus on the larger point, this omission of the possibility of new reference points for political struggle, this overhang of previously fixed positions—so massive a sedimentation that its very existence as well as its potential irrelevance cease altogether to be noticed—allows us to begin to gauge the actual pragmatics of Derrida's discourse, the real, not imaginary, politico-theoretical situation in which it took place. Fukuyama's belief in the coming or arrival of a neoliberal "endless summer" (since recanted), Derrida's avowal of a future for Marx, no matter what (and at no matter at how high a price to much actual Marxist doctrine), attests to something different than that an exhaustion of the political imagination informs our time, though this may to some extent be true. Rather, deep difficulties of conception and apprehension today genuinely beset any attempt to frame a clear path forward. Whether ultimately simulacrum or no, a feeling indeed exists that a kind of limit in these matters has been reached, that no truly new political and social alternatives can be propounded—or, if these are to arise, that only subsequent events and unexpected transformations of currently existing systems can bring them forth, not the participants themselves.[6] It is almost as if we find ourselves in a kind of hole in history, where doing for our own time what Marx did for his, framing a meaningful, future-oriented, comprehensive political vision (including new systems, new regimes of rule), envisioning radical political change and the tactics to accomplish it, lies beyond our grasp.[7]

This impasse of our present political imagination, as the prior chapters suggest, has its roots in modernity, which today unfolds exponentially (not, I should emphasize, postmodernity, the common understanding of which as some kind of *Zeitgeist*, as the presumptive totality of what we are today able to think or believe only exacerbates our current disorientation, in my view). The uncertainties existing in regard to modernity's status—as a genuinely universal or merely local transformation, as what sort of mix of history and truth—today, it may be ventured, rain down upon us with a vengeance. This impasse also bears on Derrida's thought, the investigation of which, in the following text, should ultimately lead to a firmer grasp of where we find ourselves, of why insight into these problems is so difficult, and why the rare solutions proferred appear so friable. Derrida's work, more than any of his French peers, singularly envisions our present, in a way that brings it close to much contemporary Marxism (especially in its concern with the materiality and technologies of the transformative causes at work in our current moment), even as other aspects of his interpretation depart from Marx and just about every other contemporary project.

Indeed, a comprehensive account of today, the goal of capturing our present situation in its full complexity—philosophically, technologically, historically, globally—has always been central to Derrida's project.[8] The enormous ambition, the breathtaking scope that rang out in Derrida's 1967 pronouncement in *Of Grammatology*—that what was demanded today was the thought of the greatest totality, at once both history and structure, from a point simultaneously beyond and within it—caught the attention of the world, and it echoes throughout the rest of Derrida's writings, including his last (*OG* 161–62; cf. *OG* 99). Derrida has consistently framed, with the utmost seriousness and rigor, a novel account of our own time, of where we find ourselves, at a moment when this seems vexed, even impossible.

Derrida's vision of the present also ventured, however, to a place no simply historical account went, indeed to where no historical account *can* go; for Derrida's understanding of the current moment necessitated questioning the framework of history itself: such things as linear temporality, periodization, the punctuality and stable identity of any historical present, including our own. The times themselves demand that time itself be thought otherwise, Derrida insisted; our own present, he argued, superordinately flows over into what has never been and never can be present, upending the very historical orientation upon which this notion depends. This insistence reappears in *Specters* with Derrida's repeated Shakespearean declaration that "the time is out of joint" (usually quoted in English in his otherwise French text)—Derrida once more in this work mounting a diagnosis of our present (specifically with respect to its political reference points), alongside the presentation of a structure and / or genesis (the specter "appearing" within such out-of-jointness) that eludes every strictly historical confine (*SM* 17ff, 49).

Now, this characterization of the present, it should emphasized, particularly in the early writings, implies something like a subscription, or at least a considerable proximity, to a thought of the end of history. Derrida often embraces Husserl's version of this notion and Hegel's, even as he alters them.[9] Accordingly, well before penning *Specters*, Derrida already stood in a distinct proximity to Fukuyama's standpoint. In fact, though this has been little noticed, Derrida, in *Specters*, actually states that he experienced "déjà vu" reading Fukuyama's book, precisely because this talk of the end of history (including, with it, the limits of a certain Marxism), supplied the atmosphere in which his own thinking was formed. The "bread of apocalypse was daily in our mouths," as Derrida colorfully puts it, speaking of that epoch (*SM* 14)—a contributing factor indeed being the coming to an end of a certain Marxism (of a version of Marxism as a straightforward political program), thanks to its actually existing versions manifesting an undeniably totalitarian character. These convictions long held by Derrida—of in some way being at history's end, but also Marxism's—thus overlap Fukuyama's stance, such that in *Specters*, Fukuyama ultimately serves as Derrida's own twin or double: that self-specter that Derrida most desires to disavow. Fukuyama indeed plays Max Stirner to Derrida's Karl Marx (according to a characterization of Marx's relation to

Stirner Derrida offers [*SM* 139]) in an ongoing battle over the right way to think the ends of history and of Marxism.

It is not this battle nor these differences, however, though differences there surely are, upon which the following will focus. Rather, my subsequent discussion targets a topic abutting Derrida's unique understanding of the present as possibly bearing history's end: namely, the future, the future in the plural, "futures" as found in Derrida's writing. Due to his unique understanding of our present as at once historical and not—owing to the demand, inscribed within our now, to turn away from the shaping value of presence, and thereby distance oneself from the present's historical identity—the future as a category, from the beginning of Derrida's thought, has itself registered as something of a question mark. How, after all, can Derrida have continuing access to this term, to "the future," once the present has been understood by him in this split fashion (both historical and not) and the end of history-as-it-has-always-been-known declared? How can any notion of a collective future cohabitate with the trope or theme of an end or closure of history (however the latter may be understood)?

To be sure, Derrida was never simply paralyzed by this problem. Early on, he affirmed a quasi-Foucauldian (or neo-Heideggerean) stance: the embrace of the future as sheer, absolute (even monstrous) novelty. Striking a Nietzschean note, in *Of Grammatology* Derrida repeatedly invokes a wholly unknown, explicitly monstrous future—and the cry of "dissemination" in the '70s underscores both the importance of this dimension and its recalcitrance to any further determination. This notion of the future's absolute novelty, of its radical unanticipatibility, and thus its fundamental unspeakability (since Derrida repeatedly advises silence on this score), rather than foreclose the being-in-history of Derrida's own thinking, its own historicity, was itself said to be an opening onto it—a sign, or better a product, of the radical historicity of his own thought, resulting from metaphysics', and the metaphysics of history's, deconstruction. Nevertheless, the problem remains: by what right speak of this result as a future, once history itself has been abandoned to metaphysics and its closure?[10]

Nor is this simply a matter of paleonyms, the continuing use of old names. Not only does the word "history" and its allied terms function far differently from, for example, the word "writing" (since history was never the subordinate term of a binary), but, unlike in the case of Foucault, whose project throughout its various metamorphoses always retains the framework of a recognizable history (including just those notions of period, of linear time, and a "thick" historical present that here come into doubt), Derrida from the first rejects just this framework; in fact, he closely questioned Foucault's own reliance on it in his now famous essay on *Histoire de la folie*.[11] Accordingly, as he himself is in the course of up-ending all standard historiographical categories, in what manner Derrida still lays claim to the future remains obscure.

What Derrida later fashions in the face of this problem, then, his subsequent "solution" to this predicament, thus constitutes one of the greatest shifts in his positions over time.[12] Derrida's early standpoint indeed gives way to, or comes to be supplemented by, a different thought of future. In part mediated by his ongoing "dialogue" with Levinas and the notion of the "to-come" (*a-venir*, which is a play on the French word for the future, *avenir*), in Derrida's last writings a futurity with more apparent content, one already at work in this still-divided present, emerges, most notably under the heading of "a messianism without a messiah." This phrase combines a vector toward a radical justice with an opening onto the future as such.

In Derrida's last work, a sort of permanent structural appendage to radical impermanence thus appears: a structure or function of futurity apart from, or after, the end of history-as-it-has-always-been-known, with an ethicopolitical content, that in fact calls forth change, according to Derrida, rather than foreclosing it. This new, additional vision of the future is already visible in fact in Derrida's treatment of Marx. Indeed, to fine-tune what was brought out above: while Derrida in *Specters* does affirm a permanent relevance of Marx, this affirmation is, of course, not meant to replace the future, or to imply an absence of further events. Rather, this relevance is owed to Marx's, or Marxism's, singular proximity to change, in Derrida's view—precisely to Marx's project's intrinsic ties to this semi-messianic to-come, which is implicated in any event and all futurity (since Derrida believes Marxism alone instantiates this moment in a secular register), as well as owed to Marx's own doctrines' capacity for radical self-transformation, for submitting to a radical historicity (though why change, even radical change, and the goal of a quasi-messianic justice, should necessarily accompany one another perhaps remains a bit opaque—cannot change, even radical change, after all, be toward the less just or simply indifferent to this value)?

An enhanced, enriched, more content-laden thought of the future appears in Derrida's late writing, which clarifies how it is possible for this temporal dimension to be at deconstruction's disposal, given deconstruction's distance from all standard history and all standard historiographical categories. Along with the workings of this standpoint—in addition to its complex mechanics—its politics, the politics of this shift and of these various versions of the future, will be investigated in the following. In Derrida's late writings both phases of the future remain in play, the earlier one becoming melded with the later. His previous diagnosis of the present, including the Nietzschean affirmation of radical discontinuity, which I sometime call "the present future" (since it stems from the present's discontinuity) comes together with this future after the end of history, this other quasi-messianic thought of futurity, harboring a vector toward an "undeconstructible" justice, which, accordingly, I call "the future future" (as coming after, though also before, this end). Within this intersection of types of futurity Derrida's late treatment of politics comes to take its stand, and the question must thus be raised of what sort of politics this complex matrix yields, of what results for a specifically political thinking from these overlapping affirmations.

Finally, the site provided by Marx and Marxism for exploring these issues proves to be no accident. Marx, and the tradition that follows him, offers one of the most powerful and comprehensive views of politics as it relates to the categories of both the present and the future, one of the most complex interactions of a knowledge with one foot in becoming and another purportedly standing beyond it. Thus asking how a Marxian analysis compares to the Derridean furnishes a living test, a trial by fire, of Derrida's own late, extraordinarily complex, difficult, and provocative political intentions, a test that should finally permit reflection on what all this means for our own understanding of the present and the impasses that we confront in today imagining or reimagining a future politics.

The Present Future: Derrida's Present and Marxism's

In what consists Derrida's understanding of our present, then (from which arises the need to turn away from history, away from the present as itself a simply historical category)? Further, how does Derrida's grasp of the present relate to Marx's, or to one identifiable as belonging to that tradition? In *Specters* the answers to both of these questions arrive together. For, as glossed by Derrida, Marx at once attained and missed the future that now is our present. His thinking alone, or best, anticipated and projected the future that has concretely arrived, yet which having arrived, or begun to arrive, necessarily outstrips even Marx's prescient prognostications.

Derrida writes, "Marx is one of the rare thinkers of the past to have taken seriously, at least in its principle, the originary indissociability of technics and language, and thus of teletechnics (for every language is a kind of teletechnics)" (*SM* 53). "It is not at all to denigrate him," he continues, "it is even to speak in what we still dare to call the spirit of Marx, it is almost to quote word for word his own predictions, it is to register and to confirm to say: as regards the tele-technics, and thus also as regards science, he could not accede to the experience and the anticipations on this subject that are ours today" (*SM* 53).

Marx had an inkling of what is coming to pass around us now, in teletechnics, media, and science, developments that, Derrida has just claimed, "affect in an essential fashion the very concept of public space in so-called liberal democracies." Marx already had an eye for this future possibility that has now enveloped our present, even if, given what these developments are, he could not anticipate them fully. Following up on this linkage, moreover, Derrida makes one of his most controversial claims in all of *Specters*. "Deconstruction has never had any sense or interest, in my view," he states later, "at least except as a radicalization, which is to say also in the *tradition of* a certain Marxism, a certain spirit of Marxism" (*SM* 92).

The affirmation of his thought, as standing within a Marxian tradition, thus flows from Derrida's analysis of the present. And this affirmation was subsequently bitterly contested, most notably by Terry Eagleton. Before arriving at any definitive evaluation of this claim, though admittedly prima facie, it has a somewhat unlikely character, three distinct aspects of it, with varying degrees of persuasiveness, must be discerned.

1. The grounds on which Derrida asserts his own Marxian filiation doubtless are long-standing and of a piece with many others in Derrida's corpus.[13] This radical, truly profound diagnosis of technology's still unfolding effects is the kind of thing most have gone in for, who consider themselves Derrideans. Our present, Derrida has long maintained, witnesses a monstrous, *ungeheuer* and *unheimlich* "advance" in technics, telecommunications, prosthesis, action at a distance.

Such an analysis has long been a cornerstone of Derrida's thinking, and, thanks to it, Derrida's thought is faithful to at least one strand of Marx's own. Marx himself, after all, in many places describes a near-apocalyptic social transformation taking place at the hands of radical developments in technology, for example in the later sections of the *Grundrisse*, section G and bits of H and I.[14] While not the sole preoccupation of Marx's writings (nor even their most central one), Derrida's talk of teletechnics does amplify an originally Marxian insight. By thinking technology as today potentially effacing all previously existing borders—between the living and the dead, the human and other animals, as well as those separating nation-states—Derrida undertakes a version of Marx's own nonreductivist materialism.

2. Eagleton's wholesale dismissal of Derrida's Marxist filiation thus proves hasty; a final decision, however, ought not too quickly be reached. For this same diagnosis of the present simultaneously licenses Derrida to depart from Marx: to swing free from an entire axis of Marx's teaching, in particular that in which *labor, production,* and *class* are foregrounded. Derrida, quite self-consciously, it must be recognized, takes an essentially divided stance toward Marx; he assumes a double and heterogeneous set of positions, both of which flow from his understanding of the present and what it demands. And unless this departure, as well as this loyalty, are taken into account, Derrida's claim to some kind of quasi-Marxian orientation of his own thought cannot be fully evaluated.

3. Matters are still more complex than the above, for Derrida's establishment of a fundamentally differentiated or divided relation to Marx, this very gesture, moreover, is itself thematized within his treatment of Marx. It is included in his handling of Marx and the Marxian tradition, in the deconstruction of one of its spirits. Derrida, that is, claims that Marx's inheritance, like every inheritance, is inherently differentiated and heterogeneous, as well as subject to ongoing transformation, thanks to the very iterability that lets it function as an inheritance in the first place. In *Specters,* accordingly, Derrida avails himself of this fault-line in the notion of inheritance with respect to Marx, with the result that Derrida can claim the response that his work on Marx received from many more orthodox Marxists is in fact set out in advance, already predicted or programmed, within *Specters* itself. A certain ontological understanding of Marx, an ontological Marxism, obviously can never accept Derrida's own "spectral" version of inheritance and the Marxist tradition, but just this disagreement is already the site of Derrida's necessary departure from orthodox Marxism, deriving from what in our present Marx himself could never have anticipated.

Holding (3) above in abeyance, however (since these themes of inheritance and tradition are treated in the following section), the brunt of evaluating Derrida's self-proclaimed Marxism clearly falls on (2). As pointed out in (1), Derrida's thought of teletechnology may well amplify Marx's own understanding of *techne* (and it may even build on the Marxian thematic of economy, as Derrida and some of his best readers sometimes claim). Can what results from Derrida's differentiating gesture, however—from his questioning of Marxian ontology, or an ontological Marx—also find a place in the Marxian tradition? Can Derrida's tactical and strategic subtraction of certain doctrines from Marx justify itself in

the court of contemporary Marxist discourse—can this gesture also identify itself as in a certain spirit of Marxism? Or is perhaps Eagleton's out-
rage, as well as that of others, in the end justified, despite having a less
than complete grasp on its object?

Derrida claims, after all, that his own analysis continues to be Marxian
even at the juncture where he breaks with Marx. This is, in fact, the form
taken by every deconstruction, an operation that fundamentally presupposes that the position in question is irreplaceable, not simply wrong or
subject to mere critique. Indeed, this unretractibility of a given position
(those of Husserl's perhaps being the most notable) is why a *deconstruction*, and not a correction in kind, is called for. Accordingly, Derrida's
point of rupture with Marx must itself be a stance already in some way
held or sensed by Marx—the divided character of Derrida's Marxism, his
Marxist filiation, ultimately reflecting a fault line in Marx's own thinking.
Derrida's departure can be true to Marx only if Marx's teachings or voices,
even before meeting up with Derrida, were themselves intrinsically divided and heterogeneous. At the grounds of Derrida's possibly ambivalent
stance toward Marxism thus lies an already ambivalent Marx, according
to Derrida. And this further claim, entailing an intrinsically split Marx,
obviously sharpens the question of whether Derrida's positioning in respect to Marxism, at once affirmation and break, can be admitted into the
Marxian fold.

The side of Marx's own thought that is supposedly self-heterogeneous
emerges most forcefully at the end of *Specters*: in Derrida's discussion of
Marx's presentation of the fetishized commodity (in Part I, Chapter 1,
Section 3, D of *Capital*).[15] The site upon which Derrida performs this
complex gesture, at once one of identification and differentiation, is provided by the twinned themes of "autonomization" and "automaticity."

Derrida introduces these themes earlier in his chapter in the course of
a line-by-line rehearsal of Marx's depiction of the commodity. To summarize in the briefest possible fashion Marx's own argument, the commodity
(here made visible in the example of "this table"), as presented by Marx,
lacks the sort of value, exchange value, normally attributed to it, a value
that, in Marx's eyes, is an inherently social one. On Marx's construal, the
commodity as such is only dead matter, mere *hule*. It nevertheless comes
to something like life, appears to take on a life of its own, to the degree it
is believed to possess such value intrinsically, thought to be worth this or
that in its own terms—a misprision constitutive of its being as such. In
addition, conversely, for these same reasons, the commodity in Marx's
analysis also represents a moment when spirit, soul—here specifically
those human and social relations that first fully appear in the commodity

in a dissimulated fashion—become immured in thingness, become dispossessed of their proper predicates and weighed down in merely dead matter.[16]

Derrida, combining these two phases of Marx's analysis, accordingly identifies the commodity as a locus in which "two genres of . . . movement intersect with one another" (SM 153). A kind of "autonomy" (a movement of autonomization) takes place in the commodity. Behaving or acting "on its own" (as being taken to perform or possess an intrinsically social value), it is treated as free—its puppet strings invisible to the gaze of those social spectators whose own relations it embodies. At the same time, of course, such "becoming-free" is but a moment of automaticity. For Marx himself, this freedom "is no more than the mask of automatism"; it is merely "automatic autonomy, mechanical freedom, technical life" (SM 153).

Returning to these themes of autonomy and automaticity at the end of his chapter, Derrida presents their workings there as more internal, more integral, to Marx's own problematic. The alienation of human labor in the commodity finds an analogy in the alienation of other "human" powers in religion—religion for Marx being the paradigmatic case of ideology. Extrapolating from this claim, Derrida advances an overall *structural congruence* of ideology, society, and production. Each sector or dimension (production, ideology, and society) will have always been at work without grounding or providing the final instance for any of the others (not society for ideology, nor production for society, and so forth). Thus each in its own right entails a coincidence of automaticity and autonomization similar to that found in the commodity .

Ideology, in the paradigmatic case of religion, for example, is at once cut off from its "origins," and thus *freed*, as originary instance, from any of its presumed sources (in class or other exploitative interests)—hence autonomized and autonomous—even as its own "life" is also "automatic," thanks to lacking this, or any other, intrinsic ground (for example, one in the deity that it invokes). Indeed, in each of these spheres, this same singular movement or gesture reveals itself, according to Derrida, in which something goes to work apart from any previously defining instance or principle, untethered from any other prior ground—hence "freely"; yet, for that very reason, also mechanically, automatically, without any "living" logic.

Having fixed on autonomization and automaticity as central to at least one phase of Marx's own thought, Derrida, on these grounds, accordingly, can highlight what he has in common with Marx. Derrida, in fact, portrays

Marx as already a thinker of *différance*. Marx "insists on respecting the originality and the proper efficacity of the specter," Derrida proclaims, "the autonomization and automatization of ideality as finite-infinite processes of *différance* (phantomatic, fantastic, fetishistic, or ideological)—and of the simulacrum that is not simply imaginary in it" (*SM* 170).

Owing to the differential, heterogeneous structure of every inheritance, however, the possibility of which is finally one with these finite-infinite processes that Derrida has just invoked, what Marx "respects," what "one Marx" respects or knows (here *différance*) another may not. Thus at this *very same moment* Derrida also decisively differentiates his own thinking from Marx's. Despite his (anagrammatic) respect for the specter and what Marx already senses as coming—our time, in which these automatic-autonomic forces have taken on an unprecedented scope, force, and acceleration—"Marx continues to want to ground his critique or his exorcism of the spectral simulacrum in an ontology," Derrida states. Marx, in his thinking of ideology and production, does recognize an originary spectrality, implying the working of *différance*. Yet he nevertheless poses against it, plays off of it "a critical but pre-deconstructive ontology of presence as actual reality and objectivity," in which Marx's own work takes on the role of "stabilized knowledge . . ." (*SM* 170).

Derrida thus takes the measure of his own distance from Marx. Marx's work exhibits an ongoing fealty to an ontology of presence, a captivity in which Marx, however, to a certain extent, could not *not* be held. Derrida's own departure from Marx thus has a unique form. Not only does it fold into itself an ongoing affirmation of Marx's thought (since, as just reviewed, Marx, too, at moments recognizes the primary character of autonomization and automaticity, and the work of *différance* in them). Moreover, Derrida explicitly avows that he is not pitting a more encompassing counterknowledge of his own against Marx's. His stance toward Marx at this moment is, again, not one of critique. Marx's positions "call . . . for questions more radical than critique itself and than the ontology that grounds critique," Derrida states (*SM* 170). Derrida's own intervention instead depends on Derrida's interpretation of our present and its relation to the future. Derrida's rupture with Marx, Derrida tells us, takes shape thanks to "seismic events come from the future," which, again, Marx could not have anticipated. It is "given from out of the unstable, chaotic, and dis-located ground of the times . . . without which there would be neither history nor event nor promise of justice" (*SM* 170).

Derrida replaces Marx's ontology with his own hauntology, finally, then, not on account of any straightforward epistemic or cognitive superiority, but thanks to his own reading of the future and the present, due to his better understanding (because closer, more proximate) of our present and its possible futures—thanks to his superior "foretellese," as I here call it, taking the term from Wallace Stevens. How Derrida's prognostication, including the status of such anticipation, comes to stand in respect to Marx's own, and what it means that such Nostradamian strife replaces all knowledge claims, will be discussed further at the close of this chapter. Remaining now within the parameters of Derrida's own discussion, let the following question instead be posed. On account of what has escaped from and is yet also recognized by Marx in our present, Derrida embraces more thoroughly, more radically, these twinned movements of automaticity and autonomization. Is this embrace, then, what separates Derrida's discourse from the mainstream of Marxist/post-Marxist thinking? Does this refusal of an "ontology of presence," of the *telos* of a wholly "actual and objective reality," as no longer fully fitting the present, establish a dividing line between the Derridean initiative and any genuinely Marxian one?

The answer to this question, I believe, clearly must be no. In the aftermath of the breakdown of Louis Althusser's attempt in the mid-sixties to explain the productivity of Marxian science, to say how Marxism could be a knowledge with its own internal historicity and genesis that neverthless allowed for the knowledge of history and historical totality as such, no advanced Marxism has been able to depend unproblematically on the cognitive status of its own stance or on the economic as a genuine last instance.[17] This is attested to by the now common coinage "Marxism/post-marxism." And in Althusser's later work, this breakdown led, moreover, now famously, to an autonomization of ideology of exactly the sort that Derrida has just described.

Now, to be sure, even within such a cognitively and ontologically flexible context as contemporary Marxism affords, Derrida's stance proves to be something of an outlier. In fact, throughout the surprisingly numerous pages comprising Derrida's treatment of Marx's example of the table (to which Marx himself devotes a single paragraph of *Capital*), the concern repeatedly emerges that Derrida may be obscuring Marx's own themes to an extent that he does not fully recognize. The very notion of the specter as it operates there threatens to substitute Derrida's own fascination with questions ontological *and* hauntological for Marx's rather different focus on the commodity and the social character of labor and production. After all, hauntology's thematics still cluster around issues raised by ontology (the stability of the entity's identity, the relation of sign, meaning, and thing), even as they sketch the latter's limits.

Thus, prior to reading *Capital*, Derrida introduces the specter in a Marxian context by arguing that in the third part of *German Ideology* both

Max Stirner (the object of Marx's critique) and Marx himself equally wish to expel the spectral dimension. Stirner wants to rid himself of those ghostly "spirits" (those handed-down conventional beliefs) that he believes have alienated him from himself; and Marx desires to chase away those ghosts that still haunt Stirner, even at this moment of supposedly maximum self-demystification—the real causes of Sterner's captivation, according to Marx, being found in a concrete social-historical realm wholly omitted by Stirner's ego-oriented philosophy. Derrida thus equates Stirner's embrace of the ego with Marx's of the social-historical—on the grounds that both equally share in one and the same privilege of presence, and equally rely on the "real and objective." Yet this analysis indeed threatens to undermine, or even dispense with, Marx's own concerns with economic being and social life. Such issues cannot appear as such within Derrida's quasi-hauntology, and they indeed depend on making concrete empirico-historical claims of the sort this talk of the specter brings into doubt.

In addition, this gesture, Derrida's "tabling" of Marx, if one may put it this way, is part of an entire constellation of positions in *Specters*, in which the notions of class and mode of production, along with the institutions and apparatuses stemming from them, are identified by Derrida as aspects of the Marxist program that he will not, and never was able to, endorse. Derrida explicitly writes, speaking of that spirit of Marxism that he *can* affirm, that he "distinguishes [it] . . . from [those] other spirits . . . that rivet it to the body of Marxist doctrine, to its supposed systemic, metaphysical, or ontological totality . . . to its fundamental concepts of labor, mode of production, and social class, and consequently, to the whole history of its apparatuses" (*SM* 88).[18]

Nevertheless, even at his apogee from Marx, Derrida has not necessarily broken free from the orbit of contemporary Marxism. Derrida's devaluation of production, his refusal to privilege it as any kind of anchor or last instance, is by no means a deal-breaker for quite a few self-described Marxians. Both Paul Virilio's analyses (which Derrida cites) as well as Jean Baudrillard's (which he does not) can and do cohabitate rather easily with certain Marxian discourses, even though these bodies of work either dispense with production and class entirely or, as in the early Baudrillard, preserve the latter in almost entirely tacit form.[19] The notion of the mode of production and of the proletariat as an inherently revolutionary class are no longer maintained by some Marxists and no longer define the scope of contemporary Marxism itself.

On the level of practice the results are similar. The thrust of Derrida's swerve away from Marx ultimately targets not only the primacy given to class, but especially those "institutions and apparatuses" associated with it and the making of a proletarian revolution. Yet the ties that bind Marxist thought to a certain type of direct revolutionary action, that coordinate Marxist theory with a living revolutionary practice, do not themselves exist today in the West. At best, these are entirely virtual projects. Indeed, unlike what was once true even within living memory, when it was immediately clear to what branch of the Communist party or splinter group any given Marxist thinker belonged, current positions in Marxist/post-Marxism remain wholly removed from any activist revolutionary stance.

Not just Derrida, then, but almost no self-proclaimed Marxists today have truck or live with Marxism tethered to a revolutionary class in this sense, to what might be called the "old international," its "institutions and apparatuses," and the proletariat as a revolutionary last instance in practice. In fact, Derrida's perhaps exceedingly ascetic version of Marxism, his fiddling with Marx's spirits—summoning some, dismissing others—on these grounds, could even appear as one of the most honest, one of the most clear-eyed of contemporary Marxist standpoints. Derrida is acutely aware, in a way highly reminiscent of Marx himself, of the pragmatic conditions under which its own discourse operates. His version of Marx takes into account those actual social and institutional arrangements under which Marxism at present functions, including what these imply as to the kind of action that can or cannot be expected in the near future under such circumstances.

But this being so, Derrida by no means standing all that far from the most up-to-date Marxist/post-Marxism, what does account for this distance, then—since I suspect Derrida's work's largely ginger, often even cold, reception by contemporary Marxists cannot safely be ignored? Does something other than a distance from the proletariat per se, the old internationale, prove decisive here?

Derrida's diagnosis of the present may not establish such a divide. His own *response* to this diagnosis, where Derrida would go from here, where he would next take us, may well do so, however. For Derrida ultimately believes that the response called for in our present circumstances—of accelerating teletechnology and *mondialisation*—is first and foremost to embark on the reconception of the political as such. Derrida indeed ultimately asserts that what alone today would be truly revolutionary (even while he rules out no particular course of action in advance), what truly preserves this notion's core semantic kernel in our time, is not any conceivable political change, even one bordering on being total, but a transformation in the very framing of the political: the discovery or invention of an alternative to every understanding of politics hitherto.

Coming down between the two poles of Marx's famous binary (change / understanding), Derrida, that is, first and foremost wants to change our understanding. This has been the case at least as far back as *Of Grammatology*, in which, famously emphasizing this seme of production, Derrida stated that what the infinite inflation of the sign occurring today demanded was to go back over the entire conceptuality of the West, and make way for new modes of thought—specifically, by showing that a previously effaced radical absence structured this entire tradition. The legacy of this conviction (with its singular stance toward history as a whole still to be further sketched), in turn lives on in *Specters*, and in all the later work, in Derrida's insistence that what is most needed today—again in the face of the teletechnic, mondializing transformations taking place around us—is not any specific political change (though, again, he rules none out), but a change in the political's very conception.

This demand, this desideratum or imperative to rethink politics, is indeed tied to Derrida's ongoing refashioning of history as a category—his break with standard historiography and his transfiguration of the end of history. And whatever else it may achieve, it opens an unbridgeable abyss between any sort of Marxian / post-Marxian thinking and Derrida's own program. Calling into question the framework of every conceivably revolutionary struggle, it ultimately implies Marxism's dissolution as an actual political program, its own "going under," as Nietzsche terms this, by subjecting all political conceptualization, including Marx's, to a version of that radical discontinuity with respect to the future that we saw Derrida, from the first embrace, following Heidegger and Foucault.

In his late work, Derrida's long-standing project of the closure of history (and his rethinking of history and historicity) thus intersects with his project of (re-)thematizing politics and, to the degree that this goes all the way down and enjoins the reshaping of the very form of time and of history itself, such intersection leaves his own political thought at a decisive remove from all previously known. Derrida's demand for a wholesale revision of the political itself continues that reconfiguring and / or deconstructing of history that he had earlier undertaken, even as with these themes of justice and of a messianism without messiah, the political contributes to history's and the future's own, novel delimitation. Both gestures are in play in Derrida's demand that a break with the political as it has always been known be mounted—and from this, arises an unbridgeable gulf between Derrida's political thinking and any program that might meaningfully be called Marxist. To this astonishing undertaking, then, to this enormous wager, rife with novelty and risk, at the center of Derrida's last thought, our attention must turn.

The Future Future: Deconstructive Historiography and the Quasi-Messianic

Two themes in the later writings generally, and in *Specters* in particular, preeminently bring forward the overarching reconceptualization of politics that Derrida contemplates, including its implications for Derrida's ongoing rethinking of history: (1) anachrony; and (2) deconstruction's relation to justice, or "deconstruction and the possibility of justice," as Derrida often terms this. The first of these, anachrony, quite explicitly designates a thought of history and the event that no longer relies on a linear and punctual historical temporality. The second establishes an intrinsic connection between justice and the work of deconstruction, including an eccentric relation on the part of the former to those greatest totalities that deconstruction originally took as its object. Sorting through these topics, which ultimately form a single whole, proves difficult, however. These themes put into play the entirety of Derrida's own project: its own ends (and basic concepts) become coordinated with this new thought of justice and the future, even as Derrida continues to draw on and ramify analyses and results from earlier phases of his thinking.

Anachrony

"Anachrony," the first theme, when taken by itself, is somewhat less complex than the other, and has a more direct, continuous connection with Derrida's earlier work. Stated most broadly, history rethought under the heading of anachrony—a term that does not occur in Derrida's early corpus—renders history-as-it-has-always-been-known tessellated, a type of mosaic. So conceived, each tile, every present, becomes internally fragmented, intrinsically complex, even as each ceases to be linked in any necessary or causal way to the other moments putatively surrounding it. That divided and frayed condition, which was once a differentiating feature of our current present (and perhaps continues to be so in some manner) has become extended to all. Every present, every moment, Derrida repeatedly emphasizes, is radically singular and unique. Accordingly, rather than each present, every moment finding its location in a broader history (as more traditionally construed), the reverse occurs: history as a whole becomes located in these otherwise dispersed moments. Its own history, all history, is closed up in each present, even as this moment never closes upon itself, never knows a closure of its own.

How such anachrony operates can be specifically seen in Derrida's comments in *Specters* on Marx's *The Eighteenth Brumaire of Louis Napoleon*. Derrida takes the framework of this essay to be rooted in an ultimately untenable appeal to a distinction between ghost and spirit

(*Gespenst* and *Geist*)—a sign of this defect being the semantic overlap of these two terms ("spirit" also being a word for a ghost), which is roughly the same in German as in English. Accordingly, Derrida rejects Marx's claim that the French Revolution of 1789 embodied an authentic spirit of revolution, and accomplished the "task of [its] time" in a way that Napoleon III's recurrence (as a mere specter or ghost of his predecessor) did not.[20] Instead every time, according to Derrida, dons masks of other times, and no time presents itself as fully self-coincident—something attested by the French Revolution having already bedecked itself in Roman garb, as did Louis Napoleon in Napoleon the First's. Each moment, each present, is thus ana-chronous—disjoint and multiply sited—with the result that the task of a time, as well as its spirit, always remains in doubt.

Derrida dubs this fundamental noncoincidence with itself the law of "fatal anachrony." He further turns it against Marx's suggestion, also in the *Eighteenth Brumaire*, that the coming revolution, the proletarian revolution will take a form unlike any other: specifically, that it will dispense with the "necromancy" that still accompanied Danton and his comrades, on account of its being the first truly complete, truly radical, and thus also final revolution. Commenting on this claim, Derrida writes: "Marx recognizes of course the law of this fatal anachrony . . . , [yet] he [Marx] wants to be done with it [anachrony], he deems that one can, he declares that one should be done with it" (*SM* 113).

In addition, then, to it being impossible to identify the task of any single time, and to cognitively distinguish an authentic from an inauthentic or factitious inheritance, no time, including that of the revolution to come, can avoid remnants from the past, can escape being haunted by multiple handed-down frameworks and legacies (what Marx himself in *the Eighteenth Brumaire* calls "the tradition of all the dead generations").[21]

Derrida's revamping of the historical present, then, decisively departs from Marx's understanding. This reconceptualization, moreover, renders questionable the schemata of history and thus of political action that Marx himself relied on, both as a practical politician and a historian. Indeed, Derrida's rupture is all the more significant, as Marx's example in the *Brumaire* and the historiographical paradigm it supplies represents the most widespread theoretical legacy of Marxism today. Much contemporary academic work in the humanities continues to follow in Marx's footsteps: it replicates the type of analysis that the *Brumaire* models, in which Marx, in order to increase our understanding of the conditions conducive to what he called "serious revolutions," explains the failure of the uprising of 1848 (and Louis Napoleon's successful counterrevolution) as owing to the (central) economic and (excluded) political status of the French peasantry of the time.²² Much current historical and cultural work, not always directly influenced by Marx, takes the measure of our present situation, as well as past ones, in a similar fashion, mobilizing analogous large scale socio-economic-political reference points.²³

Such globalizing, macrohistorical analysis, it must be stressed, is simply not possible, however, in an "historical" universe modeled by anachrony. Derrida's version of the historical present unhinges the moment from the larger contexts provided by an era or an epoch: it denies to any epoch as such (except perhaps that furnished by metaphysics in totality) the sort of intergrity upon which much historiography, including contemporary Marxian historiography, depends.

Thus, for example, Raymond Williams's now famous schema (which in fact itself aimed to complicate more traditional Marxian models of the present), in which an historical present is riven by tensions owing to emergent and residual formations, itself only works by positing the kind of dateable totality that anachrony denies.²⁴ Though emergent and residual formations themselves fissure the present, they, as well as dominant formations, after all, can only can be identified and assigned these values thanks to granting an integrity to an era as a whole. They are thus impossible, or meaningless, once a radically anachronous present has been posited.

Now, of course, Derrida's notion of anachrony keeps a distance from more standard enlightenment models that view historical change in terms of a continuous progress. So, too, this framework by no means forecloses political decision and the event. The being-out-of-joint with itself of the present is instead a necessary part of the interaction of the future and the present and thus a condition of all and any change, as viewed by Derrida. Such noncoincidence, such ana-chrony indeed opens a space for, and is coordinated with, a quasi-messianic future and the imperative of justice, according to Derrida, since justice and this future only function in the mode of the "perhaps," thus only in the milieu of the in-decision, the radical nonknowing that the nonself-coincidence-with-itself of an anachronistic present provides.

Moreover, anachrony, and its distance from standard history, often elicits quite positive and powerful effects in Derrida's own work. Such a tessellated, ana-chronic organization, in fact, structures the entirety of that book that may be the keystone of all of Derrida's late thought, his enormously ambitious *Politics of Friendship*. Organized around a single phrase in classical Greek, *w philoi ouk philos*, thought originally to be Aristotle's, *Politics* traces repeated citations of this sentence starting from Aristotle's own up through the work of Maurice Blanchot—Cicero, Montaigne, Kant, and Nietzsche provide other significant waystations.[25] *Politics* thus sketches a set of events of inheritance in which in no one instance this phrase functions in quite the same way as any other, yet a set that also defines a single, unique whole—that of the conceptualization of the political as such in something like the West.

Derrida's approach in *Politics of Friendship* thus cuts across history; its segmentation of history is entirely transversal. Accordingly, Derrida quite explicitly *refuses* to locate any one of these repetitions in even the broadest sort of period and epoch. He pointedly asserts that such divisions as ancient vs. modern, Graeco-Roman vs. Judeo-Christian, have no place in his treatment, not to mention the sort of finer periodization commonly practiced today, wherein a Nietzsche, for example, might be situated in the culture, society, and economy of the late nineteenth century.[26]

In *Politics*, then, Derrida indeed undertakes a treatment without periods, yet not without shift, change, flow, or flux. *Politics'* composition recognizes historicity (Derrida would say of a radical sort), while it eschews the apparatus of the historical epoch in its totality. Taken as a whole, *Politics* thus presents a single, although internally divided, constantly differing, *traditio*, one peppered by events taking place in wavelike series, sutured to unique presents—presents themselves essentially partial, fragmented and unlocatable on a standard historical grid.

This break with the period—in a Marxian context, but also beyond—I believe to be the most profound difference between Derrida's late work, his thought of history and politics, and that ascendant just about everywhere else today in the humanities, at least until quite recently. As we have begun to see, even the broadest sort of periodization practiced by Marx himself—his talk in the *Brumaire*, for example, of an epoch defined by the bourgeois revolution, understood as the ascendancy of a certain class based on newly emerging "relations of production"[27]—would have to be jettisoned from Derridean discourse. With anachrony Derrida thus fashions a schema of considerable historical novelty, the discontinuous, and even surprising character of which, too often, in my view, has been overlooked.

To be sure, in *Specters* and the response it has so far received, some recognition of the oddity of what Derrida proposes has been registered—largely by way of voicing objections to the politics it is presumed to imply, thanks to a criticism of this politics' purportedly mild, liberal or "reformist" tendencies. And Derrida's revision of political history and analysis (itself, by the way, only a part, and indeed the first part, of a continuous revision of these themes that Derrida sees extending far beyond his own writings), as should now be clear, does entail a departure from the sole type of diagnostics today still believed able to lead to sustained revolutionary organization and action, namely a Marxian one. Moreover, at those moments in *Specters* when something like an actual political program comes into view, for example, in Derrida's description of what he calls the new internationale, a dispiriting feeling indeed can arise due to the thin character of what these remarks offer by way of a course of action.

As noted in the previous section, however, Marxian analysis (in this case Marxian historiography) itself today swings rather wide of any kind of activist program or politics. So, too, Derrida is committed, perhaps above all, to changing our understanding, and in this register his own radicality preeminently lies. Derrida insists on his own thought's revolutionary, even hyperrevolutionary potential, and in truth this valence is not foreign to his work's impact, nor to Derrida's as an agent, at least within the academy and perhaps even beyond.

In fact, in respect to fomenting or embracing revolution as a value, on at least one plane, Derrida's work departs from traditional Marxism (assuming identifiable political directions still apply here at all) by moving toward the left rather than the right—by registering a perhaps unprecedented degree of revolutionary ardor, and affirming revolutions upon revolutions, not just one final one, as Marx did above. Derrida evinces such revolutionary zeal in *Specters* at the very moment when the difference made by this new, or newly explicit, quasi-messianic dimension of his own thinking explicitly emerges. Thus, attending to this portion of his text, two birds can be killed with one stone: our view of Derrida's politics rounded out, and this second new theme, of deconstruction and the possibility of justice canvassed.

Deconstruction and the Possibility of Justice

A critical crossroads in Derrida's discourse wells up in his gloss of Maurice Blanchot's "Marx's Three Voices," most of which was added by Derrida after he first delivered *Specters* as a lecture. Blanchot's brief essay is itself, it should be noted, a rather politically charged work-product. Originally published in October following the events of May 1968, it constitutes an endorsement of these events and, in part, proposes a rethinking of Marx's enterprise on their basis, as well as offering an analysis of these occurrences by way of Marx's own practice of *écriture*.[28] Derrida, having already translated his own insistence on spectralizing and deontologizing Marx into Blanchot's "language," and now picking up on a call, or appeal (*appel*) and a corresponding "original performativity" that he believes Blanchot also recognizes as politically fundamental (both in Blanchot's own writings and in Marx's), for his part goes on to explain how this dimension relates to one of his own best-known concepts or neologistic keywords, *différance*:

> It is there [in respect to this performativity] that *différance* if it remains irreducible, irreducibly required by the spacing of any promise and by the to-come that comes to open it, does not mean only (as some people too often have believed and so naively) deferral, lateness, delay, postponement. In the incoercible *différance* the here-now unfurls. Without lateness, without delay, but without presence, it is the precipitation of an absolute singularity, singular because differing, precisely and always other, binding itself necessarily to the form of the instant, in *imminence and in urgency*: even if it moves toward what remains to come, there is the pledge (promise, engagement, injunction and response to the engagement and so forth) (*SM* 31; his emphasis).

Striking, first of all, in this statement is the role taken on by *différance* within the temporal present. *Différance*, Derrida tells us, indeed contrary to the expectations of many, bears a unique tie to the "here-now." To be sure, the present in Derrida's early writings was itself constituted by a delay; it did not and could not enclose itself in presence, and, in this fashion, *différance* has always pertained to it. Far less clear, however, in Derrida's early phase is that *différance* had the present as the privileged site of its own operation, rather than, say, the (absolute) past, as Derrida seems to be suggesting here.[29] Derrida's aim at this moment, nevertheless, is clear. In line with Derrida's introduction of a quasi-messianic futurity, *différance*, the alterity of *différance* will now be tied to this radical futurity, such that the present itself results as an "absolute singularity." Every present now emerges with *différance* contributing to it a quasi-ethical "imminence and urgency." A divided, riven, and essentially tessellated present, owing to the effect and operation of *différance* in it, thus steps forward as central to this phase of Derrida's thought—a present indeed able to furnish a staging ground for all genuine politicoethical commitment and every event.

More specifically still, without getting too lost in the peaks of the "higher Derrida," *différance*, Derrida suggests, is fastened to the present, thought to operate on or in the here-now, insofar as its work of spacing lets be included within this temporal dimension the penetration of a singular call or demand coming at once from the future and the other (a call which here is said to be met, perhaps has always already been met, by an inaugural promise or pledge). The delayed and self-differing character of the present, of a present now worked by *différance*, is ultimately coordinated with the present moment's permeation or penetration by an ethicopolitical imperative coming from, and directed back toward, the future. Accordingly, Derrida repeatedly writes the French word for the future, *avenir*, as *a-venir* ("to-come") to emphasize this quasi-messianic moment arriving from the future. This call, the imperative to do justice to the other, is indeed futurity itself, a dimension always *to-come*. And to it, to this call, in the present, Derrida further explains, corresponds an original and perhaps essentially political performativity: one at the root of all law, all political forms and life, all "constitution" and "institution"—these latter themselves only retroactively and partially ever coming to justify their own activity.[30]

Thus an essentially futural structuration, a new kind of permanent-impermanence emerges in Derrida's late thinking, with which also arrives a perhaps surprising reassertion of an "unconditional" (of an absolute demand for justice). This "unconditional"—Derrida's own term: "an appeal as unconditional" (*SM* 30)—does not, of course, stand apart from time (or the event), as by now should be clear. It is intimately bound up with "imminence" and "urgency," with the present moment's radical singularity and the possibility of any action or change. Yet this call is itself nevertheless still *unconditional*, absolute. Apparently, it itself will never "go under" (to again use Nietzsche's phrase), never pass away through its own historicity, or suffer ultimate dissemination.

And what this specifically signifies for his politics—the political valence of Derrida's new construal of temporality, his new interpretation of the future and the present at once—can be further gleaned at a slightly later stage of this same discussion, at a moment when two themes, two threads combine that will also finally bring fully forward what Derrida understands under the heading of "deconstruction and the possibility of justice."

For, on the one hand, in regard to the political significance of this novel unconditional moment, Derrida, a little later in this same discussion, joins Blanchot himself in affirming what Derrida explicitly calls "'permanent revolution,'" albeit in scare quotes.[31] Adapting this phrase, first coined by Leon Trotsky to his own ends, Derrida's political thinking now entails a "hyper-revolutionary" stance, a permanently revolutionary character, one that extends, or fills out, his earlier affirmation of monstrous change.

Indeed Derrida insists, in all his late writings, for reasons that will only slowly become fully apparent, not on some one revolution or another, but on ongoing change, constant revolution. This is a persistent theme in all of these works, both in his reading of Marx, but also in his thematization of democracy in *Politics of Friendship*, as well as in numerous other texts (most notably, "Force of Law," which, as the first setting out of the theme of "deconstruction and the possibility of justice," might be the primary work to consult on this matter). Change, revolution, according to Derrida, must be ongoing, permanent—one reason among others being because any stopping point, any belief that sufficient steps in this regard had been taken, truly decisive change finally accomplished, would bring self-satisfaction and complacency, and thus could only entail a new failure to do justice or to be (genuinely and fully) democratic.

Derrida, then, in colloquy with Blanchot, quite willingly underwrites what he takes to be the latter's call for "permanent revolution": "an *excessive* demand or urgency that Blanchot speaks of so correctly," as Derrida puts it (*SM* 33). On the other hand, at this very same moment, Derrida also contests the fashion in which Blanchot himself thinks this unconditional, this permanent impermanence (at least as Derrida reads Blanchot). Blanchot having characterized this call, this unconditional that enjoins permanent revolution as "ever-present," Derrida in response, rejecting the metaphysical commitment that he believes is implied by Blanchot's phrase, insists that " 'permanent revolution' supposes the rupture of that which links permanence to substantial presence and more generally to ontology" (*SM* 33). Derrida enjoins a break between this demand's "permanence" (which he would also retain, and from which flows this hyperrevolutionary affirmation) and "substantial presence." And how this works, what this severance of permanence from presence entails becomes plain, when Derrida asserts (slightly earlier): "The demand . . . must implicitly, it seems to us, find itself affected by the same rupture or dislocation [of revolution] . . . it can never be always present, *it can be, only, if there is any*, it can be only possible, it must even remain a can-be or may be . . ." (*SM* 33).

Derrida may well then, in his late writings, resurrect some sort of unconditional, what appears to be a species of absolute, here designated by Derrida himself as a form of "*permanence*." Yet this unconditional, this permanence, as he is in the midst of pointing out, nevertheless must be thought in a fashion unlike any other unconditional, or ideal goal. As unconditional, it eludes every value of presence, defeats all "ontology," including that implied by Blanchot's calling it "ever-present." Call, demand there may be, but these finally exist only as aporetic, Derrida indicates, and thus break with all presence, and ever-presence.

More precisely still, both democracy and justice as ends must be thought in the mode of "perhaps," as "can-be," since, to Derrida's eyes, they harbor constitutive *contradictions*, genuine *impossibilities* (as Derrida also makes clear in other portions of his later writings). In these cases, however, such contradictions, such impasses uniquely *contribute* to these absolutes' functioning; impossibility *constitutes* these absolutes' mode of being, rather than entailing their complete nonbeing.[32] These absolutes thus *are* only insofar as they always *may or may not be*. Again, as Derrida emphasizes, "the demand . . . *can be, only if there is any*, it can be only possible, it must even remain a can-be or may be" (*SM* 33).

Along with the internal aporias that lead to this result, their inherently wavering mode of being is the most profound reason, then, that these calls (to justice, to be democratic) are unfulfillable, and the politics of Derrida's position necessitates a hypperrevolutionary call. Their appeal can never reach completion. It stands structurally, necessarily, beyond any fulfillment, such that even its own existence as a demand or imperative comes into doubt.

Derrida's unconditional with its nonachievement indeed differs from the less self-disqualifying, because less ontologically fraught, nonfulfillment built into Kant's infinite regulative ideals.[33] As Derrida emphasizes, the very *being* of the demand for justice or democracy (not just its *achievement*, as in Kant) remains in suspension, because it has as its correlate a *decision*, one that its uncertain and suspensive existence *enables*, rather than eliminates—at once permits to be, but also effaces. The imperative for these unconditionals to be decided upon, a nonalgorithmic undecidability, is traced within the internal structure of these new absolutes. In this way, they defeat presence, ultimately coming from and referring back to a more radical alterity.

This distance from the value of presence (if not the present) maintained by Derrida's futurally inflected unconditionals finally makes manifest, then, the intrinsic linkage between deconstruction and justice: what Derrida intends by the phrase "deconstruction and the possibility of justice." For, as rebarbitive to presence—as never-present rather than ever-present, impossible rather than possible—such demands are themselves *self-deconstructing*. Having an allergy to presence already built into their own functioning, they escape deconstruction. Justice is thus indeed undeconstructible, as Derrida repeatedly says—yet this only insofar as it already exists, it always already "whiles," as Heidegger would say, in an essentially self-deconstructive fashion, on account of these aporias and contradictions that constitute it and permit its unique undecidable mode of being.

Justice and deconstruction, accordingly, compose a highly complex figure, when situated in the overall trajectory of Derrida's own thought. These hyperrevolutionary *tele* or goals, according to Derrida, already have a self-deconstructive or deconstructed form. In turn, however, they, and they alone, Derrida *now* tells us, will have commanded from the first the very project of deconstruction, including Derrida's own earliest versions of this undertaking. In his last writings Derrida thus reveals an unconditional of a unique sort, a new quasi-permanent absolute ethical futurity, an essentially aporetic, undeconstructible, ethicopolitical "future future," intrinsically linked to the program of deconstruction (to its undoing of presence), which he also claims preexisted his own project, and motivated it from the first.

Yet this, the temporal unfolding of Derrida's own thinking, its development or diachrony, sits rather uneasily. After all, if this is so, if any terms or concepts (such as justice or democracy) are self-deconstructing and thus already escape on their own the value of presence, one might wonder why deconstruction was ever necessary at all. Not only might there not be further concepts about, or waiting to be invented, in no need of deconstruction, but how, as Derrida repeatedly claimed, can the privilege of presence itself constitute the greatest totality, or even any sort of totality, if these and perhaps other concepts have in fact already eluded it?

To be sure, as just emphasized, Derrida understands these as self-deconstructing concepts, and perhaps he assumes the contrary case: that these notions, these demands (of justice, of democracy) can really only be grasped in all their explicitness *after* the project of deconstruction has begun. Yet how, then, could they animate this project from the start, *before* its work got underway? If deconstruction alone renders fully articulable what is entailed by justice or democracy (perhaps not themselves simply concepts or ideas), how could these notions in their complexity have stood watch over its birth? Perhaps they only officiated latently; they implicitly surveyed the invention of that deconstruction which let be articulated their own character as non-deconstructible (because self-deconstructing). But the space of such latency is, then, enormous, and, given the importance of these notions in everyday life, one might wonder about the presumption that all have been (at least partially) mistaken about justice up until now (until deconstruction's invention) as well as about the aporetic character of justice so conceived, whose purchase on public discourse in the wake of this conceptualization raises questions as well.

Foretellese

Both Derrida's more recent formulation of the future's relation to his own project, which gives to futurity a new absoluteness, what I have here called "the future future," as well as his earlier one, that takes the present, our present, as uniquely discontinuous, quasi-epochal, which I call "the present future," are thus at work in Derrida's late phase, even as the kind of whole they form perhaps remains not entirely conspicuous. Nevertheless, this complex intersection in the structure and history of Derrida's thought illuminates Derrida's situation with respect to the alternatives proposed by Marx and Marxism, first by making evident where Derrida's thinking and contemporary Marxism may coincide (around the autonomous, yet automatic character of ideology and a certain distance, willed or no, from the apparatuses and institutions of revolution), and also, where they differ (around the Derridean enterprise of reconceiving from the ground up history and politics, for which this notion of an anachronous present intersected by a quasi-messianic future proves pivotal). Yet, when a step back from these differences is taken, a still broader context invoked, Derrida's and Marx's projects in their entirety turn out to have a profound common horizon: they share an overriding mutual trait.

Both Derrida and Marx indeed participate in what I have called foretellese: the belief that the work of thought must today engage with a diagnosis of its own present, which is simultaneously essentially futural. Both Derrida and Marx situate their discourses in respect to a reading of the present (though, for Derrida, this last is not simply historical), itself oriented by a vector toward change (and thus toward the future), including an affirmation of an absolute justice, and both, as we have just confirmed in Derrida's case, employ some sort of unconditional or quasi-permanent dimension in practicing this prognostication, a dimension that is explicitly for the sake of this temporal work (for change rather than understanding) and itself ultimately accessible only within a radically temporal horizon.

Yet, does not an irony reside here? Derrida above all stakes out his differences from Marx in regard to this very dimension of permanence. Substituting his "hauntology" for what he takes to be Marx's ontology, Derrida asserts that Marx, like Blanchot above, construes permanence too "metaphysically." Derrida's most basic question to Marx is whether Marx *can* successfully mix fixity and change in the way that Derrida, and perhaps even Marx himself, believes is necessary. The late-twentieth-century French philosopher suspects that the mid-nineteenth-century German thinker may have bowed to a premature stabilization of his own doctrine (in part inevitable), one not measuring up to the kind of relation to history, historicity, and revolution Derrida believes today is required—in addition to Marx, more understandably, as brought out in Section 2, not having been able to keep pace with the changes occurring in the future, our present, brought about by teletechnology and teletechnemedia.

Yet, as we have discovered, Derrida, thus interrogating Marx, ironically enough, at this moment himself also introduces a new sort *of fixity*, a new kind of permanence, intrinsic to his own thought. He bases his criticism on a permanent structural appendage (an undeconstructible, self-deconstructing justice) new, or at least newly explicit, in his own work. Accordingly, in *Specters*, even as Derrida takes Marx to task for incorrectly mixing fixity and change Derrida himself attempts to repeat Marx's own balancing act. Derrida explicitly affirms *permanence* as well as alteration—the former largely in order to hasten the latter—just as Marx himself wanted to do. (Marx, of course, had already performed something similar, offered a parallel diagnosis and correction in regards to stability and alteration, in the case of his own predecessor, Hegel.)

Such repetition, potentially without cessation (since this gambit clearly knows no end), leads to the question, however, of whether today this practice taken as a whole, such foretellese itself, may not prove to be a "mug's game," an enterprise whose time, if I can state it thus, has indeed come and is about to go. In such foretellese, in this gesture in its totality, in fact resides the most vexed difficulty across these debates between Derrideans and Marxians, though the controversy surrounding *Specters* to date has indeed largely taken the form of playing one of these poles off another: by asserting, for example, that Marx, not Derrida, is right (or at least more right) about the future and the type of change we want to see there; or that Derrida, not Marx, is correct as to the grounds, as to the kind of permanent impermanence, that allows for radical, truly revolutionary alteration.

Yet, to refer back to the basic theme of Part II of this volume, is it not modernity itself that has launched us on this practice, that inaugurates such foretellese, this way of doing philosophy *and* forecasting, political theory *and* prophecy, together? And may it not be just this over-rich and ever-expanding diet of theoretical-practical quasi-cognitions that today causes that breakdown in our very ability to grasp our own political situation, leading to the atrophy of the political imagination that began to be sketched above? Paradoxically, this atrophy would turn out to be a sclerosis—the effect of a clotting, an overload—brought on by the seemingly unquestioned necessity to "do politics" with an eye to some other metaphysical, humanistic totality *or its absence*, this difference here counting for naught.

Abstinence from this practice of foretellese—the cessation of invoking permanence for change's sake and engaging in new, secular forms of prophecy—thus may indeed require rethinking, along with politics, permanence as well. In the case of politics, this clearing of metaphysical efflorescences might prove salutary, first and foremost, in permitting us to further reflect on, as Chantal Mouffe and others are already attempting to do, the relation of friend / enemy to this field[34]—a distinction whose day had already seemed to be past when Fukuyama wrote and when *Specters* appeared, yet which once again appears unavoidable.[35] As to permanence, whether this means once more having recourse to the now seemingly hopeless byways of a putative metaphysical or egological absolute, or whether new modes and new frameworks of thinking—perhaps in their own way also more fleeting (more like music or literature than architecture), even as they imprint this dimension—can be discovered is a question with a far longer temporal horizon. It can only be left, I fear, to future generations, to the future practitioners of this sort of work, to those who continue to find themselves with the vocation for speculative thinking and dallying with the lasting—that is to say to the Derridas and Marxes of generations to come.

Notes

Introduction: Fielding Derrida

1. "Je suis en guerre contre moi-meme"; Jacques Derrida, in *Le Monde* (August 2004).

Chapter 1: Deconstruction as Skepticism

1. Paola Marrati's *La genèse et la trace* (Dordrecht: Kluwer, 1998) [trans. Simon Sparks, *Genesis and Trace: Derrida Reading Husserl and Heidegger* (Stanford, Calif.: Stanford University Press, 2005]) was one of the first to examine in depth the roots of Derrida's thought in phenomenology. In 1996 Leonard Lawlor declared " 'Violence and Metaphysics' is deconstruction in the making" ("Phenomenology and Metaphysics: Deconstruction in *La voix et le phénomène*," *Journal of the British Society for Phenomenology* 27, no. 2 (1996): 116–36, 118); and he expanded this claim in Chapter 6 of *Derrida and Husserl: The Basic Problem of Phenomenology* (Bloomington: Indiana University Press, 2002). In 2005, I published *Essential History: Jacques Derrida and the Development of Deconstruction* (Evanston, Ill.: Northwestern University Press, 2005).

2. One example of such criticism, which on its terms presents quite a valuable account of Derrida's project, is Jeffrey Nealon's "The Discipline of Deconstruction," in *PMLA* (October 1992): 1266–79.

3. One notable exception is Henry Staten's relatively early, and still relevant, *Wittgenstein and Derrida*, which in fact begins not from Wittgenstein, but from a careful examination of Husserl's doctrines, especially those pertaining to signification, and Derrida's deconstruction of these. Staten goes out of his way *not* to position Derrida as a skeptic in respect to Husserlian phenomenology (*Wittgenstein and Derrida* [Lincoln: University of Nebraska Press, 1984], 47–48).

4. Christopher Norris, *Derrida* (Cambridge, Mass.: Harvard University Press, 1987), 85–86.

5. Norris unequivocally affirmed deconstruction as skepticism in his earlier book; see *Deconstruction: Theory and Practice* (London: Methuen, 1982), 127–28.

6. Norris, *Derrida*, 87

7. Ibid., 86.

8. Ibid., 156.

9. Richard Rorty, *Consequences of Pragmatism* (Minneapolis: University of Minnesota Press, 1982), 98, and *Essays on Heidegger and Others: Philosophical Papers 2* (Cambridge: Cambridge University Press, 1991), 112.

10. Rorty's pointed Derrida interpretation is important, despite this. Leaving aside Rorty's Derrida "redescriptions," Rorty's questions make us think further about Derrida's project as a whole, and they raise the problem of the coherence of Derrida's thought in totality. In Chapter 1 of my *Essential History* (*Essential History: Jacques Derrida and the Development of Deconstruction* [Evanston, Ill.: Northwestern University Press, 2005]), I treat at length Rorty's interchanges with Rodolphe Gasché's and Geoffrey Bennington's quasi-transcendental interpretations of Derrida.

11. Derrida, in *Deconstruction and Pragmatism*, ed. Chantal Mouffe (London: Routledge, 1996), 81.

12. Norris, despite all that is genuinely helpful in his work, ultimately does not succeed in showing how such rationality and emancipatory discourse works in Derrida. Thus Norris, after discussing C. S. Peirce, declares: "Derrida describes it as his purpose in this essay 'to bring about a dialogue between Peirce and Heidegger,' a dialogue that would question the principle of reason without thereby giving way to an irrationalism devoid of critical force" (161). Norris remains unable to say how this "dialogue that would question the principle of reason without thereby giving way to irrationalism" is to take place, however. Norris' introduction of Habermas' neo-Kantian language shows this; Norris relies on Habermas' model of critical reason to account for the critical force Norris imputes to Derrida because Habermas' is a readily identifiable model of critical reason. The much more difficult task of isolating such a model in Derrida, especially at this epoch, is one that Norris does not pursue. Yet the Habermasian model is clearly an importation. It brings Norris back into contact with the pragmatist construal of truth Norris and Derrida supposedly reject, even in the very chapter that this rejection is enunciated.

13. Norris, *Derrida*, 156.

14. Bernasconi, "Skepticism in the Face of Philosophy," 158, in *Rereading Levinas*, eds. Robert Bernasconi and Simon Critchley (Bloomington: Indiana University Press, 1991): 149–61.

15. "Levinas (according to Derrida) like the skeptics (according to their opponents) cannot help but resort to the language he is supposed to renounce" (Bernasconi, "Skepticism," 154).

16. From the other side, in part following Bernasconi's lead, Simon Critchley, focusing primarily on *Levinas* (Levinas' view of both skepticism and of Derrida) in his *Ethics of Deconstruction* (Cambridge: Blackwell, 1992), 89–90, also encountered this same ambiguity. Levinas' thought is "similar to the logic of skepticism," Critchley claimed (Critchley, *Ethics* 164). Yet "Levinasian ethics is not a scepticism" (Critchley, *Ethics* 158). Again, how and why not is never made clear.

17. Ewa Ziarek, *The Rhetoric of Failure: Deconstruction of Skepticism, Reinvention of Modernism* (Albany: State University of New York Press, 1996), 89.

18. Jonathan Culler, *On Deconstruction: Theory and Criticism after Structuralism* (Ithaca: Cornell University Press, 1982), 155.

19. Again, this is not Culler's *only* view of deconstruction.

20. Culler, *On Deconstruction*, 88.

21. A. J. Cascardi emphasized deconstruction's difference from skepticism in an important essay a while back. Cascardi's Derrida interpretation arrives at the same result. The deconstruction of skepticism differs from Wittgenstein's dissolution of skepticism, says Cascardi. Skepticism's deconstruction is *more skeptical* than Wittgenstein's dissolution, more skeptical *than skepticism*, as Cascardi understands it. Deconstruction affirms "radical doubt (madness)." By "contrast . . . [in] the Wittgensteinian response . . . reason . . . remains the stable anchor, the pivot around which doubt and knowledge turn"; "Skepticism and Deconstruction," *Philosophy and Literature* 8, no. 1 (1984): 1–14, 11. Deconstruction is radical skepticism for Cascardi, too.

22. For example, Derrida states in another context: "I tried to indicate, in my analysis, the essential indissociability of phallocentrism and logocentrism, and to locate their effects wherever I could spot them—but these effects are everywhere . . ." ("TT" 46).

23. *Of Grammatology* (trans. Gayatri Spivak [Baltimore: Johns Hopkins University Press, 1974]). This is a translation of *De la Grammatologie* (Paris: Editions de Minuit, 1967), hereafter referred to as *DG*.

24. Two caveats: first, Derrida has presented some important *anticipatory* reflections in Part 1, Section 1 of *Of Grammatology*, particularly in its final subsection: *L'être écrit* (*DG* 31). The outcome of these reflections focuses on the relation of linguistics to Heideggerean ontology. Both regional and philosophical concerns have already been raised together by the time Derrida turns to Saussure. Derrida has sketched their mutual coordination in a provisional, open-ended way. (See Chapter 6 of my *Essential History* for a detailed discussion of this prefatory moment.)

Second, *Of Grammatology* concerns grammato*logy*. Derrida has asked about writing; he has also asked about the *science* that presumes to study writing. The question about the scientificity of the science of writing is the question that launches Derrida's argument at this moment.

25. A memorable instance is furnished by Derrida's defense of "theory and the concept" against Searle's empiricist, pragmatist construals (*AFT* 126–28).

26. Derrida begins from phonocentrism's thesis, from which logocentrism will be evinced. Phonocentrism is a thesis initially concerning *language*'s treatment. It is linguistics that is phonocentric. Linguistics' phonocentrism makes possible *philosophy*'s logocentrism in turn. "The system of language associated with the phonetic-alphabetic writing is that within which logocentric metaphysics, determining the sense of being as presence, has been produced. This logocentrism, this epoch of full speech, has always placed in parenthesis, suspended and suppressed for essential reasons, all free reflection on the origin and status of writing" (*OG* 43).

27. To be sure, as many have recognized, philosophy later plays a further, critical role. Late in the interchange with Saussure, Derrida brings philosophy back. There is "a short-of and beyond of transcendental criticism," Derrida notes (*OG* 61). Derrida insists now on the transcendental's introduction. The transcendental ought to be introduced, and its introduction "transforms even the terms of the discussion" (*OG* 64). Derrida's *outcome* is not to be decided on here, then; let's grant that. Derrida's writing's ultimate reference is not in question, then, nor is the importance of the transcendental's introduction here denied. The theses concerning phonocentrism and logocentrism come in *before* the transcendental, whatever else is true. Whatever the transcendental's introduction does, it cannot exhaust their meaning. Archi-trace, archi-writing *presuppose* phonocentrism / logocentrism talk, even if they shed a different light on it later as well.

28. One commentator, Irene Harvey, even went so far as to provide a list of these oppositions (*Derrida and the Economy of Différance* [Bloomington: Indiana University Press, 1986], 113). Harvey herself, it should be noted, also expresses doubts about Derrida's treatment of "metaphysics" as an historical and systematic unity (*Derrida and the Economy of Différance*, 8).

29. Thus see *PG* (Paris: Presses Universitaires de France, 1990), 16; *IOG*, 151n184; *WD*, 57; and *POS*, 104n32.

30. Derrida has been solicitous toward Culler's work in particular and has defended Culler publicly at least twice to my knowledge (*AFT*, 134n9; *Memoires for Paul de Man,* trans. Jonathan Culler, Cecile Lindsay, and Eduardo Cadava [New York: Columbia University Press, 1989], 88n—cited in Nealon, "Discipline of Deconstruction," 1992). Such speaking out on behalf of one of his own commentators was rare for Derrida at this epoch.

31. John Caputo, ed., *Deconstruction in a Nutshell: A Conversation with Jacques Derrida* (New York: Fordham University Press, 1997), 9.

32. Ibid.

33. Derrida, *Deconstruction and Pragmatism*, 81.

34. "Antwort an Apel," *Zeitmitschrift: Journal für Ästhetik* (Summer 1987), 83.

35. Heidegger is not an historicist, to be sure. Heidegger doesn't subject thought to historically determined conditions. He does claim all knowledge is a species of *errancy*, dependent on a deeper, nontheoretical truth, itself subject to

a radically contingent genesis. Derrida's relation to Heidegger's thought is thus more vexed than is often recognized. Historicism's explicit rejection by Derrida indicates this; Derrida retains Husserl's rationality commitment while getting right what's right in Heidegger. That may have been deconstruction's prime attraction to many of us. Deconstruction promises to get right what's right in Heidegger, while keeping faith with Husserl's commitment to modern forms of knowledge. Were Derrida really to succeed, the payoff would be enormous for philosophy, for thought, or something like these.

Chapter 2: Derrida, Husserl, and the Commentators: A Developmental Approach

1. For one example, see Derrida's defense of the ideality of concepts in *AFT*, 116–17.

2. Again, Henry Staten's fine early work, which still has much important to say about Derrida's relation to Husserl, is an exception to this rule (*Wittgenstein and Derrida* [Lincoln: University of Nebraska Press, 1984], esp. 31–63). Of late, Derrida's relation to Husserl has received more attention, gaining impetus from Claude Evans' 1991 *Strategies of Deconstruction* (Minneapolis: Minnesota University Press), and the publication of Derrida's master's thesis, *PG* (Paris: Presses Universitaires de France, 1990); and its translation by Marian Hobson, *The Problem of Genesis in the Philosophy of Husserl* (Chicago: University of Chicago Press, 2003).

3. The 1989 article of Rudolf Bernet, an eminent Husserlian, on Derrida's "Introduction" has long led the way for interpretations of this piece by Husserlians and Derrideans alike (see "On Derrida's 'Introduction' to Husserl's *Origin of Geometry*," in *Derrida and Deconstruction*, ed. Hugh Silverman [New York: Routledge, 1989]). Apart from Bernet and Françoise Dastur (see "Finitude and Repetition in Husserl and Derrida" in Leonard Lawlor, ed., *Derrida's Interpretation of Husserl, Southern Journal of Philosophy* 32 [Supplement 1994]: 113–30); the other most preeminent Husserl scholars to have weighed in on this issue, J. N. Mohanty and Thomas Seebohm, tend to have the most nuanced views. Bernet, Seebohm, and Mohanty are all acutely aware of the problems Husserl's thought leaves in its wake and thus much less closed off to assistance, wherever it may come (see Thomas Seebohm, "The Apodicticity of Absence," in William McKenna and J. Claude Evans, eds., *Derrida and Phenomenology* [Dordrecht: Kluwer, 1995]: 185–200; and J. N. Mohanty's chapter on Derrida in *Phenomenology: Between Essentialism and Transcendental Philosophy* [Evanston, Ill.: Northwestern University Press, 1997]).

4. "My aim is . . . with what Derrida . . . takes Husserl to have said"; Alan White, "Reconstructing Husserl: A Critical Response to Derrida's *Speech and Phenomena*," *Husserl Studies* 4 (1987): 45–62, 46; cf. Dane Depp, "A Husserlian Response to Derrida's Early Criticisms of Phenomenology," *Journal of the British Society for Phenomenology*, 18, no. 3 (1987): 226–44, 226; Evans' *Strategies* 1991, xv; and Mohanty, *Between*, 62. Burt Hopkins has a more nuanced view in his

"Derrida's Reading of Husserl in *Speech and Phenomena*," *Husserl Studies* 2 (1985): 193–214, 193–194, but 204.

5. Mohanty, notably, has acknowledged these differences (Mohanty, *Between*, 63). But even he has not really registered the influence on Derrida of Fink's reading of Husserl, Cavaillès critique, nor Gaston Berger's interpretation, which expands on Fink and whose book, at least, has little to do with Descartes.

6. "I will not . . . be directly concerned with Derrida's various criticisms and his deconstruction of Husserl; however to the extent such criticisms and deconstructions rest on his understanding of Husserl, they would unavoidably be affected by our evaluation of that understanding," writes Mohanty (Mohanty, *Between*, 62). Again, Hopkins is something of an exception. Even Hopkins' aim, however, is to show that "a lack of warrant characterizes Derrida's account of Husserl's thought" (Hopkins, "Derrida's Reading," 194).

7. As Rodolphe Gasché puts this, modeling his own interpretation on the style he believes to be Derrida's: "'*Through* (*à travers*) Husserl's text,' is indeed the way Derrida has characterized his reading of the first Logical Investigation in *Speech and Phenomena*. This is a reading that cuts across the text in order to go beyond it" ("On Representation, or Zigzagging with Husserl and Derrida," in *Southern Journal of Philosophy* 32 Supplement (1994), 3; Gasché's emphasis). Many other commentators work this way as well, though rarely this explicitly.

8. That was Len Lawlor's response, in a nutshell, to Claude Evans in an interchange at the end of the '90s. Evans (or any Derrida critic) must be "looking at the right thing in Derrida's text," claimed Lawlor. Otherwise "his objection is not to the point ("The Event of Deconstruction," *Journal of the British Society for Phenomenology* 27, no. 3 (1996): 313–319, 318)." "If one cannot recognize the issue . . . [that] organizes Derrida's thought, then it is impossible to identify Derrida's readings as distortions"; "Distorting Phenomenology" in Evans, Kates, and Lawlor, "A Forum on *Strategies of Deconstruction*," *Philosophy Today* 42, no. 2 (1998): 185–193, 192.

9. In response to Lawlor, Claude Evans asked how the bite of Derrida's intentions is to be felt, absent "starting with Husserl's texts and Derrida's reading of them?" ("Deconstruction: Theory and Practice," *Journal of the British Society for Phenomenology* 27, no. 3 [1996]: 313–17, 316). Evans called this the "how do we get there from here" problem, and put this problem to me as well.

10. My *Essential History: Jacques Derrida and the Development of Deconstruction* (Evanston, Ill.: Northwestern University Press, 2005), in the second chapter of which I make a similar argument to the one just presented, represents a more sustained attempt to arrive at such a "definitive" outcome. Some reviewers of that work have taken exception to this aim, branding it as inherently non-Derridean (see, esp., Diane Enns, "Notre Dame Philosophical Reviews" [May 8, 2006, online], first and final two paragraphs). Though there probably is something to that criticism, let me recall Derrida's own words from "Afterword to *Limited Inc.*": "How can he [the deconstructionist] demand that his own text be interpreted correctly? How can he accuse anyone else of having misunderstood,

simplified, deformed it, etc.? The answer is simple enough: this definition of the deconstructionist is *false* (that's right: false, not true) and feeble; it supposes a bad (that's right: bad, not good) and feeble reading of numerous texts, first of all mine, which therefore must finally be read or reread" (*AFT* 146). It is in this spirit that I attempted to arrive at a correct reading of Derrida (and Husserl) in my 2005 book, and in which I do so here.

11. I am aware that the notion of "development" upon which *Essential History* also relies has seemed foreign to Derrida and thus to Derrideans, in a fashion similar to "definitive" reading, since the concept seems to imply that a course of reading or a series of texts is reduced to a unitary *telos*. As I again indicate toward the end of this chapter—it is good to get some of this out of the way at the start—as early as *The Problem of Genesis*, in pages still worth reading, Derrida indeed analyzed and rejected the alternatives of *either* opting for teleology, for a *single, continuous revelation* across the various works comprising an author's corpus (in this case Husserl's) *or* the affirmation of a plurality of "absolute beginnings" (by multiplying breaks) (*PG*, 22, *Le problème*, xxxiii). Correspondingly, nothing has surprised me more than this criticism of my book, since *Essential History*'s argument is indeed modeled on Derrida's own response to this aporia in *Problem* (and on his similar approach to Levinas in "Violence and Metaphysics," and Rousseau in the second half of *Of Grammatology*), in a way that I assumed would be immediately recognizable to Derrideans. It includes, without being confined to, a diachronic dimension (the last two chapters do not follow a chronological sequence), in order finally to complicate widely-held schemata pertaining to Derrida's thought. Finally, *Essential History*, in accord with this model, in fact sketches (at least this was my intention) a moment of wild, unexpected, radical genesis (the advent of "deconstruction") to which access would have been impossible without such a developmental or diachronic framework.

12. Many commentators discuss Derrida's *Speech and Phenomena*, trans. David B. Allison (Evanston, Ill.: Northwestern University Press, 1973), without referring to the earlier writings at all (for example, the entirety of Evans' *Strategies*). Those who do examine the early work doubtless see *some* differences. Underlying unity is almost always asserted or assumed. Hopkins and Depp are some of the few in their camp to discuss Derrida's "Introduction" in depth. (Both assume this unity. Depp brings in *Speech and Phenomena* and *Writing and Difference* in the course of a discussion of the "Introduction" without further comment ["A Husserlian Response," 236n25]. Hopkins' discussion of the "Introduction" goes decisively wrong because Hopkins assumes agreement between the "Introduction" and *Speech and Phenomena* at a key point ["Husserl and Derrida on the Origin of Geometry," in *Derrida and Phenomenology*, 61–94, 84]. The unity thesis thus hinders what remain important achievements by these authors.)

13. Some commentators do make important distinctions among Derrida's Husserl writings. A major distinction between *Speech and Phenomena* in its entirety and Derrida's prior work on Husserl (the "Introduction") is recognized by both Bernet and Dastur. "There is . . . a clear difference in Derrida's reading

of Husserl in 1962 and in 1967. In the "Introduction" phenomenology is not unilaterally seen as a restoration of metaphysics. . . ." (Dastur, "Finitude and Repetition in Husserl and Derrida," *Southern Journal of Philosophy* 32, Supplement, 1994: 113–30, 121–22n37). It's "very striking that in the present work [the "Introduction"] Derrida still deals with these themes in the context of a transcendental philosophy—albeit one of a new kind" (Bernet, "On Derrida's 'Introduction,'" 151–52). Why even Dastur and Bernet are led to downplay the difference both see is discussed later in this chapter. J. N. Mohanty is an equally important exception. Mohanty shows an exemplary awareness of *Speech and Phenomena*'s hermeneutic situation (Mohanty, *Between*, 64–66) and arguably makes a stronger distinction between *Speech and Phenomena* and the "Introduction" than anyone else. Mohanty has no quarrel with the Husserl interpretation of the "Introduction" at all. ("Derrida's understanding . . . in his . . . "Introduction" is in my view as 'Husserlian' as any other. . . . Derrida's is a viable interpretation, faithful to the texts, aware of the enormous complexities of Husserl's thinking. . . ." [Mohanty, *Between*, 75].) Yet Mohanty has big differences with *Speech and Phenomena*. Mohanty's comments thus already point toward the possibility that a deep change of perspective on Derrida's part took place between the "Introduction" and *Speech and Phenomena*.

14. Mohanty has drawn attention to this also. "Since he [Derrida] believes in the continuity of Husserl's thought, he may be said to read—as Barry Smith, a dear friend complained of me—the earlier work of Husserl in the light of the later (Mohanty, *Between*, 65)." Mohanty, though ignoring at this moment the broader context in which this reversal takes place—Derrida's prolonged prior engagement with Husserl—agrees with Derrida about Husserl's corpus's continuity: "insisting as he [Derrida] does, and rightly in my view, on the continuity of Husserl's thought" (Mohanty, *Between*, 64). That's just one sign of the extraordinary closeness—but also, consequently, distance—between Mohanty's and Derrida's Husserl readings. Mohanty's treatment of Derrida overall is sober, serious, and respectful. On that Mohanty and Mohanty's "dear friend" unfortunately diverge (see Barry Smith et al, "Letter to the *Times* [London, 1992]," reprinted in *Points . . . Interviews, 1974–1994*, ed. Elisabeth Weber [Stanford, Calif.: Stanford University Press, 1995]: 419–21).

15. Perhaps the key example of such sedimentation is the dependence of ideality on writing for its constitution as this surfaces in *Speech and Phenomena*. Hopkins, Willard, and other Husserlians take Derrida to be denying ideal objectivity's atemporal (or omnitemporal) status by way of this claim. "For every ideal object there is a point in cosmic time when it does not exist," Willard says Derrida claims ("Is Derrida's View of Ideal Being Rationally Defensible?" in *Derrida and Phenomenology*, eds. McKenna and Evans [Kluwer, 1995]: 23–42, 38; cf. Hopkins' piece in the same book, esp. 85). Ideality's status is a vexed issue in Derrida's writings as well as Husserl's. The differing views of Hopkins, Willard, and Depp on ideality attest to the problem in Husserl. (Willard takes Husserl to be a realist when it comes to universals early and late [Willard, "Is Derrida," 32, 35]. Hopkins only discusses ideality in the context of reflection. The privilege of ideality

"vis-à-vis empirical reality" concerns "not a *Seinsmodilität* but an epistemic reflective genesis" ["Derrida's Reading of Husserl in *Speech*," 207; cf 204–5 for Hopkins construal of *Logical Investigations*]. Depp goes even further than Hopkins; he accuses Derrida of "logocentrism" due to Derrida's overly realist construal of ideality [Depp, "An Husserlian Response," 233n21]. Willard has a provocative understanding of the meaning of Being in Husserl, it should be noted; it brings him close to many of the Derrida criticisms Hopkins and Depp make from a different angle. All three denounce Derrida for a too-limited ontological understanding of Husserlian ideality.)

This much is definite. Derrida has always been aware of ideality's rights and defended them from the first. Derrida has always known there is a problem with attributing genesis to ideality in any straightforward way. "It is necessary in order that all genesis, all development, all discourse may have a sense, that this sense would be in some fashion 'already there,' from the first . . ." (*PG* 9). "The primordial passage to the limit is possible only if guided by an essence which can always be anticipated and then 'recognized,' because a *truth* of pure space is in question. That is why passages to the limit are not to be done arbitrarily or aimlessly" (Derrida's emphasis; *IOG* 135; cf. Depp's "An Husserlian Response," 227). This is doubtless not the last word on these matters. The key point is this: Derrida's 1967 writings take these claims for granted. Some of Derrida's views do change in *Speech and Phenomena* in difficult and surprising ways; but even those changes assume these earlier steps. Derrida denies his work is historicist, relativist, skepticist, even today. And Willard's powerful, though idiosyncratic, Husserl interpretation fails to hit its mark, and serves no productive end, attacking Derrida's "historicist / nominalist interpretation of Husserl (Willard, 'Is Derrida,' 35)," due to Willard's neglect of Derrida's organizing aims and the layered development of those aims.

16. Good reasons exist to think *Speech and Phenomena*, or at least *La voix et le phénomène: Introduction au problème du signe dans la phénomenologie de Husserl* (Paris: Presses Universitaires de France, 1967), hereafter *VP*, was the last written of the 1967 works. *De la grammatologie*'s first half (*DG*) and almost all the essays in *L'écriture et la différence* (Paris: Editions du Seuil, 1967) are known to have been published before 1967.

17. See Chapter 7 of this volume for a treatment of one of Derrida's final encounters with Husserl in *Le Toucher*.

18. Mohanty is aware of this as well, at least locally. "Note that the question is not whether Husserl's emphasis on monologue or soliloquy . . . is a step in the right direction or not. The question is: why did Husserl take this step, to what purpose and how does this questionable step hang together with his later moves such as epoché and transcendental phenomenology?" (Mohanty, *Between*, 69).

19. This essay, initially a conference paper, first appeared in French as "'Genèse et structure' et la phénoménologie," in Maurice de Gandillac, Lucien Goldmann, and Jean Piaget, eds., *Entretiens sur les notions de genèse et de structure* (Paris: Mouton, 1965). It became the middle essay (fifth out of ten) of *Writing*

and Difference. For a discussion of its place in Derrida's early writings and of their sequence overall, see note 14 in Chapter 3 of this volume.

20. The "Introduction" *can* be understood to examine the topics that Derrida lists here. A long note in the "Introduction" goes into the phenomenological discourse problem in great depth (*IOG* 79–80n66). Intuitionism and the living present's privilege are questioned in the "Introduction" insofar as Husserl's intuitionism answers to a teleology, and the functioning of an Idea in a Kantian sense, that this intuitionism, Husserl's principle of principles, cannot account for, such that "phenomenology cannot be reflected in a phenomenology of phenomenology" (*IOG* 141). For related reasons, "resting in the simple maintenance of a living present" is said to be impossible as well (*IOG* 153). None of this should make us overlook the following: Husserl's unthought axiomatic *does not* hold center stage in the "Introduction." The discussion of the discourse of phenomenology takes place in a footnote and ends in an ambiguous posture. Intuitionism and the living present's privilege are raised as thematic problems only at the end of the "Introduction"; its ultimate horizon (this teleology), and with it these issues, are probed and questioned; yet this teleology's rights are never decisively brought into doubt with finality in this work. This is why the "Introduction" concludes by affirming "a *primordial and pure* consciousness of difference" (*IOG* 153; my emphasis) and by announcing that "difference would be *transcendental*" (*IOG* 153; my emphasis), rather than by locating Husserl's transcendental itself in any sort of difference, or *différance*, more broadly conceived, as Derrida will do later.

21. "Ponctuations: le temps de la thèse," in *Du droit à la philosophie* (Paris: Galilee, 1990), 445.

22. See Chapter 2 of my *Essential History* for a fuller discussion of this matter.

23. Hopkins recognizes this; his discussion is confused, however, because he has Derrida's aims wrong. Hopkins recognizes Derrida is speaking about a "transcendental language"; yet he believes Derrida's point is that this talk is illicit and that Derrida is saying Husserl's transcendental language must be factical and mundane language, because Hopkins assumes Derrida's thought is everywhere the same, never taking the possibility of the development of Derrida's views' seriously (Hopkins, "Husserl and Derrida," 68).

24. See Chapter 3 for a more extended discussion of the distinction between *Leib* and *Korper* as they relate to signification, as well as related passages here in Section VII of the "Introduction."

25. Bernet has also noticed the difference between Derrida's construal of the book in the "Introduction" and in his later works (Bernet, "On Derrida's 'Introduction,'" 146n7).

26. Behind Derrida's remarks here, it appears, stand Derrida's abandoned doctoral thesis of 1957 on "the ideality of the literary object ("TT" 37)"; cf., also *IOG* 90n93, and "TT" 38).

27. This is not to deny that Derrida's analysis of the book does not push up against the boundaries and limits of Husserlian phenomenology, while remaining

within it. By dint of declaring the book neither empirical nor metaempirical, neither sensible nor intelligible, Derrida clearly sketches an innovation nowhere explicit in Husserl's thinking and perhaps not even entirely in accord with it. Nevertheless, this innovation derives from Husserl's terms and themes (pure tradition, transcendental writing, and language); and, the future fate of the book in Derrida's thought, which I am about to sketch, clearly indicates that Derrida himself found the sketch of the book he crafted in the "Introduction" at best a restricted, limited, breakthrough, not a radical one.

28. See pages 140–41, Chapter 6, of the present volume for a discussion of Derrida's recasting of Fink.

29. Derrida does want to bring the two writings together, then, and Bernet seems to think this intention echoes in Derrida's presentations from the first (Bernet, "On Derrida's 'Introduction,'" 144). To me that's unlikely, since, in addition to all the other reasons brought forward, Derrida even now continues to recognize the difference between transcendental writings' function and its mundane embodiment. "The difficulty of the description is due to writing's admitting and completing the ambiguity of all language," writes Derrida leading up to the passage cited. "Movement of *essential and constituting incorporability*, it [language] is also the place of factical and contingent incorporation for every absolutely ideal object, that is to say for truth" (*LOG* 90 / 92, altered; my emphasis). As I understand Derrida, he is claiming here that a linguistic "incorpora*bility*," a possibility of being embodied in language, contributes to the ideal object's constitution, in tandem with truth, here at the 'moment' that geometry's eidetic is inaugurated. Writing's possibility, understood according to the above stipulations—within the constraints of transcendental intelligibility—is essential to truth, which "has its origin in a *pure* right to speak and write," as Derrida goes on to say (my emphasis). *Once* that eidetic's been constituted, however, once geometry's truth comes to light, mundane language, factical and contingent incorporation is itself rather conditioned by this possibility in turn, and such factical writing exists as accidental in respect to truth's being. ("One time constituted, truth conditions in turn every expression *as an empirical fact*.") The *pure possibility* of writing and language, then, only intersect in any significant way with their worldly, factual existence, at the 'moment' geometry's eidetic is in the course of being constituted and no ambiguity remains after that, claims Derrida. Ultimately, it is a two-step process. And this is thus the crux of the disagreement I have with Bernet. Bernet, by contrast, claims in the "Introduction" "language and, in particular, writing are *always simultaneously* and *indecidably* [my emphasis] the 'movement of essential and constitutive possibility of embodiment (*Verleiblichung*)' as well as 'the place of factual and contingent sensible embodiment (*Verkörperung*)'" (Bernet, "On Derrida's 'Introduction,'" 146–47.) Bernet, that is, does not restrict this interdependence to the moment of constitution and fails to recognize that it lapses after that.

30. The possibility of the disappearance of truth in its barest form, as a forgetting within the transcendentally constituting ego, is the first case considered by

Derrida, and it is rejected straightaway, almost as soon as it is raised. The second case of "a conflagration of the worldwide library" (*LOG* 93), of a destruction of truth that would come to it through its signs, the possibility most proper to this hypothesis in the form Derrida articulates, is rejected equally unequivocally— though in the course of analysis of even greater length—precisely because, were it possible to affect truth by damage to the worldly body of truth's signs, including their total and complete annihilation, this would reduce the entirety of Husserl's thought to nonsense (*LOG* 97). And finally, even in the third hypothesis, culminating in the now-famous comparison between Joyce and Husserl, while testing the limits of Husserl's thinking, is again rejected, since the teleology upon which both Husserl and Joyce depend, the teleology of univocity and truth, is brought forward by Husserl alone; his thought thus receives an asymmetrical privilege, even as Derrida claims that he and Joyce sketch out a common possibility in other respects. Many commentators, most notably Bernet, overlook Derrida's rejection of the possibility of truth's disappearance, and Bernet's interpretation leads him to claim that truth is genuinely threatened, even under case two, by worldly writing's destruction (Bernet, "On Derrida's 'Introduction,'" 147). Compare, however, Derrida himself: "Even if all geometrical 'documents' . . . had come to ruin one day, to speak of this as an 'event' of geometry would be to commit a very serious confusion of sense and to abdicate responsibility for all rigorous discourse" (*LOG* 97).

31. The second half of Chapter 3 of this volume details how, in Chapter 7 of *Speech and Phenomena,* Derrida will finally merge his questioning of transcendental historicity with the interrogation of writing and language.

32. See Derrida's 1990 "Avertissement to *Le problème,*" vi–vii, for his conception of the relation of *Le problème* to his later works.

33. See Chapter 4 of *Essential History* for a far fuller discussion of this sketch.

34. Cf., especially, *WD* 24ff. I owe this reference to "Force," as well as the explicit question of the status of my own methodology and its relation to Derrida's thinking on these matters, to Jay Lampert.

35. Cf., especially, *Le problème,* 5–17. The (perhaps only partial) coincidence of my concern with development and Derrida's own readings extends only to Derrida's early writings. Especially with his explicit introduction of the notion of "ana-chrony" in the late '80s and early '90s, Derrida's standpoint takes on a decisively different cast. I address this phase of his thought, along with its implications for reading as well as for politics, in Chapter 8.

36. I have myself attempted this in Chapter 5 of *Essential History.*

Chapter 3: A Transcendental Sense of Death?
Derrida and the Philosophy of Language

1. I am, of course, aware that the intentions of these four authors run a wide gamut in respect to philosophy and knowledge. Yet they all do indeed also claim to depart radically from philosophy's traditional conceptions of knowledge and inquiry—whether in the guise of Deleuze's (Nietzschean) insistence on difference

and repetition, Adorno's immanent critique of reason and enlightenment, Heidegger's call for a new poetizing thinking of To Be, or Wittgenstein's conception of philosophy as therapy (albeit therapy for profound, not superficial, disquietudes)—and all of them depend on certain standard positions within philosophy itself in order to do so: Heidegger on phenomenology, Wittgenstein on findings in modern logic and analytic philosophy of language, Deleuze on a complex dualism of events and substances, Adorno on the rights of an analysis at once dialectical and empirical.

2. See *SP* 14 / 15.

3. See *SP* 57 / 51: "To restore the original and non-derivative character of signs, in opposition to classical metaphysics, is, by an apparent paradox, at the same time to *eliminate* a concept whose whole history and meaning belong to the adventure of the metaphysics of presence" (my emphasis).

4. For a relatively recent statement of Rorty's ambivalent yet insightful criticisms of Derrida, see his "Derrida and the Philosophical Tradition," a review of Geoff Bennington's "Derridabase," in *Truth and Progress: Philosophical Papers 3* (Cambridge: Cambridge University Press, 1998), 327–50, esp. 336. For a detailed discussion of Rorty's criticism of the interpretation of Derrida as a quasi-transcendental thinker, as well as of this view as such, centered on a treatment of Rodolphe Gasché's work, see Chapter 1 of my *Essential History*.

5. Fenves does not explicitly mention those sentences in which Derrida speaks of a transcendental sense of death, it should be noted. Not only, however, is a discussion of this same section of the "Introduction" central to his treatment of Derrida, and not only does he cite extensively from a paragraph soon after this one, but I take the otherwise unsubstantiated conclusion he draws in regard to writing in that paragraph, namely that it (or the wandering that Fenves says is brought by it) "exposes reason to a crisis: meaning could be forgotten and truth to disappear," in part to be based on this same statement ("Derrida and History: Some Questions Derrida Pursues in His Early Writings," in Tom Cohen, ed., *Jacques Derrida and the Humanities: A Critical Reader* [Cambridge: Cambridge University Press, 2001]: 271–95, 283).

6. Fenves, "Derrida and History," 271–95, 283–84.

7. Leonard Lawlor, *Derrida and Husserl: The Basic Problem of Phenomenology* (Bloomington: Indiana University Press, 2002), 118.

8. Fenves, "Derrida and History," 284.

9. Lawler, *Derrida and Husserl*, 118.

10. This is why the fact that Fenves does not explicitly speak of death finally does not much matter here. For him, as for Lawlor, writing in its specificity brings with it the possibility of radical unintelligibility; my question thus concerns on what reading of language and its functioning this is possible.

11. "Writing . . . does not simply make up for a lack but makes up for something that was never there in the first place" (Fenves, "Derrida and History," 283), as Fenves puts it in a nice formulation.

12. Derrida's own comments on the "Introduction" in a relatively recent interview confirm that this notion of *Leib*, or a spiritual corporeality, is central to

his interpretation here. Derrida identifies his focal question in this text as "why does the very constitution of ideal objects . . . require . . . incorporation in what is called a 'spiritual body' of what is written?" (*Points . . .* , ed. Elisabeth Weber [Stanford, Calif.: Stanford University Press, 1995], 345). In his prior occasional comments on the "Introduction," Derrida has not always been this precise about the status of writing, it should be noted (cf. *POS* 5; "TT" 39).

13. Derrida speaks of his first dissertation proposal, devoted to the "ideality of the literary object," in "Time of a Thesis" ("TT" 36–37). Derrida's long note in the "Introduction" (*LOG* 88n1 / *IOG* 90n90) and his accompanying discussion of the "bibliomenon," (containing a very different stance toward the theme of the *book* than his subsequent writings [*LOG* 88–90 / *IOG* 90–91]) clearly derive from this project. See Chapter 2, pages 40–41, for a fuller discussion of the role of the book in the "Introduction."

14. This aspect of Husserl's doctrine in a phenomenological context thus in a certain way parallels what has come to be called Gricean "implicature": H. P. Grice's claim that for linguistic signs to be meaningful in a primary sense they must be used by someone with the intention to induce a belief in another by way of getting that other to assume that belief, by dint of recognizing this intention (Paul Grice, *Studies in the Ways of Words* [Cambridge, Mass.: Harvard University Press, 1989], 26). Radicalizing and transforming this assertion, Steven Knapp and Walter Benn Michaels argued in a now-classic demonstration in "Against Theory" that randomly generated signs are neither genuine signs nor meaningful at all (Steven Knapp and Walter Michaels, "Against Theory," in *Against Theory: Literary Studies and the New Pragmatism*, W. J. T. Mitchell, ed. [Chicago: University of Chicago Press, 1985], 14 ff). Their argument, on which I focus in Chapter 4 (in part by emphasizing their difference from Grice and much speech-act theory), is thus a version of this difference that Husserl, and Derrida, long ago recognized.

15. A good deal of the confusion surrounding the positions Derrida holds at this epoch, in 1961–62, stems from the convoluted publication history of his article, " 'Genesis and Structure' and Phenomenology," not to mention the numerous revisions Derrida subsequently made to all his early writings on the occasions they were collected or republished. In particular, Fenves, despite his sensitivity to much of this context, misleadingly believes the "Introduction" to be prior to "Genesis" (he refers to the former as Derrida's "earlier commentary," "Derrida and History," 283); and on this basis he turns to Derrida's account of Husserl's late thought in "Genesis" to gloss Derrida's comments here in the "Introduction." Yet "Genesis," though only appearing in print in a conference volume in 1965, was originally given as a talk in 1959. And with the appearance of Derrida's 1954 *Le problème*, it became clear that "Genesis" is largely a précis of this earlier work. In both "Genesis" and *Le problème*, most importantly, Derrida still sees Husserl's last work (the *Origin* above all) as far more continuous with the rest of Husserl's writings than he does in the "Introduction," a difference that Derrida himself flags in a footnote he added in 1990 to *Le problème* (*PG*

267n19). Thus, as I have argued elsewhere (here in Chapter 2, and in Chapter 4 of my *Essential History*), the "Introduction" for Derrida represents a new understanding of Husserl's late history, one without which Derrida's mature thought would not be possible, and one cannot, therefore, safely take this work's conclusions to be identical with Derrida's in "Genesis" or in *Le problème*.

16. See Dan Zahavi, *Self-Awareness and Alterity: A Phenomenological Investigation* (Evanston, Ill.: Northwestern University Press), 209–210; the phrase is mine, not his.

17. Without appearing ungrateful to all the fine work John Leavey, Jr., has done as a translator of Derrida over the years—Leavey, to his credit, gives the phrase in French as well as in English in his text—this phrase runs in French, "*en ce qui l'unit à l'absolu du droit intentionnel dans l'instance meme de son échec*" (*LOG* 85): "in this which unites it [death] to the absolute of intentional right in the very instance of its [that right's] check." Compare Leavey's translation: "what unites these things to the absolute privilege of intentionality in the very instance of *its essential, juridical failure*" (*IOG* 88, my emphasis).

18. Fenves himself cites Derrida's phrase, which I am also about to quote, concerning the emergence of "empiricism and non-philosophy" in Husserl's thought (Fenves, "Derrida and History," 184), and his commentary, too, then, partially embraces this threat, which is often seen as another version of a transcendental death owed to writing. Fenves thus fails to recognize that Derrida eventually rejects the grounds on which this possibility is first evoked—namely, the worldly *Körper* of the sign—and that Derrida subsequently changes quite drastically the manner in which truth might be threatened or disappear.

19. "All factual peril," Derrida declares, "therefore stops at the threshold of its internal historicity. Even if all geometrical documents—as well as all real geometers—had come to ruin one day to speak of this as an event 'of' geometry would be to commit the most grave of confusions of sense and to abdicate responsibility for all rigorous discourse" (*LOG* 97 / *IOG* 97). At least in 1962, Derrida thus *rejects* the claim that the threat posed by a worldly writing, or the worldly sensible inscription of the sign, can affect the truth. He denies such destruction can have any effect on the validating objects of geometrical knowledge, that such destruction could in any way be deemed an actual "event *of* geometry."

20. Too often it has gone unnoticed that Derrida's three scenarios concerning the disappearance of truth, which he himself explicitly numbers, proceed dialectically, each assuming the negation of the prior one. Thus the scenario to which the numeral "3" is appended (*LOG* 97 / *IOG* 97) alone has any chance of being valid.

21. Fenves' analysis, to be fair, by no means simply ignores this side of Derrida's problematic. Fenves does recognize, more than most commentators, the association of the power of writing with that of meaning: his talk of the "wandering" inherent in writing attests to this, as does the "endless flight" spoken of above, which, most precisely, is a flight from the "reawakening" of those meanings laid down in writing (Fenves, "Derrida and History," 284).

22. See Chapter 6, page 140, for a detailed discussion of how writing as construed by Husserl boosts meaning to infinity.

23. Cf. the end of section X of the "Introduction" (*LOG* 152–55 / *IOG* 139–41). There, Derrida says of the Idea that "its own particular presence . . . cannot depend on a phenomenological type of evidence" (*LOG* 152 / *IOG* 139), a claim that eventually leads him famously to suggest that "perhaps phenomenology cannot be reflected in a phenomenology of phenomenology" (*LOG* 155 / *IOG* 141; cf. Chapter 6 of this volume for a further discussion of this claim). Nevertheless, Derrida's subsequent mention of the *Logos* as this sentence continues ("and that its *Logos* can never appear as such . . . but, like all Speech [*Parole*] can only be heard or understood through the visible") already points toward the reconception of this *telos* in Section XI and Derrida's *rapprochement* with Husserl that I am about to discuss. For Derrida's entire analysis at this moment plays off a distinction between sight and speech, the phenomenal medium of vision and the discourse that need only pass through it (cf. Derrida's earlier remarks on the Aristotelian "Diaphane" [*LOG* 152 / *IOG* 138]). Thus Derrida, while indeed questioning the scope of phenomenology's principle of principles, is also *affirming* this telos, the *transcendental logos* as the origin of all philosophical responsibility in general, thanks to an analysis that is clearly a novel Husserlian variant of Heidegger's construal of conscience as *voice*, a thematic that Derrida himself of course will later call into question.

24. Cf. *PG* 99, 99n73.

25. At the end of the "Introduction," Derrida gives this problem an interpretation that brings it finally much closer to Husserl's own thought and more in line with the architecture of his philosophy than first seemed apparent. In some of the most difficult pages Derrida has ever penned (and I am here thus saying quite a lot) Derrida argues that this *telos*, the Idea in the Kantian sense, which under certain conditions may be identified with god (with "transcendental divinity" [*LOG* 163 / *IOG* 147]), has two possible interpretations. On one interpretation it precedes the history of its passage—it simply preexists, and stands outside, its active apprehension. On the other, to be meaningful at all, this *telos*, or god, must be immanent to a transcendental history and activity. Even God (or a god) may only meaningfully be said to be thanks to its manifestation within finite acts of apprehension and thus is tied to "constituting historical transcendental subjectivity" (*LOG* 164 / *IOG* 148). Since, however, neither of these sides is finally thinkable without the other, since this *telos* gives itself within history as what stands beyond it, while it, in turn, has no existence apart from this giving or sending—these two poles must be seen as parts of a single possibility, which Derrida deems "a divine *logos* . . . [which is] yet . . . but the pure movement of its own historicity" (*LOG* 164–65 / *IOG* 148). And from this analysis thus stems Derrida's oft-cited claim that "the absolute is passage" (*LOG* 165 / *IOG* 149). Thanks to this reciprocity, what is first and last for Husserl, Derrida argues, is finally *passage*—the passage, however, of an absolute transcendental *logos*, a *pure* sense or meaning in its radical historicity.

26. Overlooking this may be the most decisive error Fenves makes when it comes to the theme in which he himself is most interested, namely that of history. Fenves writes, "But history can then have no other subject than meaning and meaning must be recovered after all—after, that is, the dangerous epoch of writing. An inquiry into the history of geometry, for example, could never begin if it did not take the *telos* of this history—the sense of geometry as we know it—for its starting point" (Fenves, "Derrida and History," 284). What Fenves neglects, however, is that matters are more nearly the reverse: this *telos* and this transcendental history could not be discovered had this sense not first been disclosed in its own right. The sense of geometry is not first and foremost a *telos*, but an eidetic intuition—a present knowledge whose existence thus serves as the transcendental condition of Husserl's own inquiry. Indeed, Husserl's analysis may show that the inauguration of idealities, such as geometrical objects, depends on the possibility of writing, but this demonstration assumes the present givenness of such ideal objects, whose rights have become known thanks to a static phenomenology. So, too, accordingly, any loss of meaning that accrues to these signs by dint of their historicity, due to their possible wandering, only becomes conceivable within the broader framework of the rights of meaning that phenomenology sets out; nor can wandering mute signs of whatever sort, consequently, have a more radical and endangered historicity than that Husserl stipulates. Indeed, it is for this reason, I would suggest, because Derrida came to accept Husserl's own view of history and historicity, that he came to doubt whether there is any history at all—moving from a certain early sympathy to transcendental or intentional history and historicity in the "Cogito and the *History of Madness*" and "Violence and Metaphysics" to a repudiation of these in *Of Grammatology* and the later works, a movement which I track in the final chapter of my *Essential History*.

27. As I indicate in the preceding chapter, a small though telling indication that Derrida's findings in the "Introduction" led Derrida to invent deconstruction is offered by Derrida's recourse to Husserl's account of the sign in Section VII of the "Introduction"—his recourse to the very same account of the sign that he takes as the starting point for his deconstruction in *Speech and Phenomena*. In 1962 Derrida footnotes, without qualm or question, Husserl's sign construal at the start of the first *Logical Investigation* (*LOG* 90n3 / *IOG* 92n96); on this basis he introduces those considerations pertaining to the worldly *Körper* of the sign and the possible disappearance of truth, discussed above. Derrida in 1962 thus had yet to question Husserl radically in regard to his conception of signification, and it may well be that the impasses that he encountered in moving beyond the limits of Husserl's thought on the basis of Husserl's own account of signification (in the manner just exhibited) caused Derrida to turn to Husserl's early work and subsequently take this same treatment of the sign as his starting point for a far more radical treatment of all phenomenology.

28. I have attempted this elsewhere in Chapter 5 of my *Essential History*, with the exception of *Speech and Phenomena*'s final chapter. That chapter eventually becomes the object of my inquiry in the present one.

29. Geoffrey Bennington, "Derridabase," in *Jacques Derrida* (Chicago: University of Chicago Press, 1993), 110.

30. The importance of death as such a condition is all the more evident if this passage is linked with an earlier one in *Speech and Phenomena*, in which death is also given a central role. Derrida himself in fact refers back to it, noting, "earlier we had acceded to the 'I am mortal' starting from the 'I am,' [while] here we understand the 'I am' out of the 'I am dead'" (*VP* 108 / *SP* 97). In the passage to which he refers, Derrida had argued that Husserl's interpretation of the so-called "living present" (the ur-form of lived time, the lowest level of absolute consciousness), by dint of its rights extending beyond all finite bounds, bore within it an index toward the (mundane) subject's death (*VP* 60 / *SP* 54). The unlimited certainty that evidence of any sort would ultimately manifest itself within a living present—thus as a phenomenon for a phenomenology—in order to have meaning on a transcendental plane has to refer to the death, to the mortality of the worldly subject as that which this domain surpasses in principle, as that which, as a form of life, it reaches beyond, and it thus implies such nonpresence in the present certainty it has about itself. Since, however, Husserl himself would refuse factical death any sort of significance on the transcendental plane, this way of seeing the certainty of the living present would be at once qualifying and disqualifying of Husserl's transcendental standpoint. It would be a genuine quasi-, or here perhaps better, hyper-, transcendental condition of transcendental self-certitude.

31. I am here drawing on David Kaplan's famous essay from the 1970s, "Demonstratives" (Xerox, UCLA Department of Philosophy, 1976; excerpted and reprinted in *Basic Topics in the Philosophy of Language*, ed. Robert M. Harnish [Prentice Hall: Englewood, New Jersey, 1994], 275–319), as well as John Perry's "Frege on Demonstratives," ("Frege on Demonstratives," *Philosophical Review* 86 [1977], reprinted in *Pragmatics: A Reader*, ed. Steven Davis [New York: Oxford University Press, 1991], 146–59) for this analysis of indexicals. Kaplan's work subsequently has been the subject of a great deal of discussion and controversy, but for my purposes here, as an alternative to the Derrida-Bennington construal of "I" rather than as a valid account, complete in itself, the theory as presented by Kaplan, and contextualized and made more accessible by Perry, suffices.

32. Perry defines the role of an indexical "as a rule taking us from an occasion of utterance to a certain object" (Perry, "Frege," 149) and goes on to show how the value it yields when used (its reference) cannot be captured in a Fregean sense or thought. Kaplan's "character" is equivalent to Perry's "role," and Kaplan calls "content" what indexicals yield on different occasions of their use. Though the terminology gets tricky, since Kaplan identifies the character of a term with its (linguistic) meaning, nevertheless Kaplan's basic point is that this meaning is in no way identical with content in the case of indexicals. What "I" signifies when a speaker says "I am alive" cannot be taken as synonymous with the rule given by language for the use of "I," since the former, for Kaplan, again has no synonyms at all, insofar as indexicals refer directly. "For two words or phrases to be

synonyms, they must have the same content in every context. In general, for indexicals it is impossible to find synonyms. This is because indexicals are directly referential, and the compound phrases which can be used to give their reference ('the person who is speaking,' 'the individual being demonstrated') are not" (Kaplan, "Demonstratives," 296).

33. After all, is it not surprising that the mere fact of saying "I" should have so strong an implication for what is being talked about that the *necessity* of it being finite or mortal follows wholly from such talk? Would this not, for example, appear to be a rather odd proof against the common theological claim of the soul's immortality? An example furnished by another indexical, "now," which Perry offers ("Frege," 155), can make clearer why these conclusions may be implausible. In the case of "now," if the "the faculty meeting starts at 12 noon" is true, there will be a moment when this and "the meeting starts now" are equivalent. Nevertheless, one can affirm the former without ever affirming the latter (if, for example one never notices the time during that part of the day); yet this fact appears to have no bearing whatsoever on the meeting actually starting, and thus no bearing on the fact that "the meeting starting now" reports. Just so little, in turn, does my inability to know to what "I" refers in some instance—such as a note found on the ground or overhearing a passing conversation—seem to have any bearing on whether its referent can or does possibly exist.

34. Cf. Fenves, "Derrida and History," 283n19.

35. Derrida concludes Chapter 2 of *Speech and Phenomena*, "The Reduction of Indication," by announcing that expression is caught in an "indicative web" (*VP* 33 / *SP* 30). Subsequently, he extends this claim to further features of Husserl's analysis, such as gestures and the intimating function, thus speaking in summary later of "indication, which covers nearly the entire surface of language" (*VP* 44 / *SP* 40).

36. For a discussion of Derrida's reading of Austin, employing similar reference points, see pages 86–89 of Chapter 4.

37. One of Searle's innovations in his *Speech Acts* was the incorporation (and transformation) of Grice's early account of meaning into speech-act theory, a development that, as Searle himself says, "makes a connection between intention and meaning": John Searle, *Speech Acts: An Essay in the Philosophy of Language* (Cambridge: Cambridge University Press, 1969), 43.

38. Kaplan goes to some length to show that the content of an utterance containing an indexical remains what it is, even in cases in which the speaker or agent of expression has in fact herself or himself misidentified that to which the object refers (cf. 289–90). Subsection E, Corollary 2 of "Demonstratives" thus bears the subtitle "Ignorance of the referent does not defeat the directly referential character of indexicals." There Kaplan tells us that "the foregoing remarks are aimed at refuting *Direct Acquaintance Theories of direct reference* . . . theories [for which] the question of whether an utterance expresses a singular proposition turns, in the first instance, on the speaker's *knowledge of the referent* rather than on the form of the reference" (Kaplan, "Demonstratives," 308).

39. This is not to deny, to be clear, that reference in the analytic tradition, including in these cases, is taken as fundamental: that successful reference is assumed to be the "normal" case, and that its possibility generally does not really come into doubt. Consequently, what Derrida calls "logocentrism"—the precomprehension of all language through the *logos*, viewing it in light of its capacity for reference and for truth—is a reasonable characterization of these construals and this tradition as a whole. Presence to a subject, however, and, with that, the privilege of speaking or oral discourse—what Derrida calls phonocentrism—would be far more foreign to this tradition than Derrida often seems to recognize. This distance from presence should not be surprising, however, since analytic philosophy itself could be said to stem from an innovation in *writing*, namely Frege's *Begriffschrift*. (See Chapter 4 for a further working out of these points on the basis of a detailed presentation of the implications of Frege's thought for how language becomes modeled in subsequent analytic philosophy.)

40. See Perry's "Frege on Demonstratives" for a detailed account of why this is the case.

41. Derrida, after drawing on Husserl's own analysis to question Husserl's construal of the "I" ("*Husserl's own premises should sanction our saying exactly the opposite*" [*VP* 107 / *SP* 96, Derrida's emphasis]), goes on to specify that "we draw this conclusion . . . from the idea of pure logical grammar, from the sharp distinction between the meaning-intention, which can always function 'emptily,' and its 'eventual' fulfillment by the 'object'" (*VP* 108 / *SP* 97). With this notion of "a pure logical grammar," Derrida is referring to the opening of Husserl's *Logical Investigations* IV, where Husserl contrasts those "laws, which govern the sphere of complex meanings, and whose role is to divide sense from nonsense" from "the so-called laws of logic in the pregnant sense of this term" (*LI*, Vol. 2, 493).

42. As recently as 1996, for example, responding to Rorty, Derrida has avowed that he is "a philosopher," "that I want to remain a philosopher and that this philosophical responsibility is something that commands me" (Mouffe, ed., *Deconstruction and Pragmatism*, 81).

43. "Q: One can put it in other terms, is there a philosophy of Jacques Derrida? A: No" (Weber, ed., *Points*, 361).

Chapter 4: Literary Theory's Language:
The Deconstruction of Sense vs. the Deconstruction of Reference

1. Eve Sedgwick, *The Epistemology of the Closet* (Berkeley: University of California Press, 1990), 202; my emphasis.

2. In the last decade or so, Jonathan Goldberg, Madhavi Menon, Valerie Rohy, and others have brought even Sedgwick's rather flexible historicization and periodization into question under the heading of queering temporality and history. (See Jonathan Goldberg and Madhavi Menon, "Queering History," *PMLA* 120.5 [2005]: 1608–1617, and Valerie Rohy, "Ahistorical," *GLQ* 12.1 [2006]: 61–83.) Whether these initiatives contest or extend Sedgwick's privileging of the semantic dimension of language, and thus how they map the interplay of history

and text, reference and meaning, are questions to my knowledge not yet posed, and which thus may call for further study.

3. Chapter 8, treating Derrida's *Specters*, offers a too-cursory appraisal of the current state of Marxist cultural studies (see pages 199–201). My current project, focused on the twentieth-century notion of historicity, examines the Marxian engagement with history at the end of the last century in greater detail.

4. For example, see Stephen Greenblatt, "Toward a Poetics of Culture," in *The New Historicism*, ed. H. Aram Veeser (New York: Routledge, 1989), 1–14, 8, and Homi Bhabha, *The Location of Culture* (New York: Routledge, 1994), 108.

5. In addition to the neopragmatist critics, who clearly had a significant acquaintance with analytic philosophy and some of whom I discuss in the present chapter, Reed Way Dasenbrock, and the theorists he has anthologized over the years—in particular Henry Staten and Samuel Wheeler, to name the ones closest to my present topic—have long been situating themselves in the divide between the analytic and Continental traditions. Among others, see Henry Staten, *Wittgenstein and Derrida* (Lincoln: University of Nebraska Press, 1984); *Redrawing the Lines: Analytic Philosophy, Deconstruction and Literary Theory*, ed. Reed Way Dasenbrock (Minneapolis: University of Minnesota Press, 1989); *Literary Theory After Davidson,* ed. Reed Way Dasenbrock (University Park: Pennsylvania State University Press, 1993); Samuel Wheeler, *Deconstruction as Analytic Philosophy* (Stanford, Calif.: Stanford University Press, 2000); Reed Way Dasenbrock, *Truth and Consequences: Intentions, Conventions and the New Thematics* (University Park: Pennsylvania State University Press, 2001).

6. In Chapter 2 of his book *Origins of Analytical Philosophy*, Michael Dummett lays out three aspects of Frege's philosophy that anticipate "the linguistic turn" (Dummett, *Origins of Analytical Philosophy* [Cambridge, Mass.: Harvard University Press, 1993], 5 [*OG*]). My first point here and Dummett's coincide; after that we diverge, though other portions of my presentation have also been influenced by Dummett's treatment.

7. Gottlob Frege, *The Foundations of Arithmetic*, trans. J. L. Austin, 2nd revised edition (Evanston, Ill.: Northwestern University Press, 1978), x.

8. See Frege, *Foundations*, 59, 71ff.

9. Frege himself generally gave priority in principle to the thought expressed by a sentence (to the meaning of a sentence) over the actual sentence—over the sentence used in German or French, to express this thought. And the thought, the content or claim, presumed to be the same across different sentences in different languages, as well as in some identical sentences multiply uttered, is sometimes referred to as "the proposition." Dummett, however, in part by looking to Frege's own practice—and I will be following Dummett here—argues that the sentence for Frege may really be primary after all (Dummett, *Origins*, 10). Moreover, to the extent Frege subscribed to such an independent realm of meanings, he brought out another set of concerns, the so-called "composition principle," in which the parts of a sentence rather than the whole would be primary, and this

may be in competition with the context principle that I stress here. Dummett famously distinguished between these two aspects of Frege's thought as applying to the "order of recognition" and the "order of explanation" of a sentence's meaning respectively (Michael Dummett, *Frege: Philosophy of Language*, 2nd edition [Cambridge, Mass.: Harvard University Press, 1981], 4). I am only focusing on the latter, "the order of explanation," in order to bring forward that aspect of Frege's thought that has had the most influence on subsequent analytic philosophy (cf. Dummett, *Origins*, 19, for what I take to be Dummett's most recent view on the status of this difference).

10. Dummett argues that the sentence in use, the importance of assertion and assertoric force, comes fully forward only thanks to the early Wittgenstein's take on Frege's original doctrine. Dummett nevertheless concludes that "a study of the use of language in communication is a legitimate development of Frege's theory" (Dummett, *Origins*, 12–13).

11. For a further discussion of the status of the word in Saussurean linguistics, see Chapter 6 of my *Essential History*. It should be noted that this problem of the status of the word, and the related one of the criteria of identity for a sign as such, were much discussed in later structuralism, particularly by André Martinet and Roman Jakobson.

12. Indeed, Frege himself, it is worth noting, in the *Foundations of Arithmetic*, is engaged in working out the consequences of a new language, or more properly a new writing that he had developed—a new *Begriffschrift* ("concept-writing") that he had introduced in an earlier work bearing this term as its title. This writing was designed to allow the novel structures of meaning proper to the sentence or the proposition—the logical syntax common to mathematical as well as other discourse—to be made manifest. Thus language itself with Frege begins to become multiple—languages about language arising, potentially reaching to infinity—language taking on a surprising third, vertical "dimension," if you will.

13. Richard Rorty's classic anthology *The Linguistic Turn: Recent Essays in Philosophical Method* (Chicago: University of Chicago Press, 1967), amply attests to this diversity.

14. Barry Smith, "On the Origins of Analytic Philosophy," in *Grazer Philosophische Studien*, 35 (1989): 153–73, 159. Smith's article is a response, written from the perspective of Husserlian phenomenology, to an earlier version of Dummett's *Origins*.

15. The *locus classicus* for Frege's setting out of these distinctions is the first half of his "On Sense and Reference"; for a translation, see *Translations from the Philosophical Writings of Gottlob Frege*, eds. Peter Geach and Max Black (Oxford: Basil Blackwell, 1977), 56–78.

16. Though Frege indeed was the first to define concepts through their extensions, a possibility that subsequently proves to play an important role in much analytic philosophy, Frege's developed doctrine of the concept was a good deal more complicated than this rather simplified view of a straightforward extensionalism that I am about to set out, in part due to the important role played for him

by the distinction between sense and reference in respect to concepts themselves (see "On Concept and Object" in Geach and Black, eds., *Translations*, 42–55, as well as Dummett, *Origins*, 1981, 245ff). It is also the case that, solely within the context of analytic philosophy, Frege's views are often contrasted with those of someone like Quine, who, rejecting sense entirely, is an extensionalist about concepts in a way that Frege never was. Nevertheless, a straight line may be drawn from one aspect of Frege to Quine—Frege's thought gives Quine's a foothold—and this is the most important thing for our purposes.

17. Wheeler, *Deconstruction as Analytic Philosophy*, 123.

18. Cf. Ludwig Wittgenstein, *Philosophical Investigations*, trans. G. E. M. Anscombe, 3rd ed. (New York: MacMillan, 1958), ¶693.

19. Geoffrey Galt Harpham, in a recent important work, *Language Alone: The Critical Fetish of Modernity* (New York: Routledge, 2002), has pursued this question of whether language exists, in an attempt to question the leading role this theme has played in the humanities generally and recent literary theory in particular. While his monumental attempt to recast the history of theory in the twentieth century is highly impressive (and I am especially sympathetic to some of the motives that underlie it), my much more modest undertaking essentially differs from his in that I do not see why this question as to what language is (and indeed whether it is) cannot be a part of theory, and thus contribute to the renewal of theory's questions through the expansion of their context, as I am endeavoring to do here.

20. Thus Dummett, embarking on his comparison of the role of truth in Frege and Davidson, stresses the importance reference already has in Frege, speaking of "the form Frege conceived a theory of reference—the basis of a theory of sense—as taking" (Dummett, *Origins*, 17 and ff.).

21. Frege's new emphasis on reference can be seen, first, in his distinguishing reference within the sentence or statement as a semi-autonomous function by establishing a heterogeneity between function (concept) and referring expression (variable). So, too, secondly, with his invention of quantification, a powerful innovation in logic that I will not otherwise here discuss, the singular proposition ("Socrates is snub-nosed") receives greater autonomy from the universal ("all humans have noses"); existence claims are distinguished syntactically, not semantically, from all other sorts. In these respects Frege's approach gave special significance to language's ability to refer, to the status of particulars and individuals within discourse (though other aspects of his theory also mitigate this emphasis); and it may be said, even in Frege, that the crucial question in respect to language when it comes to its relation to the world is already how to account for those aspects of language wherein it relates to particulars.

22. This remains the most difficult of these three traits to glimpse in Frege—not only because Frege does not explicitly speak of language as such, but also because he, famously, first distinguished sense from reference, not only in respect to sentences, but even in respect to referring expressions (names), assigning to these meanings of their own, and in this respect spawning a line of thought that

derives reference from the sense of the item talked about and that appears to put meaning before referring. Nevertheless, this very distinction between sense and reference, it could be argued, only arose because of the importance Frege himself gave to reference; and such privilege is particularly important in its contrast to the Continental tradition.

23. Thus John Searle has stated, "since Frege, the problem of reference has been regarded as the central problem in the philosophy of language," something Searle himself now thinks "was a mistake" (John Searle, *Expression and Meaning* [Cambridge: Cambridge University Press, 1979], xi).

24. Despite assigning it second-class status, fiction was not in itself as great a problem for Frege's own theory, however, as it is for much subsequent analytic philosophy, in part due to his standing before the linguistic turn, due to his sub-scription to a language-independent realm of thoughts. See, e.g., Gottlob Frege, "Introduction to Logic," in *The Frege Reader*, ed. Michael Beaney (Oxford: Oxford University Press, 1997), esp. 293.

25. The *locus classicus* for this problem in Continental philosophy remains Chapter 1 of Hegel's *Phenomenology*, his treatment of sense-certainty. There Hegel notes: "They *mean* 'this' bit of paper on which I am writing . . . but what they mean is not what they say. This that is meant cannot be reached by language which belongs to consciousness, i.e. to that which is inherently universal" (G. W. F. Hegel, *The Phenomenology of Spirit*, trans. A. V. Miller [Oxford: Oxford University Press, 1977], 66).

26. Here and in what follows, I will at times be using the term "reference" in a somewhat broader sense than is always done in the context of analytic philoso-phy. More specifically, holisms, like those of Quine and Davidson, are sometimes seen as drawing reference into question, insofar as they see referents as "ontologi-cally relative," as inseparable from the totality of a discourse, the practices of an empirical language, or from a triangulated negotiation among speaker, hearer, and world. These positions are sometimes contrasted with so-called direct or causal theories of reference, such as Saul Kripke's or the early Hilary Putnam's, in which referents retain much more autonomy. Nevertheless, even granting these differences (in themselves by no means insignificant), all these approaches start from the assumption that language is preeminently able to talk about the world and thus to refer, and they are themselves all direct heirs of the problematization of reference left by the rise and fall of verificationism in positivism. The centrality of the problem of reference indeed only grows as the analytic tradition develops, as Searle, among others, attests, and this does, to a large degree, bring about an increasing individualization or particularization, or even empiricization in respect to language itself—in initiatives like those already mentioned, but also in the later Wittgenstein or Austin. In all these otherwise highly disparate instances, language itself comes to be remodeled and seen in unexpectedly novel ways, thanks to these concerns related to how it might refer—coming to be seen, for example, as an entity embedded in forms of life; as the practice of this or that historical or empir-ical language stripped of all meaning or intention; or even as an essentially unsta-ble idiolect.

27. Cf. Stanley Fish, *Is There a Text in This Class?* (Cambridge, Mass.: Harvard University Press, 1980), 231, for a similar reading.

28. J. L. Austin, *How to Do Things with Words*, 2nd edition (Cambridge, Mass.: Harvard University Press, 1962), 151.

29. Despite its pathbreaking character in so many other respects—both in regard to his presentation of Derrida's thought and the problems posed by the future of deconstruction that he already saw—Samuel Weber, in his article "It," joins with Derrida's construal of Austin in this key respect (Samuel Weber, "It," *Glyph* 4 [1978]: 1–31, 11); and almost all subsequent commentators sympathetic to Derrida have followed him here.

30. Austin, *Words*, 9.

31. Though I am assimilating Saussure and Husserl in respect to the ability of signification or meaning to function in the absence of reference, I do not mean to suggest that Saussure's structuralism does not bring certain aspects of the traditional conceptions of language into doubt (and Husserl's stance, too, by the way, has complexities upon which I have not commented here). In Chapter 6 of *Essential History*, I examine some of these differences in the case of Saussure, and I also stress Saussure's *difference* from Husserl, both in respect to intentions—not meanings—and with regard to the status of a regional, as opposed to a transcendental, science more generally, for the sake of mapping Derrida's complex interweaving of Saussurean and Husserlian considerations in that context.

32. In regard to the workings of this "highly unexpected fashion" in which deconstruction undoes present meaning, see Chapter 3 of this volume, "A Transcendental Sense of Death: Derrida and the Philosophy of Language."

33. This has been, preeminently, Richard Rorty's question or criticism when it comes to Derrida's project. Rorty questions the philosophy of language that seems to be implied by certain strains of Derrida's texts (or at least certain, quasi-transcendental interpretations of his thought), and Rorty and I agree, at least to this extent. For one of the more recent and uncharacteristically impassioned expressions of this line of questioning, see Rorty's review of Geoffrey Bennington's *Derridabase*, in Richard Rorty, *Truth and Progress: Philosophical Papers 3* (Cambridge: Cambridge University Press, 1998), 335.

34. As in Michel Foucault, *The Order of Things; A Translation of Les Mots et Les Choses* (New York: Random House, 1970).

35. See, for example, Michel Foucault, "Introduction," in Georges Canguilhem, *The Normal and the Pathological*, trans. Carolyn R. Fawcett (New York: Zone Books, 1998), esp. 9.

36. See Steven Knapp and Walter Michaels, "Against Theory," in *Against Theory: Literary Studies and the New Pragmatism*, W. J. T. Mitchell, ed. (Chicago: Chicago University Press, 1985), 11–30, 29, and Fish's response, "Consequences," Ibid., 106–31.

37. After criticizing Fish in the first "Against Theory," and Fish having responded in his essay "Consequences," Knapp and Michaels seem to let the matter drop, at least until Walter Michaels published *The Shape of the Signifier*

(Princeton, N.J.: Princeton University Press, 2004), which only contains occasional comments on his and Fish's differences. Their position, neopragmatism (also affiliated, at times, with Rorty's), is often taken to be essentially the same as Fish's.

38. Fish's proximity to meaning, his reliance on semantics, as we shall further see, can be traced back to Fish's own early encounter with John Searle's version of speech-act theory, which in the present context may also be seen to be something of an outlier in this regard, an exception—albeit only partial, as will also be confirmed—to the privilege assigned to reference by analytic philosophy. Searle's own project, especially at the time Fish engaged with it, had a pronounced bias toward semantics, visible in what Searle called "the principle of expressibility" (Searle, *Speech Acts*, 18). As Searle himself hints (Searle, *Speech Acts*, 19, esp. n2), his insistence on the principle of expressibility and his coordinate commitment to promulgating genuine semantical rules for the illocutionary terms that determine the illocutionary force with which every sentence functions (cf. Searle, *Speech Acts*, 48, 62) goes beyond anything to be found in Austin.

39. Fish, "Text," 307.

40. As late indeed as 1999, Fish writes: "But it is also true that when you come to the end of the antiformalist road, what you will find waiting for you is formalism; that is, you will find the meanings that are perspicuous for you given your membership in what I have called an interpretive community, and as long as you inhabit that community (and if not that one, then some other), those meanings will be immediately be conveyed by public structures of language and image to which you and your peers can confidently point" (Stanley Fish, *The Trouble with Principle* [Cambridge, Mass.: Harvard University Press, 1999], 294–95; cf. Stanley Fish, *Professional Correctness* [Oxford: Oxford University Press, 1995], 13–14).

41. John Reichert, more or less in passing, voiced a similar concern (John Reichert, "But That Was in Another Ball Park: A Reply to Stanley Fish," *Critical Inquiry* [Autumn 1979]: 164–72, 168). Reichert's main point, however, was just the opposite of mine; he wanted to insist on more stable and foundational sentence meanings than Fish himself (Reichert, "Ball Park," 167).

42. This is a delicate point, for Searle, too, insists that the rules governing speech acts are "institutional," not brute, and that they depend on convention. For Searle, however, who at this time seems to be very impressed by Chomsky's program, the force of those rules governing the types of speech acts that especially interested him, while being institutional and inseparable from convention, nevertheless are not conventional in the narrowest sense. Searle is finally interested in acts that are institutional (and in that sense conventional), but not insofar as they are empirically variable, but rather universal institutions, or potentially universal "rules" (Searle, *Speech Acts*, 40). Thus Searle starts *Speech Acts* by pointing out that his is not a linguistic philosophy, with conclusions finally tied to an empirical language, but a philosophy of language (Searle, *Speech Acts*, 4); and in these ways Fish from the first importantly differs from Searle.

43. Reed Way Dasenbrock in his latest work also questions the status of Fish's conventionalism with regard to the rules or norms it assumes, from the point of view of Dasenbrock's interpretation of Davidson's philosophy, and he connects it in a more sweeping way than I do here to a number of developments in recent literary criticism, to some of which Fish himself stands opposed (Dasenbrock, *Truth and Consequences* [2001], 74–75, 137).

44. The argument that Fish makes in "Text" signals a transitional point in his own thinking, establishing the stance he takes up until 1990 and perhaps beyond, a stance evident in the essays collected in *Doing What Comes Naturally* (see especially page 6 of the Introduction, where Fish denies "that meanings are a property of language," and "that language is an abstract system that is prior to any occasion of use"), as well as his article "Rhetoric" in *Critical Terms for Literary Study*, eds. Frank Lentricchia and Thomas McLaughlin [Chicago: University of Chicago Press, 1990], 203–24). Fish will cease to rely as explicitly as he did at first on Searle's own arguments as he goes forward, but his ongoing antifoundationalism, based on this same impossibility of stable literal meanings that he asserts, will continue to be oriented toward questions of semantics and meaning, with consequences that his first work with speech-act theory makes especially visible.

45. Thus early Fish sees speech-act theory itself as giving pride of place to that "realm of values, intentions, and purposes which is often assumed to be the exclusive property of literature" (Fish, *Text*, 108).

46. Though Fish's presentations of Searle's positions are often magisterial, on this one point concerning reference it is not clear to me that he does full justice to Searle's account. Fish focuses on a distinction between "describing," which he identifies with giving a context-*independent* account of an object and that of the more contextual work of referring—"the aim of a description is to characterize an object so that it can be distinguished from all other objects in the world; the aim of a reference is to characterize an object in such a way as to identify it to a person (or persons) with whom you share a situation" (Fish, *Text*, 241). And though Fish is right that for Searle reference *is* context-specific, nevertheless, this is because Searle's point is that reference is an *illocutionary* feature of discourse, an achievement of the act of speech, and not of the proposition per se. This very feature, however, in fact pushes Searle's account of reference toward what is usually meant by describing, toward seeing reference as giving some identifying features of the referent, as opposed to theories (such as those of Putnam or Kripke) that take reference, whether in an illocutionary or a propositional mode, to be a more autonomous function. Correspondingly, due to his proximity to description, Searle himself ends up emphasizing in his account that "meaning is prior to reference; reference is in virtue of meaning" (Searle, *Speech Acts*, 92), and Fish, then, has indeed picked up on this semantic predisposition in Searle to take Searle's own position one step further and present its deconstruction.

47. In fact, at the outset of their "Reply to George Wilson" (Steven Knapp and Walter Benn Michaels, "A Reply to George Wilson," *Critical Inquiry* 19 [Autumn 1992]: 186–93) Knapp and Michaels state "our interest in 'Against

Theory,' and in all our subsequent writings on this subject, has not been in philosophy of language, but in interpretation" (186). Yet, their conclusions concerning interpretation are argued for on the basis of their views in the philosophy of language—from their example of the "wave poem" forward, theirs is a self-professedly "ontological" account of language and the text. Moreover, in addition to the instance already cited above, further reasons to believe that Knapp and Michaels are engaging in some rather grave revisionism (when they deny they were ever interested in language), are given later in this chapter, most notably in the reading I am about to offer of their treatment of the work of P. D. Juhl.

48. Knapp and Michaels, *Against Theory*, 20.

49. Ibid., 21 (my emphasis).

50. Ibid.

51. Not only do Knapp and Michaels make this case against Juhl, but, it should be noted, they extend it to the entirety of speech-act theory. They explicitly claim that their difference from "speech-act theorists" such as Grice and Searle is because the latter perform the same illicit separation of "convention" and "intention" as Juhl (Knapp and Michaels, *Against Theory*, 21n13). This dismissal, of Grice in particular, later came to be the focus of George Wilson's criticism of their position in his "Again, Theory: On Speaker's Meaning, Linguistic Meaning and the Meaning of a Text" (*Critical Inquiry* 19 [Autumn 1992]: 164–85, esp. 172–75). In the meantime, Knapp and Michaels had subsequently penned "Against Theory 2: Hermeneutics and Deconstruction," (*Critical Inquiry*, Vol. 14, no. 1 [Autumn, 1987], 49–68) and were thus in a position to deny that they held the position Wilson assigned to them (Knapp and Michaels, "Reply to George Wilson," 188), which in certain important respects agrees with the one that I have just set out. Not only, however, have other commentators also believed that this position is precisely what they were originally asserting in "Against Theory," namely that the meanings of both an utterance and a piece of language—so-called sentence meaning and utterance meaning—as well as these two entities, speech-acts and language themselves, are one and the same (Searle also, for example, thinks it so; cf. John Searle, "Literary Theory and Its Discontents," *New Literary History*, Vol. 25, no. 3 [Summer 1994], 637–67, 653), but, moreover, it seems to me their position in "Against Theory 2" is inconsistent on the deepest level with the first "Against Theory." After all, if, as they initially said, the whole thrust of theory is to distinguish what cannot be separated, if, as they explicitly state, "to make method possible . . . [is] in more general terms to imagine a separation between language and speech-acts" (Knapp and Michaels, *Against Theory*, 21), once they concede in "Against Theory 2" that such a separation *can* exist and that language may indeed be said to have meanings apart from speech acts, what becomes of their anti-methodological claim—of the claim that reflection on method is not just erroneous, but impossible?

52. For example, they explicitly insist that "a dictionary is an index of frequent usages in particular speech acts—not a matrix of abstract, pre-determined possibilities" (Mitchell, ed., *Against Theory*, 20n12).

53. Knapp and Michaels, *Against Theory*, 23.

54. In the first "Against Theory" Michaels and Knapp accused text-based theory, Paul de Man's deconstruction in particular, of adopting, in the absence of any accompanying conditions, a model of intentionless language—marks, or signs of some sort that mean even without any intentionality—and Michaels has extended this criticism to Derrida's thought in his latest theoretical work, *The Shape of the Signifier* (cf. 126 ff.). Though much exegesis of deconstruction admittedly follows Knapp and Michaels' view, whatever other limitations deconstruction may have, I myself believe that this is not one of them, despite Michaels' repeated insistence on this point (which is nevertheless salutary at least in requiring us to think further about the issue). Paul de Man does invoke autonomous, mechanical, material language; yet only *after* he has first taken into account an *intentional layer* (a two-step approach that roughly maps on to the role of speech, *Rede*, and language, *Sprache*, in Heidegger). In the case of Derrida, as Chapter 3 argues, the inclusion of intentionality on the way to something that is finally not language at all is in fact far easier to demonstrate, due to Derrida's overall reliance on Husserl as a starting point, as *Husserlian* phenomenology everywhere traces all significance and significant acts back to intentions.

55. Knapp and Michaels, *Against Theory*, 14 (my emphasis).

56. Ibid., 14, 16, 101.

57. Doing so, their account, it should be noted, brilliantly avoids all the problems with speech-act theory as a starting point for conceiving literature that Continental and deconstructive types tend to raise: in particular, the confinement of the speech act to the speech situation, the so-called privileging of presence (to a subject, to a speaker and hearer). Thanks to their repositioning of speech acts, to folding them back into language as structurally belonging to it, these acts here take on that structural possibility of the (real) author's absence, the factual default of any known, any present intention that in other contexts is believed to be the primary characteristic of "writing" or the "text."

58. Knapp and Michaels, *Against Theory*, 14 (my emphasis).

59. Ibid., 101 (my emphasis).

60. An interesting attempt at such reflection, with reference points parallel to my own, is Satya P. Mohanty's *Literary Criticism and the Claims of History* (Ithaca, N.Y.: Cornell University Press, 1997). Mohanty has more faith than I in the now-burgeoning "naturalist epistemology," to which he gives a Marxian inflection, but his, as well as Dasenbrock's, recent book, with which I also have some substantial disagreements, are both exemplary attempts by theoreticians to examine the present state of literary studies and ask where we are and where we may go.

61. Nor does this demand, as is sometimes suggested, entail a resolve to dominate all criticism (and every critic) methodologically. Rather, it affirms an ongoing irreducibly *plural* level of discourses—albeit discourses not themselves stable, not wholly of the same type nor always occupying the same positions in respect to one another. As my own work here has shown by bringing together previously

isolated debates and considerations, it is because competing and overlapping discourses exist in the first place that questions concerning their truth inevitably arise. By the same token, no alternative is at hand but to start at those specific intersections at which we find ourselves—in this sense to proceed pragmatically—and to pursue those issues for reflection and thought that have fallen to our lot. Fish uncharacteristically falls into sheer sophistry attempting to rebut what I am in part suggesting here (and which others in the *Against Theory* debate have also put forward): namely, that reflection on a given position from the perspective of another may cause people to change their assumptions without all positions necessarily having been subjected to a thoroughgoing and total theoretical reflection or subordination. Fish calls this "weak foundationalism," and against it he argues that a lot of other things besides reflection also cause people to reconsider their assumptions and to change them ("the trouble is, such reconsiderations can be brought about by almost anything and have no unique relationship to something called "theory" [Mitchell, ed., *Against Theory*, 121; cf. also Fish, *The Trouble with Principle*, 281–83]), which is of course true, but wholly beside the point. It's as if Fish were saying that because a lot of other things could close the door—the wind, a pneumatic device—it couldn't have happened because I asked him to.

Chapter 5: Jacob Klein and Jacques Derrida: The Problem of Modernity
1. Jacob Klein published Parts 1 and 2 of his masterwork "Die griechische Logistik und die Enstehung der Algebra" in Germany during the '30s. See its translation, *GMT*. He subsequently published two books on Plato, as well as a number of articles on other ancient thinkers and poets, and the history of science and mathematics. These last are collected, along with many of his lectures, in *Jacob Klein: Lectures and Essays*, ed. R. B. Williamson and E. Zuckerman (Annapolis, Md.: St. John's College Press, 1985). A recovery and reconsideration of Klein's work today is under way, with Burt Hopkins playing the leading role.
2. See Jacob Klein, "Phenomenology and The History of Science," in *Lectures and Essays*, 65–94), and *IOG*. For Husserl's *Die Ursprung*, see Beilage III in *Husserliana VI, Die Krisis der europäischen Wissenschaften und die transzendentale Phänomenologie*, ed. Walter Biemel (The Hague: Martinus Nijhoff, 1976); trans. David Carr, *The Crisis of European Sciences and Transcendental Phenomenology: An Introduction to Phenomenological Philosophy* (Evanston, Ill.: Northwestern University Press, 1970), Appendix VI. All references hereafter will give first the German and then the English page numbers.
3. See Jacques Derrida, "*De la grammatologie* I," *Critique* 21.223 (December 1965), 1019.
4. A sign of the importance of these considerations to Derrida early and late is shown in his remarks on 9/11, some of which have already proved controversial. The more sympathetic of the two journalists in the *New York Times* to comment on Derrida's life and work after his death cited critically Derrida's claim that "We do not know what we are saying or naming in this way, September 11,

le 11 Septembre . . ." (in Giovanna Borradori, *Philosophy in a Time of Terror* [Chicago: Chicago University Press, 2004], 86; and Edward Rothstein, "The Man Who Showed Us How To Take The World Apart," *New York Times* [October 11, 2004], B1). Had this critic recognized that this feature of not knowing *what* an event in history is, especially as it is unfolding in the "present," has always been part of Derrida's approach to historicity, a position that grew out of Derrida's reading of Husserl's "Origin" (see, e.g., *WD* 60), Derrida's comments would have appeared far less problematic and mysterious.

5. To be sure, much of what is powerful, especially in Derrida's later thinking, comes from overleaping, or perhaps better, from capturing the modern moment within a greater nonlinear and not strictly historical framework, that takes into its purview the ends and roots of the Abrahamic tradition, as well those of Greece, approaching them from the direction of what is yet to come. (See especially Jacques Derrida, "Faith and Knowledge: The Two Sources of 'Religion' at the Limits of Reason Alone," reprinted in Gil Anidjar, ed., *Acts of Religion* [London: Routledge, 2002]: 42–101.) Nevertheless, the question remains: can work aimed at contemporary forms of society, of politics, technology, and knowledge indeed do without a reflection on modernity in its specificity?

6. It should also be clear by now, given the authors interested in modernity whom I cite in contrast to Derrida (e.g., Foucault), that my aim in introducing this category into a discussion of Derrida's thought is not at all to celebrate it or to indulge in some kind of Western triumphalism or exceptionalism. Doubtless Derrida's allergy to this category has to do with the ethnocentrism and Eurocentrism that he believes may be implied by it, especially in the context of the talk of "modernization" of the recently noncolonized countries common from the 1950s on. (And the early postcolonialism of Gayatri Spivak, as well as Robert J. C. Young, of course, represents some of the most powerful working out and extension of the implications of this abstinence. See Gayatri Spivak, *In Other Worlds: Essays in Cultural Politics* [New York: Routledge, 1988] and Robert J. C. Young, *White Mythologies: Writing History and the West* [New York: Routledge, 1990]. But as I argue here in Part II, a fuller view, a more radical interpretation of the notion of modernity may both (a) call into question the ethnocentric historiography that identifies this as an exclusively Western, rather than an Eastern or Islamic, invention (especially given the role that algebra plays in Jacob Klein's interpretation of an epistemic modernity), and (b) question whether finally this category can be understood as a moment entirely within history, properly belonging to history, at all.

7. Apart from Jürgen Habermas, perhaps the foremost thinker today addressing these issues—confronting modernity, or he puts it, modernism as a philosophical problem—is Robert Pippin. His neo- or quasi-Hegelian schema, whereby modernity discloses a philosophical problem, namely autonomy, that proves to be fundamental, comes closest to avoiding historicism of all those treatments of which I am aware. Much in these pages is indebted to his discussion of this issue. (See, esp., *Modernism as a Philosophical Problem* [Oxford: Blackwell, 1991].)

8. See the sketch Heidegger gives in his second Introduction to *Sein und Zeit* for the project of that work as a whole (Martin Heidegger, *Sein und Zeit* [Tubingen: Max Niemeyer Verlag, 1993], 15–27). Of course, Heidegger never completed that project, and his understanding of his own work changed as he brought forward pieces of what he there called the *Destruktion* of the history of ontology. Nevertheless, this sketch remains a decisive reference point for Heidegger's broadest intentions, probably up until around 1940.

9. Apart from Robert Pippin, Jürgen Habermas's project is another instance of a treatment of modernity that does not intend to give up the claim to first philosophy—in this case, first philosophy understood in a specifically modern mode, in terms of a transformation of the Kantian model of transcendental argument. Leaving aside for the moment the rather serious question of to what extent Habermas' work is itself ultimately philosophically convincing, a comparison of Habermas' remarks on 9/11 with those of Derrida is enlightening as to the different consequences of their respective positions. For Habermas clearly sees these events, and the current global situation, in relation to modernity in its specificity (e.g. Borradori, *Terror*, 31, 41). By contrast, Derrida, though here for one of the very few times granting what he calls "an absolute originality" to the Enlightenment in regard to its organization of faith and politics (Borradori, *Terror*, 116), nevertheless explicitly discounts the notion of "Western modernity" (Borradori, *Terror*, 115), and insists on the absolute singularity of the present moment (Borradori, *Terror*, 126), in a way that makes the primary task today one of deconstructing the tradition of onto-theology (Borradori, *Terror*, 111), and political theology as a whole (Borradori, *Terror*, 131).

10. As Chapter 6 in this volume explores in detail, Klein practices history (writes as an intellectual historian) in a way that Derrida never does. For Klein's identification of this standpoint with that very same modernity he wishes to criticize, see the first part of his lecture "History and the Liberal Arts" (Klein, *Lectures and Essays*, 133–36).

11. See, most famously, *Crisis*, Part 2, Chapter 9, section h: "The lifeworld as the forgotten meaning-fundament of the natural sciences," *Krisis* 48–54 / 48–53.

12. See, most concisely, "The Crisis of European Humanity and Philosophy," or "The Vienna Lecture," which also lays out the problem of objectivism just spoken about (in *Krisis* 314–48 / 269–300). Derrida in the "Introduction" has a nice discussion of how Husserl's seemingly disparate characterizations of the Idea of philosophy in this lecture and in the opening pages of the *Crisis* itself—the latter apparently assigning to modernity more of a discontinuity than the former—can be seen to conform to one another. Tellingly, Derrida's own treatment advocates an underlying continuity both in the Idea and in Husserl's thinking about it (*IOG* 128–31).

13. *GMT* 118; "Die griechische Logistik und die Enstehung der Algebra II" in *Quellen und Studien zur Geschichte der Mathematik, Astronomie und Physik*, Vol. 3, fascimile 2 (Berlin: 1936): 122–235, 123.

14. "The edifice of the new science," Klein writes, "is now erected in deliberate opposition to the concepts and methods" of the schools; yet "it is nevertheless

true," he goes on, "that the conceptual frame for their new insights is derived from the traditional concepts" (*GMT* 120).

15. "The new science . . . interprets [its concepts] with reference to the function each of these concepts has within the whole of science," writes Klein (*GMT* 121).

16. Klein footnotes Duhem's treatments of Medieval and Renaissance science more than once. See *GMT* 197n306, and, especially, 206n323.

17. The *locus classicus* for this view is Quine's "Two Dogmas of Empiricism" (W. V. O. Quine, *From a Logical Point of View* [Cambridge, Mass.: Harvard University Press, 1961).

18. Klein, it should be noted, thinks this view of mind mistaken. Taking mind as able to stand on its own, as a being in itself, Descartes misses the true character of mind, which, paradoxically enough, is really distinguished from all other beings by its inability to be conceived in this way. The mode of being of mind for Klein is as that being which always stands in relation to beings other than itself, to beings with a different kind of being than itself, and misconstruing this, taking the mind as *solus ipsus*, as standing on its own, Descartes in fact turns it into a being like any other.

19. See "The Concept of Number in Greek Mathematics and Philosophy" (Klein, *Lectures and Essays*, 43–52), as well as *GMT* 46 ff.

20. For a more detailed discussion of Klein's reading of Vieta, see Burt Hopkins, "Jacob Klein on François Vieta's Establishment of Algebra as the General Analytical Art," in the *Graduate Faculty Philosophy Journal* (Summer 2004): 25.2.

21. For Klein, from this specifically mathematical inception, it should be noted, stems the predominance of the symbolic in all other walks of modern life, such as capitalism, as well as much of our western social and political organization (see Klein's "Modern Rationalism," in Klein, *Lectures and Essays*, 53–64).

22. Chapter 6 pursues in detail Klein's relation to history and the reading of the late Husserl upon which it rests, and it contrasts these topics with the role they play in Derrida's thought and its development.

23. See Klein's essay on Husserl, "Phenomenology and the History of Science" (Klein, *Lectures and Essays*, 65–84) as well as his discussion of genealogy in "History and the Liberal Arts," (Klein, *Lectures and Essays*, 129–30).

24. *FTL* (*Husserliana*, Vol. 17).

25. Klein, *Lectures and Essays*, 75–76.

26. Ibid., 74.

27. Ibid., 77–78.

28. See the crucial Section VI of the "Introduction," where Derrida, rejecting Maurice Merleau-Ponty's contention that Husserl's thought underwent a revolution and embraced a kind of empiricism in its last phase, insists instead on the specifically transcendental character of language and culture, as they function in Husserl's last works (*IOG* 77–79).

29. "Husserl can at one and the same time speak of a pure sense and an internal historicity of geometry, and can say . . . that a universal teleology of reason

was at work in human history before the Greco-European coming to consciousness" (*IOG* 131).

30. Derrida's own footnote to *Le problème de la genèse dans la philosophie de Husserl* (Paris: Presses Universitaires de France, 1990), 264n12, the only one of substance that he added when this work was published, confirms this interpretation.

31. Klein contrasts Husserl's interest in roots, *rizomata* (defined as that from which other things grow to perfection), to an interest in *arche* (which pertains directly to the *perfections* these things attain), and this preference, Klein tells us, "is the attitude of the true historian" (Klein, *Lectures and Essays*, 69).

Chapter 6: Jacob Klein and Jacques Derrida: Historicism and History in Two Interpretations of Husserl's Late Writings

1. Klein, *Lectures and Essays*, 71.

2. As note 51 below further specifies, Alain Badiou's project may be viewed as a perhaps illicit generalization of modernity's intermixing of the event and truth, even as it remains questionable whether Badiou successfully gets out from under the shadow that the modern casts over his own work.

3. Klein speaks of Husserl, again highly positively, in his important, now-published late lecture, "Speech, Its Strength and Weaknesses" (Klein, *Lectures and Essays*, 361–74), where Klein revisits his earlier treatment of history, as well as in his discussion of the *logos* in his 1962 "Aristotle, an Introduction" (Klein, *Lectures and Essays*, 171–93).

4. Klein, *Lectures and Essays*, 65.

5. Ibid., 79.

6. Though for Klein both the scope and validity of Husserl's project may be limited, it seems safe to say that some kind of limited or partial endorsement of Husserl's enterprise is implied by the opening and conclusion of Klein's article. In a similar vein, Klein, in "Speech, Its Strength, and Its Weaknesses," after calling Husserl's philosophy "a most remarkable attempt to restore the integrity of knowledge," adds that "it has remained an attempt" (Klein, *Lectures and Essays*, 372). Nevertheless, Klein goes on to depend on conclusions drawn from Husserl's philosophy in his own discussion.

7. This preference, Klein tells us, "is the attitude of the true historian" (Klein, *Lectures and Essays*, 69).

8. In respect to these limits, see also Klein's remarks on Husserl's unacknowledged debt to symbolic mathematics (Klein, *Lectures and Essays*, 70–71).

9. Ibid, 65.

10. *FTL* (*Husserliana*, Vol. 17).

11. Klein, *Lectures and Essays*, 66.

12. Ibid, 67. This notion, the *eidos*, seems to apply as much to a set of invariant modes of intellectual activity (such as the insight that all perceptions can be returned to in memory but never with their objects or even their acts again perceived as such), as it does to the objects of these activities, such as the spatial object (which can never be given from all sides at once), or the genus color; and

this ambiguity as to which sort of essences are meant is owed to the fact that Klein at this moment is drawing on an appendix to *Formal and Transcendental Logic* primarily concerned with phenomenology's own methodology.

13. Klein, *Lectures and Essays*, 67.

14. Ibid., 74, my emphasis. It sometimes appears that Klein believes that constitution, at least genetically, applies only to what Husserl calls idealities—or that Klein himself wishes to limit it to these formations. Thus it is unclear whether at this moment Klein means by a significant unit solely one that is *Bedeutungsvoll*, logically significant, able to enter into propositions, or includes *Sinn* (sense), having a broader scope under which perceived particulars fall.

15. Ibid., 73.

16. Ibid.

17. Ibid.

18. Ibid, my emphasis.

19. Thus Klein claims that the inventor of geometry must possess "an anticipation of what comes into being through his accomplishment" (Klein, *Lectures and Essays*, 75). And "since the product, in the case of geometry is an ideal product," he further states, "'anticipation' and the corresponding 'accomplishment,' as 'acts' of the subject," must be "founded upon the work of transcendental subjectivity" (Klein, *Lectures and Essays*, 76).

20. Ibid.

21. This word is apparently never used by Husserl himself. In his commentary on *The Origin of Geometry*, Derrida claims it is found in Fink's initial transcription of the *Origin*, which appeared in the *Revue Internationale de Philosophie* in 1939, and that Fink himself there speaks of "*Erstmaligkeitmodus*" (*LOG* 32n1 / *IOG* 48n40).

22. "This experience," as so far described, in which the intentional constitution, at work at the moment of any actual science's historical invention, steps over to the real, "does not [yet] . . . ," Klein tells us, "transcend the personal sphere of the subject," of the one founding geometry. Thus, according to him, a "second necessary—and decisive—step" is needed for real history: "the embodiment of that [subject's] experience in words, which makes it communicable to other subjects" (Klein, *Lectures and Essays*, 77).

23. Ibid., 77, my emphasis.

24. Ibid.

25. Ibid., 78.

26. Ibid., 77.

27. Ibid., 78.

28. Ibid.

29. Ibid.

30. Some of these matters have already been discussed in my *Essential History*, particularly in Chapter 3, as well as at the beginning of Chapter 3 of the present volume. Both of these treatments focus on section VII of the "Introduction," where (transcendental) writing is discussed. The present treatment, thanks to the

comparison with Klein, elucidates the stance taken by Derrida in 1962 toward history as a whole. Moreover, some reviewers have decried the highly technical nature of the discussions of *Essential History*. Thus, I thought it worthwhile, while comparing Klein's and Derrida's thinking on modernity and history, to "leverage" my discussion of Klein to set forth what I believe to be crucial and still overlooked aspects of Derrida's early thought in a manner that would be more accessible to those not deeply steeped in Husserlian phenomenology.

31. Chapter 6 explores in detail Derrida's treatment of Husserl's transcendental subject and the problem of intersubjectivity in Derrida's work *Le Toucher: Jean Luc Nancy* (Paris: Galilée, 2000) (*LT*).

32. Even Derrida's account, though thinking a transcendental "first time," does not restrict the validity of essences to any finite block of history. Derrida is most of all concerned with the kind of conditions that must be in place on a transcendental level for the style of objectivity appropriate to essences to be constituted: the transcendental-intentional conditions of the objectivity pertaining to ideality. The contents of these objects, the truths of geometry and its formation, do not themselves as such ever wholly come into doubt.

33. See *IOG* 72ff.

34. As is about to become clearer, writing can perform this function only under the stipulations (of pertaining to a transcendental consciousness in general and understood as a spiritual corporeality) discussed in such detail in Chapters 2 and 3.

35. Cf. Peter Fenves's discussion of this same set of claims in his "Derrida and History," a portion of which has already been discussed in Chapter 3. His assertion that "writing . . . does not simply make up for a lack but makes up for something that was never there in the first place" captures a good deal of what Derrida is aiming at, but seems inflected by Fenves' belief that this is more Derrida than Husserl, that writing's transcendental role is an "almost inadvertent result of Husserl's search" ("Derrida and History: Some Questions Derrida Pursues in His Early Writings," in Tom Cohen, ed., *Jacques Derrida and the Humanities: A Critical Reader* [Cambridge: Cambridge University Press, 2001]: 271–95, 283). That does not seem to me to be how Derrida himself presents it in 1962.

36. Compare Klein's view of the corrigibility of sedimentation, stated in a passage already quoted above: "Yet it [the original mental activity] is there, in every word, somehow 'forgotten' but still at the bottom of our speaking and our understanding, however vague the meaning conveyed by our speech might be" (Klein, *Lectures and Essays*, 77).

37. Derrida's detailed, extensive, and complex account of this—one of the most important extended phenomenological analyses to be encountered in his early work—is to be found at the conclusion of Section VII of the "Introduction" (*IOG* 99ff.). For a detailed discussion of it, see my *Essential History*, 74–82, as well as the penultimate sections of Chapters 2 and 3 above.

38. For Husserl's account of this teleology, see, especially, "The Vienna Lecture," as well as some of the other texts included as appendixes in the English

(and German) version of the *Crisis* (*The Crisis of the European Sciences: An Intro-duction into Phenomenological Philosophy*, trans. David Carr [Evanston, Ill: Northwestern University Press, 1970]). For a useful, relatively brief treatment of the problems accompanying this phase of Husserl's work, see Paul Ricoeur, "Husserl and the Sense of History" (in *Husserl: An Analysis of his Phenomenology*, trans. Edward G. Ballard and Lester E. Embree [Evanston, Ill: Northwestern University Press, 1967]).

39. This issue, of course, is the one to which the ending of Chapter 3 recurs. Note that Derrida in the "Introduction" cites Husserl as declaring, in respect to our ability to overcome such sedimentation, that there is the possibility of "an idealization: namely the removal of limits from our capacity, in a certain sense its infinitization" (*IOG* 106).

40. Derrida writes: "A secondary idealizing operation then comes to relieve the reactivative ability of its finitude and lets it go beyond itself. . . . This move-ment is analogous to the production of geometry's exactitude, the passage to the infinite limit of a finite and qualitative sensible intuition. Strictly speaking, even here it is geometrical idealization which permits infinitizing the reactivative abil-ity" (*IOG* 106).

41. "The institution of geometry could only be a *philosophical* act" (*IOG* 127).

42. Cf. *IOG* 134–35. Derrida argues there that the power of anticipation that begins to recognize within the vague shape a possible ideal essence must itself have been idealized (seen as an anticipatory power without limit) and this is owed to an idea in a Kantian sense, to the advent of an (infinite) theoretical standpoint having taken hold on a practical plane.

43. Edmund Husserl, *Ideas Pertaining to a Pure Phenomenology and to a Phe-nomenological Philosophy*, first book, trans. F. Kersten (Dordrecht: Kluwer, 1983), 44–45.

44. A sign of this is Derrida's defense of Husserl's late thought (specifically against a critique mounted by Jean Cavaillès, with which Derrida had previously sided). This defense culminates in Derrida's much misunderstood declaration: "the absolute is passage." (For a reprise of the details of this argument see Chap-ter 3 above, n25.)

45. See, most notably, Rudolf Bernet, "On Derrida's 'Introduction' to Hus-serl's *Origin of Geometry*" (*Derrida and Deconstruction*, ed. Hugh Silverman [New York: Routledge, 1989], 151ff.).

46. They also clearly reprise the ending of " 'Genesis and Structure' and Phe-nomenology" (in *WD*, 154–68, 168).

47. See pages 168–97 of Kates, *Essential History*, for one version of it.

48. Chapter 8 examines the historicity of Derrida's late thought in compari-son to Marx's and Marxism's in the context of a discussion of *Specters* (see, esp., pages 203–6).

49. See Chapter 7 for a sustained demonstration of the "Cartesianism" (in-herited from Husserl) implied in the later Derrida, especially visible in his cons-trual of the Other, the constitution of intersubjectivity, which is there contrasted to Merleau-Ponty's treatment.

50. These twin possibilities—of a certain retention of Descartes and of a more radical historicity—are what Derrida pits against Foucault's historicism in "The Cogito and the *History of Madness*." The second half of the final chapter of *Essential History* examines Derrida's stance toward history at this period in detail, both in this essay and in "Violence and Metaphysics" (see esp. Kates, *Essential History* 197–215).

51. Alain Badiou's *Being and Event* (trans. Oliver Feltham [London: Continuum, 2005]) offers an interesting further example in this regard. Even as Badiou apparently intends to restore and fulfill philosophy's oldest pretensions, furnishing, through a highly creative reading of mathematical logic, a present-day ontology, he nevertheless historicizes his own activity and views it as a result corresponding to our modern moment in knowledge (as well as society, politics, and culture), and not, in any way, as far as I can tell, a finding that goes beyond these historical parameters. (On the relation of his project to the history of science and category of modernity, see Badiou 2005, 123–29, 340, 435.)

Chapter 7: Derrida's Contribution to Phenomenology: A Problem of No Species?

1. Edmund Husserl, *Ideas Pertaining to a Pure Phenomenology and to a Phenomenological Philosophy, Second Book*, trans R. Rojcewicz and A. Schuwer (Dordrecht: Kluwer Academic Publishers, 1989) (*Husserliana* IV), 365.

2. For this last point, see Hannah Arendt's *Origins of Totalitarianism* (New York: Harcourt Brace Jovanovich, 1973), where she claims this instability—in her eyes the ultimate political hollowness of the notion of humanity—played a decisive role in the success of fascist anti-Semitism (see, especially, Part II, Chapter 9, Section 2, "The Perplexities of the Rights of Man").

3. See, for example, Descartes' preface to the French edition of the *Principles of Philosophy* (in *The Philosophical Writings of Descartes 1*, John Cottingham, Robert Stoothoff, Dugald Murdoch, eds. [Cambridge: Cambridge University Press, 1985], where, outlining the consequences of this paradox, he likens research to a tree: it being "not the roots or the trunk of a tree from which one gathers the fruit, but only the ends of the branches," and "so the principal usefulness of philosophy depends on those parts of it which can only be learned last" (Adam-Tannery IXB 15).

4. See Jean Petitot, Francisco J. Varela, Bernard Pachoud, and Jean-Michel Roy, eds., *Naturalizing Phenomenology: Issues in Contemporary Phenomenology and Cognitive Science* (Stanford, Calif.: Stanford University Press, 1999) for an approach to this problem from the regional and empirical, rather than the philosophical, side.

5. Perhaps paradoxically, it is the recent attempt by leading Husserl scholars, as one of them, Dan Zahavi puts it, to see "Husserl as a thinker who . . . anticipated and contributed to the central post-Husserlian discussions in phenomenology" (Zahavi, *Self-Awareness and Alterity: A Phenomenological Investigation* [Evanston, Ill.: Northwestern University Press], 201) that gives this question its

particular urgency. That Husserl altered his own positions and the focus of his inquiry somewhat, thereby treating themes (often for the first time) that would become central to those who followed after him, is not to be doubted. Yet, the consequences of this shift (whose degree remains an open question), how it affects the epistemic and philosophical architecture of Husserl's own thought—in particular what results from the role played by the factical existence of human being in his later investigations—are questions still not adequately resolved.

6. This last fact, Derrida's affirmation of the (philosophical) truth of the position that he therefore does not refute, but deconstructs, is masked to a degree by the order of Derrida's argument, which begins, as for example in *Speech and Phenomena*, by laying out the participation of the position in question in what Derrida calls the history and system of metaphysics, as defined by a teleology of presence. Thus Husserl, it is claimed, insofar as he distinguishes indications from expressions, is thought to betray a fealty to such metaphysics. However, as I have repeatedly argued elsewhere (see esp. Chapter 5 of my *Essential History: Jacques Derrida and the Development of Deconstruction* [Evanston, Ill.: Northwestern University Press, 2005]) since there are no working alternatives even in Derrida's mind to this history and system, no other positions (in the philosophy of language) that are more tenable, the central phase of Derrida's deconstruction (while referring back to this earlier one) must employ Husserl's own findings and reference points, indeed rely on his framework as a whole, in order to broach a space beyond such metaphysics, and this reliance on Husserl is in fact especially profound (and is to be distinguished from Derrida's relation to all other thinkers), when the role Husserl's thought plays in the development of Derrida's own is taken into account.

7. Leonard Lawlor, rightfully in my view (for reasons that will become clearer below), distinguishes what he calls Derrida's "meta-humanism" from so-called "anti-humanism," which Lawlor in this instance ascribes to Jean Hyppolite (*Derrida and Husserl: The Basic Problem of Phenomenology* [Bloomington: Indiana University Press, 2002], 90).

8. Etienne Balibar has raised a parallel question concerning Derrida's proximity to the modern moment, in an essay that unexpectedly and provocatively connects Derrida's concerns (with the subject and its undoing) to Lockean individualism. (See his "Possessive Individualism Reversed: From Locke to Derrida," *Constellations* 9.3 (2002): 299–317.)

9. This is, of course, Husserl's view of modernity in the *Crisis* and other late works. Husserl sees modernity as a further unfolding of the "European Idea," thus granting it a specificity of its own, even as for him it does not represent any sort of radical discontinuity or break. Less well-known, however, is that this is also Derrida's view of the place of the modern within what he sometimes calls "the tradition and history of Western metaphysics." Husserl's interpretation of this in its totality (even more than Hegel's) and the subsidiary role of the modern played in it, in fact, allow Derrida to speak of this "tradition" as such, even as Derrida also complicates this schema, in respect to its origins and ends, in part by way of questioning and transforming the notion of "origin" itself.

10. *LT*; the notes for this chapter were taken before the appearance of the English translation and thus refer only to the French.

11. At the beginning of Tangent II, it should be noted, Derrida explicitly addresses the relation of haptocentrism to the privilege of sight and "optical intuitionism" (*LT* 185), making reference to Plato and Husserl.

12. Maurice Merleau-Ponty, *Phenomenology of Perception*, trans. Colin Smith (London: Routledge, 1962), 250.

13. Merleau-Ponty, *Perception*, 251.

14. See *IOG* 111ff.

15. See Husserl, *Ideas* II, 158. Husserl himself does not use this phrase at this moment.

16. Husserl, *Ideas* II, 157.

17. Dan Zahavi, to whose remarks on Derrida's Husserl interpretation I am about to refer, in *Self-Awareness and Alterity*, examines the status of self-awareness at all levels in Husserl's thought, including Bodily self-awareness, and in this work Zahavi defends his version of Husserl's approach against a host of phenomenological (and other philosophical) competitors. Zahavi thus offers a response to the question that is also Derrida's: namely, of the relation of auto- to hetero-affection (in the Body and generally as conceived by Husserl). Zahavi's answer seems to be that hetero-affection always exists alongside auto-affection; the one always *accompanies* the other, but that this fact does not thereby impugn or "contaminate" the singularity of auto-affection, self-relation, instead in some sense permitting it—hetero-affection being the condition for auto-affection making itself manifest (198ff). Whether Zahavi's response, however, meets the concerns that Derrida is in the course of raising in respect to the foundational status that Husserl ultimately wants to give such "auto-affection," including this self-relation's, or self-awareness's ultimate epistemic autonomy and authority, is finally less clear, as Zahavi himself never addresses this second problem explicitly. Thus Zahavi claims that "Husserl . . . unequivocally stat[es] that subjectivity is dependent on and penetrated by alterity" [Zahavi, *Self*-Awareness, 118], which, if true, it seems to me would ramify, not alleviate, Derrida's concerns.

18. Merleau-Ponty's assimilation of touch and sight at this juncture is at least defensible, insofar as what is at issue at this moment in Husserl's text, as I understand it, is finally the emergence of the whole Body, embodiment generally: the localization of all the senses, and indeed eventually the psyche itself, in Body. Touch may be the gateway to this, the focal sensory experience that brings about such localization, something that Merleau-Ponty's text indeed elides (see "The Philosopher and His Shadow" in *Signs*, trans. Richard C. McCleary [Evanston, Ill.: Northwestern University Press, 1964], 166). Nevertheless, insofar as sensory experiences of all sorts have already been drawn upon in the preceding, and it is the embodiment of the *solus ipse* (the solitary experiencing ego) in its entirety that is at stake, the privilege of touch is arguably provisional, even transitory. Indeed, this same set of circumstances, Husserl's assumption that all perceptual experience is already at work, is what also makes possible Derrida's own counterprivileging of sight at this juncture. Husserl having assigned to touch alone the

condition for embodied self-relation (though all the embodied senses have already been in play), Derrida, in turn, assigns to sight alone a relation to the nonself, to the other, to a nonegocentric exteriority, albeit such relation, as he himself will note, is and has been a feature of all sensing generally.

19. Zahavi, *Self-Awareness*, 135.

20. This matter of a difference in register is one I follow up further in the next section of this chapter. Both Derrida and Merleau-Ponty, as we shall see, in some way assume that what is at stake at this moment is the embodiment of Husserl's transcendental subject, and this, in part, allows for the continuity of Derrida's remarks here and in *SP*. I have bracketed for now the question of this potential difference and have tried instead to present the strongest possible version of Derrida's position without doubting that other interpretations than his are possible and further interrogation of these matters might be fruitful.

21. Zahavi would contest this characterization, and certainly it should not be taken to mean relation in the narrow logical sense, formalizable as "aRb." Whether this stipulation thus meets all of Zahavi's criticisms of such a construal cannot here be adjudicated, however.

22. The famous final chapter of *The Visible and the Invisible*, "The Intertwining—the Chiasm," probably represents the most advanced statement of Merleau-Ponty's thought. See, in particular, 138ff for a discussion of a "flesh" that would precede and condition the individual subject, this so-called "flesh of the world"; Merleau-Ponty, *The Visible and the Invisible*, trans. A. Lingis (Evanston, Ill.: Northwestern University Press, 1973).

23. In addition to Merleau-Ponty's famous remark in the introduction to the *Phenomenology of Perception* that "the most important lesson that the reduction teaches us is the impossibility of a complete reduction" (Merleau-Ponty, *Perception*, xiv), see, among others, from the same work the beginning of "Space," the chapter referred to earlier in this chapter: "Reflection does not follow in the reverse direction of a path already traced by the constitutive act," Merleau-Ponty stipulates, clearly having Husserl in mind. Instead, "the natural reference of the stuff to the world leads us to a new conception of intentionality," an intentionality in place of "the classical conception," the latter being explicitly defined by Merleau-Ponty as that "of Husserl in the second period of his philosophy" (Merleau-Ponty, *Perception*, 243 and note).

24. See most recently, *Deconstruction and Pragmatism*, ed. Chantal Mouffe (London: Routledge, 1996), 81, and John Caputo, ed., *Deconstruction in a Nutshell: A Conversation with Jacques Derrida* (New York: Fordham University Press, 1997). I discuss these passages in the opening pages of Chapter 1 of my *Essential History*, as well as in Chapter 1 of this volume.

25. In addition to the three volumes of *Husserliana* drawn from the *Nachlass* pertaining to transcendental intersubjectivity (vols. 13–15), many of the problems touched on here are taken up again by Husserl in his *Phenomenological Psychology* (trans. John Scanlon [Martinus Nijhoff: The Hague, 1977]), not to mention, of course, *Cartesian Meditations* V, trans. Dorion Cairns (The Hague:

Martinus Nijhoff, 1960); *Husserliana* 1. With the exception of the last, none of these writings will be explicitly taken into account here.

26. Merleau-Ponty, *Signs*, 166 (my emphasis).

27. Ibid., 165.

28. "Introjection" (German "*Introjektion*," French "*introjection*") refers to the imparting of a psychic inwardness to a body, usually the body of another, here on the basis of an original similarity between one's own Body and the other's (Husserl, *Ideas* II, 172). (See Iso Kern's entry "Intersubjectivity" in *The Encyclopedia of Phenomenology* [Dordrecht: Kluwer Academic Publishers, 1997] for a brief historical and systematic overview of Husserl's treatments of these themes [350–55]. My account later of Husserl's analysis in *Ideas* II stresses aspects of Husserl's presentation that Kern does not, without disagreeing with him directly, as far as I can tell.)

29. Merleau-Ponty, *Signs*, 168.

30. Merleau-Ponty quite self-consciously is in the course of rejecting the account of the constitution of the Other on the basis of the transcendental monad that Husserl had offered in *Cartesian Meditations* V. In this same article, he asserts that "*there is no constituting of a mind for a mind, but of a man for a man* (Merleau-Ponty, *Signs*, 169, his emphasis). Here, it should be noted, confirmation emerges concerning Merleau-Ponty's own position as entailing human being (the embodied human being and perhaps the human species as such) as an absolute. Man, "*l'homme*," is indeed the entity in the face of which the other arises (on ground common to all human beings, that "aesthesiological dimension," which Merleau-Ponty himself calls a "universal"); and human identity (in some manner prior to any biology and before being grasped in the naturalistic attitude, though nevertheless still pointing toward a latent nature), thus subtends that absolute, that primary being or ontological ground, that Merleau-Ponty's own writings repeatedly work to expose.

31. I might mention that Derrida's endorsement of Husserl's analysis "of *Fremdverfahrung* as *Vergegenwartigung* in the fifth Cartesian Meditation" Len Lawlor evinces as central to his own substantial body of work on Derrida, in response to criticisms of some, by no means all, of that work, that I had previously made—specifically concerning what I took to be Lawlor's failure to recognize the degree to which Derrida's early writings depend on a profound acquaintance with Husserl's philosophy and indeed the endorsement of that philosophy as true (Leonard Lawlor, *The Implications of Innocence: Toward a New Concept of Life* [New York: Fordham University Press, 2006] 150n7; cf. Joshua Kates, "Review of *Derrida and Husserl: The Basic Problem of Phenomenology*," *Husserl Studies* 21.1 [April 2005]: 55–64). Lawlor's own footnote, however, confirms these worries rather than allays them. Picking out one point in the entirety of Husserl's corpus to which he assigns a positive role in Derrida's own thinking, not only does Lawlor in fact demonstrate how little dependence overall he takes there to be between Derrida and Husserl, but he also indicates that he does not really grasp what I have been in the course of emphasizing here: namely that this

interpretation of the constitution of intersubjectivity stands and falls with Husserl's transcendental-constitutive perspective as a whole. To be sure, Lawlor will go on to claim this reliance is more massive, in that "throughout *Derrida and Husserl*" he argues "that Derrida's thought is precisely a generalization of *Vergegenwärtigung* to all forms of experience" (*The Implications of Immanence* [New York: Fordham University Press, 2006], 150n7). Not only does this somewhat novel claim sit uneasily, it seems to me, with the sweeping methodological weight that Lawlor himself gives to experience at the outset of his earlier book, beginning with the statement that "deconstruction consists in limiting claims . . . with experience" (Lawlor, *Derrida and Husserl: The Basic Problem of Phenomenology* [Bloomington: Indiana University Press, 2002], 3); moreover, it fails to recognize that the concept of re-presentation, making present again (*Vergegenwärtigung*), only takes on its sense, is only identifiable as an operation (of consciousness) within the context of Husserl's transcendental researches, researches whose truth and content would dissolve into nothing were all *experience* (in Husserl's sense) *Vergegenwärtigüng* (also in Husserl's sense). The whole problem is thus to figure out how Derrida can contest aspects of Husserl's thought while also depending so heavily on that thought—a problem to which Lawlor has never really proposed any solution at all, never really even acknowledges as a problem, as far as I am aware, despite the undoubted importance of his work in so many other aspects of Derrida studies.

32. *WD* 123–24; *Discovering Existence with Husserl*, trans. Richard A. Cohen and Michael Smith (Evanston, Ill: Northwestern University Press, 1998), 108–9, 120–21.

33. For example, Dan Zahavi speaks of "Husserl's realization that every constitution entails and presupposes a moment of facticity, the affection of the primal hyletic fact," at something like this same epoch (Zahavi, *Self-Awareness*, 118).

34. Husserl, *Ideas* II, 171–72.

35. So, too, a little later, now speaking of some of the complexities this localization can undergo in the solipsistic subject's own experience—the interior of my body being felt and discovered as sensitive and inwardly spatial; or, sight and touch coming to be further coordinated, when I see my hand touch something else—Husserl will again speak of what is thus given to me in "copresence" in these experiences being "transferred over in empathy" to the other (Husserl, *Ideas* II, 174). This point, also seemingly in accord with Derrida's interpretation, is more delicate than the earlier one, however, since Merleau-Ponty also gives a role to empathy (*Einfuhlung, Intropathie*) (Merleau-Ponty, *Signs*, 169). Yet he takes it as utterly spontaneous, not prepared by any other constitutive work: as surging forth and bringing about the recognition of the other, simply on the basis of the immediate common aesthesiological dimension discussed above.

36. Husserl, *Ideas* II, 174; my emphasis.

37. Ibid., 177.

38. The full sentence in English reads: "Since here this manifold expression appresents psychic *existence* in Corporeality, thus there is constituted with all that

an objectivity which is precisely double and unitary: the man—without 'introjection'" (Husserl, *Ideas* II, 175). I have been stressing the "unitary" aspect, which is what is new here and what Husserl aims to bring out. More generally, according to Husserl, while human being is double (both genuinely spiritual—since in part the "site" of a pure ego's activity—as well as physical), its unity (psychophysical unity) is also an authentic one. It forms a genuinely inseparable whole (albeit of a new sort) in the causal nexus. (See, for example, the end of §14, where Husserl, after denying that humans and animals are material things [since some of what serves as their "properties" cannot be thought as a function of extension] nevertheless declares: "Men and animals are *spatially localized*; and even what is psychic about them, in virtue of its essential foundedness in the Bodily, partakes of the spatial order" [Husserl, *Ideas* II, 36]; and §33, where he concludes that what is to be "oppose[d] to [simply] material nature . . . is the *concrete* unity of Body and soul" [Husserl, *Ideas* II, 146; his emphases].) This modified, even anti-Cartesian strand of Husserl's thought (refusing as it does, to simply liberate thought from the Bodily, at the moment that it subjects the latter to possible total causal determination) is doubtless provocative and the one that Merleau-Ponty's thought was dedicated to building upon.

39. In Part 3 of *Ideas* II, Husserl shows that all of these—persons, equipment, social and political formations (such as stools, the King, or the congress)—are what they are for us, immediately as expressions. (Husserl cashes this out in great detail in Husserl, *Ideas* II, 249–55, in particular the parallel between the meaning of linguistic expressions and all these other sorts, and my argument above thus relies heavily, albeit implicitly, on this analysis.) This accords with his opening description of the lifeworld in Part 1. In both cases Husserl is aware of the immediacy with which the significances of the everyday world present themselves. (The chair gives itself originally as a chair, and *not* as a natural object with human uses subsequently projected on it [Husserl, *Ideas* II, 4ff].) His decision to isolate a bare material thing as his starting point (a decision that Heidegger contests at the outset of *Being and Time,* in the course of setting forth a different account of this same immediate significance or meaningfulness) is thus a methodological one, aimed at giving a variety of theoretical attitudes, and the sciences or knowledges corresponding to them, their rights—a problem Heidegger does not so much resolve but rather expels or banishes (on the grounds of its being, in his eyes, superficial).

40. Husserl (*Ideas* II, 101, 257).

41. Though obviously akin to it in important ways, this reading and these questions should be distinguished from the ones brought forth by Ludwig Landgrebe, in his deservedly well-known piece "Regions of Being and Regional Ontologies in Husserl's Phenomenology," in Donn Welton, ed., *The Phenomenology of Edmund Husserl: Six Essays* (Ithaca, N.Y.: Cornell University Press, 1981). Landgrebe, in some respects not unlike Merleau-Ponty, finally brings forward a problem with the order of Husserl's constitutional analyses (Landgrebe, *Essays*, 170), in order to affirm (seemingly once and for all) the priority of the lifeworld and the

body over and against what he takes to be Husserl's illicit theoretism, especially as this informs his "metaphysical" notion of constitution, which Landgrebe argues cannot finally be separated from a methodological one. For a number of reasons, some of which have been alluded to in this essay, I myself am less worried about an excess of "theoretism" (or at least genuinely valid "theory") than Landgrebe, this problem perhaps no longer today having the urgency it did when Landgrebe wrote. The more pressing question, I believe, is whether in its present form (in Husserl's phenomenology, and even in Derrida's strange deconstructive recuperation of this aspect of it), a valid stance for theory has indeed really been found.

42. Though written much later, compare, for example, Rudolph Carnap's "Testability and Meaning," in *Classics of Analytic Philosophy*, Robert R. Ammerman, ed. (New York: McGraw Hill, 1965): 130–95), where, at the basis of his reconstruction of the language of modern physics, Carnap places primitive descriptive predicates flowing from an experience of the most general (and empty formal) type, thus also related, but not necessarily identical to those of our species (cf. especially 165–66 and the discussion preceding it).

43. Husserl encapsulates this line of argument at a critical moment as follows: "Whereas . . . the *state* is identical with the space that is filled with sensuous qualities (schema), a space which can be an intersubjective unity only as related to a totality of normal 'like-sensing' subjects . . . the real possibility and actuality of subjects endowed with different sense faculties . . . lead[s] to a consideration of this dependence precisely as *a new dimension of relativities* and lead[s] to a construction in *thought* of the purely physicalistic thing" (Husserl, *Ideas* II, 91–92).

44. Husserl, *Ideas* II, 86.

45. To be sure, Husserl also wants to claim that there is a sense in which this version of nature, physicalistic nature, remains intelligible even under those solipsistic conditions that he started out by positing, since "logical Objectivity" (of which the solipsistic subject is capable) is "*eo ipso* Objectivity in the intersubjective sense as well" (Husserl, *Ideas* II, 87; cf. 94–95, where he maintains that, on the solipistic level there is already the possibility of advancing this far, while on the intersubjective level we still do not encounter any necessity to do so). Nevertheless, while such comprehension may remain possible, whether the *solus ipse* as such could ever arrive at this conception on its own, whether the genesis of such a standpoint and the ability to conceive it in the first place is in its grasp—even if, when somehow presented with it, it could make sense of it and see its truth—is less clear. As Steven Galt Crowell also notes in his article "The Mythical and the Meaningless: Husserl and the Two Faces of Nature," the full assignment of this possibility to the solipsistic subject does not appear wholly convincing (in *Issues in Husserl's Ideas II*, Thomas Nenon and Lester Embree, eds. [Boston: Kluwer Academic Publishers, 1996], 101n41).

46. Husserl himself, it should be noted, at key transitional moments throughout *Ideas* II, acknowledges that themes yet to be investigated have already been relied on. For example, in reference to the first point above, he ends the whole

of Section II and makes his transition to Section III by asserting that "the analysis of nature . . . proves to be in need of supplementation; it harbors presuppositions and consequently points to another realm of being and research, i.e., the field of subjectivity, which is no longer nature" (Husserl, *Ideas* II, 180). And though my question obviously aims to be more fundamental than this, in *Conversations with Husserl and Fink* (The Hague: Nijhoff, 1976), Dorion Cairns reports that Husserl said "that the *Ideen II* lacks methodological *Sauberkeit* [cleanliness] in that progressive and regressive analyses are mixed indiscriminately" (Cairns, *Conversations*, 57), which is why perhaps Husserl himself never allowed this work to be published during his lifetime, despite the many marvelous, concrete analyses that it contains and the huge influence on subsequent phenomenology (notably that of Heidegger and Merleau-Ponty) that it exerted.

47. An economical indication of this is given at the end of Section II, where Husserl states: "Nature is a unity of appearances posited by subjects and to be posited by them, to be posited, specifically, in acts of reason. But these absolutely presupposed subjects are not subjects as nature, men, for the latter are themselves intersubjective Objectivities. The Bodies are the identical x's as indices of lawful regulations of Bodily appearances of subjects in the nexus of the whole of physical nature. The souls . . . are also Objectively determinable . . ." (*Ideas II*, 180).

48. See Chapter 5 of my *Essential History: Jacques Derrida and the Development of Deconstruction* for an interpretation of *Speech and Phenomena*, as well as Chapter 3 of the present volume.

49. My "Philosophy First, Last, and Counting: Edmund Husserl, Jacob Klein, and Plato's Arithmological *Eide*," offers a sketch of what one version of such knowledge might look like, by following up on Jacob Klein's pathbreaking reconception of Plato's *eidē* (*Graduate Faculty Philosophy Journal* 25.1 [Spring 2004]: 65–97).

Chapter 8: Foretellese: Futures of Derrida and Marx

1. Francis Fukuyama, *The End of History and the Last Man* (New York: Harper Collins, 1992). The book expanded greatly a previous article, "The End of History?" (*National Interest* 16 [Summer 1989], 3–18), and the latter proved to be the focal point of most discussion, including Derrida's.

2. See Perry Anderson's thoughtful response to Fukuyama, "The Ends of History," which reasonably concluded that whether Marxism is or is not still a meaningfully political alternative at present is simply not known, in *A Zone of Engagement* (London: Verso, 1991): 279–375, 374–75).

3. Many of these pieces, some originally responding to the article-length version of *Specters*, have now been helpfully collected in *Ghostly Demarcations*, ed. Michael Sprinker (London: Verso, 1999), which includes a response essay by Derrida, amusingly titled "Marx and Sons." See also, notably, Gayatri Spivak, "Ghostwriting," *diacritics* 25.2 (Summer 1995): 65–83; and Slavoj Žižek, "Melancholy and the Act," *Critical Inquiry* 26.4 (Summer 2000): 657–81.

4. Notable in this regard are Aijaz Ahmad's sober "Reconciling Derrida: 'Specters of Marx' and Deconstructive Politics" (Sprinker, ed., *Demarcations*,

88–109) and Terry Eagleton's vituperative and dismissive, though cleverly titled "Marxism without Marxism" (Sprinker, ed., *Demarcations*, 83–87). Tom Lewis, in his "The Politics of Hauntology" (Sprinker, ed., *Demarcations*, 134–67) might also seem to fall into this camp, except that he makes an actual argument for Marxism as a "living tradition" being better at analyzing and affecting our current situation than Derrida's alternative.

5. Tom Keenan's highly inventive "The Point is to (Ex) Change It" (written before *Specters* appeared) is one example of this, *Fables of Responsibility* (Stanford, Calif.: Stanford University Press, 1997). Werner Hamacher's thoughtful and erudite "Lingua Amissa: The Messianism of Commodity-Language and Derrida's *Specters of Marx*" (Sprinker, ed., *Demarcations*, 168–212), which tries to fill the seeming gaps between Derrida's Marx and Marx's Marx, is to some degree another.

6. Alain Badiou's writings on politics have the virtue of recognizing this absence and the need for a new political direction, which, under the heading of an affirmative (rather than dialectical) politics, Badiou himself seeks to sketch. Whether beyond his diagnosis of what is lacking and what alternatives are no longer available, Badiou manages to meaningfully set out a new direction for political thought, may be doubtful, however. For further discussion of these matters, see my review of Badiou's *Polemics* in *Postmodern Cultures* 2007 (ejournal; http://www.iath.virginia.edu/pmc/current.issue/).

7. In addition to Badiou, Michael Hardt and Antonio Negri, in their recent writings, have attempted to frame this sort of novel vision, and Negri's piece on Derrida in *Ghostly Demarcations*, "The Specter's Smile" (*GD* 5–16), is one of the most provocative. Yet whether events have not already outrun their confidence that the mechanisms of world order that emerged in the '90s will indeed be successful, as well as their hope that they may lead to something radically different and more desirable, are suspicions that tend to confirm my central point: just how difficult it is to imaginatively conceive our contemporary politic situation today.

8. Thus, for example, in *The Other Heading: Reflections on Today's Europe* (trans. Pascale-Anne Brault and Michael B. Naas [Bloomington: Indiana University Press, 1992]), Derrida again explores the notion of our present, specifically of "the today," here through a reading of Valery.

9. Derrida brings Hegel and Husserl together in this way in *SP* 101–2, and in "The Ends of Man" (Jacques Derrida, *Margins of Philosophy*, trans. Alan Bass [Chicago: University of Chicago Press, 1980]: 109–36).

10. Derrida's trajectory when it comes to anticipation is telling here—at first the event as event must know such a horizon and thus what will not be anticipated also cannot be spoken of at all. Later Derrida seems to think that an event must be unanticipatable or combine both anticipation and the unanticipatable; whether he would still agree that its form *qua* event is necessarily known is not clear. Minimally finding in this instance as well (like the decision, justice and democracy) what he claims to be a self-deconstructing notion permits him to say more about the event and the future than he was able previously.

11. Michel Foucault, *Histoire de la folie à l'âge classique* (Paris: Gallimards, 1972); for Derrida's essay "The Cogito and *The History of* Madness," see *WD* 31–63.

12. Leonard Lawlor speaks of Derrida moving from a philosophy of "the question" to a philosophy of the "promise," which nicely formulates this change (*Derrida and Husserl: The Basic Problem of Phenomenology* [Bloomington: Indiana University Press, 2002], 211).

13. Thus, to take but one notable instance, in the opening pages of *Of Grammatology*, after announcing an "inflation of the sign 'language,'" an "absolute inflation," presently overtaking us, Derrida indeed goes on to introduce a certain tele-technology, a congruence of technics and writing, by substituting writing and the gramme for all that has hitherto been known as sign, language, information, and so forth (*OG* 6–8). This inflation and its symptoms thus belie an event of the archive, a transformation of what would have once been called the "recording or reproductive apparatus" of a wholly unprecedented magnitude. Such an event indeed takes up wthin itself the entire conceptuality to which the recording apparatus was previously supposed subordinate (the thoughts, things, persons, believed to command or use it) and the outer or inner edge of this transformation, according to Derrida, indeed uniquely marks our time, our present, even if in other respects it has always already been taking place, and has left its trace on all times, every present, not just our own.

14. Karl Marx, *Grundrisse: Foundations of the Critique of Political Economy*, trans. Martin Nicolaus (London: Penguin, 1973).

15. Marx, *Capital: A Critique of Political Economy* (New York: International Publishers, 1967): 71–83.

16. Both pieces mentioned above, Hamacher's and Keenan's (see note 5), offer important and genuinely valuable insights into this stretch of Marx's text. For other recent interpretations of it, see Spivak 1995, and Catherine Malabou's "Violence of Economy, Economy and Violence (Derrida and Marx)," trans J. Lampert and O. Serafinowicz, in *Jacques Derrida: Critical Assessments*, ed. Zeynep Direk and Leonard Lawlor (New York: Routledge, 2002).

17. Neither E. P. Thompson (*The Poverty of Theory* [London: Merlin Press, 1995]), nor Raymond Williams (see his chapter "Determination," in *Marxism and Literature* [Oxford: Oxford University Press, 1977], 83–89), nor Stuart Hall's responses to Althusser (among many: "Signification, Representation, Ideology: Althusser and the Post-Structuralist Debates" [*Critical Studies in Mass Communication* 2.2. (June 1985): 91–114]; cf. "New Ethnicities," in *Critical Dialogues: Critical Dialogues in Cultural Studies* [New York: Routledge, 1996], 441–49, esp. 442–43) seem to me to have advanced beyond his statement of the problem on a theoretical plane. Only Fredric Jameson, to my knowledge, has formulated something like a persuasive theoretical counterposition, but this has led him to root Marxian historical analyis in fictitious narrative structures and categories of rhetoricity to a degree that would shock an earlier generation of Marxists. (For a recent, concise, and provocative statement of Jameson's position

see *A Singular Modernity: Essay on the Ontology of the Present* [London: Verso, 2002].)

18. Derrida nuances his stance on the topics of class and production in "Marx and Sons" (Sprinker, ed., *Demarcations*, 252ff).

19. See Jean Baudrillard, *For a Critique of the Political Economy of the Sign* (New York: Telos Press, 1981); and Paul Virilio, *Vitesse et politique: essai de dromologie* (Paris: Galilée, 1977). John Guillory in his *Cultural Capital* employs early Baudrillard at a decisive moment late in his argument, despite the latter's break with the category of production (cf. *Cultural Capital: The Problem of Literary Canon Formation* [Chicago: University of Chicago Press, 1993] 301ff).

20. Karl Marx, "The Eighteenth Brumaire" in *The Marx-Engels Reader*, ed. Robert C. Tucker (New York: Norton, 1978), 595 (all references hereafter will be to this edition).

21. Marx, "Brumaire," 595.

22. Ibid., 607ff.

23. A number of trends have been prominent within the field of history, of course, in the last twenty years. Among them is a style of history more focused on the detail than the big picture. For a recent overview, which highlights this sort of "micro-history," see Anthony Grafton, "History's Postmodern Fates," *Daedalus* 2006 (Spring): 54–126.

24. See Raymond Williams, *Marxism and Literature* (Oxford: Oxford University Press, 1977), 121–27.

25. First cited on page vii of the Preface, this phrase recurs too many times to note. Its interpretation, indeed its very grammatical construction, undergoes a rather startling transformation at the beginning of Chapter 8 (Jacques Derrida, *Politics of Friendship*, trans. George Collins [London: Verso, 1997], 194ff). For a very useful treatment of this work and thus of Derrida's late political thought generally, see Alex Thomson, *Deconstruction and Democracy* (London: Continuum, 2005).

26. See, especially, Derrida's discussion of Montaigne in Chapter 7, "He Who Accompanies Me." There, after noting that "it might be tempting to recognize [in Montaigne's thought] a rupture with Greek *philia*," Derrida goes on to explicitly reject this alternative ("it would be difficult, indeed more reckless than might be believed, to oppose a Christian fraternity to some form of Greek fraternity"), in favor of the affirmation of an "originary" (my scare quotes) and hence otherwise historically unperiodizable "generative graft" (Derrida, *Politics of Friendship*, 185).

27. Marx, "Brumaire," 610.

28. Maurice Blanchot, "Marx's Three Voices," trans. Tom Keenan, *New Political Science* 15 (Summer 1986): 17–20.

29. I should note that my own reading of the operation of *différance* in the first half of *Of Grammatology*, examining its ties to a certain mutual production and interweaving of *parole* and *langue*, did see it at work in something like the

present, the present of enunciation (Joshua Kates, *Essential History: Jacques Derrida and the Development of Deconstruction* [Evanston, Ill.: Northwestern University Press, 2005]), 191ff). Derrida may well, then, have shifted his own views less than it at first appears.

30. Right before the passage quoted above, Derrida had just spoken of "an original performativity . . . whose force of rupture produces the institution or constitution, the law itself . . ." (*SM* 31).

31. As found in Blanchot's text, this claim obviously has Maoist overtones, and serves to underscore its sympathies with this aspect of May 1968. Derrida writes it in quotation marks, doubtless for these reasons. And while this distances his own position from a Maoist one, the notion of permanent revolution itself, as we are about to see, Derrida himself clearly endorses.

32. See especially the three aporias that Derrida sets out in "Force of Law," *Acts of Religion*, ed. Gil Anidjar (New York: Routledge, 2002), 249–58.

33. In *Rogues*, Derrida gives his own highly useful and more detailed account of how these notions, specifically those of a democracy to come, differ from Kant's regulative Idea, despite his own occasional invocation of this term (see *Rogues*, trans. Pascale-Anne Brault and Michael Naas [Stanford, Calif.: Stanford University Press, 2005], 83–86).

34. Perhaps most notably, see *The Challenge of Carl Schmitt*, ed. Chantal Mouffe (London: Verso, 1999) and Mouffe's own *The Return of the Political* (London: Verso, 2006).

35. Though this would require another essay to properly investigate, Derrida's own remarks on the current political situation seem to me to hasten a revisitation of how the distinction friend / enemy is understood in his own thought. Thus in *Rogues* (*Rogues: Two Essays on Reason*, trans. Pascale-Anne Brault and Michael Naas [Stanford, Calif.: Stanford University Press, 2005]), despite his obviously capacious and progressive intentions, when Derrida announces that 9/11 made clear what had already been true after the end of the Cold War, namely that "the absolute threat no longer took state form" (Derrida, *Rogues*, 104), does not this pronouncement, with its relocation of an "absolute threat," perhaps made out of a too-great eagerness to hail the passing of the nation-state, not come dangerously close to one George H. W. Bush (not to mention Osama bin Laden) today would also endorse? Does it not, that is, play into the hyperbole of the enemy at the very moment it attempts to rise above just this perspective, by not recognizing that Bin Laden and, let us say, the Soviet Union of the '60s, are not really equivalent as threats, a refusal, again, to which both Bin Laden himself and Bush subscribe? And perhaps this occurs, precisely because Derrida did not give enough weight to the perdurance and seriousness of this opposition friend/enemy as such?

Index

Diophantus, 117–18
Double apprehension, 162, 165
Duhem, Pierre, 115
Dummett, Michael, 79, 237–38n9, 238n10, 239n16, 239n20

Eagleton, Terry, 194, 195–96, 263n4
écriture, 5, 117, 118–19, 149, 207. See also Writing
Ego, the, 64, 130, 133, 154–55, 174, 175
  alter ego, 172–73
  ego-oriented philosophy, 200
  partially embodied, 177
  See also "I"
Eidos, 130, 131, 145
Empiricism, 151, 168, 181, 183
  Derrida rejects, 21, 23–24, 249n28
  empirical sciences, 185
  literary studies' relation to, 104
  radical, 158
  "third dogma" of, 90
  transcendental, 156
Engels, Friedrich, 6
  Communist Manifesto, 188
  The German Ideology, 199
Enlightenment, the, 14, 248n9
Enns, Diane, 222n10
Equivocity, 59–60, 62, 71
Essences, issue of, 138–42, 145
"Eternal" time, 121, 131–32, 134, 139
  eternality, 140
Ethnocentrism, 247n6
Evans, Claude J., 221n2, 221n4, 222n8, 222n9, 223n12
"Extension" as term, 82

Facticity
  of Husserl's thought, 156, 171, 181–82
  radical, 148
  of the world, 85, 185
  worldly writing, 38
Fenves, Peter, 53–55, 58, 230n15, 231n21, 233n26, 252n35
Fiction. See Writing
Fink, Eugen, 40, 140–41, 222n5, 251n21
First-timeliness (Erstmaligkeit), 134, 139, 141
Fish, Stanley, 4, 78, 99, 102, 103, 246n61

Is There a Text in This Class?, 95, 96
  neo-pragmatism of, 93–97
"Foretellese." See Future, the
Formalism, 96
Foucault, Michel, 2, 23, 102, 110, 191–92, 202, 247n6, 254n50
  and deconstruction (vs. Derrida), 78, 90–91
  Histoire de la folie, 192
Foundationalism
  anti-, 14, 143n44
  weak, 246n61
Franck, Didier, 160
Frege, Gottlob, 4, 5, 69–70, 234n32, 236n39
  and analytic philosophy (reconception of logic), 79–85, 86, 88–90
  The Foundations of Arithmetic, 80
  and language, 87, 97, 99, 103
French Revolution (1789), 204
Freud, Sigmund, 77
Fukuyama, Francis, 215
  The Ends of History, 187–88, 190
Future, the, 105, 186, 215
  circumstances determinative for, 187
  Derrida's view of, 189, 191–93, 208–9
  quasi-messianic, 123, 205, 213
  "fortellese," 7, 199, 213–14
  "present" and "future," 193, 212–13
  unanticipatibility of, 191
  See also Modernity

Gadamer, Hans Georg, 153
Galileo, 112
Gasché, Rodolphe, 157, 218n10, 222n7, 229n4
Genesis, transcendental-historical, 138–39
  problem of, 24, 121–22, 128–30, 133–34. See also Derrida, Jacques: works
Geometry, 60, 137, 143
  geometrical science, 139, 145–46
  Galileo and, 112
  geometrical triangle or circle, 131, 133, 145
  origin of, 62, 121, 134, 144–45, 146. See also Husserl, Edmund: works
  protogeometer, 120, 133–34, 135, 146

truths of, 141, 252*n*32
See also Mathematics
Gödel, Kurt, 116
Goldberg, Jonathan, 236*n*2
Grafton, Anthony, 265*n*23
Greek thought, 113, 117, 118
    Greco-European, 250*n*29
    See also Aristotle; Plato
Greenblatt, Stephen, 77
Grice, H. P., 68, 230*n*14, 244*n*51
Guillory, John, 265*n*19

Habermas, Jürgen, 110, 218*n*12, 247*n*7,
    248*n*9
Hall, Stuart, 91, 264*n*17
Hamacher, Werner, 263*n*5, 264*n*16
Haptocentrism, 160, 163
Hardt, Michael, 263*n*7
Harpham, Geoffrey Galt, 239*n*19
Harvey, Irene, 220*n*28
Hauntology. *See* Ontology
Hegel, Georg W. F., 83, 149, 187, 190,
    214, 240*n*25, 255*n*9
    neo- or quasi-Hegelian schema, 247*n*7
Heidegger, Martin, 51, 91, 153, 186,
    218*n*12, 245*n*54
    Being and Time, 172, 183, 260*n*39
    Derrida differs from, 6, 24, 32, 156, 173
        moves closer to, 111, 148, 150, 185,
        191, 202
    Husserl's influence on, 262*n*46
    Husserl vs., 157
    ontology of, 219*n*24, 248*n*8
    questioned, 50
Hermeneutics, 26, 48, 163
    hermeneuin, 111
Hermeticism, 52–53
Hirsch, E. D., 102
History/historicity/historicism
    Derrida's stance toward, 53, 110–11,
        122, 185, 202
        rejects, later accepts, Husserl's view,
        14, 21, 23–25, 233*n*26
        rethinks, 203–7
    end of, 190–91, 192, 202
    framework questioned, 190, 191–92
    geometry and, 62
    historical self-consciousness, 125, 126

Husserl's thought and, 46, 122,
    136–37, 190
    intentional history, 62, 129–30,
        132–33, 138, 144
    Klein's modernity (anti-historicist) and,
        112, 119–20, 124–26, 248*n*10
    and meaning, 233*n*26
    of metaphysics, Heidegger on, 32
    micro-, 265*n*23
    new, 79, 92, 97, 102–3, 105
    of philosophy, 143–44, 150
    philosophy and, 122–23, 151
    of science, 116, 134–36, 137, 145
    transcendental, 45, 58–62, 133,
        138–39, 143, 145
    twentieth-century notion of, 237*n*3
Hobbes, Thomas, 159
Hopkins, Burt, 222*n*4, 222*n*6, 223*n*12,
    224–25*n*15, 226*n*23, 246*n*1, 249*n*20
Human being, 154–59, 177–82, 185
    absolute human science, 153–54, 156
    embodied, 155, 171, 176–78
    identity and fate of, 186
    Man as entity, 177, 258*n*30
    problem of human as issue, 155–56
    senses of touch and sight, 160–68, 170,
        175
    See also Ego, the; *Leib*
Humanism, 177
    humanistic absolute, 161
    phenomenological, 160, 183–84
        Derrida's critique of, 169
Hume, David, 17
Husserl, Edmund, 65
    absolute of, 132, 154, 182
        absolute *logos*, 144
    Derrida's interpretation of/engagement
        with, 3–6, 11, 26–48, 51
        critics' disagreement about, 26–29
        and *différance*, 73, 148
        distinctions among writings, 29–33
        interpretation attacked, 225*n*15
    Klein's interpretation differs from,
        128–29, 139, 142–43, 150–52
    and Merleau-Ponty, 161, 166–78
    Derrida's break with, 25, 148–50,
        157–59, 161–65
    approach to philosophy, 32–33, 113

commentators' view of, 29
construals of meaning, 64, 67, 69–70, 73
deconstruction and, 4
in treatment of writing and language, 37, 40–44
Derrida's deconstruction of, 43, 182
facticity of, 156, 171, 181–82
French and German studies of, 27
and history, 46, 122, 136–37, 190
intentional, 129–30, 132–33, 138, 144
influences Derrida, 23–24, 26, 47–48, 56–57, 112–13, 120
in deconstruction's invention, 26, 34, 56–57, 63
and issue of ideality, 65
and meaning of language, 66
Husserlian model of, 4, 89–90
"I," 71
methodology of, 144
and modernity, 159
and objectivism, 55, 112–13
phenomenology of. *See* Husserlian phenomenology
philosophy of, 129, 143, 156–57, 164, 174
and sedimentation, 60, 137, 143–44
and signification/the sign, 39, 43–44, 52, 54, 56–57, 63, 67
and transcendental thinking, 40–41, 46, 57–58, 60–61, 178, 180–83
Derrida interprets, reappropriates, 121, 157, 223*n*20, 223*n*23
order of presentation, 179–80
writing's role in work of, 140
Husserl, Edmund: works
Cartesian Meditations, 129, 172–73, 175, 257–58*n*25
The Crisis of the European Sciences (Krisis), 127, 144, 248*n*11, 248*n*12, 253*n*38, 255*n*9
Formal and Transcendental Logic (FTL), 56, 120, 129–30
Ideas I, 146
Ideas II, 163, 170, 179, 181, 182–83
"absolute human science," 153–54
intersubjectivity discussed in, 6, 171–72, 175, 177

last writings, Klein's interpretation of, 5–6, 119, 120–23, 125–26, 127–37
Logical Investigations (LI), 31, 43–44, 63, 71–72, 236*n*41
Logische Untersuchungen (LU), 71
Origin of Geometry (Die Ursprung der Geometrie) (LOG/IOG), 62, 109, 134, 144–45, 147
Cairns's interpretations of, 5
Derrida's Introduction to. *See* Derrida, Jacques: works
Klein's discussion of, 116, 120–21
Phenomenological Psychology, 246*n*25
Husserlian phenomenology, 245*n*54
critics' disregard of, 27
Derrida and, 47, 128, 130, 161, 173, 226–27*n*27
influenced by Husserl, 24
Staten on, 217*n*3
Derrida departs from, 6, 61–64, 156–65
Derrida–Merleau-Ponty debate on, 163, 166–78
and history of philosophy, 143–44
Husserl's self-understanding of, 147
and invention of deconstruction, 33
and principle of principles, 146, 150
as research, 52
"static" phase of, 62
"unthought axiomatic" of, 35–36, 37
Hyppolite, Jean, 255*n*7

"I"
meaning of, 64, 65–66, 68–71, 73
and the other, 173, 174. *See also* Other, the or an
and self-awareness, 162, 165–66, 176
Idea, the, 61, 143
Kantian, 61, 72, 121, 145, 146, 147, 226*n*20
of reason, 113
Ideality(ies), 58, 251*n*14
Derrida's thesis on, 226*n*26, 230*n*13
and meaning, 65, 69–72
status of, as issue, 69, 71, 224–25*n*15
writing and, 42, 233*n*26
Idealization, geometrical, 145
Ideal objects, 133

Ideology, 197–99, 213
Indexicals, 4, 65–66, 68–69, 73
Indicative signs, 67–69. *See also* Sign(s), concept of
Infinity, idea of, 147
Ingarden, Roman, 156
Intentionality, 121, 251*n*22
    access to intentions, 88–89
    intentional history, 62, 129–30, 132–33, 138, 144
    new conception of, 257*n*23
    transcendental, 138, 185
    and writing, 39, 140
        authors' intentions, 98, 100–2
Intersubjectivity. *See* Subjectivity
Introjection, 172, 176
Intuitionism, 36, 103

Jakobson, Roman, 238*n*11
James, Henry, 75, 76
Jameson, Fredric, 91, 264–65*n*17
Joyce, James, 143, 228*n*30
Juhl, P. D., 98
Justice
    absolute, 213
    call for, 185
    and deconstruction, 203, 210, 211–12

Kant, Immanuel
    and deconstruction, 13
    and the Idea, 61, 72, 121, 145, 146, 147, 226*n*20
    and Kantianism, 83, 110, 154, 206, 211, 218*n*12
    and transcendentalism, 185, 248*n*9
Kaplan, David, 68–69, 234–35*n*31, 234–35*n*32
Kates, Joshua, 258*n*31
    Essential History, 217*n*1, 219*n*24, 222*n*10, 223*n*11, 231*n*15, 233*n*26, 233*n*28, 241*n*31, 251–52*n*30, 252*n*37, 254*n*50, 255*n*6, 257*n*24, 262*n*48, 266*n*29
    "Philosophy First, Last, and Counting," 262*n*49
Keenan, Tom, 263*n*5, 264*n*16
Kern, Iso, 258*n*28
Klein, Jacob, 2, 109–23, 124, 146

interprets Husserl's last writings, 5–6, 119, 120–23, 125–26, 127–37
    Derrida's interpretation differentiated from, 128–29, 139, 142–43, 150–52
Klein, Jacob: works
    Greek Mathematical Thought and the Origins of Algebra (GMT), 112, 114–16, 117–18, 127
    "History and the Liberal Arts," 125
    Lectures and Essays, 116, 250*n*6
    "Phenomenology and the History of Science," 125, 127
    "Speech, Its Strengths, and Its Weaknesses," 250*n*6
Knapp, Steven, 4, 79, 230*n*14
    "Against Theory," 78, 93, 97–104, 246*n*61
Kojève, Alexander, 109
Körper (matter), 39, 57, 58–59, 162–63, 233*n*27
Kripke, Saul, 240*n*26, 243*n*46

Landgrebe, Ludwig, 260–61*n*41
Language
    analytic model of, 4, 85, 93, 99, 101, 102
    Aristotelian model of, 80
    deconstruction of, 80, 86, 103
        two sorts, 90
    Derrida's concern with, 51–53, 66
        indicative dimension within, 67–69
    Derrida's discussion of, 38, 264*n*13
    "endless supplementarity" of, 13
    focus on, 3, 51
    Husserlian model of, 4, 89
    as language, recognition of, 100–1
    langue and *parole*, 265*n*29
    as literature, argument against, 98–99
    living flesh of, 44. See also *Leib*
    meaning correlated with, 89–90
    of metaphysics, 20
    multiplicity of languages, 81
    ontology of, 104
    paradoxes of, 13
    philosophy of, 4, 49–52, 55–58, 62, 229*n*1
        context principle and, 81, 99

ideality and, 65, 69–72
independent of truth, 83, 90
indexicals and, 65–66
of language, Husserl and, 66
	Husserlian model of, 4, 89–90
present, 89
reactivation of, 60
reference as basis for, 84–85
	priority of, over reference, 96
sedimentation of, 60, 135–36
of sentence, 69, 82
as sign of a sign, 12
See also Language; Reference; Sense
	(*Sinn*)
Melville, Herman: *Moby-Dick*, 56
Menon, Madhavi, 236*n*2
Merleau-Ponty, Maurice, 6, 150, 157,
	159–60, 182–84
debate with Derrida, 161, 166–78
follows Husserl, 153, 156
	contributes to his thought, 181,
	249*n*28
Merleau-Ponty, Maurice: works
	Phenomenology of Perception, 161, 168,
		257*n*23
	"The Philosopher and His Shadow,"
		163, 171
	Signs, 259*n*35
	The Visible and the Invisible, 167,
		257*n*22
Metaphysics, 51, 205, 255*n*6
	"closure of," 71, 113, 150, 185, 191
	Derrida's view of, 110
	Heidegger on history of, 32
	language of, 20
	"of presence," 51, 63, 150
	the sign enclosed in, 52
	Western, 63, 255*n*9
Michaels, Walter Benn, 4, 79, 230*n*14
	"Against Theory," 78, 93, 97–104,
		246*n*61
Milton, John, 103
Modernity
	Derrida's relation to, 5, 110–20, 185,
		189
		downplays, 110, 112, 119
	and "European" tradition (Husserl's
		view), 159

"foretellese" and, 7
and the future, 123
	vs. postmodernity, 189
as hybrid of event and theory, 120,
	126–27
Klein's emphasis on, 110, 112–17, 142
	and history, 112, 119–20, 124–26,
	248*n*10
and "new science," 248–49*n*14, 249*n*15
unresolved question of, 151–52
Western, 248*n*9
See also Future, the
Mohanty, J. N., 221–22*nn*3–6, 224*n*13,
	224*n*14, 225*n*18
Mohanty, Satya P., 245*n*60
Monad, the, 180
Le Monde (*2004* interview with Derrida
	in), 1
Mondialisation, 201, 202
Montaigne, Michel de, 206
Mouffe, Chantal, 215

Nancy, Jean-Luc, 160
Napoleon I (Napoleon Bonaparte), 204
Nealon, Jeffrey, 217*n*2
Negri, Antonio, 263*n*7
New York Times, 246–47*n*4
Nietzsche, Friedrich, 17, 186, 202, 206,
	209, 228*n*1
	and the future, 191, 193
Nihilism, 14, 21, 46, 184
9/11, Derrida's remarks on, 246–47*n*4,
	266*n*35
Nominalism, 14
Norris, Christopher, 3, 11–16, 18–22
Nostradamus, 199
Number, concept of, 137. *See also*
	Mathematics

Objectivity(ies), 131, 147, 252*n*32,
	260*n*38
	ideal, 55
	logical, 261*n*45
	men as, 262*n*47
	objectivist tradition, 91
		Husserl's objectivism, 55, 112–13
	theoretical determination of, 72
Objectlessness, 64

Ontology, 100, 114
Heidegerrean, 219n24, 248n8
of language, 104
of Marxism, 195, 198
permanence defeats, 210
of presence, 198, 199
replaced by Derrida's hauntology, 198–200, 213
Other, the or an, 155, 162, 171, 172–74, 177–78
as alter ego, 172–73
and intersubjectivity, 155, 174, 253n49
otherness, 167, 175
"absolute," 168
See also Alterity; Différance

Parole. See Speech
Peirce, C. S., 218n12
Perfection, 128
Permanence, 210, 213–15
Perry, John, 234–35nn31–33
Phenomenology
"European" tradition, 159
genetic, 129, 138
of phenomenology, 147–48, 226n20, 232n23
problem of human as issue for, 155–56
transcendental, 47, 128, 174. See also Husserlian phenomenology
Ur-phenomenon, 168, 171, 181
Philosophy
age-old aim of, 169
Derrida insists on retaining, 170
analytic, 52, 64, 79, 236n39
Derrida's relation to, 63, 67
Frege's influence on, 79–85, 86, 88–89
and language, 81–87
Continental, 84, 86, 89, 99, 245n57
deconstruction surpasses, 90
departure from, deconstruction and, 50–51
Derrida's views on, 20–21, 70, 74, 220n27
and break with Husserl, 32–33
philosophical responsibility, 14, 22, 23, 169
ego-oriented, 200

first, 111, 114
founding (Urstiftung) of, 147
and history, 122–23, 151
history of, 143–44, 150
Husserl's, 129, 143, 156–57, 164, 174
of language. See Language
mathematics seen as replacing, 115
post-, 49, 50, 70, 74, 157
of reflection, 51
as therapy, 229n1
traditional, 51
Phonocentrism, 16, 20–22, 32, 220n26, 220n27, 236n39
Derrida's contestation of, 63
Pippin, Robert, 247n7, 248n9
Plato, 2, 22–23, 109, 123, 256n11, 262n49
Positivism, 95, 119, 179
Poststructuralism, 77, 78
Pragmatism, 13–14, 69, 114, 181
deconstruction differentiated from, 16
Derrida's, 157, 188, 201
neo-, 78, 79, 92, 103
Stanley Fish's brand of, 93–97
pragmatic holism, 115
Presence, function of, 68–70
metaphysics of, 51, 63, 150
ontology of, 198, 199
teleology of, 149
Presentism, 110, 122
"Principle of principles," 146, 150
Production, Derrida's devaluation of in Marx, 200, 202
Proletarian revolution, 201
Psychologism, 128
Derrida denounces, 21
Putnam, Hilary, 240n26, 243n46

Quantification in logic, 239n21
Quine, Willard Van Orman, 83, 90, 96, 115, 116, 156, 239n16, 240n26

Ravaisson, Felix, 160
Reading, Derrida's respect for, 22, 23
Reason
deconstruction's involvement with, 17–18
Idea of, 113

as sign of radical coercion, 21
or *theorein*, 111, 113–14, 120, 144
Reference
 deconstruction of, 78, 90–91, 102
 in literary theory, 101, 103
  literature's relation to, 104
 meaning depending on, 84–85
 meaning's priority over, 96
 referential theories, 95–97
Reichert, John, 242*n*41
Relativism, 14, 15, 46
 Derrida rejects, 21, 23–24, 150
Religion, 197
Research
 Husserlian phenomenology seen as, 52
 See also Science
Revolution
 permanent, 209–10
 proletarian, 201
Ricoeur, Paul, 253*n*38
Rohy, Valerie, 236*n*2
Roots *(rizomata)*, 129
 Husserl's fixation on, 122, 128
Rorty, Richard, 4, 22, 52, 156, 236*n*42,
  241*n*33
 pragmatism of, 13–14, 242*n*37
Rothstein, Edward, 247*n*4
Rousseau, Jean-Jacques, 47, 99, 110,
  223*n*11

Sartre, Jean-Paul, 6, 153, 156
Saussure, Ferdinand de, 19–20, 37, 77, 80,
  84, 86, 89
Scarpetta, Guy, 24
Scheler, Max, 6, 156
Schutz, Alfred, 6, 156, 173
 "The Problem of Transcendental
  Intersubjectivity in Husserl," 172
Science
 "absolute human," 153–54, 156
 empirical, 185
 facticity and, 182
 geometrical, 112, 139, 145–46. *See also*
  Geometry
 history of, 116, 134–36, 137, 145
 "new," 248–49*n*14, 249*n*15
 "regional," 77, 154
 research and, 142, 153, 154

Searle, John, 52, 68, 89, 93, 95–96,
  240*n*23, 240*n*26, 244*n*51
 Derrida vs., 67, 219*n*25
 Speech Acts, 95
Sedgwick, Eve, 4, 77, 78, 91
 "The Beast in the Closet," 75–76
Sedimentation, 112, 145, 188
 definitions of, 31, 121
 in Husserl's analysis, 60, 137, 143–44
 of meanings, 60, 135–36
 of writing and language, 141–43
Seebohm, Thomas, 221*n*3
Self-awareness. *See* "I"
Semantics. *See* Language
Sense *(Sinn)*, 251*n*14
 death of, 58
 deconstruction of, 78, 93, 96
 univocal, 72
 See also Meaning
Sentences
 meaning of, 69, 82
 rules shaping, 96
 truth value of, 81
 See also Language; Meaning
Shakespeare, William, 159, 190
Sight
 speech distinguished from, 232*n*23
 touch and, 162–68, 170
Sign(s)
 body of. See *Körper; Leib*
 concept of; disappearance of, 51
 Husserl's notion of, 39, 43–44, 52, 54,
  56–57
  Derrida follows, turns away from, 57,
   63, 67
 indicative, 67–69
 linguistic, 55–60, 62–63, 67, 73
 "lost and mute," 53
 in metaphysics, 52
 "sign-expression," 43
 sign-function, 51
 significant-sign, 43
 "sign of a sign," 12–13
 "sign-thing," 57
 See also Language; Writing
Signification, 54
 Derrida on, 39, 43–44, 52
  Aristotelian model, 80

language and, 46, 88
    truth value of sentence, 81
meaning independent of, 83, 90
skepticism and, 12–13, 15
telos, teleology of, 13, 24, 25, 41,
    142–43, 228n30
transcendental contribution to, 39
writing and, 40–42, 45–46, 55

Undecidability, 18, 20
Univocity, 60–62, 143, 228n30
    questioned, 72; teleology of, 71
Unthought axiomatic (of Husserl), 35–36,
    37
Ur-phenomenon, 168, 171, 181

Valéry, Paul, 263n8
Vergegenwärtigüng, 259n31
Verleiblichung, 59
Vico, Giambattista, 125
Vieta, François, 115–16, 117–18
Villanova University, 1994 roundtable at,
    22
Virilio, Paul, 200
Vorhaben, 133, 146

Wave poem, 98, 100
Weak foundationalism, 246n61
Weber, Samuel, 241n29
Wheeler, Samuel, 83, 237n5
White, Alan, 221n4
Willard, Dallas, 224–25n15
Williams, Raymond, 205, 264n17
Wilmore, David, 3
Wilson, George, 244n51
Wittgenstein, Ludwig, 50, 83, 156, 217n3,
    219n21, 238n10, 240n26

Wordsworth, William, 100
    "Lucy poems," 98, 101
World-horizon, 155
Writing
    and analytic philosophy, 236n39
    concept-writing, 238n12
    Derrida's treatment of, 19–20, 34–35,
        135, 149
    fiction, 93, 102, 240n24
    given priority over speech, 63
    Husserl's treatment of, 37–38, 139–40
    and idealities, 42, 233n26
    intentionality and, 39, 140
        authors' intentions, 98, 100–2
    as *Leib*, 38–39, 252n34
    as paleonym, 19
    problematic of, 35, 37, 44–45, 231n21
    "regional," "worldly," 19, 37, 38, 46
    sedimentation of, 141–43
    as theme of deconstruction, 13
    as threat (absence, loss, or death brought
        by), 53–54, 58–60
    and the trace, 35, 37, 44, 45, 148
        archi-trace, archi-writing, 220n27
    transcendental, 40–44, 45–46, 139–42
    and truth, 40–42, 45–46, 55.
    See also *écriture*

Young, Robert J.C., 247n6

Zahavi, Dan, 57, 254n5
    Self-Awareness and Alterity, 165, 166,
        256n17, 259n33
Ziarek, Ewa, 3, 15–16
Žižek, Slavoj, 262n3

Perspectives in Continental Philosophy Series
John D. Caputo, series editor

Karl Jaspers, *The Question of German Guilt*. Introduction by Joseph W. Koterski, S.J.

Jean-Luc Marion, *The Idol and Distance: Five Studies*. Translated with an introduction by Thomas A. Carlson.

Jeffrey Dudiak, *The Intrigue of Ethics: A Reading of the Idea of Discourse in the Thought of Emmanuel Levinas*.

Robyn Horner, *Rethinking God as Gift: Marion, Derrida, and the Limits of Phenomenology*.

Mark Dooley, *The Politics of Exodus: Søren Keirkegaard's Ethics of Responsibility*.

Merold Westphal, *Overcoming Onto-Theology: Toward a Postmodern Christian Faith*.

Edith Wyschogrod, Jean-Joseph Goux and Eric Boynton, eds., *The Enigma of Gift and Sacrifice*.

Stanislas Breton, *The Word and the Cross*. Translated with an introduction by Jacquelyn Porter.

Jean-Luc Marion, *Prolegomena to Charity*. Translated by Stephen E. Lewis.

Peter H. Spader, *Scheler's Ethical Personalism: Its Logic, Development, and Promise*.

Jean-Louis Chrétien, *The Unforgettable and the Unhoped For*. Translated by Jeffrey Bloechl.

Don Cupitt, *Is Nothing Sacred? The Non-Realist Philosophy of Religion: Selected Essays*.

Jean-Luc Marion, *In Excess: Studies of Saturated Phenomena*. Translated by Robyn Horner and Vincent Berraud.

Phillip Goodchild, *Rethinking Philosophy of Religion: Approaches from Continental Philosophy*.

William J. Richardson, S.J., *Heidegger: Through Phenomenology to Thought*.

Jeffrey Andrew Barash, *Martin Heidegger and the Problem of Historical Meaning*.

Jean-Louis Chrétien, *Hand to Hand: Listening to the Work of Art*. Translated by Stephen E. Lewis.

Jean-Louis Chrétien, *The Call and the Response*. Translated with an introduction by Anne Davenport.

D. C. Schindler, *Han Urs von Balthasar and the Dramatic Structure of Truth: A Philosophical Investigation*.

Julian Wolfreys, ed., *Thinking Difference: Critics in Conversation*.

Allen Scult, *Being Jewish/Reading Heidegger: An Ontological Encounter*.

Richard Kearney, *Debates in Continental Philosophy: Conversations with Contemporary Thinkers*.

Jennifer Anna Gosetti-Ferencei, *Heidegger, Hölderlin, and the Subject of Poetic Language: Towards a New Poetics of Dasein*.

Jolita Pons, *Stealing a Gift: Kirkegaard's Pseudonyms and the Bible*.

Jean-Yves Lacoste, *Experience and the Absolute: Disputed Questions on the Humanity of Man*. Translated by Mark Raftery-Skehan.

Charles P. Bigger, *Between Chora and the Good: Metaphor's Metaphysical Neighborhood*.

Dominique Janicaud, *Phenomenology "Wide Open": After the French Debate.* Translated by Charles N. Cabral.

Ian Leask and Eoin Cassidy, eds., *Givenness and God: Questions of Jean-Luc Marion.*

Jacques Derrida, *Sovereignties in Question: The Poetics of Paul Celan.* Edited by Thomas Dutoit and Outi Pasanen.

William Desmond, *Is There a Sabbath for Thought? Between Religion and Philosophy.*

Bruce Ellis Benson and Norman Wirzba, eds. *The Phenomoenology of Prayer.*

S. Clark Buckner and Matthew Statler, eds. *Styles of Piety: Practicing Philosophy after the Death of God.*

Kevin Hart and Barbara Wall, eds. *The Experience of God: A Postmodern Response.*

John Panteleimon Manoussakis, *After God: Richard Kearney and the Religious Turn in Continental Philosophy.*

John Martis, *Philippe Lacoue-Labarthe: Representation and the Loss of the Subject.*

Jean-Luc Nancy, *The Ground of the Image.*

Edith Wyschogrod, *Crossover Queries: Dwelling with Negatives, Embodying Philosophy's Others.*

Gerald Bruns, *On the Anarchy of Poetry and Philosophy: A Guide for the Unruly.*

Brian Treanor, *Aspects of Alterity: Levinas, Marcel, and the Contemporary Debate.*

Simon Morgan Wortham, *Counter-Institutions: Jacques Derrida and the Question of the University.*

Leonard Lawlor, *The Implications of Immanence: Toward a New Concept of Life.*

Clayton Crockett, *Interstices of the Sublime: Theology and Psychoanalytic Theory.*

Bettina Bergo, Joseph Cohen, and Raphael Zagury-Orly, eds., *Judeities: Questions for Jacques Derrida.* Translated by Bettina Bergo, and Michael B. Smith.

Jean-Luc Marion, *On the Ego and on God: Further Cartesian Questions.* Translated by Christina M. Gschwandtner.

Jean-Luc Nancy, *Philosophical Chronicles.* Translated by Franson Manjali.

Jean-Luc Nancy, *Dis-Enclosure: The Deconstruction of Christianity.* Translated by Bettina Bergo, Gabriel Malenfant, and Michael B. Smith.

Andrea Hurst, *Derrida Vis-à-vis Lacan: Interweaving Deconstruction and Psychoanalysis.*

Jean-Luc Nancy, *Noli me tangere: On the Raising of the Body.* Translated by Sarah Clift, Pascale-Anne Brault, and Michael Naas.

Jacques Derrida, *The Animal That Therefore I Am.* Edited by Marie-Louise Mallet, translated by David Wills.

Jean-Luc Marion, *The Visible and the Revealed.* Translated by Christina M. Gschwandtner and others.

Michel Henry, *Material Phenomenology.* Translated by Scott Davidson.